The Beginning of History

THE BEGINNING OF HISTORY

Value Struggles and Global Capital

MASSIMO DE ANGELIS

Pluto Press

LONDON • ANN ARBOR, MI

First published 2007 by Pluto Press
345 Archway Road, London N6 5AA
and 839 Greene Street, Ann Arbor, MI 48106

www.plutobooks.com

British Library Cataloguing in Publication Data
A catalogue record for this book is available from the British Library

Hardback
ISBN-13 978 0 7453 2036 6
ISBN-10 0 7453 2036 8

Paperback
ISBN-13 978 0 7453 2035 9
ISBN-10 0 7453 2035 X

Library of Congress Cataloging in Publication Data applied for

10 9 8 7 6 5 4 3 2 1

Designed and produced for Pluto Press by
Chase Publishing Services Ltd, Fortescue, Sidmouth, EX10 9QG, England
Typeset from disk by Newgen Imaging Systems (P) Ltd, Chennai, India
Printed and bound in India

Contents

List of figures

List of tables and boxes

Preface

In 1969, more than a year after the mythical French May, and about the time of the Italian Hot Autumn, I was sitting at my desk in my fourth grade during one of those short breaks conceded to us by our teacher. I was nine years old, and growing up in Milan. I was diligently sticking the little picture cards of my 'history of Italy' collection into the album, making sure that the right card matched the right caption. Suddenly, I remember very vividly, I could not believe it: in my hand I held the image of a man dressed in a large white shirt who seemed to be shouting. In his hand was a banner, and on it, written in clear capital letters, the word 'SCIOPERO', strike. The caption that matched the picture said '1908'. I looked up, and, pointing at the picture, with all a child's wonder I asked my teacher, who was walking up and down with a grim look on his face: 'But then, there were strikes before?' He looked down at the picture, briefly nodded, made a low sound in his throat and continued his inspector's walk.

I did not know then, but that was perhaps the first time I encountered what in this book I call 'the outside'. As a child, I grew up believing this myth I heard repeated that the strikes, demonstrations and protests that were mushrooming in the late 1960s and early 1970s were something new, something that 'was not like it used to be'. And yet, from the second floor balcony of the small apartment where I was living with my family, I could hear and often see the demonstrations, with their slogans and the red colours of the marchers, before they disappeared around the corner. During our family Sunday walks in the park, I was puzzled by these older youths with long hair and flowers in their mouths, sharing ice creams and playing guitars. They looked quite 'cool' to me. Before going to bed after 'carosello' – the packaged entertainment ads that signalled for most Italian children the approach of the time to retire from the world of the grown-ups – I often thought about the alarming reports of the newsreader about the world out there. But I was told, all this is odd, and new, and it should not be happening. Hence the discovery of that picture dated 1908 was indeed revealing.

I would soon be going out into the world to find out for myself what all that shouting, and long hair, and faded blue jeans, and guitars, and little red books, and ice creams passed around in the park was about. I felt somehow comforted by the fact that all this had a long history; hence it was pretty much normal. Indeed, it soon became normal to me.

During much of the 1970s, Italy was bubbling with revolutionary ideas and practices. I was lucky to grow up in that period. In high school, we were on strike every other week (if not every other day) for every imaginable reason: in protest about a classroom roof leaking, in solidarity with the nearby factory workers on strike, against hikes in the transport fares, against a despotic teacher, as part of a general strike, or, simply, because it was a nice spring day. We were learning to take decision making into our own hands. And we were also studying: pamphlets, leaflets, revolutionary books and magazines, arguments and theories confronted, debated, ridiculed and promoted. No ministerial curricula were allowed to envelop our imagination: students from technical schools were studying Hegel and those from classical schools were studying technical issues of solar energy. Studying what you were not supposed to became one of many subversive activities. When in Britain, a few years ago, during the protests against the war in Iraq, outraged voices were raised in the press about high school students 'daring' to skip class and so getting the convivial education of the streets, I was bemused: what had these kids been losing all this time, putting their energy into the national curriculum, rigidly measured by pervasive exams?

Perhaps the most important thing for me as a teenager in those years was that revolution was the context of my daily life while growing up, whatever I was doing: revolution everywhere, what a great time to become a man! In retrospect, the revolution that I was breathing in as part of my daily life has implanted in me a key intellectual attitude, one that is most important in postmodern academia: 'problematisation'. And indeed, in those years people were 'problematising' social relations everywhere. Factory workers were 'problematising' relations of production, low wages and the wage hierarchy; women were 'problematising' patriarchal relations, social control over their bodies and exclusion from the wage; gays were 'problematising' their invisibility and discrimination in a heterosexual society; youths were 'problematising' social relations in authoritarian families; and so on. Growing up in those years meant you had to take a side in a ongoing debate, you had to find a place in a fluid movement of ideas, discussions, affects, relations, while at the same time enduring the pressure of traditional normative systems of authority (patriarchal, political, economic, cultural) that resisted this 'problematisation' of relations. Hence the creative revolution my generation experienced in the 1970s was also a problematisation of borderlines; indeed, I grew up with the awareness of borderlines as front lines: clear demarcations of different and often clashing practices grounded on different values.

This revolutionary ground and existential context was shaken away from my feet as soon as I started to learn how to make sense of it. In the early 1980s, the years of *riflusso*, criminalisation of the movement through anti-terrorist laws, and 'yuppification', I found myself in the student canteen of the university I was attending in Milan, having an animated discussion with another student, who was in his late thirties. He was a member of the Italian Communist Party (PCI) who, while attending the evening courses in political sciences as I was, during the day was a foreman at Alfa Romeo. We were having a very animated discussion. While he was repeating the PCI line that we needed national solidarity to end the crisis, embrace wage moderation and increase competitiveness, I argued that to be interested in competitiveness did not go very well with the 'internationalism' professed by the PCI since the implication of its achievement would have been the ruin of some other worker somewhere else in the world. After debating along these lines for a while, he stood up in front of me, pointed his finger at me, and, with his big moustaches making him resemble 'Uncle Joe', he shouted: 'You are a terrorist!' The canteen fell silent and I feared that someone might have believed him. In the climate of state intimidation of those years – when the emergency laws were imprisoning thousands on the whim of a police inspector – it was not difficult to get yourself into trouble.

Today, a quarter of a century later, I live and work in London, yet the same odd feeling of impasse I had felt on that occasion took me while witnessing a public meeting with the British secretary of state for development, Hilary Benn. On 19 January 2006 in London, the minister confidently faced an audience of critical NGOs and government advisers for 'consultation' on the government White Paper on development. The Labour minister highlighted progress, winked at the critics and spelled out policies that, in the usual neoliberal style, are all geared towards and justified in terms of creating 'effective competition', a condition, we were told, that is indispensable for fighting world poverty. When challenged to explain what happens when a country has an 'absolute trade advantage', like China, and the consequence of that is, for example, the ruin of Bangladeshi workers in the textile industry and their communities, he explained that 'competition is a fact of life'. Right, I can imagine what a woman in the struggle in the 1970s would have said to a man claiming that patriarchy 'is a fact of life', or a black about racism being a 'fact of life', or a migrant about border control being a 'fact of life', or a gay about homophobia being a 'fact of life', or an indigenous person about privatised sacred land being a 'fact of life'. In all these cases, in a wide range of modalities, what these struggling subjects would have said and done is to contest a *relational* mode they did not value, indeed, that they abhorred. Yet, we seem to be speechless in relation to the dominant relational modes through which we articulate life practices and that we call 'the economy'. We seem to be para-lysed before the domain of the relational modes implicit in 'economics'. And so, critics who feel there is something wrong with the way we live and operate on this planet emphasise the effects produced by these relational modes, such as poverty or environmental catastrophe, and their critical stance is focused on correcting the facts they are given and trying to uncover the 'lies' of power. And this is of course very good. However, they seldom look at power in its 'truth', that is, in the fact that it stands for something that we, the critics, do not. To do so would require measuring it with the yardstick of what we value, and being reconciled to the fact that the borderline is a line of conflict, a front line.

For migrants too, the borderline is, potentially, a line of conflict. They can be taken, beaten, confined and humiliated in detention camps, deported. But if they pass through, they can hope to reconstruct a life, reproduce their livelihoods and that of their communities back home, and contaminate the other side with their desires, their values, their passions. We need to learn from the migrants crossing borders, despite those in power arguing that borders are a 'fact of life'.

This book is about 'problematising' the borderlines running through our lives, in so far as our daily actions are linked to the systemic forces we call capitalism. The 'beginning of history' is the social process through which the contestations of these borderlines are at the same time the constitution of something new.

* * *

It has taken a long time to see this book into print, and many people have contributed in many ways to its production, more than I can name. It goes without saying that in my acknowledgments and thanks below all the usual caveats apply.

In the first place, I would like to thank the editors of the journals and books that published some of the material appearing here. In particular, Chapters 10 and 11 are drawn from the article published in the journal *Historical Materialism* (De Angelis 2004a). Chapter 14 is drawn from a paper published in *Research of Political Economy* (De Angelis 2002), edited by Paul Zarembka, while Chapter 15 is from an article that appeared in the collection *The Labour Debate*, edited by Ana Dinerstein and Michael Neary (De Angelis 2001b.). The section on governance in Chapter 7 is drawn from an article published in *Review* (De Angelis 2005a), and the second section of Chapter 13 is from an article published in the *International Social Sciences Journal* (De Angelis 2004c). The first section of Chapter 2 is drawn from an article written with Dagmar Diesner and published in the collection *Shut them down!* on the anti-G8 events at Gleaneagles, edited by David Harvie, Keir Milburn, Ben Trott and David Watts (De Angelis and Diesner 2005). The section on labour commanded in Chapter 8 is drawn from a paper David Harvie and I presented at the Heterodox economic conference in 2004.

In many years of teaching, my students have been fundamental in helping me to develop key aspects of this work. Many came from so-called 'disadvantaged' backgrounds, such as the poorer areas of East London, or as migrants from West Africa. Often, they joined my political economy class with no sense of why they were there, perhaps because it had 'economy' in the title and there was no maths requirement. The only certain thing is that at some point they would be instructed to fill a questionnaire and measure me in terms of their 'customer satisfaction'. I wonder whether they realised that in the end I also was their 'customer', that is, the direct beneficiary of their service: whenever they could identify their concrete experiences – of debt, of stressed out overwork, of abuse at home, of the borders they crossed and of struggles – with my 'abstract academic' stories, they confirmed to me that there was a sense and a meaning in what I was trying to do.

Despite the increasingly voracious pressure that UK higher education has exerted on its administrative staff, June Daniels has offered me good-spirited help on many occasions. Georgina Salah, a postgraduate studying global governance, has helped to sort out a messy bibliography. Through many years, my colleagues in economics at the University of East London have supported me in following my drive to do 'research' in a context in which so many conflicting and, from an educational and scholarly point of view, often meaningless demands are dumped on the academic staff of the sector.

Many people have helped to sharpen my argument, by giving voice to measures that my measures of things seemed to hide away. During copy-editing, Anthony Winder spotted trouble and suggested solutions. Coady Buckley-Zistel has brought the measure of critical philosophy, while Werner Bonefeld that of philosophical and polemical critique. John McMurtry has offered me valuable comments on an earlier draft. Over the years, in email exchanges and conversations with Gioacchino Toni I have been able to keep alive a youthful laughter, and share a light-hearted sarcasm and parody of the stupid paths we are supposed to follow while we reproduce our livelihoods. With her balanced and empirically grounded comments, Anne Gray gave me no excuse to avoid dealing with issues. On the other hand, David Harvie's enthusiasm for the category of 'excess' gave me an excuse to avoid dealing with them (on balance I hope it turned out right).

It was encouraging to hear Olivier de Marcellus's comments on an old draft of my conclusions, and to share his enthusiasm for grass-roots democracy and common sense. I learned never to lose sight of the invisible subjects of reproduction from Silvia Federici's insistence, a healthy counterweight in a world enchanted by subjectless parables. Peter Linebaugh gave me the confidence only a historian of struggles and commons could give, blessing my non-historical work with the sense that it is all about history. It is difficult to pinpoint the gifts I have received from George Caffentzis, so many insights that I gained in correspondence and conversation with him are woven into this book. But perhaps most important is the idea that philosophy is born of struggle, an idea shared by many, but by far fewer followed through in intellectual work.

In the last few months, I have met with a small group of people to read together and discuss parts of my book in draft. This has offered me a last chance to measure and fine-tune my arguments with the measures of like-minded people: the most amazingly sensible critics! In particular, I would like to thank Klara Brekke, Sharad Chari, Emma Dowling and Nicola Montagna for their convivial insights on a number of occasions.

The book has also being a ghostly presence for those who share their lives with me. My *compagna* Dagmar Diesner would have much to tell about the coupling of production and reproduction, in much less abstract terms than I have been able to in this book. Her support in this enterprise has been so tremendously grounded that the insights I got from her have no comparison. Our two-year-old son Leonardo is the greatest intellectual I have met: when he speaks his 'addah', 'oooh' or 'c-tat' he provides me with the most convincing arguments a philosopher of immanence could give me. This book is dedicated to Dagmar and Leonardo.

London, 16 April 2006.

1
The beginning of history

OTHER DIMENSIONS

Other dimensions! The problematic of the *beginning of history* is all about the beginning of *other dimensions* of living and co-production of livelihoods. A beginning that does not reside in texts and learned words, but arises out of diverse struggles emerging from within the global social body, and is thrown in the face of those who have proclaimed with crass certainty and ideological conviction that the era of the *end of history* has arrived. Yes, because the *end of history*[1] is not simply the title of a scholarly book coinciding with the planting of the banner of neoliberal capital on the ruins of 'real socialism' and the Eastern bloc. It also signals the largest attack on the commons in the West, East and in the global South through a quarter of a century of privatisations, cuts in entitlements, structural adjustment, financial discipline, public transfers shifted from social entitlements to meet needs of reproduction (health, education among them) to subsidise corporations, and the general increase in wealth polarisation, poverty, environmental degradation, war and political stupidity.

To pose the problematic of the beginning of history is to refuse the construction of the world in the image of the end of history, it is to posit other values and embrace other horizons than democracy corrupted by money, social co-production corrupted by livelihood-threatening competition, and structural adjustment enclosing non-market commons. The process of social constitution of a reality beyond capitalism can only be the creation, the production of other dimensions of living, of other *modes* of doing and relating, valuing and judging, and co-producing livelihoods. All the rest, regulations, reforms, 'alternatives', the party, elections, social movements, 'Europe' and even 'revolutions', are just words with no meaning if not taken back to the question of other dimensions of living.

Children are often said to be living in another dimension. Leonardo, my 20-months-old child, teaches me something very important when I observe his praxis of time and reflect on how it is articulated to mine. He seems to be living in 'phase time' all the time, his attention being enthusiastically taken by new objects to which he points, to new directions to walk the street's walk. This of course means that my partner and I must constantly invent new ways of keeping him happy while we take him on our daily trivial yet necessary pursuits rooted in linear time (going to the shop, washing dishes, etc.) and circular time (the alternating of the rhythms of daily life, going to bed, eating, and so on). Phase time is the time of emergence of new dimensions and is part of life, as is linear and circular time. When we scale up this little domestic vignette to the problems of the making of a new world, what becomes clear is that none of these dimensions of time is *specifically* the time of revolution, the time of new modes of social co-production. Revolution is a mode of their articulation, a re-articulation of phase, linear and circular time. On the other hand, the widespread commodity production in the social system we call capitalism, subsumes and articulates all three dimensions of time in its own peculiar way.

Linear time characterises the sequence of transformations leading to output, the articulation of functions, the structuring of plans through timetables and schedules. Continuous acceleration of social doing registered by several observers of postmodernity and globalisation is what turns this linearity into delirium, even more so today in the age of globalisation, in which an increased number of social practices are subordinated to the calculus embedded in mission statements, objectives, market benchmarks and speeded up turnover. *But this speeded up linearity that we are accustomed to lament could not come to dominate social practices if it were not for the modes of circular time to which it is articulated.*

While linear time is the dimension of purposeful action, of achieving goals, of performing functions, circular time is the time in which action returns to itself, thus defining and giving shape to norms and values without which those actions and goals would be meaningless. 'True journey,' writes Ursula Le Guinn in her novel *The Dispossessed*, 'is return', and she could not be more insightful. The return of the action or practice to itself is the activity of measurement, loosely defined, in which the subjects compare, contrast, evaluate and hence create the conditions for new action and new processes. Circular time is therefore the time of measure, and for this reason it is the time that defines norms. The return of action to itself creating norms and values happens in many ways, depending on the mode of circularity at different scales of action, yet in whatever way, we see feedback processes occurring which in this book we shall simply refer to as *loops*. Thus, for example, the return of action can be overwhelmingly defined by the rhythms of nature, the alternating of nights and days as well as of the seasons, as for agricultural activities with little technological input. The sun is not yet high, and I am still in bed, but I can hear the mooing of my cows as they demand their daily milking. I am measured by a rhythm that is largely given to me by the coupling of human production to nature's cycles. I must get up and do my daily job, and so tomorrow and the next day. Or in a different context, loops are constituted by patterns of engagement, collision, and encounters with neighbours, friends and colleagues, in which a variety of direct exchanges and relational practices may end up forming patterns and coalesce into norms of given types. The acceleration of sequences of social production we are witnessing in today's capitalism is one with the increased number of loops in which actions and social practices return to themselves and in thus doing are *measured*. The pervasive commodification of new realms of social practices, many of which depend on enforcing enclosures on the social body (Chapter 10 and 11), inserts new practices in the type of circular time as defined by capitalist *mode* of measurement (Chapters 12 and 13). The main enemy that the struggles for the beginning of history are up against is *this mode* of measurement, which is disciplinary in character and therefore to a large extent interiorised by subjects in the pursuit of their daily affairs.[2]

But mentioning subjects inserted into the normalising mechanisms of the markets, does not mean forgetting struggles. On the contrary, subjects do struggle against the modes of measurement and valuing of market cyclical time, and they do it all the time. Normalisation is normalisation of struggling subjects and struggles are set up against/beyond normalisations. What might seem a paradox, the contemporary presence of normalisation *and* struggle, is in fact the lifeblood of capitalism, what gives it energy and pulse, the claustro-phobic dialectic that needs to be overcome. Phase time is the time of emergence, of 'excess', of tangents, 'exodus' and 'lines of flight', the rupture of linearity and circularity redefining and repositing goals and telos, as well as norms and values.[3] It is the time of creative acts, the emergence of the new that the subject might experience in terms of what Foucault calls limit-experience, the experience of transformation.[4] But in capitalism, and more so in contemporary 'postmodern' global capitalism, phase time is taken back to the measure of capital (Chapter 13). Neoliberal policies at different scales of social action attempt to tie the creativity of the social body to market loops, emergence to market-type cycles, circularity and market measure. Lines of flight thus risk turning into curves of landing, and the land is the old terrain of capitalist homeostatic processes. What is the lament about 'de-professionalisation' of the professions and the rise of 'managerialism' in public services but the pain of this process of *coupling* between the cyclical time of the professions and the corresponding value practices, with the cyclical time of the markets and the subordination of the former to the latter? Hence in this book we are clearly dis-tancing ourselves from the view that regards postmodernity as communism in waiting. Indeed, this is what the approach of Hardt and Negri (2000) may at times seem to imply. If this approach were correct, the project of this book, that is of making sense of capital's categories for our times, would be pointless, since in the world of global multitudes defined in purely positive terms, the categories of capital (value, rent, interest, profit, etc.) are not symbols but ciphers; for the very objects of categorical reference no longer exist in this period, and we need to push through Empire to actually see that we live in communism. On the contrary, for this book the objects of categorical references do exist, perhaps mutated, but they are alive and kicking, and are reproduced in the daily practices and their articulation through which the reproduction of planetary livelihoods occur. Unlike Hardt and Negri, a central tenet of this book is that despite all the morphological mutations, the social force we call capital is still today more than ever based on processes of *measurement* of social practice, a measure that turns the doing, whether 'material' or 'immaterial', waged or unwaged, into work (Chapter 12).

Thus, despite a common root in the theoretical milieu of what has been called autonomist Marxism,[5] there is a difference between, say, a politics that looks to the 'creative,' 'immaterial' workers almost as the 'vanguard' of the revolution and those like myself who look instead to the Zapatistas and other similar commoners, especially the indigenous, the peasants, the just-in-time factory workers in the 'free trade zones' of the third world, the peasant mothers, the slum communities struggling in a variety of contexts for livelihoods and dignity. Not because the struggles of immaterial precarious workers in Europe are less important, or because I want to minimise the organisational innovations of 'swarm tactics' on the urban battlefield of an anti-G8/WTO/IMF/WB day of action. Rather, because the struggles of those commoners point with maximum clarity for *all of us* at the ruptures of the *coupling* between the measure of capital and other measures, between capital's values and other values. Hence they pose the urgent question of the decoupling of cyclical time as defined by the 'end of history' perspective and the cyclical time promoted by a struggling social body and its 'beginning of history' horizons. This maximum clarity is perhaps achieved because in these struggles the problematic of the decoupling from capital, the problem of how to keep it at a distance, often becomes a question of life and death. Here, the reproduction of livelihoods on the basis of value practices other than capital, and the safeguard or promotion of livelihoods *autonomously* from capital circuits, become the only terrain for the preservation of bodies and the regeneration of their webs of relations, communities. These struggles therefore allow us to focus on the *front line*, a front line that also traverses the lives of precarious 'immaterial workers', but that often does not appear so neat – apart from the instances in which they get together and are able to seize common spaces and turn them into projects of welfare from below, as for example in the cases of the movement of social centres in Italy, or when they seize the streets and set up a barrier to neoliberal policies promoting further precariousness, as in France in the first months of 2006. This because in a context of pervading markets, 'lifelong learning' policies or 'small business loans' help to recast the individual's puzzlement over how to access means of livelihoods, from being one opening to new modes of co-production and common access to means of existence, to one necessitating instead business acumen, risk-taking within a given market structure and consequent successful outperformance of *others*. The beginning of history instead peeps through the struggles for commons, that is relations to nature, 'things' and each other that are not mediated by the market measures that individualise and normalise, commons in which bodies can live, nurture, prosper, desire and even collide without being measured by money, but instead make up their own measurement of each other and 'things'.

FRONT LINE AND ALTERNATIVES

This book also takes issue with traditional Marxism, the version that conceives history beginning only after the smoke from the rubbles of the old capitalist system settles. The 'prehistory' of humanity, to use Marx's famous expression, which we shall discuss below, is an old order that has come to an end, and a new one is built on its ruins. Alternatively, the course towards the beginning of history is a gentler one, with progressive reforms promoted by progressive parties having won political power. They both belong to the 'seizing power' mythology extensively criticised by John Holloway (2002) and in different ways by the politics of immanence in Hardt and Negri (2000; 2004). These two classic strategies, which for a long time have been seen as opposites, shared indeed few important elements in that they understood the relation between a political party and the masses as one of indoctrination. The party knew what the beginning of history looked like, and it was taking the masses towards that destiny. This generally implied the application of a model that believed in 'stages' of development from pre-capitalist, through the 'necessary' transition of primitive accumulation, land expropriation and forced collectivisation, to socialist accumulation at rates of growth possibly higher than the Western counterpart and finally, in a far distant future, communism, with the disappearance of the state and the 'realisation' of all the repressed fantasies of the present projected into a future rising sun.[6] In other words, the classical radical tradition, whether reformist or revolutionary, embraces a concept of time that is overwhelmingly linear because stageist, 'progressive', while the socialist masses have to endure linearity by being subjected to a cyclical time that measures their activities on the shop floor in pretty much the same way that cyclical time measures the activities of the capitalist masses: stopwatches, attentive foremen and disciplinary practices were the ingredients constituting this measure. Lenin, after all, fell in love with Taylorism.

Whether this 'progress' is believed to occur through reforms or revolution is here secondary. In both cases, by keeping out circular time, the problematic of value and norm creation, and displacing the emergence of the new to the future, socialist models were founded on a political practice that was based on a split between organisational means and aspirational ends. The organisational means (gulags, political killing, repression, vertical hierarchy within the party, (un)democratic centralism, etc.) did not have to reflect the aspirations for justice, freedom, equality, *commune*-ism displaced into linear time. Extreme Machiavellism was embedded in the structure of the production of social transformation. The action of the socialist *prince* did not require conforming to the aspirations for different modes of doing of the socialist masses. The radical tradition based on this disjunction regards the subjects of history as *input*, and the beginning of human history as an *output* rather than as a living force giving shape to new value practices.

The approach of this book is thus that history is not an output, and people are not inputs. History does not begin *after* the revolution, but it begins any time there are social forces whose practices rearticulate phase, cyclical and linear time autonomously from capital, whatever their scale of action. And since, as we shall see in Chapter 2, every social practice is a *value* practice, that is a social practice that selects 'goods' and 'bads' and constructs correspondent measures and relational practices, to pose the problematic of the beginning of history is to pose the problematic of the overcoming of the value practices of capital.

The first task of this book is therefore to talk about a front line and the social processes emerging therein. On one side, a life-colonising force we call capital (Chapter 3), using an arsenal of a variety of means, sometimes brutal, sometimes seductive and appealing, for the sole purpose of the endless growth and reproduction of its monetary value. On the other side, life-reclaiming forces, whose practices seem to strive to cut loose their links with the colonists and rearrange the web of life on their own terms, but often enchanted or overwhelmed by the parables of the opposing camps whispering that, actually, there is no alternative. It sounds like the struggle between good and evil, but it is not: it is fundamentally a struggle to *define* what is good and what is evil, or, better, what we value and what we do not. There is no need to conceive of this front line as a straight border, with a clear-cut division between sides. Indeed, the fractal nature of the mechanisms of normalisation to commodity production, as discussed in Chapter 15, implies that this front line of struggle passes through diverse scales of actions, traverses subjects and institutions, and the problematic of its identification is one with the problematic of positing value practices that are incompatible with those of capital.

The second task of this book is to engage with the problematic of alternatives to capitalism recently posed with urgency by the life-reclaiming forces of the alter-globalisation movement. But this will not be done through a critical analysis of 'advantages' and 'disadvantages' of different alternative models, nor with the proposal of a new manifesto, an ingenuous scheme or a brilliant new idea that if all were to follow it would certainly solve all human problems. Instead, I want to problematise the question of alternatives by posing the question of their co-optation. The beginning of history, as any beginning, cannot be defined in terms of its results. The emergence of something new can be understood in terms of the values it posits, the goals it strives towards *and* the organisational means its adopts. A 'something' that begins today can end tomorrow, if it faces a counter-force that is able to end its development, by co-opting or replacing its values, by obscuring or rechannelling its goals, and repressing or using its organisational means. For this reason, and since the author of this book explicitly sides with struggles and alternatives to life-colonisation of global capital, the second task of this book, the engagement with the problematic posed by the alter-globalisation movement, is to analyse not so much what the forces striving to give history a beginning are *against* (capitalism and its horrors) but rather, what is the general character of what the life-reclaiming forces are *up against* (capital and its drive to colonise life). In other words, this book does not want to make a case against capitalism – indeed there is an abundant and well-documented literature in 'againstology' that does not need a new addition – but assumes this case from the start and moves instead to focus on the problematic of overcoming it. However, we cannot engage with this problematic through empty formulas or grand proclamations. We need to be radical and dare to go to the root of things. The overcoming of capitalism is ultimately the overcoming of a mode of co-producing our livelihoods. To problematise this overcoming is, first of all, to problematise how we co-produce our livelihoods and how even our struggles – however necessary they are – might have a role in reproducing the system.

EMANATING ANTAGONISM

In this book therefore we shall discuss capitalist dominant arrangements not so much in terms of their *effects*, as it is often discussed in the critical literature, effects summarised in the endless horror statistics to which we are growing accustomed. This is not to negate the descriptive importance of these 'effects' or the 'impacts' of global markets in specific discursive contexts (in Chapter 2, I myself use some of these for the purpose of illustration). However, the elevation of 'impact analysis' to a dominant critical weapon in the arsenal of radical theory, as it seems to be today in so far as the critique of political economy is concerned, is an indication not only of increasing world 'poverty', but also of the poverty of theory. This is for two interrelated reasons. First, a theoretical critique focusing uniquely on the effects or impacts of capitalist globalising processes on various social subjects is one that constructs these subjects *purely* as victims, not *also* as 'agents' or as *struggling* subjects.[7] In so doing, second, social practices such as 'globalised capitalism', that are supposed to have an impact on these subjects, are always defined as something *independent* from the struggles of these subjects themselves. From the methodological perspective of this book, this is nonsense. An apprehension of the processes constituting global capitalism must understand *how* struggles, conflict, subjects or, to put it more generally, in the aseptic terms loved by social theorists, 'agency' is a constituent element of the social processes we call capitalism.

It is only by recognising antagonism and conflict as constituent of the social forms taken by the social body that we can pose the problematic of the beginning of history. It is only by inscribing struggle in our discourses that we can problematise the types of social relations and correspondent social processes that the reproduction of interconnected planetary livelihoods involves. In other words, the problematic of the beginning of history is the problematic of the overcoming of the capitalist *mode* of social co-production of our livelihoods, and this is one with the overcoming of a mode of social co-production that is *emanating* antagonism. This is, I believe, what Marx was hinting at in one famous passage in which he identified the beginning of human history with the end of what he called the 'prehistory' of human society:

The bourgeois relations of production are the last antagonistic form of the social process of production – antagonistic not in the sense of individual antagonism but of an antagonism that emanates from the individuals' social conditions of existence – but the productive forces developing within bourgeois society create also the material conditions for a solution of this antagonism. The prehistory of human society accordingly closes with this social formation. (Marx 1987: 263–4)

The break between prehistory and history is here understood in terms of the end of the social *process* of production as organised in antagonistic forms – not in the sense of conscious antagonism between particular individuals, rather as an antagonism which 'emanates from the individuals' social conditions of existence'. In other words, this is an antagonism that is rooted in the ways people interact with each other while producing and reproducing the conditions of their existence. The beginning of history, in this sense, coincides with the overcoming of *this* antagonism and the positing of new forms of social cooperation. To address the question of how this antagonism plays out in our times is in a sense the specific subject matter of this book, bearing in mind that a basic central assumption of my argument, which I take as being self-evident (discussed under the guise of the horror statistics of the second type in Chapter 2), is that social powers have developed to such an extent and in so many forms that the 'productive forces developing within bourgeois society', taken as a planetary social body, have *already* for some time now created 'the material conditions for a solution of this antagonism'.

There are two interrelated ways to understand this antagonism. Firstly, the antagonism as class struggle traditionally defined, employed versus employees, bourgeoisie versus proletariat, capitalist class versus working class, however the different traditions define the latter. Here the clash takes the linear form of two arrows pointing in different directions, interests against interests, higher wages versus lower wages, social security and good pensions versus precarious conditions of work, access to land and food sovereignty for a population of small farmers versus enclosure of the land, large agribusiness and urban squalor. In this domain, there is plenty of scope for discourses that attempt to reconcile the two poles with an economic rationale. American liberals still look at Europe with envy, despite 25 years of neoliberal reforms, and argue that it is in the best interests of the American economy – hence of the global bourgeoisie having interests in the USA – to concede universal health care and cheap education, since this implies lower costs for firms who wish to invest. One has for example to read Paul Krugman's columns in *The New York Times* on this. Or efficiency wage theorists believing that it is possible to increase workers' productivity not just with the stick of threatened unemployment embedded in flexible labour markets, but also with the carrot of wage incentives. Or NGOs' development economists thinking that the European Union and the United States should help the global South to become more competitive before ruining their industries and agriculture by flooding them with cheap imports following trade liberalisation. Or all the 'good' arguments used by 'good' people believing that people are ultimately 'good' if only they are given a chance to 'perform', to be 'efficient', to 'compete'– that is, to be 'bad' to others for the sake of 'economic growth'. As soon as we concede on the 'goodness' and we break a deal with our opponents on the terrain of the value practices reproduced by capitalist markets, we realise that 'the antagonism that emanates from the individuals' social conditions of existence' is not overcome, only reconfigured. My successful deal with my boss or government means de facto threatening ruin for those of my class against whom my boss and I are competing.[8]

By looking at this circularity in time, the fact that actions are part of feedback loops and a system of interrelations, we discover that linear time alone is insufficient to problematise the present and open the horizon of the beginning of history. If the clash between arrows can be reconciled in the linear time of purposeful action, by making opposite interests become common interests and moving in the same direction, this is not possible when we are looking at the same antagonism in circular time.

Here is the second meaning of antagonism and reconceptualisation of class. The antagonism that emanates from the conditions of livelihood reproduction corresponds to *divisions* within the working class, and these divisions are not only ideological divisions that can be overcome by abstract calls for unity; they are not simply material divisions of the social body within a hierarchy of the waged and the unwaged with their corresponding degrees of access to social wealth. Articulated and reproduced by pervasive markets, they are organisational arrangements of the social body, given forms of articulation of the plurality of *powers to* making up the social body – the co-producing multitude. These divisions are the condition and result of social *practices* that first enclose commons and commodify life (enclosures) and then pit livelihoods against each other, what is generally called market competition, and through which capital can exercise social control on lives and follow its telos: profit, accumulation. Without tackling *this* mode of social cooperation – which today, despite its structural distortions in relation to the theoretical models that represent it, is becoming increasingly planetary – we cannot even start to imagine alternatives. Without 'coming out' to challenge the values embedded in this practice, and the practices it values, we shall never be able to pose *other* values. The beginning of history is constituted on the ruin of competitive practices concerning the reproduction of livelihoods, because these practices, when universalised on the social body to an extent that the social body depends on these practices to reproduce livelihoods, always imply someone's ruin or fear of ruin. The planetary working class here – waged and unwaged – does indeed appear as a multitude, as a 'whole' or 'set of singularities' (Hardt and Negri 2004: 99). But the extent to which the constitution of the whole occurs through singularities' practices that are pitted against each other and divided in a planetary wage hierarchy, *this* multitude does need to be overcome, as much as, we were taught, the overcoming of capital meant at the same time the overcoming of the working class, since class struggle is the central moment of *capitalist* development and capital's valorisation processes.[9]

FALSE POLARITIES

The focus on the antagonism that 'emanates from the individual's social condition of existence' implies that several other oppositions, dichotomies and polarities informing political discourses reflecting on current affairs are discursive constructions, which are inadequate to pose the problematic of the beginning of history. For example, the 'horror statistics' we are growing accustomed to (see Chapter 2) define for us a reality we generally call 'third world', and define it in the usual way of definitions, that is by excluding something while we discursively construct that picture.[10] It goes without saying that what is left out from this picture is what the 'global poor' are doing for themselves, the many stories of community empowerment and struggle, ingenuity, wit, cunning and sharing, in a word, the cyclical time of value creation beyond capital's value (Chapter 16). In thus doing, the 'third world' appears to us only as that world in which a large number of 'needs' are not met, in which the bodies of subjects decay in ruin, in which not only something needs to be done, but must be done, as commanded by books and the conventional wisdom of learned economists from international institutions based in New York and Geneva.

The 'first world' on the other hand, appears to us as the place of glamour, lights, abundance, however you judge this. 'There are so many lights here,' Meda Patcar told me some years ago when visiting Geneva for a political conference, 'so much waste'.[11] Coming from India, where she is a leading activist in the struggle for the survival of thousands of communities in the Narmada Valley threatened by planned dam construction to increase India's power generation to feed its export industry, the observation was particularly poignant. But 'So what? it is the place of plenty', say the migrants, investing their hope in a passport, a visa or a passage across the border hidden in a truck. However you judge it, the 'first world' then appear to us as the place of plenty, the place in which needs having being met, desires can roam freely. We know of course that there is a 'third world' in the 'first', from the tales of poor workers, of growing debt to meet basic needs, from the stressed out lives, from the tales of children living in poverty while targeted by manipulative corporate salesmen.[12] Or from the dry statistics of income and wealth polarisation that have accompanied the neoliberal reforms in the last 25 years, as a *basso continuo* accompanies a baroque concerto.[13] There seem to be so many 'needs' in the first world that are not met. And there seem to be so many 'desires' roaming the shopping malls of the 'third world', constructed right in the centre of needy *bidonvilles* and shanty towns. Thus, if from the perspective of the mind normalised to markets the third word is only the realm of horror qua needs unmet, from the perspective of the mind normalised to horrors the first world is the realm of desires and their enchantment. Both in the South and in the North, shopping malls tell us a tale of plenty, abundance in a rainbow of colours and styles: smiley faces of customer satisfaction, pure nomadic space for body-subjects projecting their desires as lines tangent to price tags. The space of needs unmet vs. the space of desires, the space of death of the body vs. the space of the death of the spirit, absolute vs. absolute, *either–or* – there seems to be no alternative. The contraposition of third world vs. first world is one example of a discourse of *false alternatives*: it asks 'them' to be like 'us', and it reminds 'us' to be grateful for not being like 'them'. It is a polarity of structural adjustment and normalisation, so we keep running the race without asking questions.

There are other examples of false polarities. Indeed, contemporary critical discourses are often trapped in them in that they embrace one side of a polarity against the other. From the methodological perspective I am taking in this book, *false* polarities do not represent true alternatives to the systemic dynamics that in fact generate them. Take for example the following polarities we often encounter in debates between the 'right' and the 'left' of the political spectrum regarding different aspects of what we conventionally call 'the economy':

- Self-interest and competition vs. cooperation
- Laissez-faire vs. state intervention
- Free trade vs. protectionism

Generally speaking, economic liberals have embraced the first pole of the contradiction while their critics have tended to make the case for the opposite. In reality, economic liberalism and the market system have been actualised through their opposites: self-interest and competition through cooperation of labour in production;[14] creation of markets through the state;[15] free trade through protectionism.[16] To the extent that the critics do not question the systemic bond between the two poles (that is, the fact that the two poles take the form they take because of the dynamic relations between the two), and instead embrace one of the poles without problematising the nature of its relationship with the other, they perform a service for their opponents, by opening a space for the reproduction of this dynamic relation.

Thus, for example, to oppose trade liberalisation on the grounds that the proponents of free trade such as the United States and the European Union practice various forms of protectionism (in agriculture through farm subsidies for example) might score points in a two-minute radio interview where sound bites are important, but is not a critique of a system that pits livelihoods against each other (at most it is evidence of hypocrisy). Rather, it is to hold the 'big players' to account for their own free trade rhetoric. If these critical discourses are taken seriously by those in power, the outcome is not the undermining of the *value practices* upon which the current system of interrelation we call 'economy' is based, but on the contrary, the advancement of this system through the dismantlement of 'barriers' and 'rigidities' that prevent it from operating as in the fictional narratives of standard economics textbooks. A further step towards dystopia! Neo-con president of the World Bank Paul Wolfowitz is today advocating precisely this. We need instead to look at these and other polarities as a whole. To do so is to look at *the processes* that articulate the two poles as well as the processes that disrupt that articulation.

STRUCTURE OF THE BOOK

The overcoming of the antagonism that 'emanates from the individual's social condition of existence' is the overcoming of the capitalist *mode* of exercising human powers: the positing of the new cannot be anything else but the positing of different modes of exercising and articulating social powers. The basic condition for this is access to social resources independently from disciplinary markets. In other words, we need to extend the realm of commons in more and more spheres of our social doing, at any scale of social action, to reduce the level of dependence on the markets and run our lives as free social individuals.

In this book we shall study the opposite of this process, that is, how capitalist markets are a systemic ordering of doing, articulating the exercise of human powers and corresponding needs, desires and aspirations. An ordering that is predicated on the enclosure of commons, pursuing a telos called accumulation, reproduced through pitting livelihoods against each other and resulting in the production of scarcity in the midst of plenty.

This book is divided into four parts. In Part I, I discuss the broad features of the capitalist mode of doing and social co-production with the preoccupation of showing how social conflict and the struggle of both waged and unwaged subjects are integral in the constitution of capitalist homeostatic loops and thus the dynamic reproduction of the system. In Chapter 2, I discuss the ontological starting point of this study of capitalist social processes of co-production. Here I recast notions of conflict in terms of struggles between value practices – clashes between modes of doing, relating, giving meaning and articulating social powers. I also argue that interpreting diverse struggles as value struggles allows us to acknowledge 'the outside', the 'other than capital', and thereby regain a dignified sanity and autonomy from the delirium of a social force that all want to subordinate to its ends. In Chapter 3, I show that when posed in these terms, the 'enemy' of those who want to pursue new forms of social cooperation is not 'capitalism', which is the name for a system *emerging* from struggles among value practices, but capital, a social force that aspires to colonise life with its peculiar mode of doing and articulating social powers. I also want to restore a dimension of hope in our politics, and take issue with those who believe that capitalism is an all-encompassing system ruling our lives, while in fact it is only one among many social systems of production and exchange. I here also discuss some basic terminology used throughout the book and clarify my understanding of social forces. In Chapter 4, using Marx's circuit of money capital, I discuss the boundless character of capital's accumulation, how this boundlessness implies strategies – contested by struggles – for the constitution of colonised subjects, and I provide a historical illustration of the global articulation of powers through processes of separation and enclosure. In Chapter 5, I extend the analysis to discuss the basic coupling between circuits of production and reproduction, that is the activity of waged and unwaged producers. I argue that historically the division between waged and unwaged activities was fundamental in the reproduction of the capitalist system as a whole and the constitution of the 'emanating antagonism' pitting livelihoods against each other along a global division of labour. In Chapter 6, I discuss the general relation between production and reproduction circuits on a planetary level. Here I outline the basic framework within which to conceive capitalist market feedback processes articulating struggles among value practices and provide a general framework to read the contemporary global division of labour in terms of these struggles and their displacement. In these last three chapters, in which I make use of the money circuit of capital, and indeed later on in the discussion of the fractal panopticon in Chapter 15, the reader might have the impression that I am theorising a structure within which individual subjectivities are trapped. My argument rather is the opposite, and is more in the spirit of Marx: the individual subjectivities articulate their social cooperation in social forms that aim at entrapping them, but at no point is entrapment all that exists, since it is continuously disrupted and other spaces are continuously created.

Part II first builds on the overall framework developed in Part I and then addresses some of the issues debated in the globalisation literature on the basis of the framework I propose. In Chapter 7, I identify the basic coordinates of capital's value practices as enclosures and disciplinary integration and discuss the general features of the relation between capitalist homeostatic processes and struggles understood as clashes among value practices. I then offer a critical analysis of today's discourse of neoliberal governance. In Chapter 8, I critically review some major tenets of the literature on globalisation and recast them in terms of the theoretical framework proposed. While in Chapter 8 the objects of analysis are the general trends and discourses of globalisation, in Chapter 9 I study in more detail global capitalist production, understood now as the coupling of the waged and unwaged loops. Here I show how current patterns of trade and the structure of global commodity chains are instrumental to homeostatic mechanisms through which value struggles are displaced.

Part III has a strange title: Context, Contest and Text. While in the previous parts I looked at the broad social dynamics that value struggles gave rise to through circuits of production and reproduction, here I zoom in to study the main processes that give rise to and reproduce capital's value practices. In Chapters 10 and 11, I argue, against traditional Marxism, that what Marx calls primitive accumulation, or, more briefly, enclosures, is a continuous feature of capitalist production. While in Chapter 10 I outline the theoretical argument and rationale, in Chapter 11 I provide an illustration and analytical framework for the analysis of contemporary enclosures. Capital's value practices find in enclosures their genealogy, something we can understand in terms of Foucault's definition of power as 'action upon action'. These two chapters thus address the theme of 'context', since the (successful) action of enclosures creates a context (acts upon the actions of others) for reproducing livelihoods and articulating doing in specific forms (disciplinary markets). In Chapters 12 and 13, the value practices of capital are uncovered through the discussion of capital's own measure. In Chapter 12, while maintaining a distance from the 'economic reductionists' and more orthodox interpreters of Marx's theory of value, I critically review some of the contemporary critics of the 'law of value', especially those who argue that with post-Fordism, immaterial labour and the rise of the service economy capital can no longer measure its own values and thus impose work on the social body. In this and in Chapter 13 instead I regard disciplinary markets as a social process through which individual agents measure the doing, and hence classify it and structure it in a social hierarchy giving rise to the global disciplinary loops discussed in previous chapters. The ongoing process of the capitalist *mode* of measurement coincides with the formation of what Marx calls socially necessary labour time. This is a blind process that gives rise to the norms of social co-production behind the back of the waged and unwaged co-producers themselves: to them, the 'how', the 'what', the 'how much' and the 'who' of social co-production turn into alien forces, making a mockery of democracy and freedom. 'Contest' refers here to the fact that this process of measurement, capital's own mode of measurement, is constituted by an ongoing struggle among value practices, an ongoing civil war within the social body.

Finally, 'text', that is the analysis of and reflection on two classic texts, which enable us to uncover how the emergent result of capitalist processes of measurement, founded on what Hayek calls the market order, is an organisational geometry, a 'meta-action' of social control with organisational principles similar to that of a particular type of prison, Bentham's panopticon. In this organisational order of pervasive disciplinary markets, which we call 'fractal panopticon' (Chapters 14 and 15), subjectivity and struggle are channelled in a mode of co-production that creates scarcity in the midst of plenty, and plenty in the midst of scarcity, with corresponding impact on the actions, fears and dispositions of subjects whose livelihoods are woven together in such an antagonistic form.

In Part IV, I return to the problematic of the beginning of history, that is of the decoupling from capital's value practices. In these two tentative chapters, my effort is not to come up with programmatic answers, but to contribute to the framing of questions that 'make us walk', to paraphrase the Zapatista's slogan that provides the title for this section. The problematic of the production of commons and of 'becoming outside' of capital's value practices is discussed, together with an eye to the conditions of this becoming, on the basis of the discussion in previous chapters.

I hope it is clear to the reader that even if this book employs categories such as exchange value, socially necessary labour and the market, and even if my professional training as an economist might at times weigh on my language and style, I have tried as much as I can to avoid committing the classic Marxist sin of 'the economic reduction of Marx's critical social theory'. Instead of reducing Marx's critique of political economy into political economy, I have tried to amplify as much as is possible the categories of political economy into vehicles of critical social theory.

Part I

Orientations: Co-production of Livelihoods as Contested Terrain

2
Value struggles

The Stirling camp during the anti-G8 action in Gleneagles in July 2005 was a temporary autonomous zone, a temporary time–space commons in which the three dimensions of cyclical, phase and linear time were re-articulated. The participants were the actors of this re-articulation, and the participants were also parents and their children. The experience in this commons can be useful in measuring the daily practices on the upside-down common of global markets. Through the re-articulation of time, the Stirling camp became a place in which *other* values were dominating social cooperation, or co-production. It was a place of peace from which to launch a peaceful war.

That it was a place of peace was obvious to us as soon as we arrived in the late afternoon. We could sense the buzz of chaotic order, the vibes typical of a laboratory of social and relational experimentation. Entering the camp was to enter a collective phase time. We parked our small van next to a large sandpit, which was a bonus for our child. Leonardo began to run up and down, interacting with other children, picking up the neighbour's things and having fun. One of the things that parents gain in getting involved in these events is that the communal dimension here is not a fantasy or an ideology: it affects the body. You realise what we miss in our daily lives structured around places of confinement, 'rules and regulations' and over-codified 'health and safety' procedures, especially if you live in an urban environment in the global North. Instead, you tend to relax your control over the child, giving it up, since you know that around you other eyes and other ears are ready to interface the dangers implicit in phase time with the 'responsibility' of linear time, and act if necessary. It is as if as an individual you amplify your powers and diminish your worries simply by virtue of being closer to others, others who are there not simply as bodies having things to do and directions to follow (as when you are close to others in a tube carriage), but others with whom you also are together in circular time, the time of norms and value creation. The camp, in other words, was a relational field in two interrelated senses. First, at the 'structural level', because the camp was organised into neighbourhoods within which people took decisions and coordinated work, ranging from garbage collection and food provision to direct-action activities. Second, in terms of a widespread communicational tension, a widespread easiness in talking and relating that overcame the fixed images we have of 'the other'. Just a few minutes after we arrived, for example, two young people approached the sandpit and started throwing spears to see how far they could get. They were the spitting image of what you might see on the front pages of ranting British tabloid newspapers, hoods pulled up over their heads and a swaggering walk that said: Do not mess with me. I grabbed Leonardo's hand, since they were throwing their spears precisely in our direction. Just when I was about to say something, they noticed Leonardo, asked politely whether it was OK to play, or perhaps, would it be more appropriate to throw them in the other direction? Middle-aged intellectual meets the image of the housing estate 'yob' as portrayed by tabloid papers and the prime minister's office and the funny thing is that they can communicate; they share a *common* discourse, the safety of children!

As parents, the decision to go to the anti-G8 demonstration and, especially, to stay at the Stirling camp surrounded by police and by media hungry for 'violence'-tainted pictures was not easy to make. My *compagna* and I have been involved in demonstrations and actions before, and escaped just by sheer luck the worst of police brutality in Genoa in 2001. Others were not so lucky. We both had stories to tell. But for the first time in our lives we were confronted with the non-theoretical problematic of 'safety' concerning those little creatures who live in phase time all the time, and for whom every experience is formative, every event is potentially traumatic or enriching. This is of course a risk that many children, their parents, friends and relatives around the world face on a daily basis, the brutality and stupidity unleashed against the needs and desires of a social body that does not regard global markets, financial discipline and 'competitiveness' as gods. We heard one journalist asking a mother whether she wasn't behaving irresponsibly by taking her child to the demonstration. What a photo opportunity that would be, a young mother with two children splashed on the front page of a tabloid next to the picture of a cop beating a black-dressed activist with a balaclava! 'Shame!', we could imagine the title. Doesn't she know that anti-G8 means trouble?

The journalist of course did not understand the function of the G8 in promoting structural adjustment, marketisation of lives and war, and the irresponsible effect this has on the lives of millions of children around the world, the horror statistics: snap your fingers, there a child has died of preventable disease, snap again, ... and so on. Talk about being 'irresponsible'! Yet, these are horror statistics widely reported by our media, and they are repeated in scandal by 'testimonials' from right and left of the political spectrum, as well as their court jesters. Liberal Bill Clinton, neo-con Paul

Wolfowitz and court jesters Bono and Bob Geldof all share the same platform to cry scandal and promote market reform as the solution.[1] They know what the headlines let us all know: for example, on the occasion of a previous G8 meeting at Evian, the British newspaper the *Guardian* reported on its front page some of the horror statistics we are growing accustomed to. Here is a sample: '2147, the year when, on current trends, sub-Saharan Africa can hope to halve the number of people in poverty'; '20,000 children die daily of preventable illness'; '500,000 women a year, one for each minute, die in pregnancy or childbirth'; '13 million children were killed by diarrhoea in the 1990s – more than all the people lost to armed conflict since the second world war' (Elliott 2003). And every year, with every G8 meeting, the same scandal, the same outrage, the same list of solutions tied to market reforms.[2]

Our journalist puzzling about mothers and protests could also have reflected on a second type of horror statistics which, unlike the ones we have just mentioned, do not make us recoil in despair. Rather, they make us puzzle for an instant, before we are drawn back into the vortex of our daily *busy*ness that forces us to close the newspaper and focus on our survival and not that of others, or are rationalised away by rigid ideological constructs with easy answers. The horror statistics of the second type point at a reality that is hard to digest: the major problems of the world, technically speaking, are peanuts. There is no *necessity* behind the dying from malnutrition, Aids and malaria; there is no *necessity* for generations of children to go to war instead of playing and going to school. The many horrors of the world are both preventable *and* treatable. Preventable by stopping structural adjustment of everybody's lives, that is those powers that enforce market competition in every sphere of life by withdrawing alternative means of livelihood. And curable since these are incredibly cheap problems to deal with: for example, to abolish malnutrition and major world diseases killing millions, what is needed is the same amount of resources we spend on the consumption of perfume.[3]

The reader should not jump to the conclusion that I am suggesting that the problems could be dealt with simply by giving up deodorants. I am using the metaphor of horror statistics as a way to *contextualise* what we perceive to be the most terrible problems of social reproduction on the planet. In the face of the almost 3 trillion dollars passing through the financial centres of the world *every day*, in search of monetary value, i.e., profit, these *annual* billions necessary to preserve the basic conditions of life look really pretty irrelevant, almost like scratching an itch. Hence, from the perspective of the reproduction of the social body as a whole, scarcity is inexistent, it is a fiction, it is an invention. It is however a hard reality for each of the individuals and communities comprising this social body and facing resource constraints, and it is experienced at each scale of social interaction in so far it is an interaction dominated by capital's measure, by capital's own mode of cyclical time.[4] For this reason, bear in mind that the horror statistics of the second type are expressed in a unit of measurement, money, that is not neutral, but, as we shall see in this book, a constituent part of the set of social relations that leads to the patterns and phenomena summarised by horror statistics.

Our troubled journalist could not see the bridge between these mothers with children protesting against the G8 and the tension within the global social body that these same mothers were trying to give voice to by being there: the tension between the tremendous *powers* we have developed as humanity and the delirious lives we have to live as co-producers of our world, a delirium that find its more tangible effect in the misery that many have to suffer.[5]

There is however another problem with the journalist's scandal in seeing mothers and children at the Stirling camp. And this has to do with the notion and construction of 'risk'. In mainstream financial and economic disciplines, 'risk assessment' is something that entrepreneurs and business people do all the time. When they talk about 'risk', they generally talk about the probability of losing assets or money, following an investment decision by an individual agent. In our case, 'risk assessment' was not something we could have done before taking the decision to join the camp and the actions. Because once you are part of an autonomous zone, of that *other* dimension, of a different articulation between cyclical, phase and linear time, together with others you contribute to create a context in which that risk is not only *evaluated* from a multiplicity of perspectives and needs, but also constructed. You become an actor together with others with whom you socially constitute 'risk'.

The affinity group with parents and children emerged precisely out of the necessity to be a united front against possible brutal police tactics. Many of the participants (mostly women and mothers) had experiences from previous counter-summits and demonstrations, which were directly aimed against economic, military and global power, and hence knew to what extent our governments use police forces to repress social movements and keep popular protest away from the red zones of their meetings. Since many of us have been engaged for many years in the movement, becoming a parent does not change the way we regard the G8 and the institutions of global capitalism. Above all, as a parent the anger intensifies, acquires more concrete depth and mixes with a deeper sense of sorrow as you more easily empathise with the pains of the victims of structural adjustment and understand the extent to which the struggles of our sisters and brothers in other parts of the world for food, water, health and education also acquire the value of preserving the bodies, spirit, dignity and future of children.

Our determination to be there meant that the fear of police brutality was something that we had to confront, not escape from. Many other parents reflected this attitude, and thus, together with the children we put together what someone wanted to call the 'babies' block – a name that was turned down however because the older children could not identify with the young ones. The 'children' block was therefore born, although we preferred to call it the 'brat block'.

At least 50 families were at the first meeting called in the middle of the camp by word of mouth, and the issue of 'safety' and how to participate in the protest and the direct action activities became top priority in our agenda. The first important decision was made through easily achieved consensus. While most of the other affinity groups were planning to leave the camp in the middle of the night or in the early hours of the morning, to avoid being surrounded by police before they could reach the motorways they intended to block, we did not have any doubt: our children would not have allowed us to do anything but leave *after* breakfast! Then followed discussions, decisions, and sound no-nonsense problematisation of the issues, tasks, dangers and opportunities. When children and the problematic of reproduction are centre stage, all the nonsense of political talk vaporises, and decisions become a matter of *common* sense, not ideological divisions, that is the sense that is constructed around a *shared* condition of living, a *shared* articulation of times.

One of the central questions was of course how to deal with police brutality in case another Genoa scenario evolved, either in the streets or if the camp was raided. In either case we hoped the police would not touch us if we visibly stood our ground as a group. Had the Stirling camp been raided, we would have gathered in an open area in the middle of the camp, to make our children visible to the police. Since rumours and speculation about police raids were mounting, we made sure that both the media and the police knew that there were children in the camp. We also made sure that we had a police and media liaison, so as to ensure that our actions and intentions were clear. It is funny how in these cases you rely on what is *common* between you and the police: they have children too, don't they? they know what it means, there are even policewomen there, aren't there? We remember having read in some tabloid newspaper that demonstrators were accused of opportunistically using children as a shield. Far from the truth. When mothers and fathers bring their children onto the streets it is not to use them as a shield. It is to hold to account the individual members of the police force they are confronting for their *values*; they are forcing them to acknowledge or reject that the safety of children is a *common* between the two camps, and that the enemy really lies somewhere else.

One can easily dismiss the practices of temporary space–time commons as ineffective and naive, and indeed, most of the traditional left does precisely that. To me, their/our presence there was similar to standing on a hill and contemplating the scenery: *outside* the spectator there lies the same world to which the spectator will have to return; but from the vantage point of this panoramic position, we can see more clearly how things are related, so that on our return into the midst of the scenery, we can measure ourselves and others, our relations of co-production, and the values that give meaning to our actions more thoughtfully. Experiencing commons in which we have to take responsibility for our daily actions and reproduction, safety, goals and aspirations means articulating linear, cyclical and phase time on a different dimension, it means articulating social co-production according to different values, it means experimenting and trying out different value practices, it means making an *outside* dimension to the value practices of capital *visible*, by virtue of our being there and declaring our presence as *other*. Temporary space–time commons allows the clash of value practices to be identified. We can then point at capital and say: We are outside it!

THE MARKET AS AN ETHICAL SYSTEM

Indeed, the outside seems so foggy in the daily pursuit of those activities through which the so-called 'economy' is constructed. In those world regions in which capitalist markets have greater reach over people's lives, it is difficult to perceive an *outside* of the economic calculus guiding the doing of social co-production. The tautology proclaiming that business is business, goes hand in hand with regarding market rationalities as a 'fact of life', rather than a value practice among many others and in conflict with others.

Value practices

By value practices I mean those actions and processes, as well as correspondent webs of relations, that are both predicated on a given value system and in turn (re)produce it. These are, in other words, social practices and correspondent relations that articulate individual bodies and the wholes of social bodies *in particular ways*. This articulation is produced by individual singularities discursively selecting what is 'good' and what is 'bad' within a value system and actually *acting upon this selection*. This action in turn goes through feed-back mechanisms across the social body in such a way as to articulate social practices and *constitute* anew these 'goods' and 'bads' or, given the nature of feedback mechanisms, to set a limit to these 'goods' and 'bads'. To talk about value practices is therefore to talk about how social form, organisational reach, mode of doing, modes of co-producing and relating, forms of articulation of powers, are constituted through social *processes*.

To talk about value practices is simply to highlight the fact that social practice, or social doing, or social co-production, is grounded on systems of evaluation that select 'goods' and 'bads', in which individual singularities act on the basis of these evaluations, and that the effects of these actions are in turn measured within the parameters of this value system and of clashes against other value practices. It is in other words to highlight the fact that it is the meaning people give to their action that in the end guides their action. In a general sense, I here understand 'value' as this action-guiding meaning. Value, anthropologists tell us, is the way people represent the importance of their own actions to themselves (Graeber 2001). By representing this importance they have a guide to their action. Value however does not spring out of individuals isolated from the rest of society. Any action, or process, 'only becomes meaningful (in Hegelian language, takes on "concrete, specific form") by being integrated into some larger system of action' (Graeber 2001: 68). *The articulation between individuals and whole, parts and totality, implies that it is by pursuing value that we reproduce wholes, that is webs of co-production. Therefore, different types of value pursuit reproduce different types of wholes, of different self-organising systems, of 'societies'.* Hence the study of how we reproduce the capitalist mode of production – the only mode of production in human history that has given rise to those horror statistics of the second type, scarcity in the midst of plenty – is a study of how we pursue the values that are characteristic of it. The politics of alternative is ultimately a politics of value, a politics to establish what the value practices are, that is those social practices and correspondent relations that articulate individual bodies and the wholes of social bodies.

The market as an ethical system

The Canadian philosopher John McMurtry helps us here to clarify these issues in so far as markets are concerned. His critical work argues, against the positivist and objectivist illusions of various schools of economics, that *the market is an ethical system*. Therefore, whatever we do *within the market* involves a value judgement and a consequent relation to the other, even if this other often remains invisible to us. McMurtry's work helps us to see through the soporific veil of the *pensée unique* that sees the market as the norm, helps us to dent the value programme of those social forces that want us to believe that indeed there is no alternative to a mode of articulating the activities in the social body predicated on *market values*.[6]

His argument in a nutshell is this: various schools of economics believe in the existence of economic laws that are independent of our choice (as society) and values. Indeed, 'economists explicitly deny that any value judgment is at work in their analyses, even though they presuppose a value system in every step of the analysis they make' (McMurtry 1998: 13), by making the other 'invisible'. In reality however, *all* market decisions are an expression of the market value system. To the extent that we are embedded in this value system, to the extent that we act within its codified language and parameters, we are like a fish that cannot see the sea it is swimming in. In order to see the value system we are operating with, we must step *outside* the parameters given by the market, and refuse it as given. McMurtry sees this stepping outside as a conceptual operation, much like when Marx urges readers of *Capital* that in order to see the social forms of the capitalist mode of production that we take for natural and given, we must use the conceptual power of abstraction. However, as I will argue later and have exemplified in the story of the Stirling camp, the conceptual stepping outside of market values also finds a parallel in many concrete social practices and struggles that are in direct opposition to the value practices of the market.

McMurtry distinguishes between the two concepts of value system and value programme. While the general term 'value' is something that we consider important, desirable, a priority, or valuable (and that in our economic life we measure in terms of money), when values are joined together into an overall structure of thinking, they give rise to *value systems*.[7] A value system thus is a conceptual grid through which we see the world; it defines (even unconsciously) what is good and what is bad, what is normal and what is abnormal, what we must resign ourselves to, and what it is possible to change. As we shall see in Chapter 12, it provides the grid, the principles of selection of what is 'good' and what is 'bad', within which singularities *measure* and order things, and, consequently, give a reference point to their action. A value programme, on the other hand, is a value system that cannot *conceive* an outside beyond itself.[8]

Thus, with reference to the value system/programme that rules the production and reproduction of the social body, the so called 'economy', McMurtry gives the example of Vietnamese bomb craters being used for aquaculture in the production of shrimps for export. Here, the conceptual grid provided by the economic discourse allows evaluating this production as a success. Export earning has increased, efficiency is raised, capital investment has been attracted, and so on. However, there are many problems that are and remain invisible to this market-oriented value system that are selected out by this conceptual grid: measured in terms of life's well-being – that is, values that are *other than* market values – the story of shrimp production is a story of loss and disaster: ground water polluted, farmers lands turned into desert, and livelihoods destroyed.[9]

There are of course plenty of similar cases; indeed the World Bank, the IMF, UN and government agencies and ministries have all encouraged such 'innovative' use of land throughout South-East Asia, Africa and Latin America, and, consequently, similar horror stories are reported from these regions. Now, we can ask, has the market value system gone wrong in this case? No, because the conceptual framework of the market does not include natural resources and self-subsistence plots as *values*, as something that is *valuable*, and thus it considers the effects of profit-driven enterprise simply as *externalities* – as economists call them – to the market value system. Incidentally, to appease the possible social upheaval brought about by these 'externalities', compensation may be devised. However, compensation does not prevent the next round of capital movement to create the same 'externalities' again and again. The key point is therefore that these are not defects that are due to poor implementation of market rules, 'market failures', as economists call them. Rather, they are constituent of the market structure of value. Examples like these abound and point to the fact that market value practices, as we shall see, do indeed clash with other value practices.

Also, it is important to keep in mind that individual 'goods' and 'bads' are discursively articulated in systems of value that link together 'goods' and 'bads'. These in turn are then functionally and structurally related in such a way that if we define something as 'good', the conditions necessary for its occurrence are also considered 'goods'. For example, when transnational business invests, almost everyone is pleased: it is said to bring jobs, it is said to revive communities, it is said it is good for the prosperity of the country, it is even said – especially if the business in question has an effective public relations strategy on the labour and environmental front – that it is good for the environment. Certainly, some will have reason to protest. Suspicious environmentalist groups will protest at the likely environmental impact on the nearby river, or the environmental destruction brought by new roads. Neighbourhood associations will be worried by the noise and the disruption to life, or even worse, about the health hazards that living next to the new plant will entail. Others will be concerned by the effect that a nearby factory will have on the monetary value of their houses. But by and large, at best these concerns will be brushed aside and assuaged through various promises of future intervention and other tactics by politicians. After all, in the area live people with needs like you, who perhaps have families and children to raise. Some needs must take precedence over others, and the needs of giving everybody 'opportunity' of a 'decent' life is top priority for any government.

This little vignette points to the fact that in our society the belief that jobs creation is the landmark precondition for what constitutes 'decent life', and therefore 'good' is rooted in our common-sense way to look at the world. And this does not seem to me to be less true with the increase in casualisation of labour, which in the last quarter of a century in the European Union and the United States has replaced the Fordist deal of job tenure and 'full employment'. It goes without saying that this is a common sense that is directly proportional to our socially and historically determined *dependence* on the wage for the means of livelihoods. Thus, and consequently, that investment is *good* per se nobody seems to question, not even the editors of newspapers and magazines otherwise very keen to report horror statistics, many of which are the direct result of investments that displace communities from their land. And since in our economic systems investments do not come free, but in search of profit vis-à-vis other agents who are trying to do the same (the so called 'competitive environment'), other 'goods' (and their invisible complements) must include efficiency (and stressed-out lives), cost effectiveness (and austerity), a 'good business environment' (and subdued compliance to business dictate), low business tax rate (and cuts in social spending), prioritisation of transport and communication infrastructures (and greenhouse gases, more traffic jams and more concrete over forests) and all other factors that are said to attract capital in search of profit. Once a 'good' has been discursively established, here come the 'bads': disinvestment (including disinvestment in arms production or population-uprooting dams), inefficiency (and convivial doing), higher *monetary* costs (and lower unmonetised 'life' costs), a 'bad' 'business environment' (and governments who concede to demands for justice), high business taxes (and free education and health care), stringent environmental and labour regulations (a cleaner environment and more laid-back and healthier lives), and all other factors that are said to repel capital in search for profit. These in fact are not necessarily bad from the perspective of other value systems.

POSITING THE OUTSIDE

How can we recognise the value system through which our own security and livelihoods are reproduced? Claude Lévi-Srauss argued that 'he had to leave France to study man'.[10] To recognise the value system that pervades our lives, we must step outside it. There seems to be a difficulty here however: one cannot take a stand from the outside of the dominant value programme – to recognise its 'pathological structures', using McMurtry's cancer metaphor – *'without putting the self at risk'* (McMurtry 1998, my emphasis).[11] Our earlier example of the Stirling camp is a case in point here, since much of the discussion held in this temporary space–time commons outside the commodified space of the 'economy' had to do with the risk of being raided. This is also obvious to indigenous communities struggling for autonomy and against neoliberal enclosures of their lands and resources and who are thus struggling for a dimension *outside* capitalist markets, such as the Zapatistas in Chiapas. This is also obvious to many waged or unwaged communities involved in struggles, to the extent that they push the line to the point of questioning the values of the market. There is indeed a double risk here. In the first place, a risk vis-à-vis the state and its repressive apparatus threatening one's freedom of movement, life and physical and psychological integrity. In the second place, a risk in relation to the means of one's livelihood. These two risks are evident in the analysis of how a value system hardens into a value programme. When this happens, the value programme 'imposes its patterns of behaviour as "necessary"' (McMurtry 1999: 19) even if this involves destroying livelihoods and killing, imprisoning and torturing those who resist it. Indeed, as Marx's analysis of the so-called primitive accumulation shows – here sketched in Chapter 10 – it is *because* it involves the force of the state that the market value system can harden into a value programme, into what looks to many of us today as a 'normal' state of affair. Also, the mental block against exposing the mindset, presuppositions of a value programme created in those who have been 'indoctrinated day in and day out as … native member[s] of society' (McMurtry 1999: 20), cannot be understood simply as a conceptual and ideological indoctrination. The market value programme *articulates* social doing, and it does it in particular ways. Individual nodes in society produce and *reproduce* their livelihoods guided by the parameters and mores of this value programme: to the worker, high wages are 'good', low wages are 'bad' and unemployment is often 'worst'. To the shareholder, high profit return is 'good' and low price is 'bad'. To the 'customer', cheap is 'good', brand is 'good' and expensive is 'bad'. To the executive director low cost is 'good', high cost is 'bad' and customer loyalty is 'good'. By attributing meanings through the dominant market value system turned into a programme, these and other sociological groups' abstractions measure and calculate, make choices and, generally, these are choices the effect of which is the co-production of their livelihoods.

But the story does not end here. As we shall see in Chapter 13, the practices grounded in a market value programme are constituent parts of disciplinary processes that create social norms of cooperation. In other words, all practices and correspondent choices are articulated in a system of doing in which the individual parts are exposed to the threat of punishment *and* the promise of a reward. This is what Foucault calls the *normalising* sanction, the repetitive process that creates normalised subjects. But these are also processes through which people recreate – or hope to recreate – their livelihoods.

In order to theorise these processes, we need to shift our focus from value systems to *value practices*. While with the term *value system* McMurtry defines the system of values as a totality that is a given structure of signification and meanings, with the term *value practices* I refer to the actions, processes and webs of relations that are both predicated on that value system and in turn (re)produce it. These are, in other words, social practices and correspondent relations that articulate individual bodies and whole social bodies, and they do so not simply by conceptually and discursively selecting what is 'good' and what is 'bad', but by actually *acting upon this selection* and thus, through feedback mechanisms, articulating social practices so as *to constitute* these 'goods' and 'bads'. To talk about value practices is therefore not only to talk about social form, organisational reach, mode of doing, modes of co-producing and relating, but about the *processes* giving rise to this form.

Individuals are singular agents and bearers of capitalist value practices in many instances of their lives, as they are agents and bearers of alternative value practices. For example, when I enter a supermarket and buy some coffee I select my brand and become the last link of a long planetary chain of co-production connecting me to instances of a million life practices that were functional in bringing that coffee there, in that form, under that brand and correspondent group of signifiers. The act of purchasing is thus an act of articulation to others, even if in my sleepy shopper consciousness it is simply buying an item on my shopping list.

Articulation within the social body occurs through information and communication, that is systems of feedback. Indeed in all systems of relations, there are flows of information and relations of communication that travel across their components. Information in human systems travel through different means: speech, radio waves, written words, signs of different types, of which *prices* constitute an example in so far as market exchanges are concerned. Whatever type of information, and whatever means adopted for its communication, one key difference between social systems and biological systems is that in social systems there is no way to use information – that is to act upon it – without interpreting its meaning.[12] But, and here is the crux of the matter, any interpretative system is a system that is based on specific *values*, whether in daily action social actors are aware of this or not. From the perspective of agents acting through these values, values can be understood as principles of selection, codes through which they select information *which is relevant to their action* understood as action within a system, within a mode of relation to others. Thus, for example, let us suppose I am the purchasing director of a major supermarket chain. The information that is relevant to me regarding a sudden drop in coffee prices is that I can stock up coffee before any recovery in the price. In other words, it is information that is relevant to my action, that *means* something to me, that I value in one way or another. The information that is not relevant to me qua market agent, the information that I therefore filter out in carrying out my *social role*, and that is therefore *not* relevant to my action, that I do not value, is that the fall in coffee prices *means* the ruin of many small producers and agricultural farmers around the world. This information of course *means* something to someone else, not just those directly hit by the phenomenon, but also those who in different ways enter into relations of solidarity with them. These two different ways to read information, to give it meaning, to act upon it, represent of course two different ways to participate in the construction of reality (information that means something and therefore is acted upon) and give rise to different systems of relations. Indeed, we could say that different value practices actually constitute the boundaries of systems of relations and that social conflict is the clash that occurs at the intersection between these boundaries.[13]

Indeed, in this book we understand conflicting value practices – or *value struggles* – as constituting an ongoing tension in the social body. This means that there is an 'outside' and, to paraphrase Hardt and Negri (2000), it is 'in the flesh of the social body', in its own practices, and is not confined to the conceptual realm. Also, because, as we have seen, value practices connect singularities and wholes, in doing so they constitute social forces. As we shall see in the next chapter, these are articulations of *powers to*, endowed with a *telos*, a sense of direction. This *telos* is not a metaphysical quality but is immanent in value practices of relating singularities who constitute wholes. Social doing is constituted across singularities related to each other through particular value practices, and the whole of this articulation constitutes what we may call social forces. Within this framework therefore, social subjects are not either 'good' or 'bad', either 'us' or 'them', either 'working class' or 'capitalists'. To the extent that the real is constituted by a plurality of value practices, we can regard social subjects as being traversed by the social forces they contribute towards constituting, social forces often in conflict with each other. This is to give credit to those who theorise the subject as a battlefield (Virno 2004), a site of contradiction and struggle (Laing 1960), and theorise individuals as ongoing processes, not as fixed entities (Simondon 2002). These conceptualisations of subjectivity will however remain in the background of this work, which deals instead with the link between subjectivities as expressed in struggles and systemic forces emerging from their interactions.

VALUE STRUGGLES

When we observe the ethics of capital from the outside, that is from the perspective of other value practices and modes of articulating singularities, we begin to uncover the social mechanisms through which this ethical system that aims at ruling social co-production is itself produced and reproduced. We thus start to ask questions: how is this system of values and correspondent discourses and guides to action sustained against our best judgements and struggles? how is it that, willingly or unwillingly, we become *bearers* of these value practices, despite our diverse values and dreams? what are the conditions for overcoming the craziness indicated by those horror statistics of the second type that seem to be the incessant product of this ethical system that we have never been asked to subscribe to? and, more importantly, how can we begin a different history, of engaging in processes of co-production of other value practices through which life-interactions can be re-articulated?

However, the bottom-line question, the one that allows us to ask an infinite number of other practically relevant questions by virtue of the fact that it helps construct reality from the vantage point of radical transformation, is this: where will we find *an outside* to the self-reproducing ethics of capital, so that we can look at it from the vantage point of a refreshingly different bias? It is a difficult task, made even more difficult if we follow those critics of capital who assure us that certainly today there is no outside, only global capital and its Empire (Hardt and Negri 2000). Surely, this claim offers a healthy counter-weight to those who frame the political problem of a new world emancipated from capital in the traditional terms of attack at the heart of nation states and seizure of power, whether through reformist or revolutionary means, and to those who cannot see that the problematic of sovereignty and power from the top has not been erased with globalised processes, only displaced in a new networked mode of ruling, what Hardt and Negri call *Empire*. But the claim that there is no outside is highly problematic. The reason advocated for this – that today's capital is a form of global rule and rests on a pervasive biopolitics that include all spheres of social life and interaction and that therefore as a pervasive power is a *normalised* power – is controversial: capital has always been global, it has always relied on biopolitical reproduction of labour power, and it has always relied on strategies of normalisation. This does not imply that there are no important differences in the way today capital attempts its self-reproduction: on the contrary. The point is that by announcing the end of an outside, the authors force us into accepting the end of history as a de facto exhaustion of the real. For this reason, in their view, and in the view of the classical deterministic Marxism they criticise, alternatives can be built by 'pushing through' empire and meeting at the other end of the tunnel: not something you want to recommend to the Central American indigenous, for example, struggling against the enclosure of their lands through Plan Puebla-Panama.[14]

I want here to propose that indeed there is an outside, an alternative realm in which material and social life is re-produced outside capital. This realm does not necessarily have a fixed space, although it might, and does not necessarily have a fixed identity. Since the realm of the outside is here our observation point of capital's value practices, of what capital values and the correspondent process and system of social relations, this outside must as well have to do with values. But these values are not simply a list of mores whose emergence is indifferent to the needs of reproduction of human life. It is not simply a question of debating abstractly defined 'shoulds' and 'oughts'. As the values of capital, also the values of *the outside* are values that are grounded in material practices for the reproduction of life and its needs. They may emerge simply as discourse, or be expressed as needs and in practices of objectivation that are limited in time and space due to the limited access to resources in given power relations. They may inhabit the phase time of emergent properties but be unable to mature into the cyclical time of norm creation, but still they are there, they are real and they are a social force.

The values of the 'outside' that I am talking about are obvious to all those who have reflected on the experience of their participation in struggles. Here these values are collectively perceived and constructed through continuous processes of feedback and engagement, debates and criticism constituting the relational practices of individual singularities within a movement. For example, the struggles against environmental degradation, patriarchy or racism throughout society are also ongoing occasions of problematisation of one's own practices within the movement. Difference within a struggling movement is also the condition for the production of new common values.[15] But the emergence of 'other' values is also evident in the many practices of micro-conflictuality that everybody is involved in on a daily basis, in which, as we shall see in Chapter 13, conflicting 'measuring' practices are articulated.

My impression is that the immediate horizon of any waged or unwaged struggle (such as for preserving livelihoods of communities, for entitlement and freedom of movement, and so on), is a line drawn to constitute an outside in which 'our values' (what we stand for) are clearly separated from 'their values' (what they stand for): 'we are for needs, they are for profit'; 'we are for justice, they are for injustice'; 'we are for freedom, they are for repression'; 'we are for solidarity, they are for competition'; and so forth. This clarity may or may not correspond to the clarity of mind of the participants in the struggle, to their self-awareness of the values they posit. But the point here is that whatever is the degree of self-awareness of struggling subjects, once the struggling social bodies are counterpoised we can observe, as in a chemical reaction, the emergence of different values for the self-preservation of the social body. Struggles bring values, their tensions and boundary lines to the forefront, and this creates the *outside* as an emergent property.

My hypothesis here has touched upon neither the means nor the concrete goals of these values. Concrete goals and means are the fundamental realm of disagreement among the different tendencies of the struggling social body, disagreements often marked by rigid ideological prejudgements. Also, I do not want to pass judgement on the types of struggles and their own values. Here the issue is simply this: *an outside* is constituted anytime social subjects are engaged in a struggle vis-à-vis a social force whose own *telos* and *conatus* demands the dismantlement and colonisation of anything outside itself. The outside is thus constituted by living subjects in struggle; it is, in this sense, a social force. By positing itself as a social force outside dominant values, this social force is a subject that turns these other values into their own *object*, and thus lays down the indispensable conditions for change. Conditions of course, since the actualisation of these conditions and their development depend on a myriad of other factors.

3
Capital as a social force

CAPITALISM AS SUBSYSTEM

The outside of 'values' emerging in struggles make us aware of a fundamental link rarely pinpointed by discourses dealing with 'the economy', namely that 'values' and endeavours of 'doing' are complementary. We cannot have one without the other. In the following chapters we will explore in detail how the values and strategies of that social force we call *capital* are articulated with and are in opposition to other values and strategies. Here, however, we must reflect on this link, and be prepared to pay the consequences of making it the true ontological starting point of our investigation, a starting point that is rooted in struggle. When we talk about the articulation between social doing and values, we are talking about human co-production (a broad concept of human production, not tied to receiving a pay check, and one that includes direct reproduction of life), of *how* social co-production is articulated, of *how* relations among the co-producers are reproduced while they reproduce the conditions of their livelihoods.

Our emphasis on value struggles leads us to make a fundamental point that we must never lose in our analysis: our world, our system of social relations, *is not* capitalism; it is far greater and more encompassing than that. There are three themes that this opening up of the notion of capitalism allows us to explore. First, the non-capitalism of our lives; second the problematisation of the conditions of emergence of alternatives; third the recognition of the pervasiveness of conflict.

In reading the critical literature from the alter-globalisation movement, as well as more broadly political and economic commentaries about the world we live in, it is easy to come across the misconception that we live in capital*ism*. I believe we don't.[1] This for a very simple reason: when we call our own world 'capitalism', we forget the 'non-capitalism' of our lives, the spheres of relations, value practices, affects as well as forms of power relations, conflict and mutual aid that we constitute beyond capitalist relations of production, perhaps within its reach, but yet constituted in different *modes* and therefore articulated by different value practices. These are the social fields in which the *norms* of social interaction are not defined by homeostatic mechanisms of the markets, or by money, monetary gain, and accumulation. These fields are not necessarily separate and distinct spheres, which we can associate with particular classes, groups, and collectives. In other words, when I am talking about non-capitalist fields, I am not referring to particular communities who are de-linked from capitalist production, although this might *also* be the case. Instead, I am talking about the complexity of the web of relations with others, and the intertwined diversity of their modes of relations and corresponding types of feedback process. We must recognise that as individual 'singularities', waged and unwaged producers relate with the world outside them in diverse *modes*, and they are both created and creators within these feedback loops. We thus do not live in an 'ism' but instead at the crossroads of many real or potential 'isms', many systems of feedback relations among human beings, social webs, and between human beings and environments, with different homeostatic processes.

In the last three decades, an abundant literature has developed that theorises and documents this other-than-capitalism, this relational field in which not commodity and money, but commons, gifts, conviviality, affects as well as traditional forms of oppression such as patriarchy are the prime shapers, makers and breakers of norms of social relations, the prime context of *value* and meaning creation.[2] Some of this literature has explored the connection and articulation between the capitalist and the non-capitalist fields, sometimes to highlight how the former has intervened in the latter in order to colonise it and exploit it.[3] Some other contributions highlight constructive practices and modes of relating that seems to be far from capitalist relations.[4] In other instances, social subjects develop these other-than-capitalism relations in their struggles vis-à-vis capital.[5] Sometimes we discover this other-than-capitalism as a practice right at the heart of capital, in its shopfloors and offices, a practice of gift, mutual aid and solidarity among workers themselves. At other times we find it outside, or running across capitalist organisations via circulation of struggles. Often, this force of community and gift is a social force that capitalist firms must be able to tap into for competitive advantage over others.[6] An extensive review of this literature is not the subject of this study. For our purposes, what is important is that the problematic of this wide-ranging literature allows us to acknowledge the existence of a borderline emerging from the heat of a struggle among value practices.

Not only does the word 'capitalism' risk blinding us to the complexity and diversity of our social existence, thus bowing in a sense to the discursive practices of our opponents, those who reduce the view of our relational webs by calling them the 'economy'. My problem with the word capitalism is also, and consequentially, political. The term carries an imagery of defeat that is absorbed into political thinking and discourse, a defeat that is digested only through voluntaristic calls to the cause of 'revolution' on the one hand, or non-strategic and uncritical laissez-faire of the global multitude on the other. This is because it projects coherence and closure into the world outside any single co-producer and outside their diverse associations and communities, when in fact political thinking should be able to identify cracks and openings in any context and scale of social doing, those cracks and openings necessary to produce new commons. It also encourages us into thinking of alternatives as alternative 'systems' through manifestos of all kind (and corresponding 'isms'). Such enterprises of course are often good intellectual exercise, and can help to frame different models to compare to the systemic forces faced by those pushing for alternatives to capital. But it would be absurd to think that, were the historical conditions ripe for *any* of these alternative 'systems' to be 'implemented', we would not find someone who was not taken into account, a voice not heard, whose needs and aspirations were invisible to the designer of the 'system'. The fundamental discourse of a politics beyond capital should not be the proposal of or the fight *for a* system (always relying on a class of intellectuals who 'know' what that system is about, hence subordinating to it the specific knowledge of those who do not, or a class of bureaucrats and technicians who are qualified to implement that system, a class of law enforcers who will persecute those left out and reluctant to acquiesce). Rather, it should be the identification of and the fight for the *conditions* making up a *context* of human interaction in which value practices that are alternative to those of capital can flourish and prosper. And this context can only be one that takes the desires, needs and aspirations of current strugglers vis-à-vis capital as its starting point.

If capitalism is not our world, then it is a subset of it. Indeed, general systems theory tells us that any system is a *holon*. This means that if when seen from within the system it appears to be a whole, from the outside one sees it as part of a larger and more inclusive system (Koestler 1967: 48). Systems of different scale thus interlock and are in a relation of hierarchy with each other.[7]

Observing levels of hierarchy among systems lead us to ask a fundamental question. If capitalism is a system, what is it a component of? Seen historically, capitalism (understood loosely as a social system of production, distribution, and exchange based on the profit motive and a concentration of control of the means of producing, distributing and exchanging in few hands) is a form of social cooperation. Indeed, what is common to capitalism, as it is to tribal, feudal or whatever forms of production, is that they are all forms of 'social cooperation'. What these systems have in common with each other is that through their processes, people apply their skills, develop forms of organisation and *powers to* and in so doing they (re)produce their livelihoods. In other words, all different modes of production are different forms (including different ways of articulating hierarchies of powers within them) of the same thing: people's social relation with each other and with nature. But then, if we shift our gaze from history to the present, from diachronic to synchronic comparison, we still cannot avoid noticing that capitalism is one system of social cooperation among many. For example, our livelihoods are reproduced through a variety of exchanges that certainly include (and perhaps increasingly so) market exchanges, and corresponding social relations of production, but cannot be reduced to these. When we think in these terms then, we discover that capitalism as a mode of production is only a *subsystem* of something much larger and all-encompassing, that is the system of social reproduction within which different subsystems are articulated. Community relations, gift exchanges, family and kin relations of different types, relations of solidarity and mutual aids, both existing and *imaginable*, all these comprise systems of production and social cooperation that live alongside, often intersect to a variety of degrees, are co-opted into or enter into direct conflict with the systems of production and social cooperation that we identify as capitalism. The set of all these systems, as well as their articulation, defines the way we reproduce our livelihoods on the planet. The whole therefore is not capitalism. *A variety of alternatives to capitalism also comprise the whole, and among these the systems of relations we are able to posit and constitute based on different value practices.*

CAPITAL

If capitalism is not an all-pervasive system, the social force that leads to the emergence of this system, capital, does *aspire* to be pervasive, to insinuate itself into all realms of human and non-human life, and colonise them all with its *mode* of doing, hence with its peculiar social relations, its own way to value and thus order things. Capital is about boundless accumulation, it is about money value that grows, that seeks growth, that strives to grow, that in the absence of growth will decline and perish. Capital therefore identifies something twofold, both a *social force* that aspires to subordinate all value practices to its own type of value practice and, correspondingly, a mode of doing things, hence of relating with one another, a set of *social relations*. In this book I understand social forces in terms of a *concatenation* or *articulation* of social powers (*powers to*, as in Holloway (2002)) endowed with a *telos* or, as I shall explain later, a *conatus* of self-preservation. On the other hand, I understand capital*ism* as the system that emerges out of the coupling, interrelation, meshing, among different social forces and value practices – often with different and clashing *teloi* and value practices – and corresponding emergent homeostatic loops through which capital is regulated, preserved and extended.

This is of course an unconventional way to talk about capital, which goes back at least to Marx. In conventional wisdom and its corresponding discourses, capital means anything but social relations of particular types or a social force. It is generally understood as a thing, a set of machines, instruments, raw materials and so on which are necessary for the production of a particular good.[8] It also means a certain sum of money, a stock of financial assets. It even means skills and knowledge ('human capital') and relations of trust ('social capital').[9] But, of course, the reason why we do call 'capital' all these *different* 'things' (machines or pieces of paper, human knowledge or social bonds), is that they have something in common, and this common does not have the character of thing-hood, but of a much less solid reality. These things are discursively constituted as capital when their owners – or their bank managers, who expect a share of the profits for their loan, or the economist, who sees the world with no other eyes but those of *economic man* – recognise in them the possibility of returning a profit, that is, a net flow of monetary value. Despite the insistence of economists on relabelling the contents of my kitchen with their categories, in my ordinary daily life I do not consider pots and cooking ingredients as 'capital', precisely because I expect a contented stomach and a convivial time with my guests from the dinner I have produced, and not a monetary profit and a consequently increased bank balance. Those who seek profit instead want to be able to harvest a higher monetary *value* than the value they sow ('advance'). The realisation of profit means that, *from the perspective of the owners of those things that we conventionally call capital, (or their bank managers or the economist)*, capital has valorised itself, has grown in value, and the expectation of profit is the expectation of this valorisation.

From this perspective therefore, capital is value that aspires to valorise itself, and in this way it sets in motion and articulates corresponding social *powers to*, in specific forms. At this very general level of analysis therefore, capital as social force has two constituent elements. One that gives it direction and that we may call the *drive, telos* or *conatus* of self-preservation, that is, profit – or, as Marx would put it, self-valorising value. The other that gives it leverage, *potentia*, organisational reach, the ability to pursue what it stands for. These two elements are of course interrelated. The aspiration of capital – generally referred to as the 'profit motive' – becomes a social force when the practices of a multiplicity of social subjects are interlaced together to give it concrete forms, to allow the social body to act along this aspiration, to articulate the multiplicity of social powers with its capital-specific value practices. It is irrelevant here whether the individual singularities (i.e., real 'body subjects' or, at larger scales, groups and networks of individuals, communities, organisations, companies, etc.) share or do not share this motive or aspiration. For capital to be constituted as a social force what matters is that the mental and manual activities of these singularities, their *doing*, constituted in a web of social relations, *are coupled* to these value practices so as to reproduce capital itself in its endless drive for self-expansion. Before formally describing this coupling or docking, in what follows I want to briefly explain the categories used in this book to describe the direction of this social force we call capital.

TELOS, DRIVE AND CONATUS

I use the terms *telos, drive* and *conatus* often interchangeably, although, when applied to the social force that we call capital, they do express different nuances of the same thing: capital's boundless thirst for self-expansion. In all three cases we refer to a constituent property of capital as social force, one that is linked to what we identify as being a *conditio sine qua non* of its existence, a condition without which capital is not capital. In this sense, these are terms that aim to emphasise Marx's reference to capital as 'self-valorising value' as 'production for production's sake.'

The term *telos* associated with capital is intended to highlight the aspirational horizons of this social force. Following one of Husserl's uses, *telos* indicates the 'aim of a particular constitutive process' (Tymieniecka 1976). However, I neither regard *telos* as the property of an individual, nor as a transhistorical essence. On the contrary, I read it as an aim that is continuously socially constituted out of the interaction of diverse life worlds. For example, to say that the *telos* of capital is profit is not to comment on the goal of this or that capitalist. Rather, it is to highlight that a multiplicity of experiences, life worlds and goals are articulated in such a way, that is constitute a social process, whose aim is self-expansion of capital, whatever are the aims and life worlds of individual actors in it. I find useful the differentiation between *telos* and goals. While the *telos* of capitalist production is profit, its goal may be different – for example the maximisation of market share in a particular battle against a given competitor, as classic industrial economics reminds us. While goals are contingent to a particular context, *teloi* are contingent to the social constitution of particular social actors.

An aspirational horizon is a drive when it is attached to a socially constituted sense of urgency. To say that the drive of capital is profit is to say that capital *must* accumulate. And it must accumulate even in those times when the *telos* of accumulation depends on the contingent lack of it, that is the establishment of a crisis that *creates* the condition of new accumulation. Indeed, Marx's extensive work shows that it is part of the constituent life process of this social force we call capital to enter into crisis, just as for living beings the act of breathing is constituted by both moments of breathing in and moments of breathing out. In Chapter 7 we shall call crises of this type 'disequilibrium' crises, and we understand them as part of the embedded regulatory function of capitalism in relation to social conflict. On the other hand, we will see that crises of another type, which we shall call 'crises of social stability', are a direct threat to the basic assumptions upon which capital's order of things is constructed.

The word 'drive', as in capital's 'drive', gives us a sense of the constant state of urgency that capital as a social force seems to diffuse in the social body, a sense of urgency very much linked to its constituting the social as the realm of scarcity. This drive is not an abstract metaphysical definition, but emerges out of concrete mechanisms of social cooperation, of particular configurations of property rights and access to resources to the exclusion of the vast majority of people. We must keep in mind that the act of driving is associated with impelling, urging onward. To be driven is the state of being harried. To drive someone mad is to force them into madness. We should however avoid the danger of naturalising this drive, by making it the inevitable result of human nature. Certainly, an organised effort to gain a particular end – whether this is money, profit, market shares – could be read as the result of adding up internal individuals' drives. This, for example, is the way mainstream economics' methodological individualism constructs the social, by adding up what it conceptualises to be a naturalised individual's profit- or utility-optimisation calculus.[10] When I talk about capital's drive instead, I do not intend to describe the drive of individual actors, but the drive that *emerges* out of their interaction in so far as they act for capital. The most laid-back actor working in a capitalist web of co-production (at whatever level of the social hierarchy) still has to confront the driving demands of the system this web gives rise to. The extent to which individual actors' discourses give voice to these systemic drives depends on the degree of normalisation of these actors to the requirement of the system, as well as their powers and strategies of refusal, survival, exit and so on. As will become clear, the degree of normalisation in turn is largely grounded on disciplinary mechanisms, that is those homeostatic processes that overcome and capture struggles and channel them into the production of capitalist values.

Finally, the term *conatus* (of capital) combines together the meanings of the aspirational horizon (*telos*) and the sense of urgency (drive) of capital, with the strategic problematic faced by any social force vis-à-vis other forces in their struggles for existence. The term *conatus* is used by Spinoza with reference to the tendency, or endeavour, of self-preservation.[11] In contemporary literature it has been used to conceptualise feedback mechanisms of living organisms and neurological homeodynamics. For example, in the words of neurobiologist Antonio Damasio, Spinoza's notion of *conatus* encapsulates the intuition that 'all living organisms endeavor to preserve themselves without conscious knowledge of the undertaking and without having decided, as individual selves, to undertake anything. In short, they do not know the problem they are trying to solve' (Damasio 2003: 79). The importance of this category for us is that it neatly conceptualises capital *as a social force that continuously faces the threat of its extinction.*[12] Spinoza's notion, 'interpreted with the advantages of current hindsight, ... implies that the living organism is constructed so as to maintain the coherence of its structures and functions against numerous life-threatening odds' (Damasio 2003: 36).

Thus, when I use this term in relation to social forces such as capital, I mean to emphasise the fact that social forces, like living organisms, have an impulse to preserve themselves, in the face of socially constituted dangers. Often, this *conatus* of self-preservation is expressed in forms and patterns of social action that emerge out of a multitude of interactions, without any single planner (a capitalist, a government, any human actor in the form of an individual or an institution). For example, homeostatic patterns such as the business cycle and periodic crises, even if they bankrupt the lives of many, from the perspective of the capitalist system as a whole they help to keep in check wages and working conditions as well as social entitlements, and to recreate conditions for the preservation of capital. The 'moderating' effect that these crises (or threatened crises) have on all forms of social entitlement and wage demand make sure that conditions of profitability, on which the preservation of capital as a social force depends, are not excessively threatened. This is something that is obvious common sense to the managers and planners of the international economy in their praise for 'discipline'.[13] The design and operationalisation of the *conditions for* this 'discipline', in given historical contexts, belong to the varied arsenal of what we might call capital's *strategies*.[14] The need for these strategies is obvious as soon as social forces *other than capital* emerge to refuse the logic of the homeostatic processes of capital, to set up barriers to its compulsion to accumulate – such as the struggles of both waged and unwaged for better living conditions, *despite* the great depression of the 1930s; despite austerity policies of the 1970s; despite the debt crisis in many countries of the global South; and despite disciplinary markets as in the early twenty-first century.[15]

Indeed, the concept of *conatus* of capital highlights the intrinsic difficulty we face when attempting to problematise a politics of alternatives to capital. On one hand, social forces that constitute themselves in opposition to capital and immediate conditions of accumulation (for example, struggles for higher wages, for less work, for more stringent environmental regulations, for commons and entitlements) represent 'life threats' to conditions of profitability and therefore threaten capital's immediate conditions of existence. On the other hand capital, like living organisms facing external dangers, must strive to adapt for the sake of its self-preservation. In this adaptation there emerge self-organising patterns that strive to capture this conflict, to co-opt it, to acknowledge some of its demands to the exclusion of others, to subsume them and make them the condition of a new round of accumulation, predicated on qualitative new organisational forms of labour and social cooperation, but reproducing the same basic life form for the social body, the same relations of production, the same rat race within the social body and artificial production of scarcity, that are fundamental in keeping mechanisms of homeostasis alive. The same social creation of scarcity, just at a greater scale and with qualitatively new instruments and organisational forms, the same compulsion to work for work's sake, to be busy for *busy*ness's sake, in an endless rat race that makes pitting livelihoods against each others the normal form of our human social cooperation. From the old liberal regime to Keynesianism, and from Keynesianism to neoliberalism, capital has survived and extended its reach and mobilised social powers through a variety of social forms. *The* problem of alternatives therefore becomes a problem of how we disentangle from this dialectic, of how within the social body conflict is not tied back in to capital's *conatus*, but instead becomes a force for the social constitution of value practices that are *autonomous* and independent from those of capital.[16]

4

With no limits

In the following effort to come to grip with the value practices of capital, we should not lose sight of our previous point, which I reiterate here: when we are talking about capital we are talking about a social force that *aspires* to colonise the whole of life practices. We are not talking about a *state*, a fixed condition in which *the whole* of these life practices are actually colonised. If we do not keep this distinction in mind, and confuse a *conatus* of self-preservation with a given all-pervasive condition of life, our critical stance has lost efficacy, since it has allowed the struggling subject and its current or potential threat to the self-preservation of capital to disappear from view.

The simplest way to represent the value practices of capital is to portray the sequence of transformations that *must take place* in order to preserve and reproduce its being, bearing in mind that reproduction of capital involves the production of a monetary sum which is larger than the one advanced, which is what we call *profit*.

We can use Marx's circuit of capital[1] to illustrate the basic feature of capital self-expansion, what is otherwise called accumulation. Thus, we could write:

1. $$M–C–M'$$

that is, in its simplest form, the process of accumulation starts with a sum of money M that individual investors inject into the process of circulation of commodities (the so called market), which buys commodities C. From the point of view of individual investors we have a transformation of money M into commodities C, illustrated by M-C, the act of 'buying'. The individual *telos* of our investors, though, was not to use these commodities to satisfy needs, but to earn a profit, that is a sum of money M' that is greater than the sum of money originally anticipated, M. The commodity C in their possession therefore, must be put back onto the market in the hope of finding buyers. If buyers are found and the sale realised ($C-M'$) at a sufficient unit price, investors will be able to pocket the difference between the two sums of money as profit. In fact, $M' = M + \Delta M$, in which ΔM is the extra amount of money (profit) obtained.

The cycle M-C-M′ cannot stop there. Individual investors may retire to make better use of their time if they have accumulated enough, but the 'class' of investors must keep feeding the system. While individuals may recognise when it is time to quit, the 'profit motive' that constitutes the *system* interlacing individual circuits of capital does not.[2]

Thus, the ΔM will be reinvested[3] with the intention – here again the *telos* of capital is working – of gaining more money. A new cycle is thus started:

2.   M′–C′–M″

that is, the buying of commodities of a greater value C-M′ and putting these back onto the market for sale in return for a greater sum of money. Again, the investors are ready for a new cycle, and so on endlessly.

This inherently endless process of accumulation of commodities and money is illustrated in Figure 1.

In Figure 1 we can continue to add M terms and C terms without limitations, precisely because there is no limitation in the pursuit of profit. Thus, the profit-making activity is inherently boundless, limitless.[4] When I say 'inherently' here, I mean to say that *within the value practice* of the profit motive it is not possible to recognise any limit; the limit *must come from the outside* of this value practice.[5]

The boundless nature of capital was a feature recognised by Aristotle almost 2,500 years ago, when the value practices of capital were very marginal in relation to the dominant ones based on household farming, which were regulated by the principle of self-sufficiency and autarchy (Polanyi 1968), as was the custom in ancient Greece and, indeed, in most of the ancient world,[6] as well as governed by patriarchal relations and slavery. We can imagine Aristotle observing traders in the docks of Athens supervising the cargoes of wine, pottery and olives ready to go to the Black Sea, while others were just arriving with barley and wheat from Sicily, and pondering about whether their monetary calculus and obsession with monetary gains had any relation to happiness. He decided that 'The money-maker's life is in

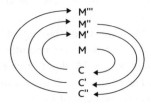

Figure 1   Boundless accumulation

a way forced on him [not chosen for itself]; and clearly wealth is not the good we are seeking, since it is [merely] useful, [choiceworthy only] for some other end' (Aristotle 1985: 8). In commerce for profit, money becomes money for money's sake, an end in itself, and thus cannot be the source of human happiness. In such monetary commercial activities driven by profit, the wealth striven for as a means to money making is also unlimited. However, 'true wealth' – the wealth that Aristotle associates with householding activities predicated on self-sufficiency–

[has a limit of size, determined by the purpose of the association it serves]; and the amount of household property which suffices for a good life is not unlimited ... All the instruments needed by all the arts are limited, both in number and size, by the requirements of the art they serve; and wealth may be defined as a number of instruments used in a household or state [and needed for their respective 'arts']. (Aristotle 1948: 26)

Whether it is the *use value* (the useful properties of a product of labour) or the *exchange value* (the monetary value that is obtainable with the alienation of a product) that constitutes the *telos* of the human process of doing and human exchange makes a great difference. Class societies, in which exploitation takes a toll on the doing of the people, can be differentiated according to whether the value practices constituting exploitation and oppression are *limited* by the set of needs of the ruling classes (however grand and decadent) or are instead *boundless*, the ruling classes thus *always* striving to acquire more.[7] In both cases class struggle, if able to deploy enough social power, can set a check on the greed of the masters and create spaces of autonomy. But while in the first case this check is a clear boundary to exploitation, in the second it is a *fuzzy* boundary, that is the value practices of M-C-M' will seek not only to destroy, but also to bypass and co-opt it since capital's *conatus* of self-preservation regards any limit as a barrier to overcome, and seeks boundless accumulation.

Before proceeding to an illustration of how the boundless character of capital concretises itself in historical form, it must be pointed out that the absence of limits constitutes from the start a particular *mode* of relation and production of subjectivity, one that constitutes *the other* in a peculiar way. Any singularity that posits itself in relation to the world outside itself as *boundless* in its drive and aspirations is one that is posited to *erase* the subjectivity of *others*, that is either to physically obliterate them or to *integrate* them into and subordinate them to their own mode of doing things. But physical obliteration and subordinate integration are also the means of constituting patriarchal or state 'illusionary communities'. States, patriarchy and capitalist markets thus complement and reinforce each other in the definition of a rule *outside* individual subjects.[8]

GLOBAL M–C–M': A CLASSIC ILLUSTRATION

An illustration of the principle of boundless accumulation – which also opens up for a reflection on the planetary reach of M–C–M' circuits and reveals how this accumulation is one with state violence and production of patriarchy – is the so-called 'transition' between feudalism and capitalism, that is the process of blood and plunder occurring in the sixteenth century, in which the European ruling classes were able to use the punishment of capital as well as capital's punishment (Linebaugh 1991) to overcome a limit to the feudal rule posed by peasants and urban workers in the struggles of the previous centuries. Indeed, the limit that European feudal rule could not bypass was a limit brought about by a long series of class conflicts running through the Middle Ages (Hilton 1978), which saw peasants' revolts and heretic and millenarian movements, as well as urban artisans' struggles against landlords, the church and political rulers, shifting considerably the power balance between the classes. In particular, the endemic peasants' revolt throughout Europe managed to win 'privileges and charters' that fixed the burden of the surplus work that was extracted to the benefit of the landowners as well as broadening the sphere of economic and judicial rights. Customary rights for the use of commons by the great bulk of the population were also established. Peter Linebaugh (forthcoming) shows how the commoners' struggles for and through commons are at the basis of founding constitutional documents such as the Magna Carta. As Federici puts it, after surveying the literature on the crisis of feudalism,

by the late Middle Ages the feudal economy was doomed, faced with an accumulation crisis that stretched for more than a century. We deduce its dimensions from some basic estimates indicating that between 1350 and 1500 a major shift occurred in the power-relation between workers and masters. The real wage increased by 100%, prices declined by 33%, rents also declined, the length of the working-day decreased, and a tendency appeared towards local self-sufficiency. (Federici 2004: 62)

Starting with the sixteenth century, with the age of mercantile capital and the beginning of the great waves of exploration, colonisation and subjection of the people of the 'new world', M–C–M' trade circuits driven by corresponding value practices began to extend their global reach as a way out of the crisis faced by the European ruling classes. This is the period of the emergence of a symbiosis still with us, that between capital accumulation and war, or, more generally, the 'economy' and the 'state', 'economic power' and 'political power' backed by force. It is a symbiosis theorised by the Mercantilist writers, the first 'economists' to voice to kings and emperors the concerns of the economic elites of the time, the great merchants, in the newly invented discourse that we call today 'economics' (Latouche 2001). This is a discourse that not only 'invents' the economy as an independent sphere of social activity, separated from the spheres of 'culture', 'politics' and indeed 'society',[9] but that in making this separation and constructing its corresponding narratives acts upon the social body in such a way as to *create* this separation. For the early Mercantilists, the separation is created by domestic policies that promote enclosures and expropriation of the commons, the setting of maximum levels of wages, and the discursive construction of workers as inputs of production to feed the economic rationale of accumulation.[10] But the real 'contribution' of the Mercantilists is at the planetary level, by establishing a synergy between war and international trade. War became instrumental in opening up access to distant lands and their resources, and in establishing and defending trade routes against pirates and opposing state powers. On the other hand, trade would bring the monetary resources, gold, to supply the military with new fleets and soldiers, and contribute to the strength of the state. A virtuous cycle made of might and gold and mediated by trade, very much similar to the cycle of awe and oil mediated by trade and financial liberalisation, as attempted in the second Iraq war of the new millennium.

From the late sixteenth century, and especially in the seventeenth and eighteenth centuries, M-C-M′ circuits began to weave a web of human doing across the globe, seeking to couple together life practices and conditions of livelihoods with the inherently boundless value practices of capital on a scale never seen before. The M-C-M′ circuits that began to embrace the globe were obviously predicated on the existence of commodities to sell, and the latter on the human labour that produced them. In a world in which the vast majority of people lived and worked in conditions of self-sufficiency, whether as members of tribes, clans or parishes, and whatever the surplus labour extracted from them by their masters when they had any, commodity production, especially that destined for distant trade, was a marginal activity for the vast majority of the world's populations, one that scarcely contributed to the core of their reproduction. After an initial period of direct predation of already produced luxuries, especially at the hands of the early Spanish conquistadores, the M-C-M′ circuits of the great merchants began therefore to be fed by the increasing supplies of gold, silver, sugar and cotton extracted by local indigenous people forced to work to death in mines and plantations.

But the local indigenous were a difficult 'input of production'. They were not only rebels in a land of their own, which they knew and which could offer them protection and sustenance for escape, but were also increasingly scarce, as a result of the massacres perpetrated and diseases brought by the Europeans. With the limited population of Europe in the context of the demographic and economic crises of the seventeenth century, 'the free labourers necessary to cultivate the staple crops of sugar, tobacco and cotton in the "New World" could not have been supplied in quantities adequate to permit large-scale production. Slavery was necessary for this' (Williams 1964: 6). Capital's value practices are inherently boundless, and therefore do not stop when faced with a barrier such as the available population to put to work.

The transnational slave trade took place between the sixteenth century and the first half of the nineteenth century, and its peak was in the eighteenth and early nineteenth century (the period of the industrial revolution) (Potts and Bond 1990: 41). The drive to accumulate bypassed the constraint given by the lack of sufficient willing and available suppliers of labour power and led to the kidnapping of between 10 and 20 million people from the African continent into the largest forced migration in the history of humanity. Basically the same evaluation processes, the same calculations that current operation managers apply with sophisticated information technology to minimise costs across a transnational commodity chain, were applied to the human cargoes of the mercantilist era. The same measuring activities, the same principles of selection, defining 'goods', which bring in profits and must be maximised, and 'bads', which reduce costs and must be minimised. The ship's captain would make his calculation, taking into account the many men, women and children who would die as a result of this transportation, 'pack' the ship with what he thought to be the 'optimum' number of bodies, and 'discount' the economic loss (brought about by the percentage of the human cargo dying on the trip) from the forecast revenue.

At its peak during the eighteenth century, the most important countries involved in the slave trade were England, Portugal and France, taking 41.3 per cent, 29.3 per cent and 19.2 per cent of the trade respectively, followed by Holland, British North America (USA), Denmark, Sweden and Brandenburg (Potts and Bond 1990). The transatlantic slave trade soon became part of a triangular or circular trade between the west coast of Africa, the Americas and Caribbean, and Europe. The English ports of Liverpool, London and Bristol were the most important European nodes of the triangular trade, which consisted of a flow of manufacturing commodities from Europe (many manufactured in the sweatshops of the English industrial revolution). These were the final payment for slaves captured by African and Arab middlemen. Slaves in turn were shipped to the Americas and Caribbean, and were purchased by landowners with the proceeds they got from selling their products to Europe. Flows of gold of course travelled in the opposite direction, as any sale is someone else's purchase.

We can see in this trade circuit an early example of capitalist globalisation processes. Three continents were tied together by M-C-M' value practices that disseminated rewards and punishments, although still at a crude and unsophisticated level, that is, one that had not yet been normalised. The livelihoods of several communities across the two sides of the Atlantic were following an interlinked destiny, in a situation in which the victims were also subjects of struggles.[11] The same of course later applied, with some modifications but no less bloody implications, with the M-C-M' circuits of the Asian colonies.

The linkages among the communities across the globe could be seen through what is common to them all. In the first place, all of them had to endure historical processes of enclosure, of forceful separation from non-market conditions for reproducing their livelihoods. At the peak of the slave trade, coinciding with the English industrial revolution, the men, women and children entering Manchester's sweatshops and working daily for 14 or 16 hours in exchange for a pittance were the result of the proletarisation of the preceding three centuries of enclosure of land, state repression of the struggles for commons and criminalisation of 'indigence' and 'vagrancy', all means that increased dependency on the market (this time the 'labour market') as a means for the reproduction of livelihood. Also the mines, plantations and other 'business operations' in the 'new world' were put in place on lands and along rivers expropriated from the local populations, while the slave-bodies shipped to work in them were themselves 'enclosed', forcefully separated from their communities. Furthermore, it is not only modern slavery that is born out of capital identifying a barrier, whatever its nature, as a business opportunity. The other unwaged activity that the economic calculus and its accounting tools systematically hides from sight also becomes the target of restructuring and subordination to it. Reproduction, that is the activity of giving life and nurturing it, but also of caring for the community and creating and advancing the corresponding forms of knowledge, an activity historically centred on women's labour, is subjected to the structural adjustment of the witch-hunt *both* in the 'old' and the 'new world', to the criminalisation of women's control over procreation and to the discursive definition of women as non-workers (Federici 2004). This is a period in which the semi-autonomous communities of the village are fragmented and, in a movement that will reach its climax during the nineteenth and early twentieth centuries, the family begins to be turned into a 'micro-state', opening the way for the patriarchy of the wage within working-class families, where control over wages plays the same role as property in upper-class families, as men's source of power vis-à-vis women.

In the second place, the transatlantic trade circuit M-C-M' is an early example of *global articulation* of *different conditions* and *activities* of production and reproduction, different socio-economic compositions of labour, different class compositions, different cultural languages of struggles, different subjectivities. From the perspective of capital and its reproduction, it is a global articulation of different techniques and strategies to make people work as efficiently as possible in the face of their resistance and struggles, so as to maximise the monetary profit of the owners of capital employing them and operating in the buying and selling of commodities in the trade circuits. M-C-M' value practices, in other words, started to pervade production and reproduction and increasingly turn life practices into 'work' (Cleaver 1979).

This point must be emphasised, since we have grown accustomed to theorising capitalism through historical narratives of *national* capitalisms.[12]

From Marx's focus on the stages and conditions of English industrial capitalism to modern and contemporary theorisations of Fordism and post-Fordism,
capitalism has not been sufficiently problematised as global *articulation* of a
multitude of techniques and strategies, from slavery to wage labour, from
unwaged work of reproduction to post-Fordist temporary work, from unwaged
third world petty commodity producers on the breadline to the highly skilled
'systems analysts' of high-tech capitalism, from Fordist sweatshops to
cognitive precarious labour. Today, when this articulation of different positionalities in the global wage hierarchy is the truly constituent moment of capital's
discipline, we can no longer hesitate. The general problematic of the overcoming of capitalism, the problematic of the *exodus* from its value practices, is all
captured by the problematic of the overcoming of this articulation dividing the
global social body and pitting co-producing communities against each other.

5
Production and reproduction

CIRCUIT COUPLING

The slave trade does indeed prefigure a variety of modern themes that we find in relation to contemporary globalisation processes. In particular, the planta-tion system sets 'a model of labour management, export-oriented production, economic integration and international division of labour that have since become paradigmatic for capitalist class relations' (Federici 2004: 104). Furthermore, it 'was a key step in the formation of an international division of labour that (through the reproduction of 'consumer goods') integrated the work of the slaves into the reproduction of the European work-force, while keeping enslaved and waged workers geographically and socially divided' (ibid.). Thus, Federici continues, the colonial production of the most important commodities for the reproduction of labour power in Europe besides bread, that is sugar, tea, tobacco, rum and cotton, took off only after slavery was institutionalised and wages in Europe started to rise modestly.[1] But Federici's important point here is that the reproduction of labour power began to be rooted in an international division of labour and a disciplinary process that was instrumental in the accumulation of capital. In the first place, the cost to capitalism of labour power in Europe was cut, through the establishment of a global assembly line that articulated the work of enslaved and waged workers, in ways that 'pre-figured capitalism's present use of Asian, African and Latin American workers as providers of "cheap" "consumer" goods (cheapened by the death squads and military violence) for the "advanced" capitalist countries' (ibid.). In the second place,

the metropolitan wage became the vehicle by which the goods produced by enslaved workers went to the market, and the value of the products of enslaved-labor was realized. In this way, as with female domestic work, the integration of enslaved labor into the production and reproduction of the metropolitan work-force was further established, and the wage was further redefined as an instrument of accumulation, that is, as a lever for mobilizing not only the labor of the workers paid by it, but also for the labor of a

51

multitude of workers hidden by it, because of the unwaged conditions of their work. (ibid.)

In order to capture this link between production and reproduction within the framework of our analysis of capital and its planetary dimension, we must extend Formula 1 to make explicit and visible the process of co-production that takes the form of capital's accumulation.

Capital accumulation is possible if ...

As before, in Formula 3 we follow Marx and represent money capital by M, while the sum value of commodity capital – that is a quantum of money and commodities understood as moments of the self-expansion of capital – is represented by C. Here however we also have LP, representing labour power – a given articulation of human powers, of *powers to*, whether material or immaterial, and whatever the level of skills, ability and complexity of work required – sold on the labour market by wage workers. MP stands for means of production, that is all the other 'fragments of nature' used in the process of production, whether as raw materials or the result of a more elaborate process of transformation by social production: tools, machines, computers, buildings, and so on. Means of production and labour powers come together in the process of production (...P...) which, from the perspective of the human subjects involved, is nothing else but a sensuous process of life practices, in which human energy is consumed (brain, muscles and nerves, as the classic Marxian text puts it) through a variety of emotional states and driven by a variety of often conflicting value practices.

The production process ends with new commodities C′ being produced, which their owner will put onto the market in the hope of selling them and pocket the money M′ and profit ΔM as before.

3. $M–C \{LP; MP\} ... P ... C′–M′$

This circuit of capital illustrated in Formula 3 should not be taken as an illustration of what at a given time actually occurs, but simply as the sequence of conditions which are necessary for capital – as a particular form of human co-production – to reproduce itself on a greater scale. In order to do this, each moment must turn into another. Capital reproduces itself only *if* the previous phase is accomplished. Failing this, there is a crisis.[2] Thus, the valorisation process – the actual phase of production (... P ...) in which life energies are expended in the form of living labour through what we will see are conflicting value practices – *presupposes* the fact that capital is able to find workers who are willing and in a position to sell their labour power and supply a given set of skills. The phase of realisation C′-M′ presupposes that actual living labour has been extracted out of the workers and objectified in the form of monetary value. The phase of purchase M-C presupposes that money is concentrated as accumulated wealth, is available and is thrown into the process as investment. The overall circuit of capital thus represented in its sequential process tells us what *must* happen *if* capital is to be reproduced on a larger and larger scale, *if* growth is to proceed. It does not tell us what will in fact happen.

Indeed, each of the phases in this general formula is not only situated in and constructed in time, but is constructed through struggle and therefore is open to the possibility of a rupture, of a crisis or of bottlenecks. As Bell and Cleaver (2002) have pointed out, each moment of the circuit of capital is a moment of struggle which, depending on intensity, composition and organisational reach, can *circulate* to other moments and will impact on the rate and form of capital's accumulation.

So for example, struggles for wages affects profitability, as do the struggles for working time and rhythms in ...P... . Investment M-C depends on profit expectations, which in turn depends on a combination of past profits, the 'cost-effectiveness' of the expected ability to extract work from workers in relation to others in another place during the moment ...P... . Depending on the different contexts in which the circuit of capital operates, profit expectation and investment also depend on making workers accept new restructuring and job cuts, the ability to make cost-effective the extraction of raw materials, the ability to increase social productivity by the building of infrastructures that might be contested by environmental groups, and so on. In turn, the moment of realisation C-M' depends on the ability to sell, which depends both on purchasing power, and also on the struggles among competitive capitals. The latter in turn is a reflection on the differential ability of individual capitals to turn their workers into objects of production (objects of restructuring which increases productivity, or objects of wage cuts), their differential ability to discipline the command over their living labour. Formula 3 thus implies that capitalist accumulation, in order to occur, *requires strategic intervention* to overcome the inherent crisis of each of its moments. The clash between these strategic interventions and purposeful actions predicated on the value practices of capital and the value practices of the co-producers running in the opposite direction is what Marx called the class struggle, and gives rise to what has been referred to as the 'law of value' (Chapter 13), although, as we shall see, nothing deterministic should be implied in this 'law'.

... more ifs ...

Marx's money circuit of capital however abstracts from what we have seen is a central component of capitalist production, namely the work of reproduction of labour power, which is mostly unwaged. Cleaver (1979), building on the insight of Dalla Costa and James (1972), represented the process of reproduction of labour power as a circuit coupled to the money circuit of capital. In this

way, it is possible to visualise and problematise the relation between the work
of reproduction and the capital valorisation process and also the strategic
importance that struggles in reproduction have in relation to the overall coupled circuits.[3] This is illustrated in Formula 4, where a circuit of reproduction
is written above the money circuit of capital.

4.   LP–M–C ... P* ... LP*
                           M–C {LP; MP} ... P ... C′–M

   In the circuit of reproduction, the money (M) obtained in exchange for
labour power (LP) is used to buy commodities (C). Commodities however
need to be processed in the household through an expenditure of labour P*.
This expenditure of reproduction labour allows the physical and psychological
reproduction of labour power (LP* = regenerated labour power), which then
can be sold again to capitalists.

   It goes without saying that the production of labour power is not the only
thing that goes on in this circuit. While reproducing bodies, minds and spirits
in their many facets, we also reproduce and build upon value practices other
than capital. Whether in kin, friendship or other networks, social relations,
desires and images are (re)produced anew through co-productions that *only to
certain degrees* are coupled to capital as reproducing labour power with certain
characteristics. At the same time, there is much of the reproduction of our bodies that is beyond and, in fact, in opposition to being labour power *for* capital.
So for example, despite the increasing pressures parents face to make their
children compete for grades to meet skills and educational standards that train
them to 'compete in the global economy', I cannot reduce the ongoing
relational practices that 'we' as parents have to our children in terms of reproduction of labour power, of facilitating their future coupling to the rhythms,
concept of times and skill portfolio necessary for them to survive in a money-
centred society. Through the games we play with them, the stories we read to
them, the silences in which they observe us interacting with the world, they
will also develop skills, horizons and values against which, in their own ways,
they will be the ones who will measure the value practices of capital.

   To go back to the circuit of reproduction, this does not tell us who is
performing this work of reproduction, although within the dominant patriarchal relations between the sexes, women do the great bulk of this work. In any
case, the interlinked circuits of capital described in Formula 4 only give us a
broad theoretical framework in which to conceptualise the link between reproduction labour and capital's accumulation. The top circuit could in principle be
used to illustrate other forms of unwaged labour, such as student work.
Capitalism, after all, 'is the first productive system where the children of the
exploited are disciplined and educated in institutions organized and controlled
by the ruling classes' (Dalla Costa and James 1972: 25). Here, the flow of

money from the bottom to the top circuit can take the form of transfers (students grants) or be simply erased with the abolition of student grants, while the process of production P* represents the process of producing what economists call 'human capital'. Also, the time-frame required to produce human capital through schoolwork may extent beyond the time period assumed in Formula 4. We must also notice that, as all productions are forms of social cooperation, so is the reproduction of labour power. Capitalist cooperation however is structured through a wage hierarchy. So for example, the increasing pressures on children to perform to given *measurable* standards across schools competing for resources is transferred into parents being co-opted as unpaid teachers.[4] As Frank Furedi puts it, 'from day one in primary schools, [parents] are told that the performance of their children is intimately linked to how much support they get at home. In a desperate attempt to improve standards of education, parents' concern for their children is manipulated to draw them in as unpaid teachers' (Furedi 2006: 28).[5]

While Marx's analysis allows us to put at the centre what mainstream economics makes invisible (the work of production), this modification of Marx's circuit of capital allows us to throw light on the other mass of human activity made invisible by mainstream economics (and mainstream Marxism!): unwaged labour. Correspondingly, while Marx's analysis of the circuit of capital points at the genealogical moment of enclosure of communities from resources held in common (primitive accumulation), the genealogical moment of the circuit of reproduction of labour power is the enclosure of the body. It is this specific form of enclosure that ultimately is at the root of the constitution of social co-production as divided into a 'private' and a 'public' sphere.

Formula 4 highlights the fact that both waged and unwaged work are moments of capital's sequence of transformation and therefore they become complementary targets of capital's strategies, realms for capital's value practices and value struggles. It also suggests that capital's working day was 24/7 much before the emergence of post-Fordism and 'immaterial' or 'cognitive' labour.[6]

Thus, capital's strategies on the side of reproduction, such as the shape of the educational system or the level of population growth, or the shape and size of expenditure on public services – strategies that pass through the discipline and control of real bodies, or, to put it in Foucault's terms (1981: 135–45), that define the realm of *biopolitics* – are complementary to strategies on the side of production to define which sectors to promote or to regulate the social wage. On the other hand, cuts in social wages and transfers to families, accompanied by an increase in transfers and subsidies to companies, has the double effect of restructuring production and reproduction work. All the same, struggles in one circuit can and often will circulate in the other, or define a point of resistance to a strategy initiated in the other, as, for example, women's struggles in Europe and the United States in the 1960s, which, by disrupting and subverting the micro-state of the patriarchal family, have also shaken the overall social fabric which facilitated capital's accumulation. This by threatening the reproduction of male workers in particular forms and routines that then contribute to shake the 'social peace' predicated on collectively bargained growth in wages and productivity for the unionised workers of the Fordist deal.

It is also important to anticipate that in the current neoliberal era of global capital, the disciplinary mechanisms that regulate social cooperation through the markets are also increasingly pervading the realm of unwaged labour, especially through the disciplinary role of international finance in the global North and debt in the global South. Indeed, international competition at every scale of social doing is *not only* made possible by a reservoir of unwaged labourers doing the work of reproduction in the global factory. Also, competitive relations with the other at different scales of social action are increasingly constituted as *biopolitical* competition, that is, are subjected to a governance of the body loosely understood (read questions of demography, health, education, environment), that is differential, a governance that attempts to articulate and couple needs and desires emerging from a place-specific class composition to the needs of competitive battle.

WAGED AND UNWAGED WORK AND THE REALM OF THE INVISIBLE

When looking at the split between the work of production and reproduction, the monetised and the non-monetised, the waged and the unwaged, we are staring at a socially constructed division of doing that cuts through the social body. From the perspective of the preservation of the social body, of the meeting of needs and the following of desires, this division simply does not make sense, it is 'crazy', if not delirious, and it is produced and maintained only by virtue of an exercise of power that drives to separate as well as to reproduce and maintain separation in varying degrees.

When we look at it from the perspective of value practices that are distinct from capital, and are rooted in the needs and desires of producing bodies, playing with children and preparing food contribute as much to the reproduction of a 'community' as playing a musical instrument at a wedding, designing a piece of software or laying a railroad track. In all these cases we are, to paraphrase Marx, appropriating nature's production in a form adapted to our wants (Marx 1976a: 171–3). From the perspective of 'use values' therefore, all these are contributions to the livelihoods of a community broadly defined. But from the perspective of 'exchange value', from the perspective of use values produced for the purpose/*telos* of moneymaking, the form of production adapts to the wants of profit.

Adaptation is a process through which biological or social organisations become suitable for certain ends, fit specific situations. In biology, the process of adaptation is generally understood in physiological or evolutionary terms.

In the first case, it refers to the adjustment of living organisms to the environment (including other living organisms) within the lifetime of an organism. In the second case, it refers instead to the adjustment of a population over several generations. For our purposes here, the process of adapting the forms of production and cooperation to the wants of profit is also the process of *constitution* of the invisible, because, in the process of adaptation, something must be lost. And this something is often something of *value* to the producers themselves, but not central to, or perhaps even opposed to, the production of capital's values. What is lost, however, does not vanish from the face of the earth, it simply becomes *invisible* to capital's discourses and value practices that construct the world and, *to the extent* that normalisation and naturalisation to these practices extends to the co-producers, is invisible to the co-producers themselves. This condition of invisibility of social subjects, life practices, aspirations and lived experiences is a necessary condition for capital's self-preservation. Since for capital anything of value has a price tag, and since capitalism is a subsystem of co-production, the recognition that the value of something does not depends on its price tag can only turn into a precondition of its commodification and/or an invisible (i.e., non-monetised) articulation to the system of commodities.

There are perhaps three interrelated realms of the invisible when we look at social co-production through the eyes of capital's value practices, but without losing the perspective of *other* values: the doing for which there is no corresponding monetary value going to the doers, that is the unpaid labour defining exploitation; the lived experience of co-production; and actualised, desired or imagined alternative modes of co-production and corresponding social relations.

Division between waged and unwaged work

To begin with the first, the division between waged and unwaged activities, between public and private, between working for money and 'in your own time', between production and reproduction, between work and housework, between what is valued by capital through a corresponding price tag and what is not, is the true material basis upon which the realm of the invisible that is at the basis of capital's exploitation is constructed. Because if, following Marx, it is true that surplus value is the invisible value that is extracted from waged workers' labour and appropriated in the form of profit, it is also true that waged workers need to reproduce themselves, and this implies that they as well need to access the products of *others' labour*. Their dinner is prepared, their clothes washed, their health preserved thanks to invisible, objectified workers. This was true 'yesterday', at the height of women's enclosure in the patriarchal households, as it is true 'today' in the post-women's-liberation-movement lands. The forms are different, and today's form is quite mystifying.

Yesterday's story – in so far as the European roots of capital are concerned, but still present today in a variety of different contexts and forms[7] – is quite straightforward, as we have briefly seen in the last chapter. It is predicated on the witch-hunt that kills women and vaporises their role in the communities, thus depriving European farmers' movements defending commons of their most fervent activists, women. It also opened the door to new modes of doing what these women were doing, thus constituting new social relations. For example, through the centuries, healing and midwifery were professionalised and industrialised into the health industry. A process that was mainly communal and convivial was replaced by one that is mainly competitive and profit-oriented. A dance of direct social relations, of gift exchanges feeding into each other and constituting identities and webs, of women of different generations reflecting and sharing their experiences of childbearing and rearing creating an empowering knowledge, was replaced by an order made up of procedures, the doctor–patient hierarchy, isolated and disempowered women, global commodity chains, waiting lists and 'healing' commodities, produced for profit and enclosed by murderous patents. This is not to romanticise the past, nor to refuse a priori the use value of modern medicine. But since the latter has developed through forced experiments on rebellious bodies, and it is today straightjacketed in forms compatible with the profit-driven and rent-seeking activities of giant pharmaceutical companies, it is the uncritical acceptance of current mainstream 'healing' practices that depend on romantisation of the present.

Through these transformations, the Western patriarchal family was born, the classic model of which enclosed women in the home, and constructed their humanity within its confined sphere. Patriarchy is of course far older than the three centuries of capital's hegemony (Mies 1998). However, it is only as an instrument of the boundlessness of profit making and the corresponding value practices that we encounter generalised practices of expropriation and management of women's own forces of production, their own bodies, that creates a neat division of labour, a neat confinement of roles. The implications of this are clear:

> To the extent that women were cut off from direct socialized production and isolated in the home, all possibilities of social life outside the neighbourhood were denied to them, and hence they were denied of social knowledge and social education. When women are deprived of wide experience of organizing and planning collectively industrial and other mass struggles, they are denied a basic source of education, the experience of social revolt. And this experience is primarily the experience of learning your own capacities, that is, your power, and the capacities, the power, of your class. Thus the isolation from which women have suffered has confirmed to society and to themselves the myth of female incapacity. (Dalla Costa and James 1972: 29–30)

This 'unprecedented economic division of the sexes, ... unprecedented economic conception of the family ... unprecedented antagonism between the domestic and public spheres made wage work into a necessary adjunct of life' (Illich 1981: 107). It also turned male waged workers into foremen of housework, direct exploiters, appropriators and managers of the activity of reproduction, which had to conform to the needs and desires of a male body psychologically and physically depleted by ever increasing rhythms of waged work.[8] This means that the unwaged work of reproduction that women and, today, an increasing number of men perform must be regarded as producing value for capital, and not only use value.[9] In this framework, the struggles of women in the home therefore resulted in a direct challenge to the capacity of capital to accumulate, disrupting the synchronisation between the circuits of capital production and that of reproduction, sending waves of refusal, insubordination and constituent desires from one circuit to another (Bell and Cleaver 2002).

Today's story has not changed in substance, but in form, through a planetary restructuring of reproduction work into new hierarchies. Capital's response to Western women's struggles in the 1960s and 1970s against housework and challenging family roles had a similar impact to that of the struggles for higher wages and shorter hours of waged workers in factories and offices: globalisation, externalisation and outsourcing. The result of this is that despite the fact that in most Western countries there has been a moderate increase in men's participation in housework and women's struggles have contributed to put men and their perception of their traditional role into crisis, at the same time neoliberal discourse has offered many women a clear deal: stop fighting men's withdrawal from housework, and subcontract it instead to the market. In this way, it was argued, we have a triple-win situation: women in search of professionally rewarding and highly competitive careers can have them without giving up on having children. Women from the global South have access to jobs that, following waves of neoliberal enclosures and increasing wealth polarisation, become more and more necessary. Finally, men do not need to do more housework than the increasingly demanding waged jobs prevent even the willing from doing.

Thus, while the women's movements of the 1960s and 1970s succeeded in pointing out the unpaid labour at the point of reproduction, they did not succeed in challenging other areas of social doing in which labour is exploited. Indeed, the neoliberal solution to women's struggles is far from 'women's liberation' or indeed, anybody's liberation. In the last 30 years, just as the international division of labour of waged work has been restructured to incorporate a plurality of managerial forms of control over labour, from Fordism to craft production, from new slavery to post-Fordism, so the international division of *housework* or reproduction work takes a plurality of often interrelated forms: from TV dinners produced by poor illegal migrants in the North to the child labour of their sisters left in the home country to care for the elderly and the younger members of the family.

As Barbara Ehrenreich and Arlie Russell Hochschild write in their edited collection on women's domestic and sex work in the global economy,

> the first world takes on a role like that of the old-fashioned male in the family – pampered, entitled, unable to cook, clean, and find his socks. Poor countries take on a role like that of the traditional woman within the family – patient, nurturing, and self-denying. A division of labor feminists critiqued when it was 'local' has now, metaphorically, gone global. (Ehrenreich and Hochschild 2002: 11)

Indeed, when your liberation depends on someone else's servitude, there is a problem with the meaning of the word freedom. And we are indeed talking about servitude here. In most countries in the North, waged servants are becoming the norm for an increasing number of working families, both because highly demanding jobs for family members of all genders makes it impossible to devote enough time and energy to the housework and reproduction, and because the wage levels for migrant nannies and maids are kept down by widespread poverty in the home countries and a correspondingly large supply of labour.[10] Not to mention the increasing portion of reproduction work being commodified by profit-driven industry, which has turned mother's slow-cooking soups into the fast food industry. While the former required cooking and washing-up by invisible workers inside the home, the latter only requires a visible cash payment; the rest (including rubbish ingredients, stressed-out labour processes, brutality against animals, environmental degradation, the planetary survival circuits of migrant workers and their ongoing struggle for survival, upon which the salads we eat in the North depends) are all hidden.[11] The cost of unwaged reproduction work in other words is externalised through *outsourcing* just as much as in the case of production. Let us keep in mind that, as we shall see in Chapters 8 and 9, everyone's externalisation of costs, is someone else's *internalisation*.

What both yesterday's and today's stories of the relation between capitalism, patriarchy and the work of reproduction tell us is that capitalist development depends on the enclosure of the body, on seeing and constructing the body as an instrument, a machine, a tool that delivers socially measurable output, whether this is a British child stressed out to meet the demands of the national curriculum in competition with other children and other schools, or a Chinese woman sweating it out on an assembly line producing electronic components, or an English mother struggling to demonstrate she is looking for a job in order to keep receiving benefits to allow her to stay at home with her 12-month-old child. At the same time, both yesterday's and today's stories remind us that the construction of the *other* has a material basis, and this is grounded on the wage relation, which is also defined by the *absence* of wages in conditions in which the reproduction of livelihood increasingly depend on access to money. The wage is not only an instrument of remuneration, it is also a tool of division, hence of defining lines of vulnerabilities and strengths along the wage hierarchy; it grounds the power relation between a woman and the domestic worker whom she can hire and fire. Clearly, many women hire helpers and domestic workers because they do not have the power to avoid it (they need to bring home a wage in a context of declining social entitlements and downward pressures on the wage due to increasing competition). However, the wage here is also a way of devaluing certain types of work, such as the work of caring, in relation to others, such as the work of the lawyer, say, hiring the carer. Market forces of course play a role here; but this is precisely the point, market processes reproduce value practices. We need, therefore, to continue from where the feminist critique of domestic labour of the 1970s left off, and expand the concept of class by redefining what work is in capitalist society – to include the waged and the unwaged as they have done, but also to go beyond them in highlighting and problematising the very material processes that continuously seek to reproduce divisions across the social body and pose contingent questions of the constitution of commons.

Invisible lived experience and alternatives

This enclosure of the body, upon which the entire edifice of capitalist exploitation depends, opens up two other complementary dimensions of social doing that are invisible from the perspective of the value practices of capital. We need to turn the spotlight onto them. First, the lived experience of waged or unwaged production, of doing, of 'labour' in the capitalist sense, that is of a doing that is measured by a force external to itself, is largely irrelevant to capital's *telos* and its value practices. It is not however irrelevant to the producers themselves, nor to a critical discourse that wants to pose the question of the beginning of history. To capital, this lived experience, of course, becomes important when it is the ground for refusal, rebellion and exodus – that is, when it gets noticed and must be reined in. Managerial discourses such as human resource management (at the moment of production) and marketing (at the moment of sale and consumption) are precisely constructed to reassert and stabilise the coupling between frustrated and struggling subjects and the value practices of capital. The marginalisation of the lived experience of doing, the subordination of the awareness of the sensuous and relational *processes* to goals and ends, is a specific patriarchal character of doing. As Luce Irigaray puts it, historically, in patriarchal traditions,

the individual and collective life wants and believes to be able to organise itself outside the atmosphere of the natural world. The body, also called microcosm, is cut out of the universe, called macrocosm. It is subordinated to sociological rules, to rhythms which are aliens to its sensibility, to its lived perceptions: the day and night, the seasons, the vegetative growth ... this means that the different forms of participation to light, to sounds and music, to smells, touch, or to natural tastes, are no longer cultivated as human qualities. The body is no longer educated to develop spiritually its perceptions, but to detach itself from the sensuous in favour of a culture which is more abstract, more speculative, more logical. (Irigaray 1997: 56–7, my translation)

The link between patriarchy and capitalism is here, in the construction of a subject normalised to the subordination of the lived experience of doing, to a rationality and a calculus that priorities *other* things, to 'rhythms' and therefore cyclical times, 'which are aliens to its sensibility', hence measured in ways that are external to the body (shareholder values, profits, performance indicators, and so on). The clash in value practices that constitutes capitalism is grounded on the enclosure of the body that is produced by patriarchy. Indeed, to me this is one of the most important links between the two, in that patriarchy *is like a system of line management* and as such it inscribes itself into every capitalist organisation, wherever the economic rationale is set to filter out *other* rationales, wherever we have the privileging of rationalities, alien rhythms and measures over sensuous perceptions and relational dances, wherever these selecting processes are contested.

Second, the shadow cast over the lived experience of doers implies that alternative horizons of social doing and forms of cooperation are also in shadow, discursively selected out, trivialised, ridiculed. This is because the *material* force of transformation can only emerge as a desire to overcome the existing lived experience of the doing body, and it goes without saying that this lived experience is also directly influenced by the degree of communication among co-producers themselves. This desire is discursively obliterated. So, for example, what is the theorisation of *homo economicus* but the assumption that co-producing singularities do not desire *another* dimension of living, other modes of articulating their livelihoods, or that this desire does not act as a material force? What is the paradigm of constrained maximisation, the mantra of every economics student, but a shadow cast over the *alternatives* to the existing order of things by virtue of which economists can theorise the utter isolation of individual agents for which constraints are always *given*. From the perspective of a desiring body, of a body that lives and struggles through the experience of co-production in communication with others, *constraints are never given*. From the perspective of a desiring body in communication with others, whatever is given is socially constructed, and whatever is socially constructed is not only socially deconstructable, but also socially *reconstructable* through value practices that are other than those rigidifying the given constrains as the cage of the present.

In other words, capital's production is not only predicated on the quantitatively definable invisibility of surplus labour, the unpaid labour performed by the unwaged and by the waged over and above the paid wage. The discourse through which capital's value practice orders social co-production also casts a shadow over the lived experience of doers and hence over the desires for *other modes* of doing. To put it in classic terms, *rates* of exploitation and *degrees* of alienation are two sides of the same coin.

The production and maintenance of this double qualitative character of the invisibility of doers is predicated in turn on a more fundamental alienation and invisibility, and here is another aspect of the link between waged production and unwaged reproduction: they are both predicated on the fixation of value practices. Capital's value practices do not regard production *for profit* as a conscious interaction among human beings and among human beings and nature (the double invisibility discussed above) predicated on specific values, but rather as an activity *of* human nature. All mainstream schools of economics tend to naturalise capitalist markets, and the drives of human beings to 'truck and barter', as Adam Smith puts it in his classic *Wealth of Nations*, and to gain a 'profit'. But this ideological construction is nothing compared to the effects that the ongoing repetition of market disciplinary mechanisms has on the normalisation of this mode of life and social cooperation of labour, the fixation of the correspondent value practices in the daily activities and strategies of fragmented people attempting to reproduce their livelihood in the context of capitalist markets. In going to work or looking for a job, signing a check or queuing up at the welfare office, investing money in a pension fund or collecting discount points from the local supermarket, we are feeding back into the system what the system wants from us: participation. And to us, *only in so far as we act as singular agents*, this is to a large extent unavoidable. In living our lives within disciplinary markets without at the same time an awareness of the *outside* we also inhabit, we grow accustomed to this mode of social co-production, we normalise it and therefore naturalise and fix it.

A similar naturalisation occurs in capitalist patriarchy:

women's household and child-care work are seen as an extension of their physiology, of the fact that they give birth to children, of the fact that 'nature' has provided them with a uterus. All the labour that goes into the production of life, including the labour of giving birth to a child, is not seen as the conscious interaction of a human being *with* nature, that is a truly human activity, but rather as an activity *of* nature, which produces plants and animals unconsciously and has no control over this process. (Mies 1998: 45)

There is thus a similarity between these two different moments of social co-production even when we measure them from the perspective of capital's *telos*. In both cases, the subjects are objectified, their feedback loops, their relational dance with nature bounded by fetters that socially construct them as 'housewives', waged workers, or consumers, *that is doers whose activities have a purpose/telos defined by 'nature'*, while instead these activities are socially constructed and value-loaded.

There is of course a difference between the two types of naturalisation of activities. While in the case of production work, naturalisation implies the separation of the forces of production (means of production plus *telos*) from the social body, in the work of reproduction, the *force of production* that becomes the target of expropriation is the body! The discursive practice according to which the production of children, their rearing, etc., is the product *of* nature, implies regarding women themselves as passive recipients of nature, which opens the way for the state, population planners and the corresponding professionals, health apparatuses and witch-hunters to treat them as such.[12]

This again casts a shadow making invisible what instead is a lived experience of production:

In the course of their history, women observed the changes in their own bodies and acquired through observation and experiment a vast body of experimental knowledge about the functions of their bodies, about the rhythms of menstruation, about pregnancy and childbirth. This appropriation of their own bodily nature was closely related to the acquisition of knowledge about the generative forces of external nature, about plants, animals, the earth, water and air.

Thus, they did not simply breed children like cows, but they appropriated their own generative and productive forces, they analysed and reflected upon their own and former experiences and passed them on to their daughters. This means they were not helpless victims of the generative forces of their bodies, but learned to influence them, including the number of children they wanted to have. (Mies 1998: 54)

The basic precondition for the constitution of alternative modes of co-production is predicated on making visible what capital's value practices keep invisible.

6

Production, reproduction and global loops

In this chapter I want to give an illustration of the relation between waged and unwaged activities by locating it within a circular time rather than the linear time of Formula 4. A time, that is, in which the doing returns to itself and thus creates patterns and norms. This will open up, in the final section of this chapter, to a broader conceptualisation of the international division of labour that articulates production and reproduction across the globe.

In Figure 2 we have brought together waged and unwaged circuits, namely M-C-M' and C-M-C.[1] It is important to recognise the necessary complementarities between these two circuits. M-C-M', that is buying in order to sell, would not be anything without C-M-C, that is selling in order to buy. However, if to preserve capital is to feed its limitless thirst for new value, to preserve a body with needs is to acquire use value that satisfies those needs. While in the first case money is an end in itself, in the second case it is a means to an end; if in the first case acquisition is boundless, in the second one it is bounded. But once the circuits are articulated, the ends of the former might end up shaping the means of the latter. There are only two extreme possibilities, and reality is probably somewhere in the middle: either the boundless character of M-C-M' succeeds, through a variety of marketing and manipulative means, in turning consumption into consumerism. The drive to consume more, of course, is always subject to budget constraints, hence debt and the reproduction of an endless condition of scarcity. Or the boundaries within which we define, satisfy and produce for our needs become constituent of the boundaries within which capital must be confined, a 'barrier' that capital will need to overcome. Thus, the most general way to portray value struggles is to set them in terms of the contradiction between exchange value and use value, production for profit and production for needs, as is the case in traditional Marxism.

But this opposition between exchange value and use value only partly captures what is really going on, which is *ongoing* clashing value *practices* of doing and relating in specific forms and for specific contradictory purposes. Production for profit of a capitalist company is *at the same time* production for needs (whether these are 'engineered' needs or the 'genuine' needs and desires of buyers). Also, the work going on in this or that site of production is the activity of subjects with needs and desires, and this activity in turn produces needs and desires. On the other hands, the doing within the reproduction sphere is not only production for need. By learning and interiorising the discipline of the alarm clock, by showing up on time at school, doing exams, learning to measure ourselves and others in terms of performance criteria such as exam grades and so on, we produce bodies and minds for no other needs than those of a society organised around competition, scarcity and profit.

The 'outside' emerging from within

What I mean to underline here is the fact that the value struggles we have discussed in Chapter 2 are transverse to the waged and unwaged circuits of capital, cut across them; they are simultaneously present in both the reproduction and the production spheres. The 'outside' therefore is not this or that sphere, is not a sphere of social production, but value practices and their corresponding organisational reach that to a variety of degrees refuse their articulation to capital, that posit their autonomy from it, *wherever this practice is positioned along the wage hierarchy*: value practices that, unlike those of capital, have boundaries set by the practising subjects themselves. We can envisage these value struggles as circulating across the circuits of production and reproduction and in this way giving rise to capital's defence mechanism of self-preservation or, as we shall see in the next chapter, homeostatic mechanisms.

Bringing together the production and reproduction cycles and taking them as a whole allows us to better observe that capital's *conatus* of self-preservation has features similar to living forces endeavouring to preserve themselves. As in the case of cells or complex organisms, capital too needs to feed on an outside, to derive from it the sources of its energies and to dispose in it the waste of its processes.

The first realm of the outside we may call, for want of better words, 'the community'. The other one is the realm of 'nature'. We obviously understand these terms very loosely, and are aware of the complex and contradictory webs of meanings that these two terms necessarily evoke.

For the purpose of this analysis, I understand the community as those social practices, that social cooperation, in which the relations among the nodes of a network are not constituted by capital's way of measuring and grading human action. On the contrary, they are made up of other types of relations, unmediated by money and the value practices of capital, or, in any case, in which money measures are subordinated to other measures. My working definition of community therefore is a web of *direct* relations among subjects whose repetitive engagement and feedback processes allow them, through conflict and/or cooperation, to define the norms of their interaction on the basis of *other values* than those of capital. When commodity exchange occurs in communities, this is accidental, occasional and not constituent of the character of the relations among people. Community in this sense, is not defined by a particular form or by a particular number of members. For the purposes of this discussion, our definition could range from the nuclear family to the tribe, from networks of friends sharing particular aspects of their reproduction to international networks of solidarity and struggle – or by a specific relation among communities which can be nested inside each other in meta-communities such as indigenous nations or the 'movement of movements' or instead separated by feuds and rivalries. In other words, community for us covers that realm of human reproduction whose *conatus* of self-preservation is *not* endless expansion of monetary value but is limited by needs, directed by desires, and constituted by different value practices, whatever these are in specific contexts. *To the extent to which* this realm of human reproduction is linked to capital, then we may refer to such communities in terms of 'reproduction of labour power', whether this happens within the sphere of unwaged work or within the sphere of communal links among waged workers in opposition to the demands of their bosses. In any case, as we have seen in the last chapter, the realm of reproduction of labour power is itself a subsystem of co-production and corresponding community relations. In the next section we shall briefly explore how in the age of 'globalisation' the reproduction of labour power is displaced through an international division of labour and the extent to which it is commodified and absorbed into the *conatus* of capital's self-preservation through the 'service' sector. From the perspective of the whole, however, even this absorption does not eliminate the invisible realm of the reproduction of labour power; it only displaces it geographically and intensifies the working lives of workers.

Interlinked ecologies

The other realm 'outside' capital that we must consider is what we called 'nature'. Nature comprises a series of interlinked ecologies, of processes of homeostasis, from the cell to human society, from photosynthesis to weather patterns. When these ensembles of processes are defined in relation to human reproduction – itself an ecological system with its own features – they are called the 'environment'. The notion of the environment, in other words, refers to the notion of nature as a collection of things rather than processes.[2] From the perspective of the *conatus* of capital, this collection of things acquires a twofold meaning: first, it is an immense resource, an immense mine, from which to endlessly extract the basic raw materials necessary to feed the processes of commodity production. (Alternatively, it is a theme park to show to tourists.) Second, it is an immense dumping ground, on which to pour all sorts of waste from growing production processes.

It goes without saying that to conceptualise natural homeostatic processes outside capital does not mean that capitalist production does not have an *effect* on nature. Global warming and the corresponding changes in weather patterns are a direct result of the *interlinkages* and feedbacks between homeostatic processes of capitalist production and those of nature. It also must be noted that announcing aloud the looming ecological catastrophe as a necessary limit we have to face up to in the hope of changing the ways of social production is not a convincing argument for bringing substantial change. We must face up to the fact that capital strives to overcome limits, and its *conatus* of self-preservation can turn ecological crises into a series of 'business opportunities' that are already and will certainly be advertised and propagandised as 'job creation' devices: sea-front barriers against high waters; hotels and other tourist establishments built where there used to be fishing communities (wiped out by tsunamis); or more simply, personal air-purifiers 'wherever you go' of the type you can already buy in airport lounges.

Hypercycle

These sets of interlinkages and feedback processes of different types might be described at a general level as in Figure 2.

In Figure 2 we have what we may call a hypercycle, that is a series of processes with feedback loops that are interlinked and are interdependent.[3] There are three such processes represented here, although each of these can be seen to be constituted by thousands if not millions of others.[4] The Production I and Production II cycles illustrate money circuits of capital as discussed with reference to Formula 3. In this example, Production II might represent the capitalist production of consumer goods and services and Production I the capitalist production of means of production. There are thus here two different sectors, or 'departments', that comprise different numbers of individual capitals.

We have seen that the money circuit of capital is simply an illustration of the moments through which capital as a social force must go in order to fulfil its life preservation: profit and accumulation. We have also seen, however, that each of the moments of this required transformations is a moment of value struggle. Community – that is value practices other than capital plus organisational reach – therefore also emerges within waged work.

On the other hand, in the loop called Reproduction self-preservation also goes through a series of moments and feedback processes to satisfy the needs and follow the desires of community members. To the extent that a community of this kind depends on access to monetary income for its self-preservation, some members of the community must look for a commodity to sell, either a

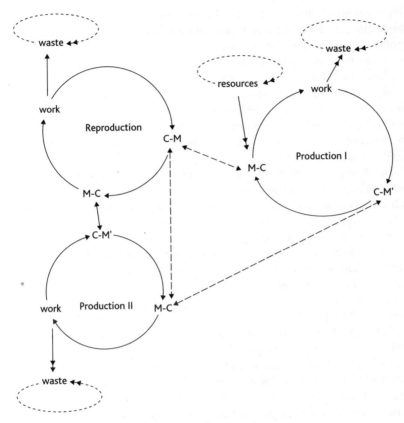

Figure 2 The articulation between *conati* of self-preservation

'thing' or a 'service' produced within the community, or a 'job'. In this latter case, the members of the community will sell their labour power which, as capacity for work, for deploying a given set of *powers to*, will enter the process of capitalist production and disciplinary integration M-C-M'. In exchange for this labour power (or petty commodities, or 'services'), the community – or a selection of its members – receives a quantum of money, a 'wage' in the case of labour power, or the market prices of the commodities sold. With this money, the community must attend some or all of the material elements of its needs, go 'shopping' so to speak, the degree to which they must do this depending on the degree of their dependence on the market or, inversely on the degree of their separation from non-market access to means of production. Once these goods are brought within the sphere of the community, they need to be transformed: housework, domestic work, community work are required. As for the case of production of commodities, the latter were produced through the productive consumption of the means of production, so the process of reproduction of labour power begins with the productive consumption of the shopping basket (in the first place, of the shoes necessary to go shopping). Their transformation into useful elements of reproduction necessitates work, i.e., housework, which, as in the case of waged work, is also a site of value struggles, as was discussed in the last chapter. Once this is done, for example in the form of a dinner, it is up to the homeostasis of our biological system to do its side of the work, which in turn allows our bodies to regenerate and be ready for another day of work in department I or II (or simply looking for a job).

The third process of homeostasis illustrated here begins with the exchange between human reproduction (as both community self-preservation and capital self-preservation) and 'the environment'. This exchange see fragments of nature going into the process of capitalist production and community reproduction as resources, and going out as 'waste' (in Figure 2 I have indicated resources going in the process of capital in department I only for convenience. In reality, although crucially, in a variety of degrees, human production regards nature as a resource in all contexts). These in turn will become the objects of the natural homeostatic processes of various ecologies, which we cannot deal with here. The degree to which resources and waste are dumped and extracted will of course have an effect on the balance of these homeostatic processes, of which global warming, disruption of weather patterns, deforestation, desertification and floods are all macro-manifestations. Here we discover that what we call the 'environment' is actually 'nature'. This is, as we have seen, not a collection of things, but a web of processes whose ordering principles comprise a series of interlinked ecologies, which, when disrupted and disarticulated, 'fight back'.

Detritus

We need to indulge a little more in this notion of waste in so far as it refers to subjects. In Chapter 2 I have argued that social reproduction is far larger than the set of life practices that are channelled into capitalist loops. This however implies that the more pervasive capitalism is, the more the 'waste' that flows out of its circuits of production and reproduction of labour power, or what economists call 'externalities', enters and colonises *the condition* of life and practices outside capital's. In Chapter 16 we shall discuss the notion of *detritus*, which attempts to capture the layers of waste inscribed in the body and in the environment and that emerges out of the articulation of life practices following their own *conatus* to capital's loops (and capital's *conatus*). The waste inscribed in the body can be understood, for example, in terms of the energy-exhausting participation in disciplinary mechanisms of the markets discussed in Part 3, what in *Capital* Marx calls the expenditure of labour power. In this sense, detritus is the common material condition (although diversified in different contexts and at different points within the wage hierarchy) in which the problematic of social reproduction is uniquely in the hands of waged and unwaged 'dispossessed' and their *organisational reach*. In other words, social reproduction dramatically depends on the effectiveness, organisational reach and communal constitution of struggles and the ability to reclaim and constitute commons in a condition of *detritus*, whether this is simply to reproduce labour power to be siphoned back into the circuits of capitals, or to *live* through practices of constitution beyond capital's value practices.

Multitude of struggles and ubiquitous revolution

In Figure 2, the loops constituting the whole hypercycle are nothing else but moments, temporally defined by a birth date, a death date and a life cycle, and spatially constituted by a set of relations within a network of people and objects. Furthermore, each of these moments, is constituted by *conflict among social forces* and *corresponding value practices running in different directions*, the general character of which depends on the type of moment, and the specific and concrete character of which depends on context, and life history. I use the term 'constituted' and not 'embedded' or 'expressed' for the reason that conflict here is really the stuff of life, what gives it dynamism and ultimately – through repetition – creates social form.

This also implies that conflict pervading the production and reproduction loops takes up different forms, but one thing that is clear is that none of the subjects engaged in conflict has the property of a 'universal subject'. It is not the industrial worker, it is not women, nor the peasantry, nor the 'immaterial workers'. In a system of feedback mechanisms like capitalist production, each part is instrumental in the production of the whole, no part therefore is *central*, yet every part is a site of struggle and, because articulated with the others, a potential moment in the circulation of struggle, its enrichment and development of form. We shall see how in the age of globalisation capital seeks to articulate these conflicts through disciplinary processes in both production and reproduction. Capitalist social relations which are predicated and reproduce capitalist value can, in a word, be anywhere. Overcoming these social relations implies overcoming a mode of life and of production of life that articulates diverse moments. Not only must the revolution be ubiquitous, but it can be triggered from anywhere, and the problematic of circulation across circuits is central to its reproduction.

INTERNATIONAL DIVISION OF LABOUR

One of the things that should be highlighted from the previous analysis is something that is pretty obvious, but little discussed, that is that each production node and value practices M-C-M′ will also be interlaced with reproduction loops. This implies that our analysis of capital must attempt to apprehend how the two are articulated, and not only be confined to the monetised realm, to what economists of mainstream or Marxist persuasion call 'the economy'. This means that if reproduction is interlinked to production through feedback processes, and if struggling subjects are in both loops, the understanding of the context-specific *conditions* within which reproduction takes place, as well the strategies deployed to change these conditions, is paramount to our understanding of capital.

Thus for example, the financial capital mobility intensified by financial deregulation that has accompanied the neoliberal era helps to keep down the cost of reproduction of labour power in the component of social wage. This is because the tax competition of different neoliberal governments aimed at attracting capital is also at the same time competition in social spending. In countries in the global North, this regime, accompanied by relatively liberal bank regulations for credit, leads to increased personal indebtedness necessary for countering the erosion of wages and other entitlements. On the other hand, in the global South, cuts in entitlements and enclosures are imposed over the social body through the management of the debt crisis and structural adjustment policies. The ongoing working of state and market forces, and the conflicts upon which each is grounded, create a world configuration of areas of reproduction with different qualitative and quantitative characteristics. To the eye of a profit-seeking agent, these can be ranked on a hierarchal scale with respect to conditions of wages, environmental standards, regulatory regimes, 'political risk', and so on.[5]

The bottom line however is that *by and large*, within a global production network, areas that offer *lower reproduction costs (which would mean, say, lower environmental standards, lower social wage, less stringent tax regimes, etc.)* are those areas in which capital has a vested interest to *externalise* transactions as moments of a global circuit M-C-M'. And given that every single area of the world – no matter whether rich or poor, in the first or in the third world – is put in a condition of scarcity by the overall financial regime, through either debt or capital movements, then different spatial areas are set against each other in a competitive race to lower the labour time necessary for their *reproduction*. This is done through either externalisation of reproduction work to the market or the shifting of the cost of reproduction to the invisible realm (unwaged work and the environment).

If different conditions of reproduction are set against each other in an endless race, it become intelligible and understandable *how* and *why* in the world of plenty of the 'new economy', in the world of biotechnologies and genetic engineering, in the world of 'immaterial labour' and 'post-Fordism', of high-tech and instant communication, the most abhorrent human practices are not simply 'still' present in some distant land, the heritage of archaic times, but become instead *constituent moments* of contemporary capitalist relations. Thus, for example, modern slavery – with features that are almost unique in the history of human production – trickles up in the global production chain by allowing cheaper food and cheaper general conditions of reproduction, thus lowering the value of labour power, say, for skilled Indian programmers connected by instant communications to their American clients. Thus, for example, the low cost of reproduction for boys and girls in many areas of the third world trickles up in the profit of transnational corporations, who profit from their direct or indirect link to the global production chain in the mines, sweatshops and fields of the world.[6]

Reproduction fields

Figure 3 builds on Figure 2 and is a stylised illustration of the articulation between and within the two spheres of production and reproduction at the planetary level, as they constitute a hierarchy of conditions of reproduction.

In Figure 3, each world region corresponds to a *reproduction field*, that is a social, political and cultural space, historically and socially produced, defining the general conditions of reproduction of labour power at given times. This may be defined by the *degree* of dependence on the market for the

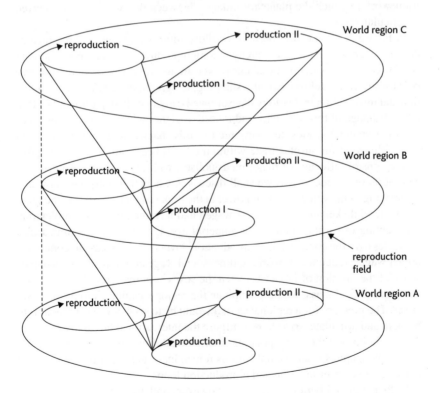

Figure 3 Stylised global linkages between production and reproduction

reproduction of people's lives and livelihoods, as well as a particular wage rate and average standard of living, that is, a particular cultural condition of the use of commodities. While, from the perspective of communities involved in reproduction, what we call *reproduction fields* comprise particular relationships, cultural norms and processes, from the perspective of capital's accumulation, reproduction fields in different world regions differ mostly in terms of the monetary value, which is necessary to reproduce labour power of an average type. In each region thus defined, reproduction and capitalist production loops are operating, as discussed in relation to Figure 2. Regions, of course, may differ in terms of what are the types of commodities produced in the two sectors of production, as well as the degree to which they are produced. But it is plausible to conceive that even in our age of globalisation, all regions have a combination of both production departments. For example, even in the most 'advanced' region A, production of raw materials of department I can still take place in the form of electricity, although the great bulk of its raw material needs is derived from other regions. The point of the figure thus is not to describe dynamics or states of world production and reproduction, but the general framework in which the planetary linkages between the two can be conceived as articulated.

In Figure 3, for the sole purpose of illustration, we postulate three regions describing an international hierarchy among reproduction fields, that is, among conditions of reproduction of labour power. In different periods in the last two centuries railway and transatlantic shipping, telegraph, telephone, communication and information technology have allowed capitalists in department I or II to take advantage of this hierarchy and indeed, together with the iron fist of states and their colonial armies, to contribute towards shaping it. This has happened first with a vent-for-surplus trade within the 'world economies' of old empires and regions of influence of major metropolises, with consequent enforced specialisation of production, as we shall discuss in Chapter 9. This has allowed a cheapening of the value of labour power in the imperial metropolis and the tying together, while keeping separate, of waged and unwaged planetary proletariat. The venting of surplus trade of the imperial age, however, had its drawbacks. Struggles over the conditions of reproduction – whether for access to commons, higher wages, reduction of working time, social wage entitlements or recomposition of the division of labour between the sexes at home – if able to mobilise sufficient critical mass, would precipitate the regions' capitals into profitability crises. The pressure for a regional capital would be to seek new world regions to bring in and articulate, so as to reconfigure the international hierarchy of reproduction fields and the corresponding international division of labour. The history of old empires is an example of this forced inclusion and articulation at the planetary level of production and reproduction loops.

With national liberation struggles however, and the demise of old-style imperial policies, neither the planetary expansion of capitalist circuits nor their articulation have stopped being necessities for capital. From the late 1970s, global elites have responded to the crisis of accumulation they faced through a planetary restructuring of global production processes to cut through a new hierarchy of reproduction fields generated through structural adjustment policies and capital market deregulation. However, unlike the international division of labour of the old empires, which was relatively fixed in the special-isations of raw materials for the periphery and industrial products for the metropolises, todays' articulation among reproduction fields is more dynamic and is constituent of global discipline, rather than merely its result. Thus, what has been called 'deep integration' allows capitalists to take advantage of this hierarchy through cost-minimising externalisation of part of their production, that is through increase in trade and transnationalisation of production, pitting reproduction communities against each other in an endless rat race increasingly pervading all spheres of human doing.

The vertical lines linking different reproduction fields and criss-crossing reproduction and production loops might be seen to inhabit what Manuel Castells called 'spaces of flows'.[7] However, we understand the movement and dynamic of these 'flowing' monetary and use values, as well as bodies, as *constituting* this space with reference to the production and reproduction loops and the problematic of capitalist accumulation and struggles for other values. Value struggles therefore also constitute the 'space of flows'. So for example, strategies such as trade liberalisation facilitate the value practices of capital by increasing the mobility of capital and the intensity of competition, contributing to reduce monetary costs and facilitating vertical integration among production loops in different regions in competition with other vertically integrated commodity chains. Furthermore, reproduction loops are also articulated at the planetary level. First, directly, through, for example, legal or illegal migration flows, bringing about a transnationalisation of the conditions of reproduction, in two senses. In the first place, because of the transfer of savings from migrants to the home communities, as represented by the dotted line across the reproduction loops in the different regions illustrated in Figure 3. Also, as we have seen, women's migration generally involves the establishment of an inter-national division of labour of reproduction work, which sees women migrants earning a wage in the reproduction of others (domestic labourers, nurses, cleaners, etc.), while the reproduction of their home communities is left to younger sisters or to the street. Also, and to a minor extent, through the purchase of commodities from another region in which different conditions of reproduction make them less expensive. These are just a few examples of current trends one can read in the framework provided by Figure 3.

Part II

Global Loops: Some Explorations on the Contemporary Work Machine

7
Enclosures and disciplinary integration

GENERATION AND HOMEOSTASIS

The value practices M-C-M', accumulation, must attend to the needs of a variety of social actors and groups, and at the same time ensure that these needs, desires and value practices, manifesting themselves in terms of struggles, do not break away from its ordering principles, but, on the contrary, become moments of its reproduction. This tension between rupture and recuperation is what constitutes the basic homeostatic processes of capital.

Homeostasis is a term introduced by cybernetics in the early 1940s to describe the *automatic* process of self-regulation of living organisms to maintain a dynamic balance.[1] It is a process in which feedback loops of circular causality are essential mechanisms. Through a sequence of self-balancing ('negative') and self-reinforcing ('positive') feedback[2], feedback loops allow all living organisms to solve the basic problems of life, from the humble amoeba to human beings:

finding sources of energy; incorporating and transforming energy; maintaining a chemical balance of the interior compatible with the life process; maintaining the organism's structure by repairing its wear and tear; and fending off external agents of disease and physical injury. The single word homeostasis is convenient shorthand for the ensemble of regulations and the resulting state of regulated life. (Damasio 2003: 30)

While the automatism of homeostatic processes in biological systems is the result of a set of instructions codified by DNA, in a social system like capitalism this automatism can only emerge out of a *social* construction. This social construction, which is certainly messy and never conforming to neat models, seems nevertheless to originate out of two main moments, one generative and the other preservative through self-organisation. The generative and self-organising moments of the system we call capitalism are enclosures and disciplinary integration. Struggles, social conflict, are not outside these two

79

moments, but to a certain extent part of them both. Or, perhaps more precisely, in so far as struggles that are born out of value practices that are outside capital are coupled back to capital's loops, they help constitute the dynamism of capital's homeostatic mechanisms. Also, the processes that go under the name of globalisation are to a large extent processes of extension and deepening of these generative and self-organising moments of capitalism.

The generative moment is the one that creates markets, that is, creates people and communities 'willing' to buy and sell commodities, creates 'proletarians', that is people with no other means of livelihood but what they can get by selling their labour power in the market, or being involved in petty commodity trade. Much of this willingness is of course the result of various forms of state practices of expropriation of commons and social engineering that reduce alternative means of livelihoods.

When we look at market values from the perspective of the market's generative principle – enclosures – they appear to us for what they are, as the order of things of a particular social force, class, elites. This is because any time an enclosure is forced on the social body, whether a privatisation, or a cut in entitlement, an expropriation of land, or a patent on a life-saving medicine, a clash of values generally surfaces with the corresponding struggles. They value privatisation, we do not. They value market forces, we do not. They value forced relocation, we do not.

With this generative moment, a set of *rules* is created, rules that are often forcibly introduced and maintained through the use of force (the state). These rules constitute a *context* for social interaction by defining *how* to access resources produced socially, sets of property rights, legal regulations filtering and channelling social action in certain ways. I discuss this generative moment in terms of enclosures extensively in Chapters 10 and 11.

Out of the activity of social production predicated on these rules, as well as the daily practices of their contestation, there follow given self-organising patterns of articulation among producing singularities constituting the social body. What is generally called 'the economy' here is a poor term to capture these patterns. As we have seen in the previous chapters, these self-organising patterns articulate both waged and unwaged work, production and reproduction. Therefore, they cannot refer to monetised production only as in the case of economic narratives of the market's patterns of self-organisation, from Adam Smith's invisible hand to Friedrich Hayek' s market order. Furthermore, unlike economists, we are interested in processes, in modes of doing, of producing and, therefore, because doing is always a social act, modes of *relations* across producing singularities. Production is always co-production.

Disciplinary integration thus refers to the integration of different value practices in a systemic 'whole' that constitutes the process of self-expansion of capital. Note that this is *integration* and not *coexistence* among different value practices. Integration implies the reduction of diverse practices to the one model that is pervasive in society (Irigaray 1997: 128). Capitalist integration implies the articulation of diversity through the common value practices of capitalist markets and their corresponding processes of measurement. As we shall see in Chapters 12 and 13, this integration is disciplinary, because it relies on disciplinary forms of command over subjects, the continuous dispensation of rewards and punishments to shape norms of interaction and social production emerging from capital's value practices in perpetual struggle with other value practices. It is also preservative of the rules generated by enclosures, because through repetition subjects tend to become normalised to them. Yet this is a normalisation that does not abolish conflict among value practices, but that turns this conflict into the driving engine of the evolution of the organisational form of capitalism while basic processes of homeostasis keep social forces and conflicting value practices coupled together. In other words, *in the daily reproduction of our livelihoods we are involved, knowingly or unknowingly, willingly or unwillingly, in a form of civil war cutting across the social body.*

This can be better seen from a brief reflection on the term homeostasis as applied to capitalism. Generally speaking, homeostasis is the property of open systems such as living organisms. Its purpose is to regulate the internal environment of such systems, so as to maintain stable conditions, by means of multiple dynamic equilibrium adjustments emerging from the playing out of *opposite forces.*[3] In the open system we termed capitalism, the ultimate forces that must be kept in dynamic balance in order to avoid breaking up the system they are part of are those social practices predicated on opposite values. In ancient Greek, the word *stasis* means 'civil war,'[4] and this is perhaps echoed in endless fables and myths of brother killing brother, as happens when the social body is ripped apart and a new beginning occurs: Cain killing Abel, Romulus killing Remus. During the fifth century B.C. '*Stasis* became politicized into conflict between those who favoured government by many (democracy), and those who desired rule by the few (oligarchy)' (Sidebottom 2004). Capitalist markets do just the opposite; they depoliticise this struggle, by making it the foundation of their dynamics. On a daily basis, they are able to articulate value practices that are predicated on and push for democratisation of the social cooperation of labour (which depends on extending access to social resources) with those that are predicated on and lead to oligarchic power over the social means of production (which depends on channelling social resources away from democratic control). From our perspective therefore, capitalist homeostasis means the *same* (homeo) *civil war* (stasis), that is, a 'civil war' within the global social body which we are increasingly forced to adopt in order to reproduce our livelihoods. Neoliberal globalisation is the intensification of this war. But this civil war is the sanitised and normalised form taken by the class struggle that Marx considered to be the ultimate driving force of history, a class struggle that is ultimately a struggle among value practices. As we shall see in Chapter 9, in the illustration of disciplinary trade and 'flying geese', by pitting livelihoods against each other, today's global capital rides on the class struggle (civil war) against and beyond its value practices, and turns it from a threat to the *condition* and *result* of everyday *busy*ness, a constituent force of its power. To refer to the homeostatic processes of capitalist markets therefore is not just to refer to the ebb and flow of business activities, cycles, and 'the economy', but to life practices and the corresponding social relations that underpin these patterns.

A CONCEPTUAL MAP

Let us try to clarify how generative and preservative practices can be seen to give rise to some general features of capitalist subsystems. Figure 4 offers a conceptual map linking the production and reproduction loops discussed in previous chapters. At the top end of the map, we link the production and reproduction loops to the historical practices constituting their geneology (enclosures) and those constituting their preservation (disciplinary processes). As we shall see in Chapters 10 and 11, enclosures occur through processes that commodify existing 'commons' (and thus introduce new laws regulating rights), or by state defence of existing enclosed spaces, vis-à-vis struggles demanding commons. In either case, the state deploys institutional force to maintain, protect or extend commodity relations and enclosures. In these chapters I shall also argue that this process of enclosure is continuous in capitalism and not only confined to some 'primitive' stage. This is for two reasons. First, because capital's *telos*, or drive, is to extend and pervade more and more spheres of human life and nature. In other words, commodification is an inherent characteristic of capital. Second, because historically the accumulated result of past struggles effectively constitutes new forms of commons that capital, if it cannot administer them on its own terms with new forms of governmentality compatible with accumulation, must enclose.

On the other hand, both spatial and temporal integration within the M-C-M' circuit requires social cooperation to occur. Cooperation occurs essentially in two ways. Either within productive 'nodes' in society – i.e., in companies, households, schools or any relatively self-contained and discrete institution – or across 'nodes'.[5] In both cases the disciplinary processes that are in place shape, channel and frame the activities of the social body into value practices that reproduce capital vis-à-vis practices predicated on *other* values. Struggle is therefore constituent of disciplinary processes. Classic examples of disciplinary processes and corresponding forms of cooperation *within* nodes are the factory, studied by Marx (1976a), the school, the clinic and the prison, these latter two studied by Foucault. I will generally abstract from cooperation *within* nodes, and will focus mainly on social cooperation across nodes. However, as will become clear in Chapters 14 and 15, in which I compare the panopticon prison and the market order, there are strong organisational

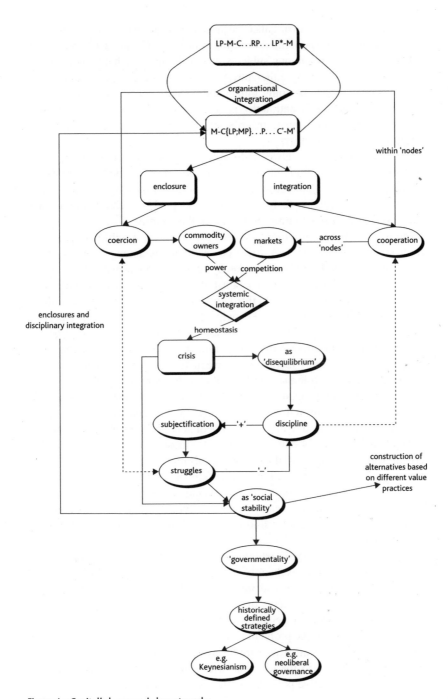

Figure 4   Capital's loops and class struggle

similarities between the two. This is because the disciplinary mechanism of the market and the corresponding measuring processes (Chapters 12 and 13) are grounded on a relation among subjects that, as argued in Chapter 4, *erase* the singularities of *others*, by either physically obliterating them or *integrating* them into alien modes of doing things and socially cooperating. Also, as we have seen in Chapter 5, patriarchy as a mode of relation to the other, as a system of line management, inscribes itself in capitalist organisations in competition with each other.

The main difference between disciplinary processes constituting social cooperation within and among nodes is in the role of money and the corresponding impersonal market mechanism. In other words, while in 'institutions of confinement' (whether factories, prisons, hospitals or schools in the traditional Foucauldian sense) everybody knows the identity of the 'rat' watching us and measuring our activities, and thus the emerging disciplinary processes are grounded on more or less *direct* power relations among subjects, in the daily experience of disciplinary market systems, it is not possible to identify a 'rat': every singularity is pitted against the others through an impersonal mechanism centred on money. In this latter case, often our immediate 'rulers', managers and bosses, through the help of the oracles of finance, become merely the spokespersons for heteronymous benchmarks that need to be met and beaten given certain resource constraints. In other words, to a large extent they become the clerics mediating between the god of the market and its people, and in such a role they are front-line instruments for work extraction.

But the source and social constitutions of both those benchmarks and the resource constraints through which work is extracted from people at the point of production and reproduction is not immediately visible from the perspective of those whose work is extracted – that is, most of us situated within the vertical wage hierarchy. If things in organisations go wrong, crises occur, bankruptcy is threatened, often the blame falls on 'bad management', as if the *successful* extraction of work from people using a variety of often instrumental, devious, and opportunistic means for what, ultimately, has the sole purpose of threatening someone else's livelihood can be classified, from an ethical point of view, as 'good'.[6]

The market order is one in which social cooperation across nodes emerges out of patterns of market exchange, grounded on real, imagined or threatened competitive modalities of social interaction, all of which nevertheless have tangible effects such as patterns of widening the polarisation of income and wealth. However, from a perspective that wants to pose the 'question of alternatives' the root of the problem is not these patterns that emerge *out of this* mode of social interaction. These are the symptoms of the problem.

We must be alerted to the fact that historically, when these symptoms are treated with redistributive policies (a rare event in the neoliberal world) under the pressure of struggles from below, the basic dynamics remain, recreating the conditions through which new patterns of unequal distribution of income and wealth emerge. Furthermore, redistributive concessions are often tied to lines of division across the wage hierarchy, excluding from the deal the weakest sections among the co-producers: migrants, women, the invisible. Finally, these concessions are accompanied by demands for corresponding productivity increases, as the balance between income received by the producers and work extraction is the key relation defining the general level of profitability. From the perspective of the alternatives, redistribution is important not so much because it represents any solution to capital's mode of doing, but because it can provide the resources necessary for empowerment vis-à-vis the demands of abstract mechanisms like capitalist markets. But this is only to the extent that these increased social resources in the hands of the commoners become the material basis for the consititution of new forms of social cooperation based on different value practices, to the extent that these resources are linked to the constitution of an 'outside' (Chapter 16).

The problem with the market as *the* central order through which the co-producing social body reproduces livelihoods is in the fact that, paradoxically, it makes people cooperate socially by threatening each others' livelihoods, subordinating each singularity to the artificial rule of an increasingly demanding clock, and thus turning any innovation, any creative idea, any new product of human communication and ingenuity, no matter how well its use values might help solve certain problems, into a force threatening someone else's livelihood, into a benchmark with the power of disciplining. In capitalist production therefore, scarcity is not as economists tell us the problem *condition* of human interaction. Rather, it is the ongoing *result* of any problem solved, of any new idea, no matter how well intended, of any new product of social cooperation. In its capitalist competitive form, social cooperation – something that we cannot avoid since we are social beings – is turned into an alien force.[7]

In any given time and place, the degree of competition depends of course on institutional context. But even in the case of near monopoly in some sector, the competitive form of the social interaction is maintained institutionally through the opening of markets to trade liberalisation, which fuels if not real at least threatened competition, or anti-monopoly laws implemented by the state, or simulation of competition as in the case of many state-owned public services. On the other hand, it is reproduced systemically through migration of capital from one sector to another, through a threat to share prices and a comparison among profit rates that accompanies the calculus of expected profitability.

Clearly, market interaction is also an expression of the configuration of power relations created and/or maintained by historically stratified enclosures and corresponding property rights. These power relations – which we can identify in specific contexts by answering questions such as, who has what entitlements? who has what commodity and in what amount? who has what financial backing and on what conditions? – play themselves out in strategic competitive interactions in the market giving rise to particular configurations of systemic integration.

Systemic integration within the social circuit of capital is thus the net result of the interaction of forces, each one of which is driven by its own plan and backed by its own powers. The emergent result of such interaction is of course unpredictable since the condition of each of the qualitative transformations necessary to allow the reproduction of social capital M-C-M' is riddled with what Marx calls the 'possibility' of crisis (Bell and Cleaver 2002). Crisis, which Marx roots in the polarity between use value and exchange value of the commodity and in the alienated character of social labour in capitalism, that is the struggles among value practices, is indeed the all-pervasive condition of commodity production, not only at times of its extreme manifestation, but also in times of relative business tranquillity. Whatever may be the various predispositions of crisis, for the purposes of this analysis they may be seen as taking one of two main forms. They either take the form of 'disequilibria' in the operations of markets, with consequent ebbs and flows in business activity, changes in market price, sector restructuring and firing and hiring of workers. Or they take the form of a crisis of social stability.

In the first case, crises are an inherent part of the disciplinary processes of markets, processes that are founded on competitive modes of interaction among productive nodes in society and, as Hayek reminds us, compel agents to adapt or die. From the point of view of people participating in market disciplinary processes, such processes correspond ultimately to processes of subjectification, that is the creation of subjects who in varying degrees accept the norms of capital's circuits in the pursuit of their own *conatus* of self-preservation. Combining Foucault's analysis of disciplinary processes with Marx's analysis of capitalist production, we can understand subjectification as those social processes through which norms of behaviour and interaction compatible with the requirement of capitalist accumulation and its value practices are reproduced.[8] For example, the role of reproduction as reproduction of labour power (e.g. getting your kids ahead of the competitive game); the unchallenged acceptance of the commodity form, its naturalisation in a particular sphere of life (e.g. 'getting a job' as a way of acquiring the means to meet needs, or paying for a social service such as health or education, or an essential resource like water, or, indeed, food items purchased in a supermarket); or the acceptance as normal of a given wage hierarchy (e.g. socially useful housework being unpaid while socially destructive arms-dealing and stock brokering are highly rewarded); the acceptance as necessary of goals and priorities that are heteronymous to the subject's goals and priorities (e.g. the 'necessity' of labour market and pension reforms for the sake of global competitiveness); the compliance with new methods of doing things for the sole purpose of 'staying ahead of the game', even if the old ways worked perfectly well, or new ways predicated on value practices *other than* capital's could be adopted.

The integration over the overall capital's circuit thus passes through a variety of processes of subjectification. In this sense, to various degrees, we are all involved in these processes and in the daily routines reproducing our livelihoods.

Following Foucault, we can interpret these strategies of norm-creating sub-jectification as disciplinary strategies, that is as repetitive practices of reward and punishment aiming at co-opting or bypassing resistance and channelling it into 'normal' patterns of behaviour. Although Foucault's analysis is confined to discrete disciplinary institutions, such as the prison, the hospital and the school, a critical analysis of what Hayek calls the 'market order' shows several fundamental similarities with the disciplinary process in these institutions (Chapter 14), the most important of which is perhaps that the market discipli-nary process contributes to creating not only normalised subjects, but also new standards of production, and what Marx referred to as the quantitative aspect of the substance of value, i.e., 'socially necessary labour time' (Chapter 13).

While market discipline, with its systems of rewards and punishments, pro-motes the production of norms and normalised subjects, this always clashes with subjectivities that escape capital's subjectification, value practices that set themselves as absolute barriers to the value practices of capital. Struggles are ubiquitous in capitalism, whether in micro and hidden forms or macro and open conflict, and the disciplinary mechanisms of the market are, in normal circumstances, only partially able to co-opt them. Thus, at any given time, the 'positive' effect – from the perspective of capital – that disciplinary processes have on the creation of 'normal subjects' is counterposed to the negative impact that struggles have on disciplinary mechanisms. The end result between disciplinary processes and struggles is open ended, and depends on historical contingency and the balance of forces. But ultimately, to maintain a balance between these 'pluses' and 'minuses' is the key rationale of disciplinary processes. As we shall discuss in Chapter 13, Marx's 'law of value' becomes intelligible once we bring struggle to its core.

GOVERNMENTALITY

There are however times in which this 'balance' cannot be maintained and conflict threatens the particular forms of disciplinary mechanism as well as their very rationale. The 'disequilibria' of flow, the cycles, the ebb and flow of business activity are no longer sufficient to discipline subjects, to channel norms of behaviour, to make them accept and internalise the normality of competitive market interaction. To the extent that this happens, crisis presents itself as a crisis of social stability, a crisis that, whatever its systemic trigger, calls into question the viability and/or legitimacy of many of the qualitative transformations necessary for accumulation (M-C-M').

From the perspective of accumulation, social stability is the stability of social arrangements and interaction in forms compatible with the accumulation process, the extensive commodification of life, particular forms of disciplinary processes of market interaction and extraction of work. It is ultimately a stability of the coupling between reproduction and production, between the value practices centred on *life* preservation in the broad sense and the value practices centred on the preservation of capital. Thus, there are potentially many instances in which social stability thus defined enters into crisis: when capital is increasingly unable to guarantee access to the goods and services necessary for reproducing bodies and social cohesion corresponding to given 'class compositions'; or when the aspirations of new generations are at odds with the 'deals' agreed by older generations and their struggles begin to shape the times; or when subjectification has gone so far as to erase all hope and bring exasperation to large sectors of the population; or when, on the contrary, hope is self-generated by social movements that challenge what they believe is the subordination of nature, dignity, peace, justice, life to greed, but that we can read as the systemic drive of accumulation; or when a combination of these and other factors emerges in particular historical circumstances so as to threaten the legitimacy of many of the enclosures and integration practices and processes at the root of accumulation. These are all the cases that, from the perspective of capital's *conatus* of self-preservation, require strategic intervention beyond mere repression and coercion. What capital needs here is an approach that allows the acknowledgment of the problems and issues at the basis of the crisis as 'social stability', but at the same time co-opts them within the mechanism of accumulation and its value practices.

This double function can be described, in general terms, using Foucault's term 'governmentality'. This is an art of government that, unlike 'enclosures', is not based on decree but on management, although this, as we shall see, is also predicated on the iron fist of the state. With governmentality, the question is 'not of imposing law on men but of disposing things:[9] that is of employing tactics rather than laws, or even of using laws themselves as tactics – to arrange things in such a way that, through a certain number of means, such-and-such ends may be achieved' (Foucault 2002: 211). We cannot here discuss this category in detail, as Foucault's work on this issue is dense with historical details and insights.[10] For our purposes here, governmentality is the management of networks of social relations on the front line of conflicting value practices.[11] This management does not come from a transcendental authority that is external to the network itself, such as in the problematic of the Machiavellian prince. Rather, the problem and solution of authority is all internal to the network, and it is for this reason that it deploys tactics rather than laws: tactics and strategies aimed at creating a context in which the nodes interact without escaping the value practices of capital. Social stability compatible with the priorities and flows necessary for accumulation is one of the rationales of capitalist governmentality.

Examples of these practices are post-war Keynesianism and the current discourses of neoliberal governance. A classic example of this 'governmentality' is the productivity deals that were at the heart of the Keynesian era. These where the result of a long institutional process grounded on the crisis and struggles of the 1930s, the worldwide revolutionary ferments following the Russian Revolution, and became the kernel not only of Keynesian policies, but also the hidden parametric assumptions of post-Second World War Keynesian models. Here the state did not implement laws establishing prices and wages (when it tried this in emergency situations it usually failed), but promoted guidelines and an institutional context in which unions and capital would negotiate within an overall framework. In other words, 'social stability' in the case of Keynesianism was seen as the output of a production process that had 'government' as its 'facilitator' and class struggle as its enforcer on the global scene. While I refer the reader to the literature for a discussion of Keynesianism,[12] in what follows I want to deal with the modern form of governmentality: neoliberal governance.

Neoliberal governance

What today is called 'governance' is the name given to the neoliberal strategies of governmentality. As in the case of the Keynesian form, governance too emerges out of a crisis that increasingly presents itself as a problem of 'social stability', a crisis that actualises the predisposition towards the rupture of accumulation, towards the interruption, slowing down, or refusal to maintain and increase the speed of flows which are necessary for the expansion of capital within the M-C-M' cycle. Neoliberal governance emerges as an attempt to manage clashing value practices in line with the requirements of capitalist priorities in an increasingly integrated world. Neoliberal governance is a central element of the neoliberal discourse in a particular phase of it, when neoliberalism and capital in general face particularly stringent problems of accumulation, growing social conflict and a crisis of reproduction. Governance sets itself the task of tackling these problems for capital by attempting to relay the disciplinary role of the market through the establishment of a 'continuity of powers' based on normalised market values as truly common values across the social body. Governance thus seeks to embed these values in the many ways in which the vast array of social and environmental problems are addressed. It thus promotes active participation of society in the reproduction of life and of our species on the basis of this market normalisation. It depends on participation on the basis of the shared values and discourse of the market. According to this logic, every problem raised by struggles can be addressed on condition that the mode of its addressing is through the market: for example, the environmental catastrophe can be dealt with by marketing pollution rights and the human catastrophe of poverty can be dealt with by microcredit and export promotion.

The last quarter of a century corresponds to the emergence, consolidation and beginning of the crisis of neoliberal policies. Governance discourse is located in this dynamic, broadly comprising three phases. The first phase, corresponding to the emergence of the neoliberal strategies between the late 1970s and mid 1980s, was characterised by heavy 'pro-market' policies both in the North and in the South. In the North, this meant a heavy process of restructuring, often accompanied by anti-union laws, anti-wage/inflation policies, cuts in social spending and the development of corporate welfare. In the South, on the other hand, the same process occurred but in the form of the management of the debt crisis which begins and intensifies in this period. Hence we have structural adjustment policies, cuts in food subsidies and, from the perspective of capital's value practices, other 'uneccessary' expenditures from public budgets. In this period we also witness the beginning of massive social movements from the South, something that will become a serious problem for many governments in the second phase.

In the second phase, roughly between the mid 1980s and the mid 1990s, we have the consolidation of neoliberal policies into what has been called the 'Washington consensus' (Williamson 1990; 2000), the elements of which are now familiar and give shape to many national policies and international agreements.[13] The Washington consensus gives more coherence to policies that were initially implemented by means of rough and often crude ideological battles (Phase 1 was, after all, the years of Margaret Thatcher and Ronald Reagan), but its implementation meets with increasing problems and resistance.

In the context of this consolidation, the IMF, the World Bank and governmental institutions' briefing papers began to refer to '*good* governance', understood as a particular system of government countries had to adopt. Ultimately, 'good governance' implied the configuration of government bodies in such a way as to facilitate the terms of the Washington consensus and make them irreversible. At the same time, a crucial aspect of this period is the emergence on the public scene of the so-called 'civil society organisations', together with an acceleration of third world social unrest now spreading also in what will be called 'transition economies'. The phenomenon, which is the true origin of what later became visible in Seattle, becomes so pervasive that academics begin to take notice of struggles (Walton and Seddon 1994) and some campaigners – in their attempt to 'persuade' the Northern public and governments of the irrationality of the debt – can wave the spectre of more 'IMF riots' or 'food riots' and social instability in general as a very likely cost if the debt crisis is not solved (George 1988).

We need to enlarge a little on this second phase, because it is here that we have the development of the context in which modern governance discourse emerges. It is useful to view the policies of the Washington consensus by reading them as three normative *prescriptions* (Chandhoke 2002: 43). First, the state, both in the North and in the global South, *should* withdraw from the social sector. Second, the market *should* be given open access to all spheres in life and social reproduction and thus be free from all constraints. Third, people *should* organise their own socio-economic reproduction instead of depending on the state.

This trinity of normative prescriptions was often met with social opposition both in the North and, especially, in the South. Also, the implementation of neoliberal policies created a vacuum in social reproduction that has opened the space for new social and political actors. Neoliberal policies of enclosures, cuts in social welfare and increases in corporate welfare have enormously increased income and wealth polarisation both within countries and between countries. This, together with the reduction in entitlements, has had devastating effects on the possibility of reproduction of livelihoods and communities. The neoliberal solution was of course based on the conviction that the market could supplant the state in providing for the needs of social reproduction. We know that this in fact was not the case, as is shown by the horror statistics regarding the state of global health, access to food, water, public services – some of which have been discussed in Chapter 2. As the market was not able to provide for people's needs of reproduction, we have a tremendous increase in the so-called 'third sector', that is that diverse and heterogeneous constellation of 'civil society organisations' (CSOs), or non-governmental organisations (NGOs), of local, national, transnational and international relevance. The latter for example has grown by about 400 per cent in the last 20 years (Anheier and Themudo 2002: 195).

As noted, the constellation of NGOs is of course highly heterogeneous, not only in terms of their reach – local, national and transnational – but also in terms of their forms of organisation – networked or hierarchical – their goals – advocacy and campaign, education, mobilisation, meeting basic needs, intervention in emergencies, and so on – as well as in their general attitudes towards political processes. This implies that although in several instances many of these NGOs dangerously share economic discursive premises with their state and corporate counterparts,[14] while others even consciously and actively promote neoliberal state and business values and agendas,[15] in many other cases they are the organisational expression of the social body striving to reproduce itself vis-à-vis capital.[16]

This is primarily because their recent growth emerged through the same process that deepened the 'globalised' market. The rationale of the vast majority of these organisations – which we must remember are diverse and heterogeneous – was thus to fill a vacuum in the need of social reproduction, a vacuum created by the restructuring of the state following neoliberal policies. Whether through charities, campaigns to raise awareness on critical issues, or direct intervention in reproduction in education, health, or replacing the welfare state through networks of churches or mosques, civil society organisations have moved into public domains to fulfil human needs. In the eyes of the neoliberals, such an emergent activity of society's self-defence against market colonisation is seen as an opportunity to build 'social capital', i.e., to promote a form of social cohesion that is compatible with capital accumulation. But in the eyes of the millions of grass-roots organisers, the opposite is true: their activities are seen – amidst all the possible contradictions, doubts and deficiencies of their actions and discourses – not as social capital but as 'social solidarity', i.e., a form of social cohesion that sets a *limit* to capital accumulation and the colonisation of life by capitalist markets. It is this contrast between two meanings attributed to the signifier 'civil society' that defines 'governance' as another terrain of struggle.

The third phase in our periodisation (from the mid 1990s to the present) reflects precisely this. In this phase we witness major world economic and non-economic institutions discussing the problems of governance, of whether a post-Washington consensus ought to be developed,[17] of how to put together civil society and business, of how corporate governance should include issues that are important to 'civil society', and, on the other hand, of how 'civil society' should meet the needs of business. At the same time, global social movements not only make their force felt on the streets and in the fields of the world, but are also undergoing a process of recomposition, a process still open-ended, but, despite the setback as a result of the war in Iraq and the consequent attack on 'civil liberties', one that is still occurring in the meshing and circulation of discourses and values practices. In this period, the movement is no longer simply a series of distinct and isolated protests against the IMF, the World Bank or neoliberal economic policies, but a meshing together of different movements, the creation of new composite identities emerging from the mixing of political and social subjectivities. What the mass global media saw in Seattle in 1999, in which students and workers, environmentalists and gays and lesbians, third world farmers and anarchists, communists and greens built bridges in a highly productive and creative swarm, was only the tip of an iceberg of a process that has been under way since at least the mid 1990s.[18]

Governance and the 'Prince'

In Foucault's terms, governance can be defined as the management of networks and flows – 'disposing things' – made of different actors (government, civil society and business institutions) – 'continuity among powers' – who are encouraged to become 'partners' in a continuum called governance.

The problem is that Foucault seems to believe that the problem of sovereignty and that of governmentality belong to different epochs,[19] that there is a kind of historical split between the time of sovereignty and the time of governmentality. I think the challenge is to see how, in moments of crisis, capital seeks to articulate these two forms, how the power to coerce, to rule and to control is articulated with the power to seduce into agreement and to establish continuity among powers in society.[20] Indeed, it may well be that the relation between the 'rule of the prince', sovereignty, and governance as governmentality may express a second-line attempt to implement the policy of the 'prince'.

The issues that have been considered as an application of governance in the last 15 years are numerous. In the case of genetically modified food, Levidow (2003) showed, for example, that in the mid 1990s the European Union was granting safety approval through lenient risk-assessment criteria similar to those used by the United States, but soon mass protest undermined that framework. In response, the EU and national authorities engaged in a governance process with civil society, even on a transatlantic scale. Although the results are still ambiguous and indeterminate, the discursive parameters feature more stringent criteria as the means of solving the problem of public confidence and legitimacy.

The UN global compact lists nine principles on environmental, labour and human rights issues, which cover a broad spectrum: social, environmental and biodiversity management; management of emergent environmental problems at every level of aggregation (local, regional and global); promotion of human rights; labour rights, child labour and forced labour; international financial management.

Another area of application worth mentioning is the production of war and the management of neoliberal peace (Duffield 2001). War here is not simply the product of an army in the war theatre, but is the co-regulation of various networks of actors, the army, the media, NGOs, charities. Often these actors have different interests and goals, yet the way they are organised into a whole constrains their choices. The way these actors are articulated, their *governance*, allows them to claim that they all 'do their job' without being able to question the rules of their functional integration into a broader mechanism.

Others point to the regulatory functions that were once the responsibility of national governments as being examples of governance networks. For example, the policing of 'dirty money' flows across countries, in which international networks of bank clerks, under pain of criminal sanction, supervise each other's activities and standards across borders (Wiener 2001: 456).

The need for governance is also evoked in the case of global financial regimes, with civil society organisations said to have a 'positive' function to play in their role as educators of the public on the intricacy of financial issues, their role as monitors of financial transactions promoting accountability and 'transparency'. Crucially, the role of 'civil society' in the governance of finance is said to enhance social cohesion[21] and legitimacy for the neoliberal international economic institutions.[22]

Finally, after the mass protests of the 1990s, governance talk is now a must in the design and implementation of controversial development projects: roads, dams, the infrastructure in general. The neoliberal project is centred on massive infrastructure projects, especially those that promote the speed of circulation of commodities (roads, railways, airports) or information for the sake of increasing the productivity and competitiveness of different regions.

These projects often meet local and translocal resistance, for reasons of the environment, the displacement of communities, and so on. The answer that governance discourse gives to that controversy is that the policy goes on anyway, but that different views are 'taken on board' through the process of consultation on how to implement it.

Governance discourse and the continuity of powers: disciplinary markets as commons

The 'continuity among powers' referred to by Foucault and that in terms of neoliberal governance allows the management of networks and flows made up of various actors (government, civil society and business institutions), encouraged to become 'partners', is established through the formation of a common discourse, one that is grounded on the coupling among the value practices of capital (the acceptance of disciplinary markets) and other value practices.

There are perhaps four operational pillars at the basis of this discourse. These are:

1. Self-regulation and co-regulation
2. Partnership among social actors
3. Principles of selection
4. Polanyi's inversion

Self-regulation and co-regulation

Like governmentality, governance is also supposed to be self-regulatory. For example, the UN Global Compact, a list of principles on environmental, human rights and labour standards to which firms and NGOs are urged to subscribe, states:

The Global Compact is not a regulatory instrument – it does not 'police', enforce or measure the behaviour or actions of companies. Rather, the Global Compact relies on public accountability, transparency and the enlightened self-interest of companies, labour and civil society to initiate and share substantive action in pursuing the principles upon which the Global Compact is based. (United Nations 2000a)

The voluntary basis of governance has been heavily criticised as ineffective, in so far as the tackling of world problems such as the environment, poverty, labour conditions, and so on is concerned (Richter 2002). It is one thing to force the oil industry to stop further explorations and invest in renewable sources of energy instead; it is quite another to invite the oil industry to embrace the principle of 'sustainability' and act with 'civil society'. But voluntary engagement in the governance process is not the sole reason for ineffectiveness on these fronts. If I am a polluting firm and I voluntarily subscribe to a principle of sustainability, I am showing that I am moving in the 'right direction' to redeem myself by putting my activities under closer scrutiny by civil society organisations. My word will be held to account. The problem however is that in this logic the accounting is simply and uniquely through media exposure, which means that 'tactics' and 'strategies' can always be employed to offset bad PR. Voluntary regulation is precisely what provides the space in which to navigate the contradictions emerging when different goals are posed, to gain time in which to deploy diverse and more media-friendly tactics, and thus to help constitute a 'continuity of powers'.

Partnership among social actors

Another important pillar of the discursive practice of governance is the idea of 'partnership'. Partnership is sponsored and promoted by UN agencies and the UN Global Compact, national governments, the global economic institutions and transnational corporations (TNCs) in a variety of ways. Its rationale is to establish 'continuity of powers' in such a way that different interest groups in partnerships (say firms and CSOs) can draw mutual benefit and their respective goals are pursued efficiently. Areas of application range from drawing up codes of conduct to social audits and particular micro-projects in the territory.

The advocates of such partnerships are of course moving from the ideological standpoint that regards existing market mechanisms and configurations of property rights as *given*, and justified by the fact that, as in the case of high-tech industry, for example, 'only private sector firms can provide the research, technology and development capacity to address global health, environmental, and information challenges of the coming decade' (Richter 2002). They can indeed, but unfortunately, apart from the fact that tax payers are subsidising private research and profits, private companies mostly engage in research that pays good financial returns rather than providing the most-needed outcomes.[23]

But the key issue here is that the idea of 'partnership' forces conflicting actors onto discursive common ground (Duffield 2001). It is for this reason that critics suggest an alternative vocabulary for use when CSOs have to deal with TNCs.[24] The neoliberal idea of 'partnership' therefore implies the ideological belief that the goals of different actors are not mutually exclusive, that is it obscures what in this book we have called the *front line*. Consequently, it closes the debate on values. By closing the debate on values, partnership has interiorised the perspective of the 'end of history'. We are thus told that the only viable way for us to deal with the major issues we are concerned about (poverty, the environment, livelihoods, and so on) is through voluntary participation in partnership with big business, its goals, its aspirations, its ways of doing things and of relating to 'the other'. But in thus doing, we override the fact that the profit-driven way of relating to the other is, from the perspective of value practices that are outside capital, quite problematic. Capital in fact constructs the 'human other' and the 'natural other' either as 'resource' or as 'competitor'. Otherwise, the other is simply 'invisible'.

Once set up, the partnership process reproduced the common terrain upon which that partnership was established. The fixing of the 'end of history' perspective upon which the partnership is constructed occurs through a process in which different actors position themselves strategically within the mutually accepted terms of the partnership – i.e., the acceptance of the market norm as the terrain for the solution of all sorts of problems. Since the mechanism of partnership is based on different actors sharing fundamental premises – partners are partners in so far as they are all 'stakeholders' of a common discourse they have constructed – whatever emerges from the process of mutual checks will in the end be measured in terms of the deviation from those common premises, and will be brought back to it. Representatives of business will focus on their bottom line – profit and growth – and will insist that the issues (on labour, poverty, the environment, and so on) concerning the representatives of 'civil society' with whom they are in 'partnership' are addressed without sacrificing their bottom lines.

We have thus a process of domestication and diffusion of the market norms/priorities through the social field, the illusion that these norms can be applied to address the 'horror statistics' continuously reproduced by disciplinary markets and enclosures, the naturalisation of those norms and the confinement of critique to the fetters of capital's *conatus*: neoliberal governance thus aims at restricting the space in which to question the social production and values of those norms. Within the neoliberal partnership discourse, just as polemics and controversy are turned into the driving force for the further expansion of capitalist markets into the colonisation of life and nature, so corporate rhetorical embrace of the values of the critiques is turned into an opportunity for corporate public relations point-scoring to acquire a 'socially responsible' image. As we are told at every juncture: 'social responsibility' is good for business – although any child knows that what matters for profit is at most that business *appears* to 'care'.

For example, Nike's website (www.nike.com, accessed June 2003) fences off its critics by boasting that Nike's Vietnamese factories are paying above the Vietnamese minimum wage ($34 a month). Perfectly legal, perfectly moral, and commendable too: Nike can rescue its reputation by paying *above* the minimum wage. It pays for corporations to invest in countries in which governments introduce minimum wages at near-starvation level. Likewise, Shell can claim it is complying with environmental regulations in Durban, South Africa, yet respiratory illnesses of school children in South Durban are four times higher than elsewhere in South Africa and there are sharp differences in air pollution levels and polluting incidents between the shell refinery at Durban and that at Frederica in Denmark (Friends of the Earth 2002). Partnership does not recognise the universality of human needs, but the universality of the market norm. It does not recognise commons as conditions for the reproduction of livelihoods, but posits disciplinary markets as the common basis on which livelihoods are pitted against each other. Disciplinary markets become the yardstick against which deviations from the norm are measured, appraised, evaluated and brought back to the market standard. In the process, the social production of this norm is internalised and left unchallenged.

Discursive common ground of this nature leaves out classic questions of political theory regarding social justice, a social contract, legitimacy, authority and power. Why have we abandoned this discussion? What sense is there in avoiding confronting disciplinary markets with other values?

Principles of selection

If 'Partnership and participation imply the mutual acceptance of shared normative standards and frameworks', then '[d]egrees of agreement, or apparent agreement, within such normative frameworks establish lines of inclusion and exclusion' (Duffield 2001). Indeed, once CSOs are confronted with the offer of partnership the key questions are, for example, the following: What are the principles of selection? Who are the agents/actors participating in the establishment of partnerships? Whom do they represent? Will they accept the common ground necessary to play 'games under rules', or will they want to play games about rules (Stoker 1998)? And if their rules are not those of the market and profit, will they then be labelled '*rouges*', 'deviants', 'terrorists', and criminalised accordingly? And if setting rules is part of the game, to what extent are participants under external pressure (such as socially constrained access to resources) that limits their space and power to set the rules they desire beyond the market?

The case of 'corporate governance' can provide us with some general principles of selection.

Principle number 1: *Discretion*. You are selected as a 'partner' if you sign a confidentiality agreement. The results of monitoring your environmental performance (or record on human or labour rights) will not be disclosed.[25]

Principle number 2: *Setting up hand-picked groups* instead of working with existing ones.[26] There is of course a long corporate tradition of companies organising their opposition and turning them into 'partners', for example, by creating new unions to undermine the less manageable ones set up by workers. The same tradition is now extended to environmental and other groups.

Principle number 3: *Enforced selection*. Working with local authorised groups in totalitarian countries. Shell's work in China is an example.[27] The UN defines this tactic as 'beneficial and silent complicity' (UN 2000a: 24).

Principle number 4: *Divide and rule*. Invite existing groups to closed-door regular consultation, thus discouraging public debate.[28]

Polanyi's inversion

Another pillar of the governance discourse is what we may call 'Polanyi's inversion'. Karl Polanyi was the institutional economist whose seminal work *The Great Transformation* represented an important criticism of the myth of self-regulating markets and the neoclassical conception of the 'economy' as a realm of human action that is independent and separated from society (Polanyi 1944). He argued that *the economy*, rather than being a distinct realm, *is embedded in society*. Governance discourse turns Polanyi's criticism of neo-classical economics on its head as it is based on the need to *embed society and the environment into the economy*, into business priorities. Embedding society and the environment into economy and business priorities is, for example, a hallmark of the UN-sponsored Global Compact 2000. 'The rationale is that a commitment to corporate citizenship should begin within the organization itself by *embedding universal principles and values* into the strategic business vision, organizational culture and daily operations' (United Nations 2000b: 3, my emphasis).

Why is there a need to embed society and the environment into economy and business priorities? Because a 'growing moral imperative to behave responsibly is allied to the recognition that a good human rights record can support improved business performance' (United Nations 2000a: 18). Human rights, environmental protection and 'universal values' are thus good for business. But what if they are not? What types of value then come first, 'universal values' or shareholder values? And how are we then supposed to deal with the issue if the latter come first, since these are only *voluntary* codes?

An illustration of the bias of such an approach can be given by visiting the website of one of the signatories of the Global Compact, Shell. After several public relations disasters concerning alleged links between the oil company and the Nigerian regime in the repression of the Ogoni people and the execution of human rights leader Ken Saro-Wiwa in 1995, Shell launched a huge public relations campaign and is now in the front line on the question of corporate governance and working with civil society. In 1997 it made a 'public commitment to contribute to sustainable development'. In 1998, it published the first Shell report 'documenting the actions we have taken to meet our responsibilities and creating value for the future'. On its website (www.shell. com, accessed June 2003) Shell boasts a commitment to sustainable development, a concept 'developed under the auspices of the UN as a way for governments to solve some of the world's most pressing problems'. Although '[b]usinesses alone cannot create a sustainable future' they have however 'an important role to play'. The pledge is thus that 'We [i.e., Shell], as part of society, intend to play our part both as a company and an energy provider.' In 2002 they published another report in which 'meeting the energy challenge' includes talks of collaboration with other parts of civil society and sustainable development projects. Sustainable development becomes a way to 'integrate the economic, environmental and societal aspects of our business to achieve sustained financial success, safeguard our environment and develop our reputation as partner and provider of first choice for all of our stakeholders'. In this sense, 'Sustainable development is not just about the environment and social concerns, it's very much about economic performance too. For these reasons it makes good business sense.' Embeddedness and continuity among powers is here a must: 'Our biggest challenges now are consistent delivery across all our operations and weaving together the economic, environmental and social strands of sustainable development, rather than addressing each in isolation.'

However, as soon as one's browser is pointed at the page listing Shell's seven principles of sustainable development, one cannot fail to notice principle number 1, 'Generating robust profitability,' or, to quote fully:

Successful financial performance is essential to our sustainable future and contributes to the prosperity of society. We use recognised measures to judge our profitability. We seek to achieve robust profitability by, for example, reducing costs, improving margins, increasing revenue and managing working capital effectively.

This is soon followed by principle number 2, 'Delivering value to customers'. All the other principles more familiar to environmentalists are subordinated to the sustainability of markets and profitability.

We can thus wonder whether this Polanyi inversion, which on the one hand acknowledges the 'values' of society – on grounds such as 'human rights', 'environment', 'labour standards' – and on the other subordinates them to the economic and business priorities of corporate capital, is just a type of public relations. For example, Shell forecasts a yearly expenditure on renewable energies of about $200 million a year, 1.7 per cent of their capital expenditure. Yet at the same time, current yearly expenditure on fossil fuel exploration and reproduction is $8 billion (Friends of the Earth 2002).

Neoliberal governance and the beginning of history

Governance, far from representing a paradigm shift away from neoliberal practices, has been shown to be a central element of the neoliberal discourse in a particular phase, when neoliberalism and capital in general face particularly stringent problems of accumulation, growing social conflict and a crisis of reproduction. Governance sets itself the task of tackling these problems for capital by relaying the disciplinary role of the market through the establishment of a 'continuity of powers' based on normalised market values as the truly universal values. Governance thus seeks to embed these values in the many ways that social and environmental problems are addressed. It thus promotes active participation of society in the reproduction of life and of our species on the basis of this market normalisation. Neoliberal governance thus seeks to co-opt the struggles for reproduction and social justice and, ultimately, promotes the perspective of the 'end of history' at the point of crisis of social stability.

Neoliberal governance is a way of dealing with the problem of 'stability of social flows' that cannot be turned into systemic disciplinary flows by the market mechanism, as in the original neoliberal project. There are also grounds for believing that the level of recomposition of the movement in the third phase of the neoliberal period has made the task of governance quite difficult. Governance is in crisis at the very beginning of its implementation. Very few NGOs can sustain close material or discursive partnership relations with business and government without at the same time alienating the support of social movements and thus undermining their legitimacy.

In this context, we could ask whether war – and especially the paradigm of permanent war that is emerging after 9/11 – can also be seen as an opportunity to push forward the project of neoliberal governance. The recent US administration's attack on NGOs,[29] coupled with the hike in the criminalisation of social movements and the pervasive patriotism brought about by the permanent 'war on terror', might represent a desperate attempt to impose the principle of selection and the discursive common ground that we have seen is necessary for governance to be operational. After all, it was the Second World War that facilitated the formation of a common discourse between unions, state and corporations, through the institutionalisation and bureacratisation of trade unions in the United States, facilitated by the state in exchange for the 'no strike pledge' and the acceptance of rules of bargaining and of companies' rights to managerial control of production (De Angelis 2000a).

The governance discourse is a discourse that constructs difference in such a way as to *integrate it*. To the World Bank or IMF operators, the 'other' who protests, fights, problematises, campaigns and takes issue with the World Bank, the IMF or the G8 must be taken inside, so that they can join the 'debate with civil society', or even, in certain rare cases, sit at the negotiating table. But in this way, the other must be knowable, predictable; their protesting 'otherness' must be formalised into a set of procedures that allow integrating *them* into the priority of capitalist growth and market promotion of the same organisations they are protesting against. To be integratable, 'the other' must be judged within the parameters and principles of selection of a market discourse, which can certainly be reformed from the 'excesses' of early neoliberism (that is to adopt the soft neoliberal approach à la Jeffrey Sachs or Joseph Stiglitz) to accommodate *dissent*, but not to the point of questioning the principle that markets must be the instruments of choice for articulating livelihoods on the planet. In this way, the integration of the struggling other implies their transformation into something else, no longer autonomous, but discursively *coupled* to the value practices of capital. It is only when the 'protesting other' claims their autonomy and irreducibility to capitalist markets and their value practices, that we can hope to make inroads into changing the institutional setting of our lives,[30] even if this must happen through compromises.

Finally, the implication of this analysis is also that governance discourse, together with the neoliberal project, can and must be problematised and opposed by reconnecting with the traditional problem of political theory, the question of what constitutes social justice. If governance is a strategy attempting to establish a 'continuity of powers' geared to accumulation, and if this continuity of social powers subordinates any value to the market as value, then governance and neoliberalism can and must be problematised by reopening the question of 'values' and 'power'. This is not a question of outlining 'universal values' and asking people to regroup beyond them. Rather, it is a question of finding organisational forms through which questions regarding the *values* governing our planetary social interactions are raised in every corner of the global social body, in every interstice of social practice. We need to push forward the process of opening the debate over how we produce and reproduce our species and our ecosystems. Which in turn poses the question of the exercise of human *powers*, of who controls what, for what purpose, for what ends, in what manner. Ultimately, it is only a question of reopening history through a political process grounded in the activity of asking fundamental questions and the reclaiming of value practices other than capital.

8
Global loops

There is general agreement that sometime between the late 1970s and early 1980s a sort of epochal transformation occurred in terms of social relations, discourses and images. This transformation has been given many names, depending on what is the discipline of the interpreter, or what are the features that the interpreter wants to highlight. For example, it is called postmodernity in order to highlight the historical and cultural condition in which 'master narratives' are dissolved, a crisis in which all the certainties of ideologies seem to have vanished (Lyotard 1984). This, as Fredric Jameson (1991) would put it, is a cultural movement that corresponds to the 'late capitalism' of transnational consumer economies. It is called post-Fordism, to convey the idea that industrial production has moved away from large factories and standardised processes, towards small flexible specialised units of production and their interconnection through information and communication technologies. It is called neoliberalism, to highlight the shift away from Keynesian policies of full employment and public spending, towards cuts in social entitlements and intensification of pro-market and pro-business policies. All these approaches grasp some important aspects of the transformation we have been through in the last quarter of a century, yet they all fail to recognise that the transformation they are highlighting was only one side of the coin of a much broader transformation. The collapse of master narratives was accompanied by the deepest and most extensive colonisation of our lives by the master narrative of capitalist markets. The post-Fordist flexibilisation of production was accompanied by a dramatic increase in production in sweatshops and factories around the world, many of which retain typical Fordist features. Increased state intervention through regulatory bodies and state subsidies accompanied global pro-market neoliberal policies towards business, not to mention the intensification of surveillance, repression and military functions of states accompanying neoliberal structural adjustment policies. In a word, it is as if the observers were looking at the element of novelty as part of a linear movement of history towards the future, in which the accumulated effect of the transformations (no master narratives, i.e., 'end of ideologies'; flexible production, neoliberal policies, and so on) would lead to a clear new social configuration having the features prefigured by these early trends. Instead, these transformations were moments of a much deeper transformation in our lives, one that combined *both elements of the old* and of the new. This transformation is a transformation in the ways capitalist relations of production (both waged and unwaged) are today maintained and reproduced. It is a transformation that aims at intensifying the coupling of the circuit of production and reproduction at different scales of social action within the planetary social body, and in thus doing articulates and channels struggles and conflict into more pervasive processes of capital homeostasis. In this and the next chapter I study only some of the features that are contributing towards the creation of this 'deepening' of market disciplinary mechanisms.

Behind 'economic' trends

It is generally accepted that three main interrelated 'economic' trends distinguish the neoliberal era from the late 1970s to today. These are: increased mobility of financial capital and third world debt, increased transnationalisation of production and increased world trade. From our perspective, these trends are not 'economic' trends, but the manifestation of how the genealogical and preservative mechanisms of capital markets discussed in the previous chapter have been operating in the last quarter of a century, of how capitalist production and reproduction loops, waged and unwaged work, have been extended, intertwined and coupled in new patterns and forms to serve capital's *conatus* of self-preservation.

The crisis of social stability of the 1970s manifested itself in high unemployment and inflationary pressures, due to capital refusing to invest and putting up prices in its resistance to higher wages, more social entitlements, lower work rhythms, and the more 'environmentally friendly' processes of social production demanded by struggles around the world. In the mid 1970s the 'masters' appointed a commission of wise people to interpret the meaning of these demands, which had led to a major profitability crisis. After long elaboration, the 'Trilateral Commission', as the committee was called, reported its findings: the problem was too much democracy! (Crozier, Huntington and Watanuki 1975).

A major reorganisation of world capitalism and class relations thus took place, of which the restructuring of 'finance', 'production' and 'trade' became the pillars through which world democracy could be taken away from the streets and popular assemblies and restricted to the realm of farcical and manipulative electoral campaigns. Nothing really substantial would be decided through the electoral system of Western democracy, because *most* of what matters for the reproduction of people's livelihoods would be decided by the 'democracy' of the market. Governments became management executive

boards of *Country X Inc.*, and politicians turned into 'technicians' whose task
was to create conditions of competitiveness and ride the 'inevitable' neoliberal
globalising processes.

The first thing required for the expansion of markets over people's lives was
to devise a mechanism that would put stricter bounds on governments' ability
to respond to popular movements demanding the socialisation of resources in
order to meet needs. 'Excessive' public spending was identified as the major
source of inflation and unemployment, together with 'excessive' wage
demands. With the election of Margaret Thatcher in the United Kingdom in
1979 and Ronald Reagan in the United States in 1981, a new 'consensus'
started to consolidate according to which national assets had to be privatised,
public spending curbed and capital markets had to be liberalised. Until then,
the post-Second World War governments could implement Keynesian policies
of full employment – whether these were successful or not – through the
manipulation of tools such as the interest rate and the exchange rate, merely on
the basis of capital control. With the opening up of capital's markets, governments decreed the abandonment of their commitment to full employment and
the welfare state. Economic and social policies had first of all to please the
financial capital markets. If governments made popular concessions that
redistributed resources from capital to the working class, financial capital
would fly away, thus inducing a fall in exchange rates and an increase in interest rates and provoking a downturn in business and an increase in unemployment. In the view of neoliberals, a 'stable economy' meant accommodation to
the desires of international financial capital. Disciplinary financial markets
thus started to exert heavy pressure on production and reproduction loops
across the different nodes through which capital increasingly migrated, pitting
conditions of reproduction against each other.

In the global South, which did not have 'advanced' capital markets through
which to impose the discipline of global capital, the same effects were obtained
through the management of what became known as the debt crisis. This has its
roots in the profitability crisis of the 1970s, when Western banks lent money to
military regimes in the South to fund their armies and repressive apparatuses
and development projects backed by the World Bank. At the time, these
regimes seemed to guarantee a safer and higher return than Western business
and government investors operating in a context of high social and political
instability. The crisis exploded in October 1979 after the US Federal Reserve,
chaired by Paul Volker, newly appointed by the Democratic president, Jimmy
Carter, dramatically raised interest rates to 'combat inflation', thus provoking
a massive global recession. In 1982, the first country to be hit by crisis was
Mexico, which defaulted. Since then, debt crises have been ongoing occur-
rences, which, from the perspective of capital's accumulation, has served the
same purpose as financial capital liberalisation. This is because the mechanisms used to deal with a liquidity crisis have in principle the same effects as

the operation of financial markets, as experienced by self-disciplined Western governments not wanting to 'upset' financial markets and trying to 'please' international investors and attract capital.

In an event of a liquidity crisis for a debtor country, the first action is to make a phone call to the International Monetary Fund (IMF) in Washington. The IMF was created in Bretton Woods in 1944 as a pillar of global Keynesianism, not of global neoliberalism. In the post-war scenario, its role was to provide short-term financial aid to Western national governments in balance of payment difficulties. The idea was that this would give them the breathing space in which to make the necessary reforms – in conjunction with business and trade unions – to increase productivity and efficiency more than wages and social entitlements, thus re-equilibrating the trade balance. Global capitalism, at least in its Western dimension, was thus conceived as the ebbing and flowing of trade deficits and surpluses, ultimately resulting from the impact of a series of 'social deals' among governments, business and bureaucratised trade unions. In the neoliberal period, since financial liberalisation replaced the regulatory role of the Keynesian deal, the IMF became the police and enforcer of market discipline for the people of the global South.

The result of the phone call that a national government in liquidity crisis would make to the IMF is well known: IMF officials would offer their help and would consider extending a loan in order for the country in question to be able to pay its due interest. This would allow it to continue to 'benefit' from existing trade agreements, aid flows, and all the perks that go with being a member of the world 'economic community'. *However*, the proviso for the loan would be a series of conditions, also known as a Structural Adjustment Programme (SAP), which the IMF forces all countries in crisis to adopt with little variation: devalue the currency, thus making imports more expensive and enforcing a cut in real wages; privatise water, education, health services and other national resources, thus opening them up to restructuring, hence unemployment; cut social spending; open up markets; promote competitive exports, which will help to service the debt. In the case of basic resources like water, their privatisation results in attempting to make poor people pay for them at prices they often cannot afford.[1] In other words, as in the case of financial liberalisation in the global North, in the global South too the management of debt crises becomes an opportunity to impose enclosures and disciplinary integration over the social body.

Global restructuring of production and reproduction

While these trends and practices on the side of finance serve to extend the rule of capitalist markets and reduce the space for social entitlements, they also increase people's dependence on markets for the reproduction of their livelihoods. In this context, the development of information and communication technologies, together with the drastic reduction in the monetised cost of global transport, has offered capital a major opportunity to restructure global production and reproduction and *escape* from zones of high social conflict. Through the late 1970s and 1980s, *export processing zones* (EPZs) began to mushroom around the world. These are areas set up by governments in the global South in which extremely favourable tax regimes for business, slack environmental regulations, and anti-union laws, in a context of widespread poverty and increased dependence on the market, all contributed to attracting industries desiring to escape the higher wages and higher regulatory regimes of the Northern countries and their corresponding reproduction fields. With the generalisation of EPZ to whole countries, multinational corporations thus increasingly turned into transnational corporations. While the former, which grew in the 1950s and 1960s, were replicating production processes in different countries so as to access national and regional markets, the latter slice up the production that once would have taken place in one area, and displace it through large *global production networks* according to cost and efficiency criteria. The productive nodes within these networks might belong to a major transnational corporation, or they might simply be subcontracted out to minor players. We shall discuss the implications of this in the next chapter. What matters here is the acknowledgment of the fact that from the late 1970s onwards, capital underwent a major restructuring for which integration *within nodes* and integration *across nodes* increasingly became substitutes for each other, thus enabling business to escape the worst of struggles over wages, environment, entitlements and conditions of reproduction and relocate in advantageous reproduction fields (see Chapter 6).

This restructuring of production and reproduction across global production networks is predicated on a labour force that is increasingly flexible, precarious and disposable. Supply chain adjustments, whether they are 'demand driven', 'supply driven', or 'technology driven', are ultimately possible through oscillations in labour *activity*. It is obvious that from the perspective of employers (i.e., cost-minimising units), the flexibility of labour they hire following the whims of the market must correspond to flexibility of contracts (i.e., increasingly precarious and temporary labour). The character of this 'flexibility' of labour changes through the global commodity chain and includes the most disparate forms, from new forms of slavery and bonded labour (which are flexible to the point of being physically disposable) to precarious and casual labour of skilled professionals employed by 'soft money'. In some contexts, 'flexibility' can accommodate *both* the needs to minimise costs by capital, as well as demands for autonomy and the refusal of factory discipline. Thus, the growing pattern of externalisation and outsourcing creates a pool of self-employed, autonomous workers who only two decades ago would have been working full time for a company and who are now portrayed as subjects undergoing an 'entrepreneurial revolution'. In reality, what this often means is the growth of heavily indebted workers, who no longer face a foreman with a stopwatch, but instead an impersonal one, with a virtual but still pressing and life-consuming stopwatch emerging from the market disciplinary mechanisms within which they are now direct actors.[2]

This ongoing restructuring of industrial production across the globe obviously accounts for the greater share of world trade, as mentioned before. This has also been facilitated by the fact that between 1944 and the present day, average tariffs for manufacturing products have dropped from about 44 per cent to about 6 per cent. Trade liberalisation became increasingly controversial in the 1990s with the discussion of new issues and new procedures. Within the Uruguay round of trade negotiations that ended in the mid 1990s and, after that, within the framework of multilateral trade agreement overseen by the WTO, or in the plethora of bilateral trade agreements between nations, new controversial issues were introduced: liberalisation of services including public services, enforcement of patents and US-style intellectual property rights, agricultural tariffs and dumping, biotechnologies, among many others. In the last few years mounting criticism has been directed towards the impact that these trade-liberalising practices have or could have on democracy, environment, labour, poverty, and so on, a critical mood that took many by surprise in November 1999 in Seattle, when the ministerial meeting of the WTO was surrounded by thousands of protestors who shut it down. The agenda of trade liberalisation on new issues has been pursued relentlessly, especially by the global North, in the subsequent WTO ministerial meetings at Doha (November 2001), Cancun (September 2003) and Hong Kong (December 2005) and in the ongoing negotiations among trade representatives.[3]

From our perspective, these current issues on trade liberalisation in services and deregulation of investment regimes have to do with the further deepening of capitalist markets across the social body. However, the discursive opposition to trade liberalisation that is being voiced by many trade unions and NGOs building on struggles from various social movements around the world is still rooted, to a large extent, in false dichotomies lacking an overall apprehension of the rationales of capitalist processes.

Trade unions, for example, often embrace rhetoric opposing some specific trade-liberalising practices while at the same time embracing principles of national competitiveness. It is clear that, at any given time, capitalist processes of trade liberalisation will raise some kind of opposition from both unions and business leaders for the sectors affected if these sectors are likely to feel the crunch coming from foreign competition. It is also clear that the opposite is true: for those sectors that have a competitive advantage in the process of liberalisation, this will be seen by both unions and business as a new opportunity for jobs and growth. Thus, partisan lines are always reproduced along predictable alliances when trade liberalisation is promoted. What is generally not seen, contested and problematised, is the meaning of the process as a whole.

Similarly, many NGOs, due to their dependence on funding from their constituencies, often cannot afford to contest the overall role of capitalist markets – whether these are promoted in specific contexts by trade liberalisation or protectionist policies – and instead embrace discourses restricting their opposition to specific trade-liberalising policies promoted by the global North.

Like capitalist strategies of protectionism of particular industries, trade liberalisation, despite the endless number of economic models formulated in its defence, is never a process that offers crystal clear and universal advantages. The overall role of trade liberalisation is that of a strategy aimed at increasing the pervasiveness of the markets, and this always favours someone and ruins others in an endless race. It is because of this common feature of protectionist policies that the reasons for its legitimisation must be found somewhere else. It would appear absurd for anybody to regard trade liberalisation, i.e., a policy designed to deepen and extend the *process* of livelihood-pitting competition within the social body into new spheres, as an end in itself. This would make sense only from the perspective of capital's value practices. In order to be understood as a rational and sensible policy, and especially in view of the fact that everybody knows that someone will lose out in the face of it, trade liberalisation has to be portrayed as a means to broader goals.

And the promised goals are really remarkable. Take for example the WTO website, which posts a brochure listing ten benefits of the WTO system among which are: 'promoting international peace', 'making life easier', 'cutting the costs of living', providing 'more choice of products and qualities', 'shielding governments from lobbying' and encouraging 'good government'.[4] A convenient, wonderful, and detritus-free world, almost like a CNN news programme, not really conforming to the experiences of those social subjects from around the world who, in the name of free trade, have become victims of war (such as in Iraq with its new neoliberal constitution), have seen their education and social entitlement cut, or their commons privatised in the name of competitiveness, have to pay skyrocketing bills for privatised water, bear on their own bodies the environmental and labour costs of export industries, or have to pay for health and education, and whose choices are restricted between detritus in their homelands or detritus in illegal migration circuits. And it goes without saying that, given the increase in planetary wealth and income polarisation, for any ten losers we can find a declining fractional number of winners.

Not to talk about the blatant hypocrisy of linking trade liberalisation with 'shielding governments from lobbying', as if massive corporate lobbying was not a constituent feature of Western democracies. But on one point we must agree. Trade liberalisation indeed promotes 'good government' – in the tautological sense that for capital's value practices, 'good' is the government that embraces, promotes and defends capitalist markets.

GLOBALISATIONS

On the basis of the previous discussion, we must reflect here on the number of different definitions of 'globalisation' that have mushroomed in the last few years, together with their associated explanations and rationalisations. This vast literature is divided across academic/intellectual disciplines and the biases inherent in each disciplinary framework have led to different conceptualisations of 'globalisation', regarding the phenomenon as principally economic, social, political or cultural, for example. Held et al. (1999: 2–10) propose a useful classification of approaches to studying globalisation, distinguishing *sceptical*, *hyperglobalist* and *transormationalist* theses. Following this classification, Hoogvelt (2001: 120) suggests that 'these approaches correspond [respectively] to whether one views globalization as primarily an economic, a social or a political phenomenon'.

Sceptics

It is interesting to note that within this classification, 'sceptics' who question the relevance of notions such as globalisation to describe global trends in foreign direct investment (FDI) and trade in the last quarter century are those who study 'globalisation' in terms of 'economic' phenomena, that is, in terms of the realms of money variables, production, distribution and market that, in popular perception, are the most 'globalised'. Their scepticism depends on the narrow conception of these realms as 'economic'. According to sceptics of the globalisation thesis, such as David Gordon (1998), Hirst and Thompson (1999) and Linda Weiss (1997; 1998), the extent of globalisation, and in particular its novelty, have been grossly overstated. Hirst and Thompson even claim that they are 'convinced that globalization, as conceived by the more extreme globalizers, is largely a myth' (1999: 2). To make their argument, the sceptics have charted quantitative historical comparisons of foreign trade and capital movements and have concluded that globalisation, as a worldwide integration of national economies, is nothing new. In fact, taking proxy measures of integration, such as the share of foreign direct investments over production, the incidence of trade on national economies, and so forth, the world was more integrated in the early part of the nineteenth century than it is now. This is even the case for many of the then colonies, which, in terms of these measures, were more integrated in the world economy than today's countries of the South.

Thus, for example, Hirst and Thompson, after examining post-war investment and trade flows, find that

between 54 per cent and 70 per cent of the world's population was in receipt of only 16 per cent of global FDI flows in the first half of the 1990s. In other words, between a half and two-thirds of the world was still virtually written off the map as far as any benefit from this form of investment was concerned. (Hirst and Thompson 1999: 74)

Kleinknecht and ter Wengel, focusing on the EU, find that

to the extent that trade [and FDI] exceeds the frontiers of the European Union, the lion's share of transaction still takes place among the rich OECD countries, notably with the US. Looking at long-run trade figures, one can also question the proposition that we are currently experiencing an historically unique stage of internationalisation. (1998: 638)[5]

In the sceptics' approach, then, globalisation as global integration is put under question or even treated as a 'myth' because the bulk of FDI and trade are concentrated in the 'triad' of North America, Europe and Japan, the dominant economic blocs. However, there are three broad problems with this economic approach to globalisation, which we shall call *nation state, reproduction* and *measure*.

The *nation state* problem concerns the fact that the unit of analysis – the nation state – used to explore the significance of worldwide integration has itself been subject to transformation. Globalisation does not simply mean greater integration of nation states' 'economies', but a reconfiguration of the capitalist 'economic' unit away from the borders of the nation state. According to this view, the nation state (and its 'economy') is a constituent moment in the overall set of social relations, whose form is determined by the developing nature of these social relations (Burnham 1996; see also Holloway 1996). This reconfiguration of the state occurs precisely *through* those 'economic' flows identified, such as trade, FDI and finance – together with systematic policies of enclosures such as the governance of structural adjustment policies and debt – which are important not so much in their absolute quantitative size, but in their ability to integrate people and livelihoods across the globe as moments of a continuously pervasive global circuit of capital, M-C-M'. As was illustrated in Figure 1 of Chapter 6, this is at the same time the integration of reproduction loops.

The *reproduction* problem concerns two linked problematics, first, that of integration and, second, that of the relationship between production and reproduction. These are ignored when globalisation is viewed solely as a question of integration of different '*economies*', that is, the *monetised* set of human activities which produce commodities, but they raise crucial questions: how, and in what forms, do globalisation processes globally integrate people's activities for the reproduction of their livelihoods? Since reproductive labour includes large chunks of unwaged work, we can no longer study the world in terms only of 'the economy', whose categories are from the start restrictive and biased towards monetised production and its world-view. (See, for example, Dalla Costa and Dalla Costa 1999.) Suffice it to say that this problematic opens up the third problem with the economic approach to globalisation, that of measure.

The problematic of *measure* permeates almost every issue of interest to (political) economists.[6] Regarding globalisation, if this phenomenon is understood as one of a modality of integration of people and livelihoods across the globe, then to what extent do patterns of FDI (and trade) flows measure it? To what extent does the knowledge of trade and investment quantities between Indonesia, the United States and India give insights into what is really important, that is the mutual *relations* between, say, a mother's work of reproduction in Indonesia and a steel worker's work of production in Indiana, USA or a call-centre worker's service labour in India?

Patterns of capital investment cannot be theorised independently of the problematisation of differentials in the conditions of reproduction, much of it unwaged, of labour power in different localities. This is because capital, i.e., money-values seeking to grow in *value*, is also attracted or repelled by differentials among broad conditions of reproduction, as discussed in Chapter 6, conditions which are in turn constituted by an assemblage of a large variety of factors, among which: social entitlements, wage rate differentials, degrees of revolt and insubordination, degrees of normalisation to markets, states of public spending, social spending and consequent tax regimes, and so on.

What is the implication of all this for our critique of the economic view of globalisation? The implication is that monetary measures for us matter more as a moment in a process (indeed, a contradictory process based on conflict and on the articulation between monetised and non-monetised reproduction) than as a static picture of a 'structure'. For this reason, to argue, as the sceptics do, that trade and FDI are concentrated in the triad, does not in fact question globalisation as a process of capitalist integration. On the contrary, this empirical evidence perhaps reveals the capitalist character of this process of integration, one based on the command over labour and its differentiation along an international division of labour that is continuously being reconfigured. Given the miserable wages of the global South in relation to those of the Northern developed countries, and the overall lower value of labour power in these countries, the fact that only 15 or 20 per cent of world FDI goes to the South may demonstrate not that investment is unfairly redistributed in the world, but rather that it is 'fairly' redistributed according to capital's value practices, that is, the capacity to *command* labour within the process of capitalist accumulation.

For example, in the United States, $20 will employ a worker for one hour, that is, it will command just a single hour of labour time. But, in China or Thailand, $20 can put four people to work each for ten hours, whilst in India that $20 is sufficient to put ten people to work, each for ten hours. When the difference that $20 makes is between commanding one hour of labour time on the one hand, and commanding 40 hours or 100 hours on the other, it matters much less that so little FDI goes to the South. This is the problematic introduced by what classical political economy calls *labour commanded* and Marx in particular refers to as a measure of the (possibly potential) quantity of living labour, which can be set in motion by a quantity of money as capital. In short, the question of the extent to which global capital is inserting itself into people's lives cannot be answered by considering only absolute quantities of money.[7] Also, as we have discussed in previous chapters, the labour that is commanded with wages is also the invisible unwaged work of reproduction of the unwaged. Hence, measuring FDI in terms of labour commanded reveals just the opposite of what the sceptics argue. In terms of labour-commanded FDI, the lion's share 'belongs' to developing countries. When we measure capitalist investments in terms of its potential to mobilise labour, i.e., in terms of the social power of money, there would seem to be no doubt: pervasive capital's globalisation can also be made intelligible quantitatively. As far as capital is concerned therefore, there is no need for greater investment in the South in relation to the North: it is already able to command masses of living labour there, and moreover is able to do so by paying pitiful wages and massively underspending on the conditions of reproduction.

This also means that we need to problematise the notion, which is held dear by conventional economic wisdom and embedded in economic discourse, that investment is uniquely associated with a 'benefit' to the recipient local population. In fact, a large quantity of FDI measured in terms of labour commanded could well be associated with poorly performing social and environmental indicators, which result in a high level of labour commanded per dollar. As one example of the double-edged nature of investment, one could reflect on the investment programme to build a series of dams along the Narmada River and its tributaries in central India. This investment can certainly be seen to 'benefit' local unemployed labourers and engineers, but hardly those thousands of families who have to be displaced to make room for the development. High displacement rates and, in general, the high vulnerability of the local population would be reflected in prevailing wage rates through something akin to the Marxian theory of the reserve army of labour (Marx 1976a).[8] The monetary figures of FDI are not able to capture the social costs associated with investment programmes. In contrast, labour-commanded FDI figures, through their emphasis on power and their link to conditions of reproduction captured by the prevailing wage rate, are better able to make us reflect on such issues.

Hyperglobalists

In contrast to the sceptics, the hyperglobalists tend to emphasise power and politics as defined from the top down, not the bottom up. Their focus is thus the nation state, the relevance of which is problematised in the context of global trends. Here the thesis advanced (see, for example, Strange 1996) is the *declinist* view of the state: comparing the power of business and transnational production networks on the one hand with that of nation states on the other, these authors conclude that the former is growing in relation to the latter. A classic illustration of this approach is the ranking of TNCs and government powers as measured by their net revenues. Such a ranking positions companies such as Ford, Texaco and GM above Brazil and other poorer states (see Sklair 2002). The declinist thesis is that nation states have 'lost power over their own economies' and instead are simple 'transmitters of global market discipline to the domestic market' (Hoogvelt 2001: 120).

There are some problems with this approach. In the first place, it poses a distinction between 'power' and 'economic' practices that, from the perspective of an analysis of capital adopted in this book, is quite problematic. As we have briefly discussed in Chapter 2 and shall see more clearly in our discussion of enclosures, the role of the state in the processes of transformation of the last 20 years or so is far more than a mere transmitter of global market discipline to national market discipline. All the practices of enclosures promoted by neoliberalism, not to mention the practices of structural adjustment, accompanied by bombs and invasion in such cases as Iraq, are, in one way or another, state policies. Furthermore, the so-called process of 'deregulation' of the neoliberal period actually amounted to a 're-regulation' in favour of business and of the processes of capitalist markets in each country.[9] In other words, the *nation state* has been and is instrumental in creating global market discipline.

In so doing, nations states have not seen their power declining. Rather, the exercise of their many powers is now subject to their rearticulation into a process of global governance and the constitution of a global sovereignty that regards the rules of the global markets as the *benchmark* criteria for government intervention. To articulate given populations to global markets implies that enclosures are enforced, markets are created and extended, and the institutions and practices regulating and overseeing people's reproduction are articulated to the global machine. But since this is a contested process (increasingly so since the rise of neoliberalism), states reconfigure and upgrade their powers to police, control and repress increasingly transnational movements against neoliberalism and capitalist value practices. The so-called 'war against terrorism', for example, provides the perfect opportunity to introduce laws that limit civil liberty and criminalise protest.

But the activity of policing is also directed towards governments that, for a variety of reasons, are recalcitrant towards full implementation of neoliberalism and market pervasiveness. Indeed, the military power of the global police state par excellence, the United States, is not in the way of global neoliberalism, but has become a fundamental instrument for the management of its internal contradictions, crisis and rebellion. This, as George Caffentzis argues, is because, for neoliberal globalisation to 'work',

the system must be global and the participating nations and corporations must follow the 'rules of the trade' (including trade in services, patents and copyrights) even when participation goes against their self-interest. In a time of crisis, however, there is a great temptation for many participants to drop out of or bend the rules of the game, especially if they perceive themselves to be chronic losers. What force is going to keep the recalcitrants ... from proliferating? Up until the 1997 'Asian Financial Crisis' most of the heavy work of control was done by the IMF and World Bank thorough the power of money. Since then it is becoming clear that there are countries that will not be controlled by structural adjustment programs (SAPs) and the fear of being exiled from the world credit market if they do not follow the instruction of the IMF and World Bank. (Caffentzis 2005: 48)

Typical examples of these countries are of course the 'Bush-baptised "axis of evil" nations', that is Baathist Iraq, Islamic fundamentalist Iran and communist North Korea; but

there are many others Islamic, national socialist and communist governments that have not transformed their economies into neoliberal form. This list will undoubtedly grow unless there is a check, in the form of a world police officer that will increase the cost of an exit. (ibid.)

In other words, increasingly the neoliberal order needs the equivalent of the role played by Britain in the nineteenth century in policing the old liberal order.

Bill Clinton and his colleagues believed that the UN could eventually be used by the US government as such a force. The Bush Administration disagrees and concludes that the US will have to act in its own name to enforce the rules of the national order ... and that action must at times be military. In the end, it is only with the construction of a terrifying US Leviathan that the crisis of neoliberalism will be overcome and the regime of free trade and total commodification will finally be established for its millennium. (ibid.)

A military Leviathan, and not declining states, seems to be the prospect for neoliberal globalisation.

Transformationalists

Finally, the transformationalists regard the process of globalisation as 'primarily a social phenomenon that has brought qualitative changes in *all* cross-border transactions' (Hoogvelt 2001: 120). The phenomenon in question is what David Harvey (1989) has called 'time–space compression'. The emergence of this phenomenon is seen in the fusion between information and telecommunication technology, as well as in the reduction in transport costs (Dicken 2003). These two factors have combined to bring the 'annihilation of space through time'. They have thus created a 'new economy' based on networks, and a consequent transformation of cross-border activities, which is then called globalisation (Castells 2000). In the next chapter, we shall discuss how this 'social phenomenon' we call globalisation is rooted in value struggles.

9

The global work machine

GLOBAL PRODUCTION NETWORKS AND TNCs

From the perspective of an individual capital, globalisation and transnationalisation of production can be illustrated with the money circuit of capital that we have studied in Formula 2. This becomes

5.
$$M - C\{LP;MP\} \overset{p_1}{\cdots}|\overset{p_2}{\cdots}|\cdots\overset{p_3}{P}\cdots|\overset{p_4}{\cdots}|\overset{p_5}{\cdots}|C' - M'$$

in which p_1, p_2, ... p_i are moments of the production processes that are *externalised* to others and therefore turn into market transactions.[1]

Each production 'transaction' between the material phases of production p_i appears as a commercial transaction M-C or C'-M'. By virtue of this externalisation the production process p_i will now be subjected to the full blast of the impersonal disciplinary power of market forces.

The overall M-C-M' will then be constituted by a set of individual capitals, which in turn will be under increased competitive pressure, since this act of splitting and externalising is universal. The last quarter of a century's growth in trade, outpacing that of global monetised output, is therefore a manifestation of the restructuring of global production.

One central driving force of this process of splitting is of course the TNCs' design of global production networks, both directly as integrated productive nodes within a TNC and indirectly through the establishment of webs of subcontractors, with the consequent spatial reconfiguration of intra-firm trade.

Understanding the specific nature of current globalisation processes relies on the understanding of the nature and characteristics of functional integration as opposed to the integration of capitalist social relations. Both are ways of looking at global integration, but the first refers to the global integration of use values and the second to the global integration of the exchange values and processes of capital's valorisation. Let us briefly examine these.

Much literature has been devoted to the study of *global production chains*, as these provide a useful map of how a sequence of productive functions are linked together within an overall process of production of goods and services

(Gereffi and Korzeniewicz 1994).[2] At the basic level, production (or commodity) chains illustrate the geographical configuration of the interconnections between individual elements (e.g. materials, procurement, transformation, marketing and sales, distribution, services) by means of various forms of technological inputs and transport and communication processes. Also, each production chain is embedded within a financial system and is regulated and coordinated by TNCs and the state (understood here as including both nation states and various levels of supranational institutions such as the IMF, WTO, etc.) (Dicken 2003: 6–7). Ultimately, production chain analysis helps us to map how TNCs are slicing up production at the global level.

Generally speaking, from the perspective of a TNC, whether this is a major retail company overseeing a global food supply chain, or a computer company overseeing the chain of its components and correspondent processes, each of the individual functions may be integrated with other functions in two main ways: by means of externalised or internalised *transactions*. In the first case, a function is performed by individual and formally independent firms linked to other firms by means of the market. In the second case, each function within a productive chain may be located within a vertically integrated firm. It is clear that these are two extreme cases, and reality is more in line with a mix of externalised and internalised transactions. In either case, both externalised and internalised transactions when organised across borders point at the central importance of trade in constituting today's capitalist production process.[3]

Cost externalisation = someone else's cost internalisation

We have a first, important result of production chain analysis: TNCs' planning departments and market mechanisms are two forms of the same thing, namely a mechanism of coordination and regulation of production chains. The reasons why a firm chooses its mix of in-house and outsourced functions depend on a range of things, all of which have to do with risk and cost assessment and ultimately with the firm's strategic evaluation of its profitability condition and opportunities. Also, it is clear that the greater the flexibility and pervasiveness of markets at the global level, the greater is the range of opportunities for TNCs to reduce costs and minimise and externalise risks. There is therefore a symbiotic relationship between the neoliberal drive towards trade liberalisation, the TNCs' vantage point, and the constitution of production processes worldwide. It is in this sense that 'transnational enterprise is evolving from company organisation to a loosely confederated network structure (global web)' (Hoogvelt 1997: 127). Trade, both internalised and externalised, is thus what keeps together geographically displaced production processes at the global level.

Yet, as we have seen, each functional node within a production chain represents at the same time a configuration of monetary value production and value struggles, i.e., of power relations, not just a technical configuration for the production of use values. In this respect, as we shall see in Chapter 13, each node of global production is a moment within loops that define socially necessary labour time (SNLT), and is thus engaged in the corresponding disciplinary processes and articulated to loops of reproduction. Not only power relations between say, subcontractor and subcontracted firms (in the case in which the market plays the coordinating role) or between various departments within a vertically integrated TNC. Also, and more tellingly, power relations and value struggles at the point of production *and* reproduction, that is, around the quality and quantity of expenditure of labour, wages, entitlements, housing, health, education, environmental conditions, and so on, both between TNCs, the subcontracted firms and their corresponding territories, and *within* them.

Indeed, if the framework of analysis is the 'whole', *every externalisation is somebody else internalisation.* Thus, for example, TNCs' externalisation of risks involved with outsourcing implies of course the internalisation of risks by subcontracted companies. For subcontracted firms to be able to internalise this risk, they must be able to rely on a workforce that is flexible enough and cheap enough to absorb required changes in production, that is, to *externalise to them* possible costs of adjustment. At the same time, they must be able to rely on environmental practices that externalise to forests, rivers and the atmosphere the cost of adjustment.

In both cases, the actual cost of adjustment trickles down to individuals and communities in charge of their own reproduction; the invisible, unaccounted realm of the reproduction of our livelihoods becomes the dumping place for capital's cost externalisation, which then coincides with the creation of *detritus*. The pursuit of flexible labour markets, capital mobility and the management of public expenditure that preclude non-market ways of gaining access to social wealth, which are at the cornerstone of profitably viable TNCs' outsourcing strategies, are at the same time grounded on processes of social labour, of doing, that internalise *at their own life-cost* what TNCs write out of their monetary cost accounts. The secret of outsourcing is that it makes capital's command over labour more invisible, removing it from inside the belly of corporate capital and instead displacing it in an archipelago of productive units in competition with each other. The command over labour thus appears in a more discrete and sanitised form as trade flows between these outsourced units and large TNCs, which have externalised control over labour. As we shall see, this does not mean the end of disciplinary society, but its greatest triumph: the planetary social body itself is organised along the principles of a panopticon prison (see Chapter 15).

There is thus a second implicit result that we can derive from production chain analysis following the twofold character of capital's integration: each functional node is a site of implicit or explicit conflict over the quantity and quality of labour expenditure, over wages, over values and meanings, over regulatory practices on the environment, over prioritising social welfare or the welfare of business, over the allocation of state finance, around conditions of reproduction. If we enlarge our view of global commodity chains so as also to include the territory and the social and political space around each node, i.e., regard global commodity chains more in terms of global production networks, which are not simply confined to monetised production (Henderson et al. 2002), then it is clear that as each node or 'place' of global production is a site of contestation and each node or place includes both production and reproduction, waged and unwaged work, then we might see how the overall competitive *articulation* between nodes or places takes the form of *biopolitical competition*. Within the overall sequence of a production chain, and it can be a long sequence with many ramifications, the degree of impact and disrupting leverage of conflict within a particular node is, *ceteris paribus*, inversely proportional to the degree of spatial substitutability of that node. The degree of spatial substitutability of capital from one node to another, facilitated and made possible by 'time–space compression' (Harvey 1989) and promoted by neoliberal strategies of liberalisation and privatisation, makes each node more vulnerable. The Zapatistas' insight of neoliberalism as a war against humanity is precisely this: the deepening of a rat race over the global social body.[4]

DISCIPLINARY TRADE

Trends

Some of the epiphenomenal effects of this splitting and spatial displacement of production (aided by trade liberalisation policies that reduce barriers and promoted by government tax incentives and other measures of corporate welfare for states in 'competition' to attract capital) make up a series of empirical trends that have been developing in the last quarter of a century up until the economic slowdown of the early twenty-first century, and which includes:

- the increased relevance of international trade in relation to global monetised production
- the increase in manufacturing trade as a proportion of overall trade
- the change in the specialisation patterns of global trading, with more low-wage 'developing' countries specialising in finished and semi-processed manufacturing to feed into global production networks
- the fall in the terms of trade in manufacturing
- the increased relevance of intra-firm and inter-product trade
- synergies between trade and foreign direct investments[5]

It goes without saying that this list is not exhaustive, as it leaves out important issues such as patterns of trade in agricultural and primary producers as well as services. However, the selection here intends to illustrate and draw attention to the historical novelty of the role taken by trade. For the case of this illustration, I focus here on trade in manufacturing. This is an area of global monetised production that has been subject to heavy restructuring during the last quarter of a century.

These empirical trends, when read within the framework here proposed centred on the *conatus* of capital self-preservation and struggles among value practices, suggest that trade today has increasingly acquired some new characteristics. In the collective imagination, when we think about trade, we think about a human activity whose main purpose is to allow people in different locations to access goods produced elsewhere. Generally we think that the reason these goods are traded is because they are produced in 'surplus', that is above the amount consumed in the location of production. This 'vent-for-surplus' trade has been a key characteristic of both pre-capitalist and capitalist forms of trade, although with the important difference that in the latter case, as we have seen in the case of the slave trade, the surplus itself was systematically, militarily and politically engineered to serve the input needs of capital and thus subsumed within a continuous and systematic flow serving boundless accumulation.[6]

A large and increasing part of contemporary trade does not have anything to do with this 'vent-for-surplus' trade. To the North–South specialisation, which saw the South specialising in cash crops and raw materials and the North in manufacturing industries, and to the vent-for-surplus trade among developed nations (each tending to specialise in particular products), must be added another aspect of capitalist trade that is acquiring increasing importance: *disciplinary trade*. Disciplinary trade is a capitalist form of 'acquisition of goods from a distance' (Polanyi's general 'transhistorical' definition of trade[7]) in a context in which the monetary (not the 'invisible' ecological and human) cost of overcoming distance has been drastically reduced due to the vast increase in productivity in communication and transportation.[8] In this context the continuous process of trading is not simply ancillary to the accumulation needs of capital, but is one of the constituent moments of capitalist *relations of production*. This means that international trade not only serves the input needs of production processes dispersed through global production networks, but also plays a central role in aiming to manage the inherent conflict of capitalist social relations of production through displacement and continuous restructuring. In thus doing, the 'technical' specifications of trade flows are increasingly becoming subordinated to the regulatory function of social antagonism at the global level. International trade increasingly assumes a disciplinary role of both production and reproduction.

Models of capitalist trade

This disciplinary function of trade is relatively new. There are perhaps three main models of capitalist trade. In the old colonialist period, semi-feudal colonial powers such as Spain and Portugal raped the 'new world' in search of precious metals and gold. These were obtained through the imposition of work in the mines on the indigenous population and the collection of tributes. The main objective of this form of 'acquisition of goods from a distance' was immediate theft, and in fact it is difficult to label it properly as trade. Then came colonialism in the wake of the industrial revolution. This established trade routes – the first of which was the infamous triangular slave trade – and an international division of labour that saw the colonised lands producing raw materials and foodstuffs while Britain and other emerging industrialised powers were producing manufactured goods. By 1870, almost all food in Great Britain came from the USA and the *dominions* (Barratt Brown 1974). This latter form of colonialism, which shaped an international division of labour and made trade an integral part of capitalist accumulation, has survived until the present day, through various forms of neocolonialism that promoted cash crops and management of the debt crisis in the poorest areas of the world.

Within this model of trade, the integration between different regions specialising in different productions can be described as 'shallow' integration. As pointed out by an UNCTAD study, shallow integration characterised international economic integration before 1913, and consisted in 'arm's length trade in goods and services between independent firms and through international movements of portfolio capital' (UNCTAD 1993: 113). This corresponded to the constitution of a series of world empires and spheres of influence, each possessing a 'north' and a 'south', a 'centre' out of which political, military and economic power was emanating and a 'periphery' in a position of subordination. Each of these formations could be seen with Braudel's spectacles and understood as 'world economies' (Braudel 1984), that is, from the perspective of use values, relatively self-sufficient areas, with the centre producing manufacturing and the periphery raw materials and tropical goods. Conflict among 'world economies' or empires would then occur in order to acquire new territories with the corresponding resources and to displace the supplies that were imported from competing imperial powers (Hudson 1992: 32–6).

A third model of trade, increasingly dominant today, disciplinary trade corresponds to what has been called the process of deepening of global integration, that is the movement away from the North–South complementarity and specialisation characteristics of the shallow integration scenario and a change in the pattern of trade, from inter-product to intra-product trade.[9] Deep integration is organised and promoted by TNCs' shaping of global production networks[10] and

extends to the level of the production of goods and services and, in addition, increases visible and invisible trade. Linkages between national economies are therefore increasingly influenced by the cross-border value adding activities within ... TNCs and within networks established by TNCs. (UNCTAD 1993: 119)[11]

As this means that 'there is no longer a neat division of labour between countries' (Hoogvelt 1997: 22), the primary function of trade is no longer simply access to resources not available on the spot, but the shaping of norms of production and therefore of social relations. With this new model of capitalist trade, the flow of commodities between the trading areas increasingly serves the purpose of a disciplinary device, a function also served in other periods of capitalist production, but not in the pervasive and structural way it does today.

Global markets: the thing-like foreman and the control society

Trade has of course always helped to shape and to regulate class relations in the history of the capitalist mode of production. Cheap imports have always ruined businesses and threatened the livelihood of communities, while at the same time giving hope to other businesses and other communities. But in the context of today's global economy, this threat has become a constant menace and, whether real or perceived, it is now a constituent part of the web of flows and interrelationships defining global production. Although deep and shallow integration of trade clearly coexist today, to the extent that comparative advantages in trade reflect the *relative* degree of acquiescence of workers and communities across the globe (weighted by the respective productive forces that they set in motion) within a planetary hierarchy of reproduction fields, as illustrated in Figure 3 of Chapter 6, pervasive trade patterns extend the market role to regulating, managing, normalising and ultimately disciplining global patterns of social conflict. Global markets increasingly become a thing-like foreman, whose raison d'être is the internalisation of mechanisms of control by workers and communities at large. Thus, measured by its strategic and operational development, neoliberalism differs from classical liberalism in that corporate capital seeks liberalisation not only in order to gain access to markets and resources, but also to shape the actions of human producers and educate and normalise them to ever new benchmarks by which to assess rhythms of work and life. International trade is becoming an impersonal foreman, since it constitutes an important element of capital command over labour. Just as at the heart of the systematic colonisation and corresponding international division of labour promoted by Gibbon Wakefield and his followers lay the fear of social revolution in Great Britain in periods of stagnation and crisis of capitalism (for example, the first 20 years and the last 30 years of the nineteenth century) (Barratt Brown 1974: 131), so the new model of trade that has erupted in the last 20 years follows the period of crisis of Keynesianism following the international social movements in the 1960s and 1970s (De Angelis 2000a). Whereas colonialism and neocolonialism aimed at the dual target of cheapening the goods entering the reproduction of labour power – thus reducing its value in the presence of working-class-led pressures to increase it through struggle – in the new model this cheapening obtained through the import of manufactured goods is supplemented by trade, which increasingly acquires the role of a mechanism for disciplining both waged and unwaged labour to work.[12]

It is an unfortunate paradox that at the time at which neoliberal strategies attempt to extend these disciplinary mechanisms of the markets to cover the world and pervade ever new spheres of life, social critics have been talking about the overcoming of disciplinary society and the movement towards the control society.

In recent years, starting from Gilles Deleuze's studies of Foucault, important contributions began to describe the epochal socio-economic transformations from the late 1970s as the passages from disciplinary to control societies, or, more synthetically, as post-disciplinary societies. This passage is also associated with a particular reading of Foucault's analysis of bio-power in the same period, a reading that has been more recently revived in a well-known version of autonomist Marxism with the book *Empire* by Hardt and Negri.

Following Deleuze (1990; 1998), Hardt and Negri suggest that, although he never explicitly says it, 'Foucault's work allows us to recognise a historical, epochal passage in social forms from *disciplinary society* to the *society of control*' (Hardt and Negri 2000: 22–3). Unlike disciplinary society (that in which 'social command is contructed through a diffuse network of *dispositifs* or apparatuses that produce and regulate customs, habits, and productive practices'), the control society is one in which

mechanisms of command become ever more 'democratic,' ever more immanent to the social field, distributed throughout the brains and bodies of the citizens. The behaviors of social integration and exclusion proper to rule are thus increasingly interiorized within the subjects themselves. (Ibid.: 23)

It is recognised that 'the society of control might thus be characterised by an intensification and generalization of the normalizing apparatuses of disciplinarity that internally animate our common and daily practices'. However, 'in contrast to discipline, this control extends well outside the structured sites of social institutions through flexible and fluctuating networks' (Ibid.).

In this sense therefore, one could argue that what defines control societies is the *pervasiveness* of disciplinary mechanisms, that is disciplinary mechanisms that extend *outside* singular institutions and pervade the social field. Manuel Castells (2000) would put it in terms of circulation of decoded flows (of money, of people, of signs, of culture), while Gilles Deleuze would emphasise how disciplinary power has not been dismantled with the increased porosity of the walls of spaces of confinement (the factory, the school, etc.) associated with increased mobility, but rather 'released through the social field', so that post-disciplinary power operates in what Castells calls the 'space of flows', in which turbulence is regulated through modulation, optimisation or, in short, control functions.

Although there is a lot of good metaphorical and descriptive sense in these approaches, the main problem is what they leave out: they do not account for, engage with, and problematise the *processes* through which the extending and sustaining disciplinary methods are possible within society and upon which social practice is constituted as 'flows' of particular types. Once we take this into consideration, we notice that these processes create the 'parameters', the norms upon which a 'control society' – like any control system – is predicated. Hence it is crucial that we expose them, because the *front line* of the beginning of history is not in the 'flow', but in the type of 'molecular structure' giving rise to those flows. A system of control of traffic flows, for example, depends on car drivers who have internalised the norms according to which red signals mean stopping at the line. Control systems cannot function without given parameters. Thus, the relation between control and discipline is *never* one of either/or, either discipline or control, or of an 'epochal passage' between the two. I believe things are subtler. If we take 'discipline' to be a *factory of ethic*, as Foucault would put it, that is, the mechanism of reward and punishment that creates norms, then control mechanisms are those that use these norms to regulate flows. An example of this would be states attempting to 'modulate' and 'optimise' migration flows, i.e., to control these 'flows' from the perspective of given specific 'national' or 'regional' conditions of valorisation of capital. This control is specified on the basis of economic norms (targets in public spending, 'degrees' of competitiveness, state of labour demands in different sectors, trade balance and inflation, and so forth) that form the parameters upon which optimisation and modulation are predicated. In a global competitive environment, these norms in turn emerge from the complex interaction of a multitude of capitals and of subjectivities working for capital.

But there are in principles two broad ways to create norms. A designer of a control system (a planner) sets these parameters, these norms *outside* the control system. Alternatively, these norms emerge as a moment of a system of feedbacks within the control system. In this second case we have a 'learning system'.[13] There are of course many types of learning system. Capitalist markets are one of these, and much of this book is devoted to analysing the disciplinary processes that go on in the daily factory of capitalist ethics.

Thus, instead of celebrating the epochal passage between disciplinary and control society as if this were some type of liberatory movement *tout court*, a more grounded understanding of the 'epochal' transformation should instead focus on the complementary extension through different social spheres of *both* disciplinary mechanisms and corresponding control systems, discipline and governmentality. Indeed, capitalism has always been a control society and therefore it has always been a disciplinary society; the point is *how* in different moments disciplinary and control functions are interrelated, what is their reach, their lines of fracture, their contradictions. The specific aspect of today's homeostasis of capital is its diffusion through the social field.

The 'control society' is thus an optical illusion. When disciplinary mechanisms extend to all aspects of life, when it appear there is no outside (Hardt and Negri 2000) to capital's disciplinary processes because discipline escapes the confinement of discrete institutions and involves all realms of social action, *then their identification requires a standpoint that creates the outside*. This is the standpoint of radically new ways of organising human co-production, the standpoint of other value practices predicated on common access to social wealth, the standpoint of the beginning of history.

SPATIAL SUBSTITUTABILITY AND 'CLASS COMPOSITION'

The basic thesis proposed in the previous section is that trade, in the age of globalisation, acquires a disciplinary character, in the sense that it is constitutive of capitalist social relations of production and articulates *both* waged and unwaged, production and reproduction work. *How* is modern trade able to discipline?

There are, I believe, three interrelated ways for trade to discipline: through its *ex post* impact; through its *ex ante* threat and from the process of continuous recomposition of the material basis of subjectivity, which results from the interaction between the two.

The *ex post* impact of trade is obvious. International competition destroys existing business, reduces the economic viability of existing ways to earn a living, it pushes people to adapt and learn new ways so that they, in turn, can survive and flourish by threatening other people's ways of earning a living in distant lands. The *ex post* impact is the hard reality of that continuous compulsion that Hayek identified in the competitive process (Chapter 14). The *ex post* impact of trade is nothing new, and goes back to the very origins of capitalist trade. To talk about the benefits of free trade in this respect is preposterous – yet this is exactly how the debate over free trade is structured. This is because although learning new ways is part of the process of human development, when the new ways are turned into means of competition among humans, the only *consistent* 'benefit' brought by trade applicable to *all* trade participants, both losers and winners, is an escalation of the competitive war.

The *ex ante* impact of trade, the anticipated threat to existing livelihood is also not new. What is new here is the interiorisation of such a threat as a part of *normal* life. Globalisation practices and discourses have enormously contributed to this normalisation of the *ex ante* threat, the acceptance, as a normal condition of life, that there is someone out there to get us. The *ex ante* threat does not need to correspond to an actually existing threat; yet it is no less real. The *ex ante* threat is the discourse of neoliberal globalisation, fuelled by policies of deregulation and trade liberalisation.[14]

By and large, the greater the degree of productive and commercial capital mobility, the greater these two types of threat will be felt, in that they shape conditions of work and life and arouse fears that our livelihoods are under continuous threat. Fear and insecurity become the constituting elements of daily working and searching-for-work practices. They are fuelled by disciplinary trade and by the consequent mantra that 'change for change's sake' is necessary. The future seems clear: there will be no stable families, no responsive communities, certainly no state safety net. There will only be individuals and the debt-enforced compulsion to plug their ever changing skills into the abstract mechanism of competitive markets. Here *fear* and insecurity become a constituent moment of the production of 'flexible' subjects alerted to 'market opportunities'.[15]

Finally, the working of the *ex ante* and *ex post* impacts of trade create continuously new socio-economic conditions, thus displacing, or at least aiming to displace, the inherent social conflict of capitalist production and reproduction.

The 'flying geese'

A way of capturing *how* in today's global factory social conflict is displaced through disciplinary trade is through a political reading of a model recently used to describe this continuous process of transnational redefinition of commodity chains: the 'flying geese development paradigm'. This paradigm, originally formulated in the 1930s by Japanese economist K. Akamatsu to describe change in industrial structure over time, has recently been used to describe patterns of regional integration in south Asia (UNCTAD 1996: 75–105). It defines trade as the most important vehicle for transferring goods and technology across countries/places following a dynamic process of 'shifting comparative advantage', and therefore as the instrument for promoting a continuous social and geographical reorganisation of production and of the division of labour within and across countries/places. Although this model does not reflect the rapid catching up of certain follower countries such as China (Peng 2000), its illustrative strength is still of great interest, as an example of a narrative embedding an alternative hidden narrative of social conflict.

The model divides countries within a region into two groups, followers and leaders (see Figure 5). Imports from a leader country (respectively, A, B, C, etc.) to follower countries allow new goods and technology into the latter. This allows production of the imported goods in the follower countries, which, eventually, will be able to export them to other countries. When eventually a country loses competitiveness in one particular product, its domestic production is phased out, workers are made redundant, and production is replaced by imports from the country that has succeeded in building up a competitive industry in that sector. One of the interesting insights of this model is that the flying geese pattern of FDI 'is governed by shifts in competitiveness', which TNCs themselves help to generate. FDI in fact (as well as trade) both shapes and is shaped by the evolution of comparative advantage between the follower countries and the lead country. Domestic investment withdraws from those sectors suffering loss of competitiveness (e.g. labour-intensive sectors such as textiles and footwear), and production is relocated where labour is cheaper in order to supply both foreign and home markets. However, aggregate investment does not diminish in the advanced economy because its industry is constantly being restructured and upgraded, and resources are reallocated to higher-skill, higher-technology products, where it now enjoys comparative advantage. In this model, therefore, there is no trade-off between aggregate domestic investment and FDI; global investment continuously increases, promoting trade flows (UNCTAD 1996: 76–7).

We can reformulate this flying geese pattern of trade and FDI in such a way as to bring to the forefront the embedded conflict of capitalist social relations of production and the hidden flesh-and-blood narrative of value struggles by rereading the narrative of the flying geese model in a way that takes into account real people and the general conditions in which they work and struggle. But before we can do this, we must briefly elaborate on a key analytical concept that gives historical and sociological texture to social conflict, that of 'class composition' (Bologna 1991), which, for the sake of the link between production and reproduction work, I shall refer to as 'community composition'.

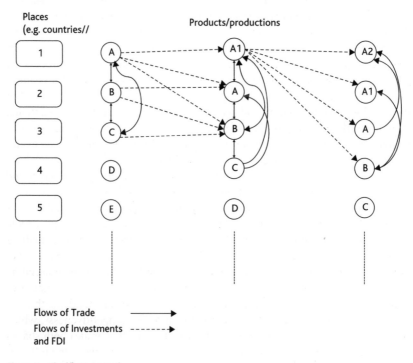

Figure 5 The 'flying geese'

The basic tenet behind this concept is that the forms, the objectives, the dynamics of social conflict are linked to the ways people relate to each other in the places of production and life within a certain historical context. For example, 1,000 workers disposed along an assembly line and confined within the walls of a single large factory relate to each other, have concrete aspirations and develop forms of organisation that are different from, say, ten workers behind computer screens in 100 factories spread over a large geographic area. Also, and certainly not less importantly, the ways these workers are part of communities, the rhythms, modalities and conflicts of reproduction work, the power relations within communities, and so forth, will have different forms depending on whether we are talking to a village living off the land, a shanty town next to sweatshops or an urban area of a service industry. One of the main targets of capital's strategies for dealing with the struggles of communities whether these struggles are around production work (at the factory, the office, etc.) or reproduction work (on the territory, for entitlements, etc.) is therefore to disrupt the composition that constituted the material basis upon which communities' struggles and their organisations were founded. These strategies, also commonly known by the term 'restructuring', lead to a historical transformation of the composition of communities, that is, a restructuring of what Italian historian Sergio Bologna has called the 'totality of socio-professional contents and its associated culture of work' (Bologna 1991: 22).

This restructuring does not eliminate conflict. It only creates the conditions for *new forms* of its reoccurrence. To each community composition corresponds a political composition, that is, 'the totality of autonomous and class conscious ways of behaving and their associated culture of working class insubordination' (ibid.). The material power and forms of organisation expressed by communities are historically specific to a particular material and political composition.

Thus, to return to the flying geese, when workers and communities in the leader countries/places succeed in imposing limits on the ability of their employers to offer low wages and appalling working conditions (through the often lengthy process of union organisation), or threaten the profitability that could be derived from a generally low cost of reproduction of labour, FDI shifts production or part of it to the follower countries. This has a twofold rationale. In the leader countries the community composition is changed, thus threatening the forms of organisation and entitlements that waged and unwaged producers were able to build on the basis of that composition. While cheaper imports from follower countries/places – together with restructuring of the class composition – allow the value of labour power in leader countries/places to be kept in check, the development of new branches of production made possible by a new configuration of labour processes starts afresh the process of accumulation with a relatively lower social unrest.

In follower countries/places, where the imported composition mixes with local cultural and socio-economic content, the community composition is relatively new; the coupling between production and reproduction work and the corresponding struggle still need to go through the lengthy work of organisation. A precondition for this shaping of production in follower countries/places is of course a previous wave of enclosures, whether this is enforced poverty on the countryside, reduction of various forms of entitlements such as food subsides, or any policy making poorly paid wage labour a desirable alternative, especially in the context of a widespread reserve army of labour.

This process of course has no inherent end. Both leader and follower countries/places will soon be hit by new waves of social unrest and struggles, whose novelty is not only in terms of their reoccurrence in time, but also in terms of the form of organisation and the nature of the aspirations of the new configuration of community composition. Also, this model not only implicitly recognises a vertical hierarchy among regions within an international division of labour, but turns this hierarchy into a driving force for capitalist accumulation. Finally, within this model, one cannot envisage an end to this structural hierarchy, only its continuous structural displacement. The socio-economic geography of the capitalist world is and always will be made up of the 'developed' and the 'underdeveloped'[16] and the dynamic principle of this development and underdevelopment is the attempt by capital to escape the class struggle.

In each group of countries the slow work of organisation of a previously fragmented workforce, and the slow work of circulation of struggle across communities within society, will reach a point at which they threaten the viability of capital's accumulation. Shifting production to a new tier of follower countries/places that offer a large pool of labour power and widespread poverty will then displace the struggles in those follower countries/places. Transferring relatively skilled labour production to lower tiers in the hierarchy and/or regulating/promoting inflows of migrants enjoying lower non-citizen rights, as well as upgrading production to new lines and processes, will displace the struggles in the leader countries/places by changing the composition of their communities.

This model reformulates at an international level the properties of regulation of class conflict that economic cycles have always had at the national level (Bell and Cleaver 2002). From the perspective of capital, the optimum management would be that of a trade region organised hierarchically, where booms and busts, composition and decomposition were synchronised in such a way as to allow a continuous aggregate flow of investment and thus accumulation, thus making local economic declines instrumental in a consistent overall growth and accumulation.

The experience of south Asia seems to confirm this pattern at a regional level. The emergence of the first-tier NICs (newly industrialised countries) (Hong Kong, the Republic of Korea, Singapore and Taiwan) was soon followed by that of a second tier (Indonesia, Malaysia and Thailand), under the impact of strong wage increases and the gaining of union rights in the first tier (especially South Korea). FDI from the first tier then moved to countries/ places in the second tier, in which wages were lower, to promote labour-intensive production – especially in Indonesia. Finally, the last ten years have seen the rise of China as a major player in the region, with both a huge reservoir of cheap labour power producing labour-intensive basic goods and skilled workers who earn relatively low wages by international standards but can still enjoy a relatively high standard of living. This, together with a strong police/military intervention in state planning promoting development of the infrastructure and corresponding enclosures in the countryside, and management of social conflict, has again shifted 'comparative advantages' and imposed a new competitive 'benchmark' for the region and beyond – until of course, as usual, the crisis hits China too: news report are now indicating that in several sectors, India might well constitute a new challenge.[17]

In conclusion, 'shifting comparative advantage' is the economists' term for the recognition of the centrality of what Marx called class struggle, its dynamic nature, and the strategies aimed at its continuous displacement within an ever changing international division of labour. As in the case of the role played by the economic cycle in a national economy in attempting to regulate social conflict, the flying geese model captures the management of social conflict through the process of economic development, through continuous shifting of technical and social compositions from leaders to followers, in such a way as to minimise workers' and communities' organisational impact. It must be observed that the disciplinary logic built into the shifting comparative advantage narrative can only work to the extent that the different points of conflict in the leader and follower countries/places are temporally displaced. If David Harvey's (1989: 284–5) 'time-space compression' were to work for organised labour and other movements within society, it would not be difficult to show in practice the Achilles heel of this strategy of capital.

The recognition of globalisation as the globalisation of capitalist social relations of production, and of trade as a disciplinary device for social relations of production, have two important implications. In the first place, we can read trade liberalisation strategies as strategies that attempt to impose capitalist work by displacing conflict. Indeed, by looking at the implications of global trade patterns it is very hard to envisage an era of the 'end of work' as suggested by some (Rifkin 1995). On the contrary, capitalist work – the doing that is tied to capital's valorisation process and its measure, is a form of social control and increasingly spans the social field. Thus, second, when looking for

alternatives we cannot simply point at the devastating effects of trade liberalisation in terms of distribution of wealth and social injustice brought by market
freedom in particular sectors and areas. The 'pluses' and 'minuses' of capitalist relations are inherently interlocked and are both moments of disciplinary
mechanisms. The key lesson for the definition of alternatives must therefore be
the redefinition of norms of co-production of livelihoods, norms that must be
redefined beyond competitive relations between people and communities
across the globe.

Part III

Context, Contest and Text: Discourses and their Clashing Practices

10
Marx and the enclosures we face

CAPITAL ENCLOSES

Capitalist disciplinary processes do not emerge spontaneously. They are made possible by active strategies of enclosure of commons that increase people's dependence on capitalist markets for the reproduction of their livelihoods. Indeed, capital encloses. The diverse movements comprising the current global justice and solidarity movement are increasingly acknowledging and fighting against this truism: by opposing the attempts to relocate communities to make space for dams; by resisting privatisation of public services and basic resources such as water; by creating new commons through occupations of land and the building of communities; by struggling against rent positions of intellectual property rights threatening the lives of millions of Aids patients; by simply downloading and sharing music and software beyond the cash limits imposed by the market; by resisting the cut in rights and entitlements won by previous generations of struggling subjects.

Despite the mounting evidence of real social struggles against the many forms of capital's enclosures, that capital encloses is not something that has been sufficiently theorised by critical social and economic theory.

The so-called 'tragedy of the commons'

On the side of mainstream research, the broad question of enclosures appears to be one of justification and modes of implementation. In the first case, we have what has been referred to as the 'tragedy of the commons.' The core of this argument, first proposed by Garret Hardin (1968), is that commons are property arrangements that provide an incentive for, and inevitably result in, environmental degradation and general resource depletion. This is because the commons are understood as resources to which there is 'free' and 'unmanaged' access. In this framework, no one has an obligation to take care of commons. In societies in which commons are prevalent, Hardin argues, people live by the principle: 'To each according to his needs' formulated by Marx in his *Critique of the Gotha Programme*. By *assuming* that commons are a free-for-all space from which competing and atomised 'economic men' take as much as they can, Hardin has engineered a justification for privatisation of the commons space rooted in an alleged natural necessity.[1] Hardin forgets that there are no commons without communities within which the modalities of access to common resources are negotiated. Incidentally, this implies that there is no enclosure of commons without *at the same time* the destruction and fragmentation of communities.[2]

In the second case, it is sufficient to mention the extensive literature on modes of privatisation and methods of implementation, and the alleged benefits that they would cause, not to mention the different fields in which enclosures of commons would emerge and be reinforced following trade liberalisation policies in new areas such as public services. In this immense literature, enclosures are the *basso continuo* of a neoliberal discourse within which we are fully immersed.

Enclosures and Marxist paralysis

On the critical side, there is of course plenty of literature opposing this or that privatisation, this or that strategy of trade liberalisation, identifying the effects of WTO-sponsored trade liberalisation policies, or the immense social cost of building a new dam and relocating millions, or the injustice involved in privatising water.[3] Yet, there are very few systematic works attempting to pull it all together, in the fashion of theoretical constructs, so as to help us to clarify the nature of the enclosing force we are facing.[4]

Apart from a few exceptions,[5] it is within Marxist literature that we find the most paradoxical deficiency in the attempt to theorise enclosures as an ongoing pillar of capitalist regimes. This is a literature that in principle should be very sensitive to issues of struggles and capitalist power, as well as alternatives to capital. There is one main fallacy in the way the traditional Marxist literature has dealt with the issue of enclosures.[6] It marginalises enclosures from theory by making them not just a question of genealogy, but a genealogy within a *linear* model of development. To simplify, the narrative goes something like this: *before* capital*ism* there are enclosures or 'primitive accumulation'. These processes of expropriation are preconditions of capitalism, because they *create* and develop markets for commodities such as labour power and land. Once the job is done, we can stop talking about enclosures (or primitive accumulation) and must instead talk about 'capital logic'. 'Primitive accumulation' and 'capital logic' are thus distinctly separated, and therefore become the subject matter of two distinct *Marxist disciplines*. Marxist historians debate issues of genealogy and the 'transition' to capitalism as being very much linked to the issue of primitive accumulation or enclosures. On the other hand, and at the same time, Marxist economists debate the intricate issues of 'capital's logic', such as questions of value, accumulation and crisis, as if the social practices in front of their noses have nothing to do with real and ongoing enclosures (since in their framework these have *already occurred* sometime in the past).

This framework is extremely problematic, both theoretically and politically. Theoretically, because as I shall argue in this chapter, enclosures are a continuous characteristic of 'capital logic', once we understand capital not as a totalised *system*,[7] *but*, as we discussed in Chapter 2, as a *social force* with totalising drives that exists together with other forces that act as a limit to it. This is so not only at the fringes of capital's reach, in the strategies of imperialism for the creation of new markets. Even if we conceptualise the domain of capital as not having a territorial outside, as *Empire*,[8] there is the theoretical and political need to recognise the central role of enclosures as part of the world we live in. In this world, enclosures are a value practice that clashes with others. It is either capital that makes the world *through commodification and enclosures*, or it is the rest of us – whoever is that 'us' – that makes the world through counter-enclosures and commons. The net results of the clashes among these social forces and their corresponding value practices Marx calls 'class struggle', while Polanyi theorises it in terms of 'double movement of society.'

The framework is problematic politically because the confinement of enclosures to a question of genealogy *within* a linear model of capitalist development paralyses Marxian-inspired contributions on the question of 'alternatives'. Paralysis is understood here as a state of powerlessness or incapacity to act. Indeed, in the linear model of historical development inherited and practised by classical Marxism, the alternative to capital*ism* can only be another 'ism'. The ongoing struggles for commons within the current global justice and solidarity movement are thus not appreciated for what they are: budding alternatives to capital. Marxian-inspired thinking cannot join the intellectual and political endeavours to shape alternatives in the here and now because its framework is *for* another 'ism' projected into an unqualified future, and generally defined by a model of power that needs a political elite to tell the rest of us why power cannot be exercised from the ground up, starting from the now.[9] Thus, while current movements around the world are practising, producing and fighting for a variety of different commons – thus posing the strategic question of their political articulation – traditional Marxist theoreticians cannot conceptualise these movements in terms of categories familiar to them. They thus endeavour to *reduce* these movements to those familiar categories, and when they do that, their contribution to the rich debate on alternatives is poor indeed, of the type: 'one solution, revolution'.

Enclosures are also marginalised in non-traditional critical (Marxist and postmodern) discourses. Indeed, as we have mentioned in Chapter 9, the Deleuze–Negri theme that regards contemporary forms of command as post-disciplinary, loses sight of strategies of enclosures upon the global social body, in a period in which neoliberal policies are instead intensifying them, by means of war and structural adjustment.

In this chapter I propose an alternative reading of Marx's analysis of 'primitive accumulation', one that shows the continuing relevance of 'enclosure' as a constituent element of capitalist relations and accumulation. From this perspective, enclosures are characteristics of capital's strategies at *whatever* level of capitalist development. In the next chapter I briefly propose an analytical framework as a way of illustration of the wide range of current new enclosures and discuss the meaning of enclosures as a front line in the struggles among value practices.

MARX AND THE CONTINUOUS CHARACTER OF ENCLOSURES

So-called primitive accumulation

According to Marxist traditional interpretation, Marx's concept of so-called primitive accumulation[10] indicates the historical process that gave birth to the preconditions of a capitalist mode of production. These preconditions refer mainly to the creation of a section of the population with no other means of livelihood than their labour power-to, to be sold in a nascent labour market, and to the accumulation of capital that may be used for nascent industries. In this conception, the adjective 'primitive' corresponds to a clear-cut temporal dimension that separates the past understood as feudal*ism* from the future understood as capital*ism*. However, by focusing on a definition of capital as social relation rather than as stock as in Smith,[11] Marx's definition of primitive accumulation leads to another possible interpretation. For primitive accumulation to be a precondition of accumulation it must be a precondition to *the exercise of capital's power*. The latter is nothing else than human production carried on through the relation of separation that characterises capital's production. With his discourse on 'primitive accumulation' Marx is thus able to point out the presupposition of this capital-*relation*: 'The capital-relation presupposes a complete separation between the workers and the ownership of the conditions for the realisation of their labour.'[12]

From this it follows that

the process ... which creates the capital-relation can be nothing other than the process which divorces the worker from the ownership of the conditions of his own labour; it is a process which operates two transformations, whereby the social means of subsistence and production are turned into capital, and the immediate producers are turned into wage-labourers.[13]

Thus, the 'so-called primitive accumulation ... is nothing else than the historical process of divorcing the producer from the means of production'.[14]

A careful examination of Marx's definition of primitive accumulation allows us to argue that although enclosures, or primitive accumulation, define a question of genealogy, for capital the problem of genealogy presents itself *continuously*.

Separation

There are three central points that I believe are central to this understanding of primitive accumulation and that at the same time are consistent with Marx's theory and political understanding of capitalist accumulation. Let us consider the first two first:

1. The separation of producers and means of production that Marx is talking about is a common characteristic of *both* accumulation and primitive accumulation. The difference between the two – important nevertheless – is however a question of degree.[15]
2. This *separation* is a central category (if not *the* central category) of Marx's critique of political economy.

What does 'separation' mean? In the context of accumulation, separation of producers and means of production means essentially that the 'objective conditions of living labour appear as *separated, independent* values opposite living labour capacity as subjective being, which therefore appears to them only as a value of *another kind*'.[16] Through enclosures in other words, objects rule subjects, deeds command the doing,[17] and the doing of human activity is channelled into forms that are compatible with the priority of capital's accumulation. This separation is clear in the fetishised categories of mainstream economics. To call 'labour' a factor of production, is to call human activity, the *life process*, a means, and the objects produced, the end. We are in full sight of what we called 'value struggles'.

At the social level, this separation means the positing of living labour and conditions of production as *independent values* standing in opposition to each other.[18] This *separation* therefore is a fundamental condition for Marx's theory of reification, of the transformation of subject into object. It is through this *separation* that 'the objective conditions of labour attain a subjective existence *vis-à-vis* living labour capacity'[19] and living labour, the 'subjective being' par excellence, is turned into a thing among things, 'it is merely a *value* of a particular use value *alongside* the conditions of its own realisation as *values* of another use value'.[20]

The idea of *separation* therefore strictly echoes Marx's analysis of alienated labour, as labour alienated from the object of production, the means of production, the product, and other producers.[21] The opposition implicit in this definition is of course a clashing opposition expressing a 'specific relationship of production, a specific social relationship in which the owners of the conditions of production treat living labour-power as a *thing*'.[22] These same owners are regarded only as 'capital personified', in which capital is understood as having 'one sole driving force, the drive to valorize itself, to create surplus-value, to make its constant part, the means of production, absorb the greatest possible amount of surplus labour'.[23]

The concept of *separation* enables us to clarify Marx's reference to capital not as a thing (as in Adam Smith), but as a social relation and consequently, of capital accumulation as accumulation of social relations:

> The capitalist process of production ... seen as a total, connected process, i.e. a process of reproduction, produces not only commodities, not only surplus-value, but it also produces and reproduces the capital-relation itself; on the one hand the capitalist, on the other the wage-labourer.[24]

3. The difference between accumulation and primitive accumulation, not being a substantive one, is a difference in the conditions and forms in which this *separation* is implemented. Marx refers to this as '*ex novo*' separation between producers and means of production requiring extra-economic force to be carried out.

Having defined the common character of both accumulation *and* primitive accumulation, we must turn to what constitutes their distinctiveness. This is located in the genealogical character of 'primitive' accumulation. As opposed to accumulation proper, what 'may be called primitive accumulation ... is the historical basis, instead of the historical result, of specifically capitalist production'.[25] While sharing the same principle – separation – the two concepts point at two different *conditions* of existence. The latter implies the *ex novo production* of the *separation*, while the latter implies the *reproduction* on a greater scale of the same *separation*.[26]

The key difference thus resides for Marx not so much in the timing of the occurrence of this separation – although a sequential element is naturally always present – rather in the *conditions, circumstances and context* in which this separation is enforced. In the *Grundrisse* for example, Marx stresses the distinction between the conditions of capital's arising (becoming), and the conditions of capital's existence (being). The former 'disappear as real capital arises', while the latter do not appear as 'conditions of its arising, but as results of its presence'.[27] Marx is emphasising here a simple but crucial point: 'Once developed historically, capital itself creates the conditions of its existence (not as conditions for its arising, but as results of its being)',[28] and therefore it drives to reproduce (at increasing scale) the separation between means of production and producers. However, the *ex novo* production of the separation implies social forces that are posited outside the realm of impersonal 'pure' economic laws. The *ex novo* separation of means of production and producers corresponds to the *ex novo* creation of the *opposition* between the two, to the *ex novo* foundation of the specific alien character acquired by social labour in capitalism.

This is the element of novelty, of 'originality' that Marx seems to indicate when he stresses that while accumulation relies *primarily* on 'the silent compulsion of economic relations [which] sets the seal on the domination of the capitalist over the worker', in the case of primitive accumulation the separation is imposed *primarily* through '[d]irect extra-economic force',[29] such as the state[30] or particular sections of the social classes.[31] In other words, primitive accumulation for Marx is a social process in which separation appears as a crystal-clear relation of expropriation, a relation that has not yet taken the fetishistic character assumed by capital's normalisation, or the 'ordinary run of things'. Or, borrowing from Foucault, it is separation that has not been normalised ... yet; or it is that normalisation of separation that has not been challenged ... yet.

When does *ex novo separation* occur? If you believe in capital*ism* as the whole comprehensive condition of our existence, the answer is very simple: it occurs *before* capital*ism*. However, as we have discussed in Chapter 2, the fact is that people do not live in capital*ism*. People live in life worlds, often overlapping. For example: the factory, the school, the neighbourhood, the family, cyberspace – that is, the realm of significant relations to objects and to other people. What capital (not capital*ism)* does is that it attempts to create life worlds in its own image (like the factory) or to colonise existing ones, to put them to work for its priorities and drives. And it has done this since the beginning of time to different degrees, and at any given historical time different life worlds result in different degrees of colonisation. Capital will not stop in its attempt to colonise until either some *other* social force will make it stop – socialised humanity, for example – or until it has colonised all life. So, paradoxically, the true realisation of capital*ism* coincides with the end of life (and therefore of any alternative to capitalism!).

The *ex novo* character of separation that characterises enclosures is that they are the entry points into new spheres of life. *Ex novo* separation occurs in two cases. The first is when capital identifies new spheres of life to potentially colonise with its priorities. The list here is endless, from land enclosures, to the enclosures of water resources through privatisation, to enclosures of knowledge through enforcement of intellectual property rights. The second case is when other social forces acting in opposition to capital are able to identify and to struggle to reclaim social spaces that have previously been normalised to capital's commodity production and turn them into spaces of commons.

In both cases, capital has to devise *strategies* of enclosures, either by promoting new areas of commodification vis-à-vis resistance, or by preserving old areas of commodification vis-à-vis *ex novo* attacks that it faces by 'commoners'. In both cases, capital needs a discourse of enclosures and consequent discursive practices that extend and/or preserve commodity production.[32] Therefore, around the issue of enclosures and their opposite – commons – we have a foundational entry point of a radical discourse on alternatives.

CONTINUITY, SOCIAL CONFLICT AND ALTERNATIVES

The above three points lead to a new understanding of the timing of primitive accumulation that allows us to appreciate its continuous character. The interpretation of Marx's analysis of primitive accumulation presented thus far has revealed two basic interconnected points: first, primitive accumulation is the *ex novo* production of the separation between producers and the means of production. Second, this implies that enclosures define a strategic terrain among social forces with conflicting value practices. The actual playing out of these strategies in given forms depends of course on the historical, geographical, cultural and social context.

The reduction of the category of primitive accumulation to a historical (rather than a political–theoretical) category is a confusion certainly due to the fact that primitive accumulation also occurs *before* the capitalist mode of production is established as the dominant mode of organising social reproduction. But the political–theoretical understanding of the concept emphasises that if a temporal dimension exists, it is in the sense that enclosures are the *basis*, the presupposition, and the basic precondition that is necessary *if* accumulation of capital must occur. It must be noted that this last definition is Marx's own and it is more general than the one adopted by the classical 'historical interpretation', and therefore it includes the latter. This is because if primitive accumulation is defined in terms of the preconditions it satisfies for the accumulation of capital, its temporal dimension includes in principle both the period of the establishment of a capitalist mode of production *and* the preservation and expansion of the capitalist mode of production *any time the co-producers set themselves up as obstacles to the reproduction of their separation from the means of production*, separation understood in the terms described before.

In other words, capital's overcoming of barriers must not be seen as *the* necessary result of its dynamic, but as both a conditioned result and a necessary *aspiration* embedded in its drives and motivation as well as in its survival instinct vis-à-vis emerging alternatives to capital. History is open, for both capital and the rest of us who are struggling for a different life on the planet.[33]

Within Marx's theoretical and critical framework therefore, the divorcing embedded in the definition of primitive accumulation can be understood not only as the origin of capital vis-à-vis pre-capitalist social relations, but also as a reassertion of capital's priorities vis-à-vis those social forces that run against this *separation*. Thus, pre-capitalist spaces of autonomy (the common land of the English yeomen; the economies of African populations targeted by the slave merchants) are not the only objects of primitive accumulation strategies. Objects of enclosure strategies also become any given balance of power among classes that constitutes 'rigidity' towards furthering the capitalist process of accumulation, or that runs in the opposite direction. If we conceive social contestation as a continuous element of capitalist relations of production, capital must continuously engage in strategies of primitive accumulation to recreate the 'basis' of accumulation itself.

This element of continuity of primitive accumulation is not only consistent with Marx's empirical analysis describing the process of primitive accumulation, but seems also to be contained in his theoretical framework. This is because accumulation is equal to primitive accumulation 'to a higher degree', and 'once capital exists, the capitalist mode of production itself evolves in such a way that it maintains and reproduces this *separation* on a constantly increasing scale *until the historical reversal takes place*'.[34] Thus, just as the 'historical reversal' is set as a *limit* to accumulation, so strategies of enclosures are set as a challenge – from capital's perspective – to that 'historical reversal'. To the extent that social conflict creates bottlenecks in the accumulation process in the sense of reducing the distance between producers and the means of production, any strategy used to reverse this movement of association is entitled to be categorised – consistently with Marx's theory and definition – as 'primitive accumulation'.

Marx's text is quite enlightening on this. The key difference between what he calls 'the ordinary run of things'[35] – that is the normalised silent compulsion of economic relations – and 'primitive accumulation' seems to be the existence of 'a working class which by education, tradition and habit looks upon the requirements of that mode of production as self-evident natural laws'.[36] Therefore, insofar as the working class accepts capital's requirement as natural laws, accumulation does not need primitive accumulation. However, working-class struggles represent precisely a rupture in that acceptance, a nonconformity to the laws of supply and demand, a refusal of subordination to the 'ordinary run of things', the positing of 'an outside' to capital's norm, an 'otherness' to the already codified. This also implies a rupture in the economic discourse, understood as discursive practice that constructs capitalist economic action and acts as a factor for the (re)-establishment and maintenance of the normalised rationality embedded in the 'ordinary run of things', or the 'natural laws of capitalist production'.[37] It is against this concrete and discursive challenge of the normality of capital that 'extra-economic means' are deployed:

Every combination between employed and unemployed disturbs the 'pure' action of this law. But on the other hand, as soon as ... adverse circumstances prevent the creation of an industrial reserve army, and with it the absolute dependence of the working class upon the capitalist class, capital, along with its platitudinous Sancho Panza, rebels against the 'sacred' law of supply and demand, and tries to make up for its inadequacies by forcible means.[38]

It follows therefore that not only is 'primitive accumulation, ... the historical basis, instead of the historical result, of specifically capitalist production',[39] but it also acquires a continuous character dependent on the inherent continuity of social conflict within capitalist production.

11
Enclosures with no limits

As we have seen, the emphasis on the 'divorcing' of people from the means of production opens the way for understanding 'primitive accumulation' as part of the continuous process of capitalist accumulation, rather than as something that took place at one point in time in the past. It is a continuous process that is rooted in capital's drive to continuous expansion – accumulation proper – as played out by M-C-M′ value practices. Both accumulation and 'primitive' accumulation pose capital as a social force that must overcome a limit. But while for accumulation the limit is merely a quantitative limit, for primitive accumulation or enclosure in a broad sense, the limit that capital must overcome is qualitative. With enclosure a new social *space* for accumulation is created, and this creation begins with the *identification of a concrete limit* and the deployment of strategies for its overcoming. The force identifying this limit may either be capital – in its attempt to colonise new spheres of life – or other social forces set in opposition to it. In either case, enclosure emerges as a strategic problem *for* capital any time capital sets itself to overcome a limit, whether this limit is identified by capital itself or by those life-reclaiming forces that attempt to de-commodify spheres of life to create commons. If capital must identify a limit in order to overcome it, our critique must identify capital's processes of identification in order to expose them and devise strategies to limit capital's overcoming of limits, and establish political practices and alternative projects in the space thus opened up.

There are two main types of *limit* that capital identifies in its drive to overcome them. One we may call, *limit as frontier*; the other, *limit as political recomposition.*

1. *Limit as frontier.* The frontier presents itself as the border dividing the colonised from the colonisable. Capital's identification of a frontier implies the identification of a space of social life that is still relatively uncolonised by capitalist relations of production and modes of doing. From this perspective, it is indifferent whether this space is clearly posed 'outside'

142

existing capital's domains – as in the definition of a potential colony in the discursive practice of imperial*ism*, or within its interstices – inside 'empire', as Hardt and Negri put it.[1] In either case, it is capital that identifies a frontier and the identification of this frontier implies the creation of a space of enclosure, a horizon within which policies and practices promote further separation between people and means of production in new spheres of life. In this case, the initiative of the identification of the limit and of the setting-out of concrete strategies of enclosure comes from capital. The *strategic* character of this identification is clearly due to the fact that the identification of a space of enclosure implies the attempt to overcome necessary resistance by what capital regards as 'enclosable' subjects. All classical examples of enclosures, such as land enclosures, as well as those enclosing entitlements won through past battles, fall into this category. Other more insidious practices also fall into this category: for example enclosures of cultural commons or hegemonic redefinition of discourse. The successful deployment of strategies of enclosure result here in a process of *deepening* of capital's relations of production across the social body.

2. *Limit as political recomposition.* Here the limit is identified *for* capital by a social force that poses its activity and value practices in opposition to it. Any time movements force a constraint on the capitalist process of production by raising a social barrier to the endless drive to commodify and accumulate, by opening up a space of entitlement and commons disconnected from market logic, capital is faced with the need and strategic problem of dismantling this barrier (or co-opting it). In this case the limit emerges as a political problem for capital. This is what Polanyi refers to as the 'dual movement' of modern liberal society, although Polanyi sees this movement mainly through its institutionalisation.

In the first case, therefore, the limit that capital must overcome is defined by capital itself. In the second case, it is defined *for* capital by a social force that opposes it. In the context of today's dynamics, the many types of 'new enclosure'[2] are defined through both these two processes of identification. In either case, we cannot think of alternatives to capital without posing the question of counter-enclosures, of spaces of commons. The *alternatives* to capital pose a *limit* to accumulation by setting up rigidities and liberating spaces. In a word, alternatives, whatever they are, act as 'counter-enclosure' force. This of course opens up the question of capital's co-optation of alternatives, which we address in Chapter 7, on the question of 'governmentality'.

TYPES OF ENCLOSURE

Enclosures emerge out of processes of commodification, but also as a reaction to struggles of anti-commodification and reclaiming of commons, by strategies that go under the name, for example, of 'privatisation', or class strategies that shift enclosures back through practices that produce commons and communities. In the first case they range from attacks on conditions of life by a World Bank-funded dam in India, threatening hundred of thousands of farming communities, to cuts in social spending for servicing international debt in a country of the South, or cuts in social expenditure in the United Kingdom, threatening hundred of thousands of metropolitan families. In the second case, as at St George's Hill[3] during the English civil war, or currently in Brazil in the waves of land occupations,[4] or in the de facto mass illegal bypassing of intellectual property rights in music and software production and the establishment of 'creative commons', it is possible to identify enclosure as an external limit, posed by capital, to the *production of commons*. It is this barrier that political and social movements need to overcome through the production of commons, and often this production is the result of practices of civil disobedience and direct action, rather than traditional party politics. Also, it is clear that these productions of commons, in the context in which capital aims at pervading the entire social field, are *at the same time* struggles against enclosure. The awareness and de facto identification of enclosures thus arises either because the production of commons problematises existing established property rights (as with past and stratified enclosures), or because the struggles to defend commons established in the past problematise the threat of new enclosures attempted by states. In other words, the extent to which we are aware of enclosures is the extent to which they confront us. In all other social interactions still rooted in commons of different types (take for example language), in other words commons that are not immediately threatened by enclosure, we live our lives undisturbed. Here we are only preoccupied by the question of *how* we relate within these commons (say, how do we speak to each other), and not whether the 'what' that constitutes the material basis of this 'how' is a common or not. We take that for granted.

As we have seen, there is a vast critical literature on processes of privatisation, marketisation, cuts in entitlement in both North and South, the effects of structural adjustment policies, biopiracy, intellectual property rights, resource privatisation, and so on. However, not much effort has gone into pulling these and other types of enclosure together into a coherent whole rooted in a critique of capital. This broad picture derives from the understanding of the role of enclosure from a capitalist systemic point of view, that is from the role played by enclosure as the birthplace of M-C-M' and in its continued reproduction. From this perspective, all these different types and consequent strategies of enclosure share a common character: *to forcibly separate people from whatever access to social wealth they have which is not mediated by competitive markets and money as capital.* Such an access empowers people to the extent that it give them a degree of autonomy and independence from the corporate sharks of the world economy and from competitive market relations.

New enclosures thus are directed towards the fragmentation and destruction of 'commons', that is, social spheres of life the main characteristics of which are to provide various degrees of protection from the market.

On the other hand, a typology of new commons is starting to be debated. Various advocates are proposing different kinds of commons as solutions to a variety of problems and issues arising from the world economy. These include, for example, civic commons,[5] environmental commons, natural resources commons (such as water), common heritage resources, and so on.[6] Often, the identification of these types of commons is made possible by the acknowledgment of struggles against their enclosure, so that these struggles have begun to be seen in their positive and propositional content, as struggles for *new commons*.[7] For example, natural commons are set in opposition to the privatisation of water. Life and knowledge commons are set in opposition to patenting the genetic structure, expropriating indigenous knowledge of plant variety, and bioprospecting. Finally, public services as commons are set against privatisation and GATS.

Although the contraposition between enclosures and commons emerges from the current literature, I do not think the radicalism of its implications is sufficiently theorised. This is for two reasons. First, because the enclosing force is generally discursively identified merely in terms of *policies* (e.g. neoliberal policies), rather than seeing these policies as particular historical forms of capital's inherent drive. In saying this I am not dismissing the importance of recognising the peculiar aspects of neoliberalism; on the contrary. Those Marxists who in the many public forums of social movements and civil society (such as the World Social Forum or the European Social Forum) remind us that the problem is not neoliberalism but 'capitalism' often make a doctrinaire connection, not a political–strategic one. Because the term 'neoliberalism' identifies a capitalist's strategy in a particular historical moment, an effective and intelligent discourse on alternatives to capital must be able to *articulate* the historically contingent with the immanent drive of capital, which is common to various historical periods. While the Marxist 'doctrinaires' fail to make this articulation, by dismissing the historical forms of strategies in preference to 'contents', many other approaches within the movement emphasise historical forms with no articulation to 'content', to capital's drive. Thus, second, in this latter approach commons are often seen as alternative 'policies', and not as social practices that are *alternatives* to capital (in the first place by posing a limit to it, *that at the same time* opens a space for alternatives and their problematisation). For it is here that lies the risk of capital's co-optation of commons, for example as a space of social relations that promotes creativity and innovation but is then articulated, through the market, against *other* commons and in opposition to them.

Third, as modes of accessing social resources that are not mediated by the market, currently emerging discourses on commons can be the entry point for

Table 1 A taxonomy of new types and modes of enclosure

Types	Modes
Land and resources	Land policies: through direct expropriation (e.g. Mexico's *ejido*) or indirect means (e.g. use of cash-tax)
	Externality: land pollution (e.g. Ogoni land in Nigeria; intensed shrimp production in India)
	Against reappropriation (e.g. against MST in Brazil)
	Water privatisation (e.g. Bolivia)
	Neoliberal war
Urban spaces	Urban design
	Road building
Social commons	Cuts in social spending
	Cuts in entitlements
Knowledge and life	Intellectual property rights
	Marketisation of education

broader discourses that help redefine the priorities of social reproduction. But in order to do so, these political discourses must be open to the possibility of opposing *all* types of enclosure, both old and new, both those stratified and normalised to different degrees by economic discourse as well as those recently emerging. This requires a process of identification of capital's enclosure through political recomposition, as discussed above.

In any case, by way of illustration, let us confine our attention to new types of enclosure. In the first column of Table 1 I offer a non-exhaustive list of types of enclosure that I will discuss in the next section.

Modes of enclosing

How does this *ex novo* separation occur? I think there are two general *modes* of implementation of enclosure: enclosure as a conscious output of 'power-over'; and enclosure as a by-product of the accumulation process. In the first case, we are talking about conscious strategies that go under many names (privatisation, export promotion, budget austerity, and so on). The English enclosure by act of parliament that became common in the eighteenth century is the archetypal mode of this type of enclosure. In the second case, enclosure is the unattended by-product of accumulation. In the language of mainstream economists this kind of enclosure may go under the name of 'negative externalities', that is costs that are not included in the market price of a good, because the costs are incurred by social agents who are external to the producing firm. Pollution is an example of an externality cost to the extent that producers are not the ones who suffer from pollution damage. Others have referred to this as 'the power of splitting' that accompanies processes of accumulation due to the fact that

Industrialization is not an independent force ... but the hammer with which nature is smashed for the sake of capital. Industrial logging destroys forests;

industrial fishing destroys fisheries; industrial chemistry makes Frankenfood; industrial use of fossil fuels creates the greenhouse effect, and so forth – all for the sake of value-expansion.[8]

In terms of this analysis, it is not only the question of resource depletion and pollution, but of the role that resource depletion and pollution and other so-called 'externalities' have in promoting the bankruptcy of independent producers, from indigenous people to farmers: resource depletion seen here as a means of enclosure. Another example is the effect of natural disasters (natural to the extent that they are the product of natural homeostatic processes, but human-made to the extent that these processes have been triggered by global warming) such as the Asian Tsunami or hurricane Katrina, that have been used to dispossess fishing communities to make space for hotels along the south Asian coasts, or to dispossess poor households in New Orleans to make space for privatised developments. Also 'negative externalities' have an archetype model in the English enclosure of land of the seventeenth and eighteenth centuries, when the landed aristocracy took their horses and dogs across fields while hunting foxes, ruining small farmers' crops.[9] These agents of 'negative externalities' and destroyers of small farmers' livelihoods were the ancestors of those that in Britain today claim to defend the 'traditional way of life' in the countryside in the face of a parliamentary bill against fox hunting.

There are of course many concrete instances and ways in which these two modes are implemented. The second column in Table 1 provides a synoptic list of some of them.

Land can be (and has been) expropriated in various ways, by direct means, as in the classic case of the English and colonial enclosures, or by indirect means. In the latter case for example, in many countries of the South, where populations are largely dependent on farming, leveraging a tax in cash may become an instrument of expropriation, by forcing mostly self-sufficient farmers into allocating part of their land to produce a so-called 'cash crop', a good produced for the sole aim of acquiring cash instead of products that would serve for people's subsistence. The same result is achieved by many of the large development projects, such as the construction of dams (as in Malaysia, India, China), or by other means of promoting cash crops. Another form of new land enclosure is that which results from environmental damages caused by multinationals.[10] Another example is the intense shrimp production occurring in some Indian and other east Asian regions. Shrimps are produced for the world market with intensive industrial methods, i.e., aquaculture. This involves large pools of salted waters in the vicinity of coastal regions. In time, the salted water penetrates the soil thus polluting the water supplies and making the land of local farmers unusable for subsistence crops. Also in this case of modern enclosures, the result is pressure to abandon the land.

Just as the old enclosures were accompanied by struggles, so in the case of new enclosures people organise themselves and build forms of resistance.

Two important examples are the Zapatistas' struggle in Mexico, catalysed by the attempt by the government to sell the common land traditionally held by the indigenous population (*ejido*),[11] and the movement for reappropriation of land in Brazil by the 'Sem tierra' movement (MST).[12] War and, in particular, the recent forms of 'neoliberal' war have also been discussed in terms of their effects as land or other types of enclosure.[13]

In order to show the pervasiveness of the new enclosures, I mention here some cases of urban enclosure. Urban design in fact is a site of important attempts to enclose human and social behaviour in forms and patterns compatible with the accumulation process and the profit motive. For example, the lack of public benches in public sites such as the large main hall of Waterloo station in London can be puzzling, unless we understand it as an attempt to minimise vagrant behaviour (which takes us back to the rationale for the Tudors' 'bloody legislation' following the early enclosures), its marginalisation to an 'invisible site', or simply as an attempt to turn tired passengers into consumers by forcing them into nearby cafes. Even the satisfaction of primary human biological functions has become the object of enclosure in train stations and other public spaces in the West. In order to have a leak we have to pay for the privilege; 20p a time is the ongoing rate in London – pretty much the daily wage of a fibre-optic ditch digger south of Mumbai, I was told. (The alternative, of course, is to reclaim MacDonald's and other fast food outlets as public toilets.) Also public benches 'enclosed' by arms as in London or with a convex surface as in Los Angeles, as pointed out by Mike Davis,[14] find a rationale as instruments of social engineering, preventing our modern 'vagrants' (especially the homeless) from stretching their legs and reinforcing 'correct' and 'acceptable' social behaviour, even while sitting and resting. Enclosing the space of benches keeps the city moving.

By 'social commons', I mean those commons that have been created as a result of past social movements and later formalised by institutional practices. A classic example is the body of rights, provisions and entitlements universally guaranteed by the welfare state in spheres such as health, unemployment benefits, education and pensions. Although these social commons served at the same time as a site for the administrative regulation of social behaviour,[15] they also to a certain extent allowed access to public wealth without a corresponding expenditure of work (that is, *direct* access). This characteristic has been under increasing attack by the neoliberal policies of the last quarter of a century. In the North, enclosure of these social commons has passed through the transformation from welfare to workfare (as in the United States and Britain), through the imposition of strict 'convergence criteria' which limit social spending in the European Union, among other cases, through massive programmes of privatisation and structural adjustment linked to the neoliberal policies of the Washington consensus, both North and South, to third world debt management, and to trade liberalisation of goods and, especially, services. On all these issues there is of course a massive literature.[16]

The enclosure of knowledge commons includes the attempt to direct and shape the creation of knowledge in terms of access, content and modes of delivery. Here of course there is a vast array of policies defining privatisation of education, the selling of public libraries and schools, the link between scarcity of public resources channelled into education and debt servicing in the South and more generally the strategies for the subordination of education and knowledge to the perpetration of competitive markets.[17]

In most cultures in the history of humanity, knowledge has been accumulated and passed on to further generations as a matter of human social interaction. Just as language, agricultural and farming methods and skills of any kind are the cultural basis of any society, without which it would not survive, so genes are the building blocks of life itself. Yet there are increasing pressures by large multinational corporations to introduce legislation that 'encloses' the 'knowledge' built into life: genes. Intellectual property rights to life itself have contributed to starting a debate about the question of enclosure of knowledge and life in general. This has also led to a debate about the meaning of investment and research. For example, despite the drug companies claiming that patenting is necessary for guaranteeing that investment in the sector is maintained, thus allowing further research, many researchers argue that patenting by promoting secrecy and channelling funds into what is commercially profitable rather than for the public good will threaten future research. Patenting of life legitimises biopiracy and the appropriation and subsequent privatisation of knowledge built up collectively by generations of anonymous experimenters, especially at the expense of the people of the South. It would provide industry with a new means of establishing control over areas of nature previously held in common by communities in the South. What these enclosures of life are showing is the completely arbitrary character of *private* property claims over what are essentially *social and historical* processes of knowledge creation. What these debates are revealing is the urgency for Marxist thinking of reconceptualising enclosures and contributing to the emerging political discourse on life and knowledge as a commons.

12

The 'law of value', immaterial labour, and the 'centre' of power

GLOBAL MARKETS AND VALUE PRACTICES

In the last two chapters we have understood the processes of capitalist market creation in terms of 'enclosures', strategies of separation between people and means of production that turns people and their powers, as well as fragments of nature, into commodities.

Enclosures only create a *context* for market social interaction to occur. If enclosures push people into increasing the degree of their dependence on markets for the reproduction of their livelihoods, then the markets integrate their activities into a system that pits all against all. In this and in the next chapter, I discuss the general features of this 'integration' that constitutes the social body (now a planetary one) as a war of all against all, an inter-locking of processes of exploitation, alienation, valorisation of capital and self-valorisation of communities in struggles and, finally, subjectification rooted in clashes among value practices. These general features go under the name of 'law of value', a term evoking a century-old debate among scholars of classical political economics as well as among radicals of many persuasions.

I will not be able to survey extensively the terms of this debate, its low and high points, the paradigmatically different discourses that have framed the meaning given to the 'law of value' in often contrasting and tragically oppos-ing ways, from the critique of the law of capitalist imposition of work on the social body (which I, among others, embrace), to the framework within which to theorise the imposition of state capitalist (i.e., 'real socialist') work (which I, among others, strongly oppose). Instead, in this and the next chapter I want to discuss the *process-like* features of this 'law of value' and highlight the fact that understanding it from the perspective of an anti-capitalist movement is, crucially, understanding what it is up against. In a word, the problematic of overcoming capitalism, of the 'beginning of history', is ultimately the problematic of overcoming that 'law of value' that wants to reduce everything to capital's measure and, at the same time, of positing other values, other measures and other ways of articulating them.

Capitalist globalisation: a form of interdependence that sucks

Before going into the details of our analysis, it is worth pointing out how this 'law of value' appears to us in this 'globalised' world, at the phenomenal level of discourses on the global dimension of our living. The increasing intensification of planetary interdependency brought about by global capitalist markets implies that any 'node' of social production, at whatever scale – whether an individual on the labour market, a company in a particular industry, a city or country in competition to attract capital and investments vis-à-vis other cities and countries – faces an external force that pushes it to adapt to certain standards of doing things, to adopt certain forms of social cooperation, in order to beat the competitor, or else to have its means of livelihood threatened. But 'beating the competitor' at the same time threatens the livelihoods of other communities we are competing with, to the extent that they also depend on markets to reproduce their own livelihoods. The more we depend on money and markets to satisfy our needs and follow our desires, the more we are exposed to a vicious circle of dependency that pits livelihoods against each other. Some of us win, and some of us lose; in either case we are involved in perpetrating the system that keeps us reproducing scarcity when in fact we could be celebrating abundance.

In looking at the 'law of value', we shall have in mind these current capitalist markets with the view of problematising the types of social relation they entail, rather than focusing only on the types of outcome they produce. When doing this, we must obviously not underplay the many 'horrors' that contemporary processes of neoliberal global integration are producing, and that are discussed by many critics and participants in the alter-globalisation movement. From the perspective of an analysis of social processes and social relations, what I am suggesting is that the key problem of capitalist markets is not so much the creation of 'losers', but *a mode of articulation of productive 'nodes' across the social body that constantly creates 'winners' and 'losers'*. Indeed, the very social constitution of capitalist markets is one of the continuous dispensations of 'rewards' and 'punishments', that is a mode of 'disciplinary integration'. This 'mode of articulation', understood in its process-like dynamism and inherent conflict among value practices, is what in general I refer to as the 'law of value'.

Importantly, if we do not ground our critique of mainstream discourse on the problematisation of this 'law of value', then we will not be able to gain discursive, practical and political *autonomy* from the interests and value practices of capital. Even more worryingly, lacking this autonomy, oppositional movements will be locked, together with those they oppose, into a certain discourse in which they play different but interrelated parts. So, for example, whether we are ideologically for or against capitalist markets, we have no difficulty, in this mode, in selecting the outcomes that weave a narrative to support our claim: those who are critics of capitalist markets tell stories of restructuring, low wages, poverty, environmental degradation, displacement and unemployment, all of which can easily be linked to market processes. And, on the contrary, those who are ideologically committed to various strands of neoliberalism will instead select out the stories of the winners, higher wages, improved local environmental and social indicators, and so forth. Both are true, because, when we look at capitalist markets as process rather than as outcome, they are two inescapable sides of the same coin. Periods of 'boom' and 'bust' make one or other class 'phenomenally truer' than the other, resulting in an endless oscillatory relativism. Until, of course, as we have seen in Chapter 7, periods of crisis of 'social stability' enter the scene, which put into question the core systemic mechanisms and their corresponding social relations.

The relational meaning of capitalist markets – often obscured by economic discourse corresponding to daily practices that Marx had called 'commodity-fetishism' (De Angelis 1996; Holloway 2002; Marx 1976a) – can also be seen, for example, when we read the conventional understanding of globalisation as increasing interdependence between people, regions, or countries in the world. Interdependence means we *depend* on each other, but it *also* implies that what we do has *effect* on others somewhere else in the world.

Indeed, the double meaning of interdependence as 'depending on each other' and 'affecting each other' is today increasingly obvious in many spheres of life, and it points at one thing: interdependence means that you and I, perhaps inhabiting life worlds apart, are caught in the same loop, and the *form* of the loop, its rules and methods of articulating our dependency – what we do and how what we do affects each other – is the invisible thread ruling our lives. This is a form of rule that is independent of our positionalities and perspectives, our own drives and passions, our own calculus and reasons, our own affects, feelings and emotions. Yet it is one that *articulates* all these positionalities, affects and desires, without us being able to say a word about the form of that articulation. This form is the sea in which we are swimming in our daily actions, and as such we do not see and problematise it.

Thus, for example, dam construction in a country in the South might be financed by Europe's future pensioners. The pension fund managers put their money into those dam companies paying high returns on the market, but this implies the uprooting of communities to make space for the dam. It is not just, as Giddens puts it (1990: 64), that 'local happenings are shaped by events occurring many miles away, and vice versa'. The fact is that when the value of my pension depends on the successful uprooting of communities in some parts of the world (Schmid, Harris and Sexton 2003), we have a form of interdependence that sucks! We have here a clear example of how capitalist markets articulate different communities' needs for livelihoods (the community of workers forced into private pension funds and the community of villagers forced out of their land) in such a way that they are opposed to each other.

The forms of *global interdependence* predicated on capitalist markets is all of this kind, an 'interdependence' among human beings whose life preservation strategies are *articulated* by a global mechanism that sets them in opposition to each other. Capital's form of global interdependence means that my going to work today and eagerly complying with all the requirements of a competitive society and economy implies that my actions have an effect on somebody else somewhere in the world. To put it bluntly, the competitive market logic implies one of three things: 'we' are more efficient than 'them' and thus we contribute to their ruin; 'they' are more efficient than us so 'they' are contributing to 'our' ruin; or the two opposites are true alternately, resulting in an endless rat race that ruins both 'their' and 'our' lives.

The 'law of value' and capital's limit to democracy and freedom

It must be noted that the competition that runs through the global social body is not similar to the competitive games we play with friends. When I play table football with my friends I aim at winning. But whether I win or lose, I end up sharing food and laughter with my friends. Competition of this type is innocuous; it is a practice that might strengthen communities' playfulness instead of destroying it, unless, of course, I am a bad loser. But 'economic' competition is ultimately a type of competition that finds its very energy in its threat to livelihoods. This is the case regardless of whether this competition is a 'function' of the degree of 'imperfection' it is said to have by economists, or whether it is real or only simulated, as is increasingly the case in public services in which there are no markets, but where government agencies simulate market dynamics by setting new benchmarks. It is a mode of social relation that is based on *pitting* livelihoods against each other. In so doing it continuously reproduces scarcity and community destruction.

This form of interdependence represents the underlying basis of the dangerous and pervasive character of globalisation that is today so widely contested. It is not interdependency per se that is the problem, not even global interdependence. More people coming closer to each other, better able to share resources, knowledge, ways of doing things, cultural forms, experiences, musical traditions, and so forth, in many cases means enriching the lives of people and communities, opening up new horizons for creativity, and deepening exchanges. Furthermore, human societies, understood more correctly as networks of individuals who cooperate and therefore *interact* to reproduce their lives, can only be understood in terms of degrees and forms of interdependency. The problem with capitalist markets is the *form* of this interdependence, the *type* of globalisation processes. The problem therefore is *how* this integration is brought about – that is, how markets are created – and *how* this integration operates once it is set in place.

The 'law of value' implies that from the perspective of any 'node', this mode of articulation across the social body is disciplinary, because the market is a mechanism in which norms are created through a social process that distributes rewards and punishments.[1] By norms of production I am here referring to the variety of principles of allocation of resources and distribution associated with social production as well as ways of doing things, rhythms and forms of cooperation that, as we shall see in the next chapter, in capitalist markets are synthesised in prices. Norms of production (that is, ways of relating to each other) are answers to fundamental questions: *what* shall we produce? *how* shall we produce it? *how much* shall we produce it? *how long* should we spend working to produce it? and *who* shall produce it? – all very concrete questions that define *processes* and *relational* matters concerning the reproduction of our social body, concerning the ways we relate to each other and to nature.

The 'law of value' ultimately implies that these questions are not answered by people themselves taking charge of their lives and their relations with each other. Thus, equally, the norms of social co-production and of people's relations with each other are defined collectively through the market, but in a way that goes behind the back of individuals and communities, because they are defined by an *abstract* mechanism that we have created and that we take as 'natural' in the daily practices of our lives. The 'law of value' thus is the limit posed by capital to democracy and freedom. It is the abstract process of disciplinary markets that articulates the social body in such a way as to constitute social norms of production, rather than individual social actors negotiating among themselves the norms of their free cooperation. In this market mechanism, individual actors must respond to existing heteronomous norms imposed by a blind mechanism by meeting or beating the market benchmark (or the simulated market benchmark imposed by neoliberal state bodies), an activity that in turn affects the market norm itself. In this continuous feedback mechanism livelihoods are pitted against each other. When rewards and punishments are repeated in a system, norms are created. This, as we shall see in Chapter 14, is a process that the paladin of market freedom, Friedrich Hayek, well understood, although he ignores the question of power and enclosure processes in explaining the emergence of capitalist markets. For him the abstract mechanism of the market is a spontaneously emerging system of freedom.

Thus, if another world is possible, the minimum condition is that we coordinate social action in a different way, one in which the norms of our interaction and cooperation in social production are defined directly by ourselves (those who are doing the interacting), and not by a blind and abstract mechanism that pits livelihoods against each other. Capital's 'law of value' is set up as the basic constraint we have to move beyond in order to constitute this other world.

WHAT IS THE 'LAW OF VALUE'?

Thus far I have used the term 'law of value' in scare quotes to indicate that we must be cautious in approaching this term, given the complex history and diverse meanings associated with diametrically opposed political projects. To frame our discussion, most of these meanings of course derive from Marx's oeuvre, especially *Capital*. However, although Marx employed a value discourse that we shall spell out later, he rarely used the term 'law of value'.[2] In the Marxist tradition, the term sometimes narrowly corresponds to the claim that the value of a commodity is the socially necessary labour time for its production. On the other hand, it sometimes includes a plurality of interrelated meanings. These maximal definitions include:

1. a 'price theory' version of the law, similar to Leontyev's definition, which claims that the exchange values and production prices of goods are 'established according to the labour socially necessary for their reproduction';
2. a version that explains the market-price mechanism in quantitative terms;
3. a version that explains class relations, alienation and impoverishment in capitalism;
4. 'the laws of development of capitalism in history (concentration, theory of crises, etc.) can be incorporated, too, so that the law of value embraces the economic law of motion of capitalist society' (Haffner 1973: 268–9 quoted in Caffentzis 2005: 90).

As I shall argue in this and the next chapter, the 'law of value' is interesting to us not because it is a method for explaining the value of commodities at a given time, so as to prove 'bourgeoise' economics wrong (as many Marxists economists have argued), or to contribute to social planning (the 'command economy', understanding of 'law of value'), but rather for making the *process* of constitution of these values critically intelligible, that is, to gain the perspective of an *outside* to the normal state of affairs constituting the reproduction of livelihoods, in so far as capital is concerned. This *process* of formation of commodity values is the process that defines socially necessary labour time (SNLT) and that we shall discuss in detail in the next chapter. The interrelation between a 'price theory' (1), the quantitative and qualitative aspects of value (2 and 3) and the macro-patterns emerging with the ongoing process of reproduction of commodity values (4), are all captured by the 'law of value' as emerging from the dynamic of this process, and this, in turn, is one with the problematic of capitalist 'measure'. Indeed, the practices and social processes defining and constituting capital's measure and giving rise to the formation of prices are *at the same time* constituted by class struggle (clashes among value practices) and give rise to the 'laws of capitalist development' that Marx refers to in terms of concentration/centralisation of capital, the creation of a 'reserve army',[3] the tendency towards a falling rate of profit, and, generally, the ongoing structuration of the social body into hierarchies of power and command over resources and the means of life.

However, in terms of the problematic we are interested in here, that of the 'beginning of history' and the overcoming of capitalism, the 'law of value' must be understood as a process *at the core* of the problematic of co-optation of struggles – a particular type, or better scale and intensity of co-optation, one that is completely normalised and appears as the *ordinary run of things*, hence cannot appear as co-optation, but as norm. It does indeed appear as distinct from other examples of co-optation, such as consumerism, public schooling or, at the level of general discursive strategies, Keynesianism. These three examples are instances of co-optation of struggles in linear time, they are, in other words, strategic *responses* developed by capital to preserve itself vis-à-vis waged and unwaged working-class struggles. Thus, historically speaking,

consumerism is a capitalist response to successful working class struggle for more income and less work, it is not just one more devious capitalist plot to expand its social control. Consumerism emerged out of the working class struggles of the 1930s which forced capital to shift from its traditional reliance on the business cycle to regulate wages to the plans of the Keynesian and welfare state. Consumerism is thus another mechanism, analogous to public schooling, of the capitalist colonization of the sphere of working class independence. Just as school subverts free time by making it into time for the production and reproduction of life as labor power, so consumerism seeks to subvert the autonomous power of the worker's wage by turning it into a vehicle of capitalist expansion and a tool of capitalist domination. ... When work took up all waking hours this was fairly obvious; there was no time for anything else. As the 'working' class succeeded in forcing down the length of the working day, week, year and life cycle, and more time became available, at least potentially, for other activities this has become less obvious. Yet, when we examine any average slice of life time (day, week, etc.) it becomes obvious that the bulk of that time is still shaped by and around work. (Cleaver 2005: 120)

The relation between consumerism, public schooling or macro-strategies such as Keynesianism and capital's measure is that, given historically specific class compositions and political subjectivities, capital's *conatus* of self-preservation develops new institutional settings within which to couple working-class subjectivity to the process of accumulation. We can recognise the development of these as instances of co-optation once we understand their historical relation (struggles → capital response) rooted in linear time. On the other hand, the 'law of value' is this ongoing process of coupling among clashing value practices rooted in circular time (hence: struggles → capital response →

struggles …) whatever the historical form taken by it within the history of capitalism. Co-optation (of subjectivities, of value practices, of human energies, of affects, of natural processes) here is not the result of a new 'institutional setting', or new 'rules of the game'. It is instead *the* lifeblood upon which the preserving, reproducing and expanding social force we call capital depends in the *ordinary run of things*. It is this daily process of co-optation articulating lives and livelihoods, rooted in capital's measure and made possible by pervasive old and new enclosures, that must be overcome.

CRITICAL APPROACHES TO THE 'LAW OF VALUE'

If Marx did not use the term 'law of value' often, his work was undoubtedly grounded on value discourse. Caffentzis (2005: 94) among others has argued for the threefold function of this discourse for Marx, namely analytical, critical and revolutionary. In particular, analytic 'labor-value discourse allows for an apparently precise and measurable definition of exploitation in capitalist society. This clarity is especially crucial in capitalism because exploitation is formally and legally hidden by the wage form'. Second, critical labour-value discourse provides

a narrative (i.e., the class struggle) that workers can use in an antagonistic way to describe themselves as fundamental actors in the drama of history and the capitalists and landlords as parasitic upon their labor, anxiety and suffering. It allows the worker to view the totality of capitalist relations from his/her point of view and not from the perspective of the capitalist.

This is also what Cleaver (1992) calls an 'inversion of class perspective' narrative.[4] As we have seen in Chapter 5, from the perspective of capital's value practices the labour, anxiety and suffering of the labourer are invisible. This invisibility is well captured by what Marx called the 'illusions of the trinity formula' of wages, capital and rent attributing to 'things' (capital, land and labour) rather than human doing the creation of value. Or, similarly, due to the fact that the application of scientific knowledge to production and reproduction loops increases productivity, leading to the fetishised impression that increases in productivity are brought about by capital, not social labour, thus legitimising capital as the force to determine the future of humanity.

Finally, and crucially,

if labor is the ultimate force of value creation (as the Law of Value claims and gives a measure to), then laborers are valuable and creative in themselves. A revolutionary corollary follows: workers are capable of creating non-capitalist 'tables of values' and, indeed, an autonomous world beyond capitalism. This conviction is crucial for the development of a revolutionary alternative to capitalism. Without it, the class struggle becomes a form of 'bad infinity,' always there, always producing the next step, but never the last step. (Caffentzis 2005: 94)

Hence, from this perspective, the overcoming of capitalism implies the overcoming of the 'law of value' and the mode of measuring human activity it is grounded on.

The 'law of value' as a particular articulation between value and work however, has been extensively criticised from a wide range of 'progressive' perspectives, and each of these criticisms has implications for an anti-capitalist perspective. It is worthwhile here to review three different types of criticism: from the perspective of those radical economists who argue that work is important but not determinant of value; from the perspective of those social scientists for whom current features of work make it no longer a central category for our understanding and for grounding emancipatory practices; and from the perspective of those political philosophers for whom these changes make the 'law of value' redundant, yet the forms of labour emerging from the recent changes are central in grounding a new political project.

'Equilibrium' Marxist political economy

In the first place, there is what we might call the 'equilibrium' economists' critique. This is the often technical and abstract criticism of political economists who, building on the century-old original critiques of Marx's system by the Austrian economist Eugen von Böhm-Bawerk and the 'solution' offered by the Russian mathematical economist Ladislaus von Bortkiewicz, opened the way, in the 1970s, to a long string of critiques judging Marx's labour theory of value as conceptually incoherent (e.g. the so-called 'transformation problem') and empirically unfounded. Sraffian economists like Ian Steedman (1977) were joined by 'analytic Marxists' like G. A. Cohen (1988) and Jon Elster (1985) to define the key question for the anti-capitalist movement as one of 'distribution' of the product, not of *mode* of production and corresponding relations. Much of these critiques as well as of solutions to the 'transformation problem' was based on an analytical framework in which *life* time as *work* time played no role, and the problematisation of the social process explaining *how* a subject's life energies and activities are extracted was replaced by the *postulation* of technical coefficients that specified the proportion of living labour among other inputs necessary for the production of a particular commodity.

By disposing of Marx's value discourse, the equilibrium interpretation and corresponding 'surplus' approach has important implications: it not only reduces exploitation to a question of distribution. It also fetishises technology by naturalising its development and reproducing the myth that an increase in productivity following continuous technical change implies – for the system as a whole – increasing profits; it is unable to provide, within its own framework, any insights on competition qua disciplinary mechanism of labour leading to the formation of socially necessary labour time; it is silent on the meaning of alienation as a founding element of value, relegating it at most to non-economic analyses; its formalism cannot help comprehend crises that are rooted in antagonistic *value* practices; unlike Marx, for whom values can express themselves *only* as monetary quantities – i.e., prices, of whatever kind (market prices or prices of production), prices and values belong to two different systems, thus again fetishising reality.

More recently, the 'transformation problem' was objected to as being a non-problem, thanks to an analytical framework called 'temporal single system interpretation', or TSSI.[5] This framework introduces time and thus rejects the dogma implicit in equilibrium economics that input and output prices must be equal. The other claim of this approach is that the sum of value transferred from used-up means of production depends on the price, not the value, of those means of production. Once these two claims are postulated, it is possible to discharge Marx of the criticism of internal inconsistency derived from the 'transformation problem' as well as to replicate all the results that were alleged to be internally inconsistent within Marx's theory. These include his theory of exploitation through the equality between social profit and social surplus value; the implication, following Marx's theory, that the source of profit is surplus labour and the determination of values and profit by labour time; and the confirmation of the falling rate of profit tendency in cases of continuous technical change that reduce the price of outputs in relation to inputs, among other things.[6]

Although this 'vindication' of Marx's internal consistency might be of value to people trained in the technicalities of Marxian economics, and, *within this framework*, might form the basis to an understanding of crisis as a necessary element of the capitalist mode of production, within the mathematical treatment of this approach there is little problematisation of both ongoing struggle among value practices and of the coupling among circuits of production and reproduction. It must be said, finally, that the ongoing debate between the equilibrium and the temporal approaches to values, cast in the technicalities of mathematical economics, risks becoming self-referential and of little use to the anti-capitalist movement. These types of ongoing debate are based either on public vindication or humiliation of Marx's texts instead of raising the questions of whether this 'transformation problem' or 'non-problem' tells the anti-capitalist movement anything useful about the processes, structure and vulnerability of capitalism.[7]

The 'end of work' and all that

The second type of critique of Marx's labour theory of value, one that gained much credence during the last two decades of the twentieth century among social critics, is indirect, in the sense that it is based on the argument that the most fundamental form of social organisation of contemporary capitalism is no longer work. The argument has been put forward in a variety of ways, in terms of both 'objective' forces (technology, changes in relative growth and importance of economic sectors, such as a shift from manufacturing to services, and so on) and 'subjective' factors (the subject's identity derived from work).

So, for example, in his *End of Work* bestseller, Jeremy Rifkin criticised those who argue that the new technological revolution of the information and communication age, together with genetic engineering and robotisation, will lead to new employment opportunities if a well-trained and flexible workforce is available to respond to the challenges of the 'information age'. His refutation is based on the idea that, unlike in earlier periods of restructuring such as the mid 1950s and the early 1980s, when the fast-growing service sector was able to re-employ many of the blue-collar workers displaced by automation, today this would be impossible, since the service sector too would fall under the heavy hammer of restructuring and automation (Rifkin 1995: 35). The consequence, when we scale up this scenario to the planetary level, would be an unemployment problem of tremendous proportions involving billions. Rifkin's analysis is problematic, in that his objectivist understanding of technology (which skates over the social constitution of technology as a class relation of struggle) and his unproblematised determinism in portraying the future trends of economic sectors (which skates over the fact that demand might well increase for 'service' goods that are not 'automised', especially if an oversupply of labour power and conditions of reproduction makes their labour cheap!) lead to an impossible solution. Because, if it is true, as Caffentzis (1999: 27) argues, that 'there is no inevitable capitalist strategy in the drive to overcome workers' struggles' and 'these struggles can lead to many futures – from the reintroduction of slavery, to a dramatic increase in the workday, to the negotiated reduction of the waged workday to the end of capitalism – depending on the class forces in the field', it is also the case that 'there is one outcome that definitely cannot be included in the menu of possible futures as long as capitalism is viable'. And this is Rifkin's vision of 'the high-tech revolution lead[ing] to the realisation of the age-old utopian dream of substituting machines for human labor, finally freeing humanity to journey into a post-market era' (Rifkin 1995: 56). Hence Rifkin proposes a utopian capitalism, in which the combination of a drastic reduction of the working day and a 'new social contract' providing financial incentives for working in 'the third sector' (made up of independent, 'non-profit' or volunteer work in the 'service industries' of the twenty-first century), could offer 'the only viable means for constructively channeling the surplus labor cast off by the global market' (ibid.: 292). That is, as Caffentzis puts it:

Rifkin's vision of the 'safe haven' for humanity is a form of capitalism where most workers are not producing profits, interest or rent ... [However] the capitalism resulting from Rifkin's 'new social contract' is impossible, for it is by definition a capitalism without profits, interest and rents. Why would capitalists agree to such a deal after they trumpeted throughout the Cold War that they would rather blow up half the planet than give up a tenth of their income?' (Caffentzis 1999: 28)

Similarly, Claus Offe (1985) makes the more theoretical point that work is no longer a central category either in terms of the changes in the objective centrality of work in the structuring of life in contemporary societies, or in terms of the subjective role of work in shaping and structuring individual lives. For both 'objective' and 'subjective' reasons therefore, the central role of work in the organisation of social life is drastically curtailed, so as to bring about a 'crisis of the work society' and the need for replacing social theories that are centred on work. It goes without saying that this includes Marx's theory and 'law of value'.

In the first case, in a way that is prescient of later arguments on immaterial labour, Offe argues among other things that the displacement of manufacturing labour by the growth of services makes it impossible to talk about work in general. 'One can no longer talk of a basically unified type of rationality' (Offe 1985: 139) since service work is fundamentally different from other types of work, in that it is 'reflexive', as it 'produces and maintains work itself' (ibid., 138). This implies, as we shall see, that capital cannot subject it to its measure. The second, related argument is that work time as a proportion of lifetime has fallen, non-work time (education, family life, leisure, consumption) has grown less structured by work, and unemployment is increasingly failing to coerce people into work, due to the existence of the welfare state.

It is interesting to investigate in more detail the rationale of these two arguments, especially the first, keeping in mind that since Offe argued his case, 20 years of neoliberal policies of privatisation of services and increasing competition, as well as cuts in welfare entitlements, have redesigned the context in which this service labour operates.

For the first argument, activities such as 'teaching, curing, planning, organizing, negotiating, controlling, administering, and counseling – that is, the activities of preventing, absorbing and processing risks and deviation from normality' (ibid., 138) are different from the 'industrial production of commodities' for two reasons. First, 'because the heterogeneity of the "cases" that are processed in service work, and due to the high levels of uncertainty concerning where and when they occur' make it difficult to establish 'control criteria of adequate work performance' (ibid., 138). Second, service work is not conducive of a 'clear and uncontroversial "criterion of economic efficiency", from which could be strategically derived the type and amount, the place and timing of "worthwhile" work'. This criterion is absent because the outcome of service work, whether in the private or the public sector, 'is not monetary 'profit' but concrete 'uses'; they often help to avoid losses, the quantitative volume of which cannot be determined precisely because they *are* avoided' (ibid.). Thus, while non-standardisation must be accepted to a large degree and 'replaced by qualities like interactive competence, consciousness of responsibility, empathy and acquired practical experience', instead of economic rationality one finds 'calculation based on convention, political discretion or professional consensus' (ibid.).

This picture of service work led Offe to conclude that service labour, although not ' "liberated" from the regime of formal, economic wage-based rationality, ... becomes a separate but functionally necessary "foreign body" which is externally limited (but not internally structured) by that economic rationality.' This leads to the conclusion that 'this differentiation within the concept of work ... consitute[s] the most crucial point supporting the argument that one can no longer talk of a basically unified type of rationality organizing and governing the whole of the work sphere' (ibid.: 138–9). In other words, the kernel of Offe's argument seems to lie in the fact that service work cannot be subjected to capital's measure. Such labour is heterogeneous (or, as we would say today, is performed by a *multitude* of subjects) and therefore it lacks a common measure of productivity and efficiency. Because of this, to talk about 'work' in general is misleading.

Offe's objective arguments are grounded on shortsightedness with respect to the history of the capitalist mode of production and the corresponding dynamic taken on by the clashes among value practices. There are three aspects of the 'novelty' of the post-Fordist period that Offe is eager to highlight. The question of labour heterogeneity; the type of 'new' services that are offered on the market; and the question of unmeasurability of service work. None of these 'novel' characters of labour are new in terms of the clash among value practices constituting these activities, that is in terms of class relations. What is new, of course, is the social organisational form through which this clash expresses itself. Thus, in the first place, useful labour has always been heterogeneous under capitalism, whatever are the tendencies towards deskilling and homogenisation. As Cleaver (2005: 115) argues, movements towards homogeneity and deskilling, such as the shifts from manufacture to machinofacture and Taylorism, 'have been complemented by a growing diversity of products and technologies which have provided the technical basis for the repeated decomposition of working class power through new divisions of labor'. Particular forms of 'segmented labour' or of international division of labour, or types of managerial authority inside specific organisations 'constitute historically specific aspects of such heterogeneity rather than new "fractures" which make it impossible to understand the organization of work in terms of the class struggle over valorization' (ibid.: 2005: 118). Second, several new services that we find today on the market fulfil a function that has been recognisable since the beginning of the dominance of the capitalist mode of production, that is the reproduction of life as labour power. From the twenty-first century lecturer who is supposed to 'manage the aspirations' of poor students after neoliberal governments have lured them into getting into debt to pay for their degrees with the promise of unrealisable rewards in increasingly competitive labour markets, to the social services officer who takes a mother to court because of her truant child, to the court and the police who fine or put the mother into prison, to the unwaged mother who is supposed to meet social expectations and rear children as law-abiding citizens (whatever the law may be) and obedient workers (whatever the social relations of production may be), we have a contemporary task of differentiation that is indistinguishable, in its basic rationale, from ways of reproducing life as labour power in previous periods of capitalism.

Finally, measure. The fact that the productivity of this 'service' work is difficult to measure – something that was heavily discussed from the late 1960s in the midst of the crisis of the welfare state and of 'productivity' – does not mean that the subjects performing these activities are not the objects of continuous measure and measuring strategies based on capital's rationality, which, in turn, affects the organisational principles and 'quality' of these services themselves. Take for example educational services. Here the 'work of teachers and administrators is primarily to produce labor power in general, i.e., the ability and willingness to work, and secondarily to produce particular skills and abilities' (Cleaver 2005: 119). Here the productivity of labour is measured

at the individual level by grades on particular and standardized tests which measure primarily the ability and willingness to study, and thus to work. The productivity of such work is also measured at the social level by the adequacy with which it tracks students into the heterogeneous categories of work required by capital, from dropouts who will do unskilled unwaged or low-waged work to highly skilled professional labor. (ibid.)

Also, even conceding Offe's claim that for the types of service activities he discusses both 'control criteria of adequate work performance' and a 'clear and uncontroversial "criterion of economic efficiency"' (Offe 1985: 138) might be difficult to establish, it is nonetheless the case that either the neoliberal introduction of markets into service sectors, or their simulation in state sectors, or, in general, the overall increased scope for competition brought about by pressures to 'globalise' services, turns this 'difficulty' into a barrier that capital must overcome. In other words, we are here confronted with a clash in value practices. Thus, with recent government policies introducing competition for funding among schools in a variety of ways, as has happened in the last decades in Britain, the 'measure' of educational labour (both for students and for teachers) becomes more insidious and alienating, markets are simulated to reproduce their *process* of measuring, benchmarks are centrally defined for all to adopt, career-minded 'cost-minimising' educational managers, with no experience of the complexities of relational and affective labour in education or research, decree curricula by culling cost-ineffective courses and dictate procedures, dressing up their uneducational practices in terms of 'best practice'; 'heads of quality' are appointed to make sure that individual staff conform to standard measures of doing things, and are not too innovative; while vice-chancellors, after dropping in to 'three-line whip' staff meetings in which they urge staff to improve on the students 'retention' statistics, otherwise funds and jobs might be threatened, run up and down the planet to allure more students from the global South to enroll in the education shopping mall they represent, in competition with other similarly eager business education PLCs or INCs. And all this of course, while the increased student participation is not accompanied by massive social investment to give a hard-pressed section of society a chance to think, reflect, do and play with life unpreoccupied by scarcity. On the contrary, scarcity becomes the condition of education. Once the 'privilege' of the wealthy, education is now a 'work' available to all, since to go through it you just need to incur debts of thousands of pounds, keep doing part-time work to pay bills, and, if you have children and cannot afford pro-hibitive child-care costs, cut down on study time and swallow up notions to regurgitate at the exam while they are taking a nap.[8]

In terms of the subjective meaning of work, Offe argues that the work ethic is less central, and people's sense of self-definition, worth and purpose is less tied to work. This is not just because the increased heterogeneity of work makes it difficult for work to provide 'a precise and shared significance for the working population' (Offe 1985: 136) and hence, makes less likely the common feeling of being part of a working class; it is also because of the struggles against capital's measure, or, in his language, people's having become increas-ingly conscious of the 'disutility' of work.

On the question of the work ethic, Offe underplays the struggles against work discipline permeating the history of capitalism from its inception. What perhaps contributed to giving Offe the impression of novelty is the fact that he wrote after a decade, the 1970s, in which workers' grass-roots power to reject that discipline grew enormously, hence making it visible to all. Also, the problematic of the emergence of a 'common feeling' among workers, and its 'difficulty' due to the heterogeneity of work, must be understood in terms of the problematic of how to overcome capital's 'measure', but not in terms of the declining importance of what this is predicated upon, that is work. It is not the useful aspects of a particular labour activity that provide the ground for the common feeling at the basis of anti-capitalism. This can be true in particu-lar branches of production, among 'educators', or 'nurses' or 'miners'. But the rules of the capitalist mode of production articulate all these labourers. To the extent that 'educators' and 'nurses' and 'farmers' and 'miners' and 'indigenous people' and 'students' and 'housewives' and 'single mothers' and so on are all subjected to a measure and a rationality alien to them and posited from the outside (the measure of capital, through the process of capitalist markets, state dispensation of social security conditional on 'evidence-based good behaviour' as job searchers, and the robbery of social entitlements and commons) – and yet, the form and discourses in which this measure is imposed on their lives is so different – to this extent, 'the common feeling' of belonging to a class vis-à-vis capital's measure is not an a priori, but a result that must be socially constructed through communication between those partaking in diverse struggles. Thus, while Offe's alternative for critical social theory is, like many others, to follow up those trends that have replaced class concepts with what have become known as single issues (gender, race and ethnicity, human rights, peace and disarmament, environment), in synchrony with the 'new social movements' and similarly to what Ernesto Laclau and Chantell Mouffe called 'agonistic democracy', in the last part of the twentieth century these same 'single issue' social movements have begun a hard process of political *class* recomposition.[9]

Immaterial labour: the end of the 'law of value'?

Among the authors who have problematised and rejected the 'law of value', Hardt and Negri (2000), among others in the post-workerist tradition, contend that the original argument for this rejection is in Marx's own work, especially in the often quoted 'Fragment on Machines' in the *Grundrisse* and in the unpublished Part 7 of Volume 1 of *Capital*, 'Results of the Immediate Process of Production'. They claim here that Marx foresaw the development of capitalism as a continuous process of displacement of labour from production due to mechanisation and the application of science. This process implies that in the end, labour will cease being at the basis of wealth creation, and therefore labour values will cease to be relevant categories. As Marx put it, 'as soon as labour in the direct form has ceased to be the great well-spring of wealth, labour time ceases and must cease to be its measure, and hence exchange value [must cease to be the measure] of use value' (Marx 1974: 705). This future, according to Hardt and Negri, is now. Indeed, it is several years since Negri argued that capital has now reached this stage.[10] And since 'the logic of capital is no longer functional to development, but is simply command for its own reproduction' (Negri 1994: 28), then nothing but sheer domination keeps the rule of capital in its place.

This development marks what Marx called the passage from formal to real subsumption of labour under capital. In terms of Hardt and Negri's rendering of this, this transformation is responsible for literally 'exploding' the 'law of value' (to use Marx's term in the *Grundrisse* 'Fragment'), by positing the immeasurable character of value. Contemporary capitalism, it is argued, is thus constituted by two 'novel' features. In the first place, the productive metabolism with nature is dominated by science and technology, know-how and savoir faire, which are the products of the 'general intellect' and 'immaterial labour', and not material labour. Secondly, perhaps by virtue of the fact that immaterial labour is 'relational' and 'affective' labour investing the body, capitalist control subsumes also the processes of social reproduction, and not only the direct sphere of production. In other words, production becomes biopolitical (a term borrowed from Foucault) in that various aspects of social reproduction (education, sexuality, communication, demography, etc.) become the terrains of struggle of the multitude vis-à-vis capital.

On the other hand, however, production's becoming biopolitical also implies that capital's control over labour does not pass through measure, since immaterial labour, and the value it produces, is beyond measure (Hardt and Negri 2000: 354–61).

This double feature of what constitutes contemporary labour for Hardt and Negri implies the rejection of Marx's labour theory of value, which is 'really a theory of the measure of value' (Hardt and Negri 2000: 355). According to them, in modern capitalism – corresponding to what Marx called the phase of real subsumption of labour under capital – the idea that a commodity value might be measured by the labour that is socially necessary for its production[11] is untenable. The 'law of value' is therefore obsolete, that is, it has lost its explanatory power and political meaning in the reality of contemporary postmodern capitalism (see Hardt and Negri 1994: 9, 175; 2000: 209, 355–9; 2004: 140–53). Production of value in this period is beyond measure, since value is now created by living *immaterial* labour, the 'cooperative aspect' of which 'is not imposed or organized from the outside' (Hardt and Negri 2000: 294) by an alien measuring force. The value produced in modern empire is beyond measure, because the immaterial living labour producing value is identified with 'general social activity', 'a common power to act' that cannot be disciplined, regimented and structured by measuring devices such as clocks. In such circumstances, exploitation still continues, but not through the subjection of labour to capital's measure, that is it continues 'outside any economic measure: its economic reality is fixed exclusively in political terms' (Negri 1994: 28). In the context of what Hardt and Negri call 'empire', value can at most be indexed 'on the basis of always contingent and purely conventional elements' imposed by 'the monopoly of nuclear arms, the control of money, and the colonization of ether' (Hardt and Negri 2000: 355).

Politically speaking, the argument put forward here is both of great appeal and also worrisome. In the first case, unlike traditional Marxist approaches fetishising technology and capital as a thing, there is the recognition – typical of autonomist Marxism – of the struggle-led development of capitalism. In particular, Hardt and Negri root their understanding of the emergence of contemporary capitalism not in a deterministic historical necessity, but as the result of struggles that brought capital into crisis from the 1970s and brought Keynesian strategies down. Struggles that in Europe and in the United States took the form of a 'refusal of work' – especially of the heavy measured factory work of Fordist factory workers – have pushed capital to reorganise itself, and have led to the decline of what Foucault called 'disciplinary society' and the emergence of the tendency towards a, 'control society' (for a critique of the latest aspect, see Chapter 9). Also, unlike traditional Marxists uniquely obsessed with 'negativity' and fixed doctrines, in their emphasis on the positive and creative character that can derive from desires, affects and communication within struggles, they are reminding us that the dimension of transformation is immanence, and the new world is constituted in the here and now thanks to *constituent subjects*, and not 'after' revolution thanks to party's central committees. However, while there is the recognition of capital's dependence on struggle for its own development and of the constituent force of subjects in struggle – thus opening up to a strategic and political reading of reality – at the same time the authors give us a deflated theoretical framework that does not help us to recognise the social forces many movements are up against, nor the strategic field into which they are inserted. By proclaiming that capital has gone beyond measure, and instead celebrating what they call immaterial labour, which they posit as a form of social cooperation 'beyond measure', the authors turn our sight away from the most central, fundamental aspect we must face in the struggle against and beyond capital as a way of articulating livelihoods and social doing: that capital, even the contemporary global capitalism of the phase of 'real subsumption' – which, incidentally, for Marx 'was not a thing of the "future," [but] was fully present in his time' (Caffentzis 2005: 104) – is constituted through a particular mode of *measuring* life activity, and therefore of articulating social powers. Correspondingly, the constituent moment can only be the positing of *other* measures the communal problematisation of which is at the bottom line of processes of political constitution beyond capital.

Indeed, the positing of immaterial labour as a given hegemonic tendency eliminates any need for this communal and constituent problematisation. For Hardt and Negri, the 'common' is directly posited by what they understand to be the central quality of immaterial labour. Their argument that immaterial labour is a hegemonic figure, that is, a tendency, 'a vortex that gradually transforms other figures to adopt to its central qualities' (Hardt and Negri 2004:107) implies that by pushing through Empire these central qualities of immaterial labour centred on life produced in common will generalise and will transform the world: 'the multitude, in its will to be against and its desire for liberation, must push through Empire to come out the other side' (Hardt and Negri 2000: 218). There is light at the end of the tunnel. Since immaterial labour is production that is directly social, its generalisation is interpreted as being nothing less than the generalisation of 'communism'.

We must pause on this question of immaterial labour as creating common relations and social forms due to its relational, communicational and affective character. I want here neither to challenge the empirical basis upon which immaterial labour is said to become hegemonic vis-à-vis 'material' labour (others have done this),[12] nor do I want to dispute the obvious claim that in so far as an activity is 'immaterial' (i.e., intellectual/linguistic or affective)[13] it is directly social, that is involving direct social relations, communication and affects. (Incidentally, car production on an assembly line involve social relations, communication and affects, although these might not be the *object* of material production, unlike in the case of some forms of immaterial production.) What I want to dispute here however is two fundamental things:

First, the claim that the 'becoming common' of the qualities of immaterial labour has nothing to do with capital's *measure* and the struggles among value practices. In Hardt and Negri, this becoming common of production is a given, that is, it is generated by the tendencies and hegemonic role of immaterial labour and its central qualities. Instead, as soon as we problematise the 'production in common' of immaterial labour within the terrain of contemporary capitalism, we discover that the extent to which immaterial production (or the transformation of communications, relational modes and affects into output of production) becomes 'hegemonic' is highly correlated with the ongoing process of capitalist measure and the corresponding struggle among *value* practices through which this form of labour, as all others under capitalism, is constituted.

Indeed, the notion of tendency and the question of measure are related. Because if the notion of tendency lays emphasis on 'direction' rather than numbers (Hardt and Negri 2004: 141), then how is this direction constituted? A tendency in Marx is always the emergent property of clashes of forces. For him, struggle is the driving force of tendency. For example, in the tendency of the rate of profit to fall, Marx counterpoises capitalist attempts to escape living labour and its struggles by introducing machines, automation and therefore raising the organic composition of capital, thus undermining its capacity for further valorisation based on exploitation of labour. Furthermore, the tendency is such precisely because capital can try to put in place countertendencies such as enclosures, new markets, reduced wages, extended working hours, neoliberal globalisation, and so on. In Hardt and Negri, measure, or the struggle over measure, is left out of the picture when in fact it is precisely this struggle that constitutes what gives rise to a tendency. The tendency they are talking about, such as the formation of the hegemonic role of a particular type of labour (immaterial or industrial), must be understood as the frontier on which the battle over measure is played out. Take the old case of the 'hegemonising' tendency of industrial labour emphasised by Marx and referred to by Hardt and Negri to argue that they are following Marx's method (Hardt and Negri 2004: 141). How could industrial labour have determined the ruin of early manufacturing and craft-based production except by posing the productivity of industrial labour as an external measure for these? The same is true of immaterial labour. What else but the fact that more and more immaterial elements of production (such as 'good service', customer 'satisfaction', the production of communication, relations and affects *in others*) are conditions for 'effective competition', hence weapons to be deployed in an ongoing battle over measure, bringing about the ruin of those competing nodes of social production that put little emphasis on these 'immaterial' factors?

Second, the question of tendency also downplays the role of hierarchy within the global multitude. Not that Hardt and Negri are unaware of the amazing disparity in wealth and access to social resources. But it seems to me that in their positing of 'tendency' as if it did not have anything to do with the question of measure, they do not provide us with a framework within which to problematise the material divisions within the global 'multitude'. And these material divisions, this hierarchy, and its continuous reproduction through the ongoing homeostatic processes of intense and pervasive competition, is perhaps the most single challenging *condition* we have to face to bring about new social relations and new modes of production. Without a problematisation of this hierarchy within the global 'multitude', and its uses and function in relation to the reproduction of the present regime, there is no new politics. As we have discussed in the previous section on Offe and in previous chapters, every 'hegemonic tendency', or any historical phase of production within the history of the capitalist mode of production, corresponds to a widely differentiated hierarchy, which can in the first instance be seen in the division between the waged and the unwaged. And this is precisely what makes the 'becoming common' of labour problematic, in that to the extent that this labour is still subject to capital's measure, its becoming common occurs in ways and forms that create hierarchy anew.

Because if it is true that global circuits of capital require an increasing emphasis and self-reflexivity on social relations, communication and affects, it is also the case that the unfolding of *this* process is predicated upon and reproduces hierarchies. This is for three reasons, all linked to capital's measure. In the first place, as argued above, immaterial forms of labour are constituted within a field of forces and made instrumental in gaining a competitive advantage to some *other*. Second, because the ongoing process of capitalist measurement constituted by the homeostasis of capital leads to crises of over-accumulation and consequent pressures for new enclosures, hence polarisation in access to the means of life. Third, the ongoing competition among immaterial workers in the global marketplace does not occur in a vacuum. Biopolitical production is also biopolitical *reproduction*. Immaterial workers, like anybody else, have bodies to nurture and need to reproduce their labour power. Part of their competitive effectiveness depends on how cheaply their labour power can be reproduced in relation to others with whom they are set in competition. Hence their 'effective competitiveness' in the market depends largely on the extent to which cheap or unwaged labour of reproduction is available to nurture or provide the means to nurture their bodies. To the extent that coupled circuits of both production and reproduction are set against other corresponding coupled circuits elsewhere in the world, we can talk about 'biopolitical competition'. But substantially, as we have seen in the first section of this book, this is nothing new for capitalism.

'Pushing through Empire' will thus certainly imply extending the 'production in common' of immaterial labour, but this is a common as constituted by capitalist social relations of production: a terrain of struggle over measure and value practices. Ultimately, without the problematisation of measure and hierarchy there is no problematisation of the overcoming of the capitalist mode of production. But we do not need to push through empire or vote for neoliberal constitutions[14] to engage in a political process of this type. I prefer to learn from the Zapatistas, for whom the 'no' to enclosures and neoliberalism is at the same time the positing of alternatives in the form of the many yeses, and the problematisation of their articulation.

It must be noted that the uncritical use of hierarchy occurs in Hardt and Negri in the replacement of the analytical devices of class composition with the notion of 'tendency'. As we have seen in Chapter 7, class composition allows us to capture both the synchronic configuration and the diachronic dynamic of a heterogeneous body of labour in relation to capital. We have seen that every social process of class struggle is grounded on a particular class composition, that is particular configurations of skills, desires and needs, and a web of relations constituting the highly heterogeneous social body of the doers. Political recomposition, in turn, is the emergence of *common* articulations, affects, desires, needs, communicational forms and so on, that allows the heterogenous social body of the doers to recognise that their 'production in common', in so far as it is shaped by capital's value practices, is not what they desire. Political recomposition therefore is the positing of other value practices and the constitution of different commons than those of capital, the constitution of a social force with a different *telos* from that of capital. But in this way of putting it, there is no tendency. Capital's restructuring and the state repressions have *decomposed* these political compositions over and over again, by destroying affects, killing bodies, or withdrawing and seizing means of livelihood. But the problem does not go away, and we still face the problematic of political recomposition in the conditions of our times: how do we produce commons beyond capital's measure? Indeed, while for Hardt and Negri the answer is given by the tendency of immaterial labour, learning from the Zapatistas, we have to hold on to the question and posit it again and again in all moments of struggle, networking and political processes. The answer can only emerge from below and can only be contingent on the desires of the struggling body.

Once we reread Hardt and Negri through the lenses of the question of measure and the ongoing struggles among value practices, we realise that their insistence on immaterial labour, despite their error, give us a great insight. We live, after all, in a time in which self-reflection on relations, for good or bad, is everywhere. Starting from the recent 'obsession' with networks in the social sciences and political activism, passing through anti-racism, feminism, and in general 'identity' politics, to the performances to be played in McJobs and other 'immaterial' productions, whatever their wages, all these are occasions of self-reflection on the *mode* of relation to the other. In some cases, the consequent problematisation of these relational modes gives rise to a movement of emancipation (feminism, anti-racism, and so on). In others, the problematisation is confined to serving the intentions embedded in its design: getting 'customer satisfaction', or 'reducing turnover time' and, ultimately, meeting corporate targets. In all these cases however, the activity involved is the problematisation of a relational mode to the other. *If only we had the courage to learn from the wisdom of our epoch and redirect it towards the active and constituent problematisation of the relational modes we employ to reproduce our livelihoods in common!* What would we discover? Isn't this process of discovery the process of making a new world? And isn't every moment of this process a beginning of history? These are the insights we get from the work of Negri in the last 20 years, the strength to raise a question about the relational, communicational and affective modes of our reproduction because the powers to begin and sustain a common process of problematisation and reconstruction are all within our reach.

But these powers are within our reach, they are *not given*. The 'production in common' that Hardt and Negri say is a quality of immaterial labour, once taken back to earth through its articulation to struggles over measure, is the problematic of a new political recomposition traversing every ripple of the global factory, every scale of the 'fractal panopticon'. It is *not* a historical tendency of emancipation, it is a power *condition* we must embrace to critically question the modes of articulating life processes and livelihoods – a power condition allowing us to question our process conditions: self-reflexivity, overcoming.

To the hegemonic discourse centred on competition as a relational mode through which livelihoods are reproduced we must counterpoise our discourse *problematising* this relational mode. It is time to seize and reclaim 'value' production and measure the relational modes predicated in capital's discourse with other relational modes springing from struggles.

THE 'CENTRE' OF POWER

One thing that emerges out of our discussion of the contemporary critics of the 'law of value', especially those emphasising in a variety of ways the recent transformations of labour, is that modern production occurs in 'networks', and networks do not have centres. We can recognise this as underlying Offe's emphasis on the heterogeneity of labour, and it is even clearer in Hardt and Negri's emphasis on the common relational and affective features of immaterial labour and in their definition of Empire as a network form of ruling (Hardt and Negri 2000). Indeed, there seems to be a general trend in the last quarter of a century towards abandoning the problematisation of the 'centre' of power as it emerges within the capitalist mode of production. For example, in diverse ways, we can discern this movement away from the problematic of the 'centre' of power in other influential authors, such as Manuel Castell's (2000) 'network society' as a 'space of flows' or in Laclau and Mouffe's (1985) postmodern critique of Marxism. Castells thinks of power as a flow, as something that moves across networks, passing through oscillators in ways that make a network resembling an electrical circuit through which the current (power) moves. When we understand power as a flow, however insightful the metaphor may be, until we pose this 'flow' in terms of a flow of social relations and the *mode* of their exercise, power remains a thing (a fluid thing, but a thing nevertheless), since it is not explained *how* its exercise as a *relation* makes it move. Thus, I can understand capital flows as a thing in terms of interest rate differentials across countries, but until I have related this movement to the broad problematic of how livelihoods in the two countries are systemically pitted against each other *by virtue* of this capital movement or the threat of this movement, and until I have understood and problematised the *rationale* of this, my concept of power is quite useless from the perspective of radical alternatives. This rationale is one with the problematic of the 'centre' of power.

The post-Marxism advocated by Ernesto Laclau and Chantal Mouffe (1985) disposes of the problematic of the centre by criticising the traditional Marxist emphasis on struggle against capital as 'economistic'. Instead, they open up the social field and see it as constituted by a plurality of struggles (on class, on gender, on the environment, on homophobia, on race, and so on) with little or no connection among themselves apart from those that can be developed contingently. The corresponding project of 'radical democracy' seeks thus to promote egalitarian relations across the social body. And since class is seen as simply one of the many sites of struggle, the project can avoid posing the question of emancipation from capital as the central problematic of any emancipatory politics.

This postmodern critique of Marxism as economistic is of course well founded, as orthodox Marxism has a long tradition of reductivist and economistic theorising. However the call for diversity and autonomy of different struggles has also emerged within non-orthodox Marxist traditions. While the postmodern approach to class had helped to give voice in academia to the many struggles that in the previous decades have developed on the ground around a plurality of issues, there is however a big political price to pay for celebrating difference in *this* way. Postmodern Marxism reproduces the very stereotypes of orthodox Marxism, its very economisticism. Instead of creating a discursive framework that facilitates the enriching of the problematic of class (that is of the limit to capital, of the constitution of new social relations, of new ways of articulating livelihoods) through the full acknowledgment of the plurality of powers and desires in the social body, as well as their spatio-temporal structuration, it is content to accept the reductionist notion of class qua waged labour as inherited from orthodox Marxism. It then 'de-centres' it by considering it as one issue among many. It thus leaves the theoretical and practical job of articulating this difference to the political project of capital, which from the 1980s onward goes under the name of neoliberalism. Capital does not have any problem in acknowledging difference and diversity, as long as it is diversity that finds the *common centre of* articulation within capitalist markets. In the postmodern discourse on class, therefore, we become blind to the political need to engage in a process of political recomposition for the constitution of alternatives to capital. It is in this political recomposition that we bring together diversity and learn *how* articulating the 'many yeses' constitutes another world. If we deprive political and theoretical thinking of this preoccupation, we contribute to making all types of struggle extremely vulnerable to co-option into new rounds of accumulation, since we do not recognise the common force that all these struggles are up against. Capitalist divide and rule is based not simply on diversity, but on a diversity in which each is pitted against the other, with a resulting hierarchy of powers and access to resources. To avoid confronting this reality is 'to evade, rather than surpass, the crucial point of Marx's analysis of "real subsumption" – the tendency of capital to impose its logic not just over the workplace, but over all areas of life' (Dyer-Witheford 1999: 188).

In reality, networks of social production and the emergence of 'centres' are always interrelated. In every social mode of cooperation, body subjects and singularities in general act through measure, and their activities are moments of feedback loops. Feedbacks are relational, that is, they put singular body subjects into given relations to each other, following certain patterns. The extent to which these loops are iterations repeated in certain ways gives rise to certain networks patterns constituting the social body. Global commodity chains (see Chapter 9) are networks emerging from measuring activities of particular types, those that reproduce capitalist values. In general, social networks are the emergent outcome of activities of singularities and in turn they are the preconditions for individual body subjects being in the world. Homeostatic processes can therefore only occur *through* networks and, vice versa, networks are the organising of the social body going through its homeostatic processes (Capra 1997: 82–3). Our study of social networks must thus always reflect the awareness of their link to some type of homeostatic process. Hence global networks of waged and unwaged labour constituting contemporary capitalist production and the struggles within it must be understood in terms of their relational links, the fact that their actions are constituents of feedback loops.

To understand networks as emergent from the repetition of homeostatic processes implies reconceptualising the problematic of 'centre' of power, not disposing of it. Traditionally, radical discourse, under the hegemony of orthodox Marxism, conceived this centre in a variety of guises: the state, the 'military–industrial' complex, the 'bourgeoisie', the particular hegemonic role of a country in relation to a regional area of influence or within an empire, and so on. This traditional notion embraced by dominant Marxist political culture that there is a 'place' from which power emanates (the centre: that is, on various scales, the state, a country, and so on), and the corresponding notion that power is something one *has* rather than a process-like *exercise*, has been extensively criticised in the last few decades from a variety of backgrounds and approaches. From Foucault, who thinks of power as a ubiquitous relationship among forces, to John Holloway's recent critique of 'power over' and emphasis on 'power to' and doing;[15] from feminist authors emphasising *relations and processes* of constitution of masculinity and femininity, to contemporary social scientists studying the 'network' society. If power can only be *exercised, the* fundamental political question becomes *how do we exercise* it? The problematisation of the mode of exercise of human power is the key to the politics of alternatives.

In the contemporary global field of social interactions, there is indeed no one visible centre of power that can be held responsible for how social relations are articulated and lived. Yet there is a multilateralism of 'centres', a plurality of institutions such as the IMF, the WB, governments, and so on, that are responsible – in different ways – for making sure that our interactions in the planet, what they call 'the economy', follow certain general modalities, and are organised around a certain *parametric centre*, the value norms emerging from the playing out of market relations. While making sure that our interactions increasingly take the form of market interactions is the realm of what we call enclosure, the sustaining and reproducing of this parametric centre is a matter of the disciplinary integration of singularities across the social body. We thus need to recast the problematic of the centre that we must overcome in a twofold way: in terms of both a *strategic* centre, which promote enclosures and commodification of life on the social body – that is, a context of social production; and also consequent emergent parametric centre, a centre of gravity of capital's homeostatic reproduction, which seems today to pervade all networks in the social body, all spheres of life. The study of this emergent parametric centre is the study of capitalist commodity production, of the valuing and measuring of capital.

13

The valuing and measuring of capital

MEASURING AND FEEDBACK

From the perspective of an individual actor or social 'agent', value is about selecting out, comparing within a system of reference, and acting upon this comparison. The question of 'measures' is therefore fundamental in any evaluation process that guides people's actions. What distinguishes different processes of value production is *how* we measure what we measure. In this section, before tackling the specific form of the capitalist measure of value, I want to provide some general reflections – not specific to capitalism – on the activity of measuring as an activity that integrates parts and wholes, individual and societies, body subject and social body.

In whatever mode of production and form of social relations, it is the meaning people give to them that ultimately guides their actions, including the actions that reproduce their livelihoods. In a general sense, we understand 'value' in terms of this meaning. Value, anthropologists tell us, is the way people represent the importance of their own actions to themselves. By representing this importance they have a guide to their action. In this first sense, value is a measure of doing from the perspective of singularities. However, we have seen in Chapter 2 that value does not spring from individuals isolated from the rest of society. Any action, or process, 'only becomes meaningful (in Hegelian language, takes on "concrete, specific form") by being integrated into some larger system of action' (Graeber 2001: 68). It is in relation to some notion of totality, a system of reference and comparison, that human values of whatever kind become intelligible. That human meaning is a matter of comparison, is something that

almost all classic traditions of the study of meaning agree on – dialectical, hermeneutic, and structuralist alike. ... Parts take on meaning in relation to each other, and that process always involves reference to some sort of whole: whether it be a matter of words in a language, episodes in a story, or goods and services' on the market. So too for value. The realization of value is always, necessarily, a process of comparison; for this reason it always, necessarily, implies an at least imagined audience. (Ibid.: 23)

In this second sense, value is a measure of doing as it emerges out of the perspective of the process-like articulation between individuals and the whole, singularities and multitudes, in an ongoing process of reference and comparison.

Third, and consequently, feedback is therefore central to the production of value. As we have seen in the last chapter on the question of the 'centre', any process-like articulation between individuals and the whole is a mode of articulation of social powers, constituting networks of singularities cooperating in certain ways. The activities of valuing singularities are moments of feedback loops. Feedback is relational, that is, it puts singular body subjects into certain relations to each other. The extent to which these loops are iterations, repeated in certain ways, gives rise to certain network patterns constituting the social body. In this third sense, *it is by pursuing value that we reproduce societies. Therefore, different types of value pursuit, hence of value practices, reproduce different types of societies, of wholes, of self-organising systems, of forms of social cooperation.* Hence the study of how we reproduce capitalist social relations is a study of how we pursue the values that are characteristic of it. The politics of alternatives is ultimately a politics of value, that is a politics of establishing what the value *is* that connects individuals and wholes.[1]

To put the question of value, or value practices, in this threefold manner, is to face up to the question of *measures*. A measure is *always* a discursive device that acts as a point of reference, a benchmark, a typical norm, a standard. It is thus a *relational* reference point that guides action of the singular body subject, yet it carries the weight of the habits, traditions and cultures of the social body. In our discourse therefore, the question of measures is the entry point for the study of the interrelation between body subjects and the social body.

We measure the distance between A and B using a socially defined standard of length, a yardstick. The child playing with fire has *learned* a physical, rather than social, norm (fire hurts), and acts accordingly. By approaching fire she measures her current action in relation to that standard she has learned: fire hurts, stay at a safe distance. Obviously, the child can also decide to play with the norm, to challenge it, and learn to fine-tune the precision of the measure: fire hurts, but if I quickly pass my finger through the candle flame I will feel only gentle warmth and impress my younger friends. The practice of measuring is in this case something utterly different from, say, the practice of measuring as conceived by a corporate manager, an economist, or a 'profit-maximising' agent.

Any of our actions can be mapped in relation to given norms; in this sense, to a variety of degrees, they are alter-norms. These norms can be set from outside and internalised or contested, welcomed or despised, forced upon the body subject or chosen by body subjects themselves. In other words, when we pose the question of measures here, we only intend to draw attention to the fact that in daily intercourse among body subjects we measure all the time and that a plurality of measuring processes is possible. Indeed, any degree of coordination and cooperation among the social body or any section of it is possible only through some type of measuring process, which allows the individuals' practices to gravitate around given norms and/or contest them and/or constitute new ones, and in any case result in *common* actions.

Also, measuring should not be intended necessarily as a rigid and mechanical comparison between a *given* norm and an object. This may be the case, of course, when we pick up a tape and measure the length of the new wardrobe to see whether it really fits in the bedroom. But from experience we can also see that a particular measure can be the result of social practice rather than its condition. A domestic vignette will do as an example: some time ago my partner and I reached an agreement always to leave a space in our small kitchen clear, to make it easier for any of us to prepare food, whatever might be the condition of the rest of the kitchen! Now, that space has become a socially defined norm, which individual body subjects use to measure their activities. Something that was the *result* of a decision-making process (in which the new was formed), has now become the standard *condition* of future production. Not only that, but the degree and form of commitment to that norm by each body subject has become the *centre of gravity* of a relational dance, in which play and conflict, pleasure and frustration, can emerge out of the social interaction *around* that norm. Norms and the activity of measuring constitute the parametric centre around which the *community* is organised. This centre is a *common*, which particular body subjects share, notwithstanding their *differences* in attitudes, needs and desires. No social relation among people can do without some types of commons that act as a centre of their interaction. Not even in capitalist production.

It goes without saying that norms need not be *decided*, they can as well emerge out of a social interaction, and become normalised without the body subjects becoming aware of these norms. All the same, social actors, depending on the powers they can exercise and their aspirations, can strive to dictate or abolish norms and corresponding measuring activities, or keep them unchanged, or modify them in changed circumstances. And circumstances will in turn depend on the interactions among body subjects redefining their needs and desires as well as the modalities of the exercise of power in the establishment of new norms and measuring activities.

To introduce the question of measures is thus to introduce the question of *process* and *feedback* in the articulation between social body and body subjects. This articulation can be conceptualised as in a *feedback* relation: this is a modern way of looking at an old insight, namely that we are *social* individuals (or subjects), and that we change the world, but in conditions that we do not choose (yet it is *we* who change it!). To introduce the problematic of measuring is to open up the question: *how* do we measure what we measure? Who or what sets the standard for the measurement? What forms of measurement are used in different discourses? What powers have been deployed and/or repressed with this or that measuring processes? And what loops articulate human practices to practices of measuring?

COMMODITY VALUES

Let us now move on to investigate in more detail the basic processes through which capital's value practices and corresponding measuring processes articulate body subjects and give form to networks of social cooperation. To do so, following Marx, we must start from the 'elementary form of bourgeois wealth', commodities, and enquire about how their exchange values are produced. When we approach the question of the production of monetary value of commodities, the form of value and value practices endlessly promoted by that social force we call capital, we have to investigate this *articulation* between the way people represent the importance of their own action to themselves in the form of monetary value, and the *whole* that constitutes their system of reference. Indeed, the problem becomes *how* the former constitutes the latter and the latter is a condition of the former.

Commodity values, process and struggle

Thus, in this and following sections we revisit a classic preoccupation of political economy, capitalist production of value, in the light of our previous discussion that emphasises the articulation between singularities and the social body and understands this articulation as a social *process* of measuring. To readers who are familiar with debates on the labour theory of value – which we cannot survey here and have briefly discussed in the last chapter – this approach may seem different from the traditional approach taken by Marxist economists. In the traditional approach, the concept of socially necessary labour time (which for Marx constitutes the quantitative measure of commodity values) is regarded as *distinct* and separated from *the process* of the constitution of commodity values, in that it is the result of *past* processes. This is not the case in the approach I take, in which socially necessary labour time is a sequential loop, which articulates the *past* and the perception of the *future* that guides the *present* action; it is a social standard as well as an individual singularity's positioning in relation to it; it is constituted by pervasive microconflictuality at the 'point of production' as well as sharp macro-conflicts; and it points at the link between production and reproduction as the terrain of this struggle. Furthermore, and as anticipated by Cleaver (1979), unlike in the approach taken by traditional Marxist economists, competition among capitals is not distinct from the process of class struggle, but is the form of its manifestation. Whether the phenomenon appears as competition or social conflict depends on the discursive political positionality of our reading.

Indeed, this 'sequential' way of looking at the formation of capitalist value – which to me is the only obvious way to look at commodity values as constituted by a continuous *social process of struggle over work* (its degree, nature, intensity, extension, rationales and pay off) – sits oddly with traditional Marxist approaches to political economy, which instead stress the 'structure' of quanta of labour values across society through input–output tables and simultaneous equations. Perhaps paradoxically, this structural approach is also the starting point of Negri's critique of the law of value, which we critically appraised in the last chapter. In *Empire*, when Antonio Negri and Michael Hardt argue that with the hegemony of immaterial labour the production of value is beyond measure, they mean that it is beyond the 'relation between labor and value in terms of corresponding quantities: a certain quantity of time of absolute labor equals a quantity of value' (Hardt and Negri 2004: 145). Marx, of course, was well aware of the fact that this correspondence did not even apply to the conditions of production of his own time, as both his work market values and prices of production show.[2] By recasting the question of the measuring of value in terms of *processes and class conflict*, I hope we can dispense with the bathwater in Negri's approach *without* throwing out the baby, that is without throwing out the emphasis on struggle, desires and immanence as the main coordinates of social constitution beyond capital.

My task here not only takes the approach that studies value as process and class struggle very seriously, but also wants to enquire *how* commodity values are about the processes of class struggle. To pose the question of the *how* is to highlight the question of the *mode* of relation/production/articulation linking up individual and society, singularities and social body; it is to understand the loops or feedback mechanisms articulating individual singularities *acting* in the *process* of reproducing their livelihoods. In a capitalist system, in which what has worth, 'wealth', takes the form of commodities, the reproduction of people's livelihoods and corresponding value practices is largely subordinated to the production of commodities.

External and immanent measures of value

As we have seen, value is the importance people attribute to action and as such is measured using discursively and culturally given units of measurement. Commodity value is this importance turned upside down: it is the importance people attribute to the *products* of their action, in so far as these products are objects of market exchange and the production is production for profit. When things have a price tag, it is these things that have value, not the human labour that has produced them. The importance of all commodities here is measured through money, i.e., units of a particular commodity (gold, silver, etc.) or, in modern times, signs of value (dollars, euros, etc.). We call this the *external* measure of value, and this is the most obvious measure of value with which we are all familiar. It is obvious that any product of human action presupposes action, but when we measure things using money, it is as it we have become myopic about this action, about *its* value. This myopia leaves us with problematic effects until we put on spectacles and realise that we socially value the actions of arms dealers hundreds of times more than those of nurses, we value the actions of stockbrokers hundreds of times more those of fire-fighters: their respective pay checks bear witness to this. We must of course be aware that there are ongoing struggles against this myopia, struggles over the visibility of the connection and articulation between non-commodity values and commodity values. These struggles are actually struggles among different value practices, and they *constitute* the social production of commodities.

It is the *way* this importance is effectively attributed, the *mode* in which this is done, that interests us here. It is in this mode that we uncover the secret of the reproduction of capitalist society and the connection between individuals and the social body peculiar to it. When we reflect on this connection, we encounter another measure of commodity value, a translation of the external one and one that shifts our attention from the done to the doing, from commodities to work, from things to life processes and their corresponding social relations. Following Marx, we can call this the *immanent* measure of value that corresponds to that labour which is socially necessary for the production of a commodity. As its corresponding external measure, *this immanent measure of value is also constituted by the ongoing working of capitalist disciplinary processes (and therefore value struggles) passing through markets*, as well as their state-implanted simulations. To appreciate this immanent measure we must look at the market as a *continuous* process of value (price) formation through the distribution of rewards and punishments and not, as in mainstream economics and a variety of strands of radical political economy, as a static structure.

This immanent measure of value is hidden from the view of the daily working of markets, from individuals' experience as commodity sellers and buyers, because it is a property that *emerges out of* the continuous process of their interaction. Yet it somehow fits in with the experience of being caught in a rat race to reproduce livelihoods. And when we bring this reflection to the foreground, we realise that the disciplinary mechanism that creates commodity values is at the same time the disciplinary mechanism that attributes value to the social actions that produced those commodities, that creates patterns of how we produce them, what we produce, how much of them we produce, how we relate to each other in producing them, what system of needs we create, and how we distribute our social doing, our *social labour* across the social body. Patterns in social cooperation in other words, to a large extent emerge from a disciplinary process to which we have subjected ourselves, a process that *includes* struggles against it.

But, as we have argued, value is the meaning people give to action. Individuals pursue value by comparing and referring to a whole. It is by pursuing value within the confinement of market relations that individual 'actors' compare monetary values of different products or compare values of the same products produced with different methods and conditions of production, and *act upon* this comparison. The *effects* of this acting enter into feedback relations with millions of others, they contribute towards producing new average prices and profits and they produce effects that act as material forces for other actors making similar comparisons and acting upon them. The ongoing process of these acts of measurement of value and the *actions* based on them is what gives rise to what we value socially, and it does so *whatever* is our individual or collective 'aggregate' *ethical* standpoint. In other words, to quote an archetypal 1960s hippy: 'It's the system, man!'

Capital's 'nervous system'

In order to see this more in detail, let us enter one of these loops among millions, and see how it articulates individuals and totality, parts and whole, hence how it creates values and reproduces the corresponding system of value. As we saw in Part I, the movement of the social force that we call capital in the pursuit of its own self-expansion can be portrayed with the money circuit M-C-M', which is composed by the act of 'buying', M-C and selling, C-M'. If buyers are found and the sale realised at sufficient unit prices, investors will be able to pocket the difference between the two sums of money as profit, that is $M' = M + \Delta M$, in which ΔM is the extra amount of money (profit) obtained. The M-C-M' circuit embeds a process of production in which, according to Marx, values are created by the activity of doing, labour. Linked to millions of similar M-C-M' loops, the money circuit of capital integrates different branches of social cooperation of labour in a broad sense. As we have seen in Chapters 5 and 6, all of these loops are organically linked to unwaged reproduction loops.

The integration occurs through the construction of a 'nervous system' across the social body called a price system, a nervous system that carries information of a particular type and that takes the form of monetary values. Prices, by representing rates of transformation of flows of commodities and money, act as signals to those involved in taking decisions. The set of prices and the set of signals they send to the different actors of the global economy constitute a sort of map of the nervous system of what we may call the global factory. The process of neoliberal globalisation has intensified market interaction across the globe, it has deepened the articulation of world regions and social practices through monetary 'nerve endings' (in the form of prices) that can signal back to the 'matrix' of the global market as to the productive state of the living productive cells (individuals) or complexes of cells (from families and communities to firms and nations, depending on the level of discursive aggregation). The global market is thus supposed to operate in this way like a central nervous system, although it is itself a network of places.

The signalling is highly complex, and is part of the homeostatic mechanism of self-preservation of capital which pits livelihoods against each other and enforces work discipline and the rat race on the social body. As with any nervous system, price signals are not just a matter of 'zeros' and 'ones'. They do not simply say that a given productive cell is on or off, that a commodity producer is out of business or is working fine, that in one region people are starving and not meeting their needs, but in another they are flourishing. Instead, price signals capture in a simple quantitative monetary expression a highly variegated range of states and their *differentials*. For example, price signals can index the cost-effectiveness with which a commodity is produced in relation to the same commodity produced in another place. They can signal the future prospective cost of producing a given commodity. They can register the effect of floods, strikes, social unrest and political instability, tax policies, advertising and similar brain-washing strategies, 'brand fidelity', and so on. They can, in other words, put order into chaos, but, of course, a particular *type* of order, one that is founded on the *self-preservation* and therefore *self-expansion* of capital.

Dear or cheap, commodities are sold or bought as a means of fulfilling particular desires by the actors in the markets, or, as Hayek puts it, particular 'plans'. Whether the end of these desires or plans is to meet the immediate needs of the body or the spirit, or instead these commodities serve as the means for the production of other commodities, is, from the perspective of the markets, irrelevant. In both cases, to individual actors in the market the information carried by prices is a condition for action. 'Shopping around' is common both to 'consumers' on a tight budget and wishing to make ends meet, as well as to capitalist investors wanting to maximise profits and needing to buy machines and hire workers. There is a difference however. While in the former case the flow of monetary value represented by those purchased commodities disappears from the consumer's pocket to allow consumption and the corresponding satisfaction of desire, in the latter case the desire or plan of the actors who purchase the commodities is to receive a greater flow of monetary value, that is, a profit. Monetary value is therefore not only retained, there is also the expectation of extra value added to it.

From the perspective of investors therefore the information received from the purchase price of the material components of production is not only measured in terms of alternative purchase prices. It is also measured in terms of the *expected* price that the commodity produced with the purchased machines and raw materials, as well as the hired or subcontracted workers, is able to fetch. An expected profit (the desire or plan of the investor) obviously corresponds to this expected sale price, profit being calculated from the difference between the expected sale price and the purchase price of the inputs of production. In turn, the expected sale price and the corresponding profit is measured by, that is, *compared to*, the given *average* price prevalent in the market. For new commodities, for which no corresponding market prices can serve as yardstick, or for commodities that take a long time to produce, a greater degree of risk is involved, a risk that investors seek to minimise, using market research about people's desires on the one hand, and advertising to 'persuade' and attempt to construct needs and desires on the other.

But the information carried by flows of monetary values in the forms of purchase and sale prices only stops at the gates of production, with the purchase of the material conditions of production, such as machines and raw materials, and of labour power, i.e., the M-C moment of the money circuit of capital. It is also a flow of monetary value that reappears in the sale of the finished product or service, that is C-M'. As Marx argues, in between these two moments there is the process of production, in which the flow of value transmutes into a flow of a different form. From flows of monetary value it turns into flow of human activity, doing, *labour*. Hence, when we look at this flow we cannot avoid interrogating the subjects of the doing and their system of relations and understanding of this flow of labour as a flow of emotions, energies, affects, whose turbulence reflects a struggle among *conflicting* value practices. On one hand, there are the value practices that aim at maximising flows of monetary value upon which survival in the market rat race depend. From *this* perpective, all other human value practices are subordinated to the monetary measure and profit. On the other hand, there are the value practices that constitute the social flows of doing, understood as a network of affects and reproduction, hence not simply as the means to an end, but as *life processes*. To put it differently, labour is a condition of endurance, and therefore a site of struggle. And the more this is so, the more the goals of labour, the means of labour, and the rhythms of labour belong to an alien *conatus* of self-preservation. In phases of political recomposition, such as crises of social stability, this pervasive struggle becomes the core disciplinary problem of *capital because struggles posit other values*. However, from a systemic point of view and from the perspective of daily working, this struggle is, as we shall see, its greatest driving engine, the life energy that gives rise to capital's own specific self-organising patterns in the attempt to preserve itself while facing the dangers posed by other value practices.

As we have seen, the lives of the doers, the subjects, are 'traversed' by different value practices that often conflict with each other, those that originate from their own experiences and images, their own bodily needs, desires, plans and corresponding modes of measuring, those in a word that constitute their own *conati* of self-preservation and well-being and are relationally linked to their own communities, and those instead that reproduce capital. To come out of the other end of the M-C-M' process and meet the plans of investors, the flow of monetary values has to go through this process of transfiguration, taming and subordinating the values and value practices of the doers and directing them towards a purposeful action the end of which is not theirs, but is to fulfil as much as possible the expectations of those who have 'invested' money in them.

An illustration

Now, let us consider this process of the transmutation of flows of monetary values into flows of doing and again into flows of monetary values as we follow the sequence M-C...P...C'-M' as a *continuous* process, and in which, following Marx, ...P... represents the production process. And as we do that let us consider the fact that this loop, this particular sequence M-C-M', is linked to others similar (M-C-M') or dissimilar (C-M-C) loops: those who sell or would like to sell them their inputs of productions (MP and LP), those who buy or could buy their commodities, and their direct or indirect competitors. All these links among loops are, in the sense that interests us here, information flows of the types described before when talking about prices. Yet let us also keep in mind that in each of these loops, whether other capitalist producers (M-C-M') or subsistence producers (C-M-C), there is a life process of doing, although in quite different organisational and motivational forms.

For example, let us imagine we are the executives of a company producing toys, say A' in Figure 6, competing with other toy firms A" and A'''. Each of the loops drawn in Figure 6 represents a specific M-C-M' cycle, although I only note the final phase C-M'. The price signals we receive from the market, b, tell us that someone out there, say A", is producing similar toys and selling them at lower prices, thus threatening our market shares and profit. In Figure 6, this is symbolised by the fact that all the toys producers A', A" and A''' try to sell their commodities at given prices in market b. As a managing director I must intervene and make sure that we take measures to defend our survival as a profit-making firm (indeed, within the present rules of the game, this is the only way for us to survive). So we act, we look at ways to reduce our unit price without affecting our profit margins (we will have here to strike a strategic balance between the short term and the expected long term), on which our existence depends, through the perceived solidity of our shares (and thus their market value). Somehow, there are always plenty of efficiency savings we can make, plenty of trimming, of things that we find redundant, that *from the perspective of the monetary value we seek and that guides our action*, are not really needed in the process of production. Somehow, there are always cheaper places, factories and offices can be relocated, there are always more cost-effective 'reproduction fields'. Of course, somehow, whenever we try to make cuts, there is always someone who complaints, who has reason to object, who counterpoises *other values* to those we seek as a competitive and profitable firm. Of course, we can always identify pockets of resistance, people who want us to live 'beyond our means', that are 'shirkers' who are undermining the competitiveness of all. The degree of resistance will of course depend on a variety of factors that do not interest us here, though they are, of course, fundamental to the definition of the actual *form* of the strategy and outcome. But the point here is that the reaction to a market signal of this kind corresponds to the deployment of strategies for overcoming some *internal resistance. The first systemic effect of our playing the role of managing director in acting from the information signals we have received is our attempt to overcome resistance.*

So let us assume that, to a variety of degrees, depending on the net result of social forces running in opposing directions and corresponding value practices, the usual menu of options is deployed: cuts are implemented, new ways of organising production are introduced, news demands for speeding up bodies and minds, new emotional strain, new forms of labour organisation, relocation and outsourcing. And if this is not sufficient, automation is introduced to increase productivity and thus reduce unit costs. Also, new product design ideas are promoted, including brand design. Finally, wages may be cut, workers may be switched from permanent to temporary contracts, or, on the contrary, those who show exceptional dedication to the monetary values pursued by the firm may be rewarded with permanent contracts. In any case, the community in which the workers reproduce their labour power will be affected; will have, for example, to compensate different rhythms and forms of work with different reproduction work. Two pay checks are needed today in a household to buy the standard of living that one wage bought yesterday, for example, and this is matched by different types of organisation of reproduction at home, different types of input of reproduction, such as the purchasing of more ready meals and less preparation of home-made dishes. A variety of processes of relational feedbacks will affect the changes occurring here. The point of this pretty obvious story is simply that whatever I am doing, the effect of the price signals I received as *benchmarks* from the market has reverberated throughout a production and reproduction chain, both of which are today increasingly taking up a global dimension, affecting the lives and livelihoods of a few people or of a few million, depending on the scale of the production and reproduction network.

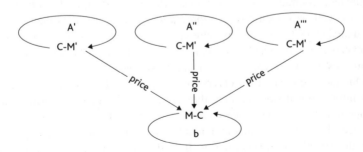

Figure 6   The formation of socially necessary labour time (SNLT)

Finally, I am ready to throw my new commodities back onto the market, but this time it is my price that will be able to send signals to the world. It will do that by virtue of a price that, to the observers and decision makers of other capitalist loops, will be the object of comparison, evaluation, measurement in the same way as it was for our original firm. After all, their own rates of profit and market share (affecting the volume of profit) will be threatened if the new resulting *average* market price puts them out of the market. Indeed, the process of restructuring in our original toy firm, a process that followed the information received by the market, has now produced information flows that have affected the market average price. However, if from the perspective of competitors this is only an information flow that informs their own action, from the perspective of the doers whose doing has allowed the production of commodities at the new price, it meant and still means particular forms of life flows and processes, work.

To us who are conceptualising this process and observing it as a whole, the two flows of monetary value and work cannot but be *related* and indeed what we have called the external and the immanent measures of value cannot but be two sides of the same coin, distinguishable when we look at things from different perspectives, two different moments and positionalities in an ongoing feedback loop. To us the new prices will signal, for example, whether and to what extent resistance has been overcome in that company, whether and to what extent the fragment of social doing that occurred within the confinement of that firm conforms to a social production norm, and to what extent and in what direction it deviates from it. Whatever is the result, one firm has now contributed towards changing the average price and thus *the benchmark* against which both our and our competitors' actions must be measured. From the perspective of the competing firms, with the ongoing process of measuring deviations from a price benchmark *and* contributing to its formation, the system creates a web of signals that constitutes the market system redistributing rewards and punishment in the forms of profits and losses.

From the perspective of the doers in all competing firms, as well as their communities, rewards and punishment in the forms of wages, job security, entitlement, contractual forms of labour, rhythms and form of work organisation, as well as conditions of reproduction make sure that their lives are articulated in a rat race ruled by values posited *outside* them. Looking at it from their perspective, the result is similar to looking at it from the perspective of the companies they work for, because from the perspective of the doing, too, new benchmarks are created for others to measure. But benchmarks here are not only informational flows; rather, they are concrete socially defined norms of production that describe *how* we produce, *what* we produce, and *how much* we produce.[3] It is also clear that individual parts of the social body might *deviate* from this social definition of norms. Indeed, in disciplinary markets the ongoing opposition among these deviations *constitutes* what Marx calls socially necessary labour time (SNLT) the norm that emerges from this ongoing opposition across the social body in the production of commodities. SNLT has a double meaning, depending on whether we look at it from the perspective of the whole of a co-producing social body or its parts. From the perspective of the whole, this is an average, the average labour time, which is necessary for the production of a particular commodity. But from the perspective of individual productive nodes, the same average is a *benchmark*, a discursive device that signals a particular type of information, an aid to decision making and action with respect to conditions of production and working rhythms. But as we have seen, these two perspectives, the perspective of the part and of the whole, are *articulated* by a *process*, a feedback loop that constitutes the value norm and that captures our life activities within it.[4]

It must be pointed out that the same mechanism can occur the other way round. Rather than receiving from the market a benchmark, firms might instead receive from communities a 'signal' of a different kind, a benchmark for 'environmental and labour standards', pollution levels or wage level and union rights. The extent to which communities are successful in making their 'signals' discipline firms to different norms, to different concepts of what is *socially necessary*, depends, of course, on the social force they are able to deploy, that they are able to mobilise, and the degree of their coordination and solidarity, which minimises the effects of their being pitted against each other. Thus, in the end, the socially necessary labour time of any commodity is the ongoing result of an interaction that passes through the market. However, at its core we find the struggles of communities over the doing of social life processes and the conditions for the reproduction of their livelihoods. Capitalist value is a relation of struggle (Cleaver 1979).

Capital's measuring of 'material' and 'immaterial' labour

We can illustrate the general features of this process of competitive interaction among different capitalists as an articulation among feedback processes as in Figure 7. Each of the phases of accumulation of branch A (the toy industry) plays a role in the formation of a SNLT, a standard of production. In the phase of sale (C-M′), each company will assess the market average, and consequently make its decision. At the same time, companies will also receive information from the market about their own inputs, and will ponder on whether it is convenient or not to continue to hire the same groups of workers, or to purchase from the same suppliers. These assessments of price deviations that occur in the two moments of circulation (M-C and C-M′) will demand different strategies, and indeed will have different implications, depending on the degree of monopoly or monopsony of the industry, but the value practices constituting this measuring process do not change in relation to market structure. The information collected in the process of circulation is then evaluated in such a way as to give rise to specific sets of strategies, all of which will have an effect on

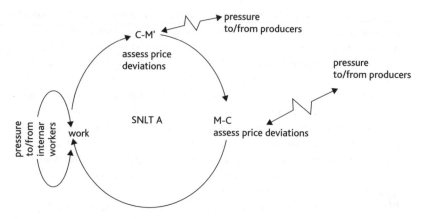

Figure 7   Homeostatic processes and SNLT

communities, near or distant, whether through changes in the composition of labour, effects on wages and entitlements, changes in suppliers or direct interventions in the patterns of work of their workers.

The communities will then have to compensate, and compensation is always through some type of struggle, whether the struggle of coping with new work patterns, the juggling of overlapping responsibilities between waged and unwaged work, or the struggles to get organised and collectively set a limit to the race.

It may appear that the discussion as presented thus far has at least two limitations. One is that our emphasis on the doing as a moment of conflict seems to portray the doers as victims of the initiative of capital, and therefore as putting up a struggle in the form of *resistance* to this initiative. I have here only followed a conventional Marxist narrative and sought to open it up. As I have indicated, from the perspective of the general features of this process the initiative can come – and indeed often does come – from the doers themselves and their communities. In this case, it is this initiative that sends a signal to the owners of capital and their administrators. But it must be pointed out that even in the classic case in which the initiatives come from the latter, the resistance which is put up by the doers can and often will take novel organisational and relational forms that give voice to new subjectivities.

There is also another limitation that may be pointed out. It is the fact that our treatment seems not to include a particular form of doing in production, a form that many observers believe is a peculiar contemporary feature of what they call post-Fordism, namely the doing that creates the new, that imagines, that innovates, and that is based on team work, forms of cooperation and relational labour among the doers, which give them a higher autonomy in conceptualisation and production than that possessed by the classic mass workers tied to assembly lines. As we have seen in Chapter 12, Hardt and Negri among others refer to this as 'immaterial labour' and argue that this form of labour is beyond capitalist measure precisely because it is a form of social cooperation that is constituted by relational and communicational patterns defined by the doers themselves (hence measured by themselves). While it might be argued that 'no transcendent power or measure will determine the values of our world [since] value will be determined only by humanity's own continuous innovation and creation' (Hardt and Negri 2000: 356), it is also true that when innovating and creating singular producers are pitted against each other in an endless rat race, the values that emerge from this ongoing clash are measurable by capital. Indeed, it is through this antagonistic mode of relation among social producers that capital values are constituted.

Thus, the ongoing creation of SNLT is a feature not only of what is called, 'material' (capitalist) production, but also of what is referred to as 'immaterial' (capitalist) production, i.e., the production of ideas and affects (see Figure 8). Here too we can have *ongoing* competition among producers who are then locked in the feedback loop of their own rat race against each other. What is continuously compared in order to give rise to differentials are here the perceived quality of ideas, whether in the form of creative work for advertising or that leading to product or process innovation, and improvements in the time and efficiency of their execution, of getting the job done. All the same, in terms of affects, what is measured is not only the speed of service, but also the per- ceived service quality as measured by given indicators: smiling, 'costumer satisfaction', and so on. In both these cases, the set of systematic pressures is the same as in the traditional case of 'material' work. The work of a waitress *having* to smile at an unpleasant customer, or a cashier instructed to utter the sentence 'how-are-you-doing-do-you-have-a-loyalty-card-have-a-nice- day' not only reproduces within the doing subjects the conflict among value practices we were talking about in the case of material workers, but also poses specific *limits* to the communicational range and forms of immaterial works. Indeed, with respect to this immaterial labour, the degree of autonomy of the doers has precise limits defined by processes of capitalist measurement and *not* by the creative workers themselves. The *selection* of new ideas that can be turned into products or processes of doing occurs with respect to the SNLT process of measurement. The communicational patterns within work teams are bounded by the priorities set by their employers and managers, who measure the results of these communicational patterns in terms of price, qual- ity and profit deviations from benchmarks. Nurses, doctors, teachers have a variety of degrees of autonomy, but are increasingly exposed to measures imposed from *outside* themselves which are heteronymous, which instruct them, *in a context of declining resources and numbers of staff*, to meet cer- tain quality targets that relate in one way or another to external benchmarks (Harvie 2005).

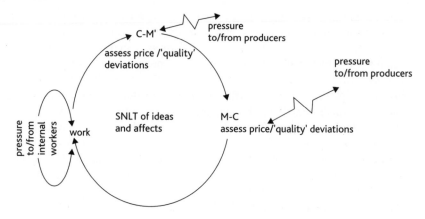

Figure 8   SNLT of ideas and affects

In many public services in which competition *does not* exist and workers
have a long tradition of cooperation (education, health), state bodies instead
simulate competition by constructing league tables according to given criteria,
and funding is linked to the meeting of these criteria. In the United Kingdom,
for example, the ultimate market punishment – bankruptcy – is 'simulated' for
those schools and hospitals that are said to 'fail' to meet these criteria and they
are closed down, with the effect that the children and the patients displaced will
go to other schools and hospitals starved of resources, thus intensifying the
waged work of teachers, nurses and doctors left on the job and the unwaged
work of communities who have now to balance their lives, sending children to
more distant schools, going through the emotional work of countering the
heteronymous forces whose reasons are difficult to rationalise.

MEASURING AND STRUGGLES

We have seen that to investigate the specific form of value of the capitalist
mode of production is to investigate this articulation between the way people
represent the importance of their own action in terms of money and the *whole*
that constitutes their system of reference. But, since the values that guide people's action are also *non-monetary values*, to investigate commodity values is
to investigate the *articulation* between them, the articulation between the
actions sparked by different *ways and meanings* that people have to represent
the importance of their own action. At any given moment, both non-monetary
and monetary values guide people's action, and they often do it in conflicting
ways, as they indicate different directions, *teloi* or *conati*. It seems to me that
this articulation between different value practices, both at the level of the
subject and at the level of the social forces that their networks give rise to, is

what we call class struggle. This struggle is *class* struggle in so far as the social forces guided by non-monetary values posit themselves as limits, in given contexts and conditions, to capital's accumulation, to the pursuit and accumulation of monetary value at whatever scale of social action.[5]

It is obvious that, stated in these terms, class struggle is pervasive in society. It is in the workers demanding higher wages, and in 'consumers' boycotting a brand. It is in environmentalists stopping the construction of a new airport terminal, and in women questioning the traditional division of labour and its corresponding relations. It is in refugees crossing borders, in landless peasants reclaiming land and in indigenous people reclaiming dignity. But it is also in the universe of micro-conflictuality happening at any scale of social cooperation. All these and many others are instances of non-monetary value practices and the corresponding social forces that in given contexts and circumstances posit a limit to capital and its own specific value practices. Unless the different value practices posited by these movements are able to weave themselves into self-sustaining social feedback processes that are alternative to the parametric centre of capital's value mechanism and its corresponding mode of relations, these struggles risk being either repressed or assimilated into capitalism's evolving forms. We need to work through a politics of value that problematises strategically how we sustain new social relations of production, new value practices through which we reproduce our individual livelihoods and their articulation, vis-à-vis the value practices of capital that, through enclosures and a pointless competitive rat race, reproduce scarcity while we could be celebrating abundance.

Unless the different values posited by these various movements are articulated in a new way to give rise to a feedback mechanism that hits at the centre of capital's value mechanism and its corresponding mode of relations, one by one these struggles will either be repressed or subsumed into capital. It is subsumption that interests us here, the subtle strategy of turning enemies into best allies (or preventing those who present themselves as best allies from turning into enemies). When this happens, class struggle does not disappear, but turns into the systemic underlying *pulse* that is converted into price, profit and interest rates indicators on some investment bank's computer screen or in the financial columns of daily newspapers. The effect of any wage rise or fall, of environmental regulation or deregulation, of technological transformation, of restructuring and corresponding productivity increases, of social, cultural and technical innovations – not to speak of the effect of budget policies or of the size and composition of fiscal expenditure and revenue – ripples through the social body constructed as market system and is codified by capital as a new deviation in *value* (*its* value as expressed in relative prices, government bonds, shares, profit indicators, and so on); hence it constitutes a guide for action (the action of some 'economic' agent who will seek to invest, disinvest, restructure, re-regulate, and so on). Depending on the extent to which the ongoing struggles are dispersed through the social field, relatively isolated from each other, with values that have not meshed and thus are not able to question the parametric centre of capital, its mode of creating value, they can be articulated systemically by disciplinary markets. That is, the activities, values and desires of struggling subjects can be pitted against each other and in thus doing create capital's value. As we have seen, the process of creating socially necessary labour time is precisely this articulation. The type of activity used to measure capital's value and the action that follows is the process of class struggle viewed *from the point of view* of capital's self-preservation. To put it bluntly, it is not that on one side there is competition among capitals and on the other there is class struggle, as in much of the Marxist vulgate, so that we can say that one causes the other or both cause something else. No, class struggle and competition (qua process and mode of social cooperation) are two ways of seeing the same thing from two different *world-views and corresponding value-guiding actions.*[6] One, competition, is a discourse that measures social cooperation with the yardstick of monetary value deviations. The other, class struggle, is a discourse that measures social cooperation as a conflict between a multitude of yardsticks and the yardstick of capital's value. At this point of conflict, one value is outside the other. However, when the points of conflict are pitted against each other through their systemic integration in disciplinary markets (that pit livelihoods, needs, desires and needs against each other), then the multitude of values is subsumed in capital's self-preservation: capital evolves by channelling the values singularly opposed to it, and the corresponding actions, into webs of market relations. Thus the values singularly opposed to it can find expression in new commodities and corresponding use values, or new modes of organisation of production that take into account environmental targets, and so on, and corresponding modes of regulation. Yet this multitude of values and corresponding practices is subsumed as capital's value deviations. Capital thus evolves and changes its forms of social organisation, takes on board new cultural mores and turns the newly acquired freedoms in the social body into new creative ideas for selling commodities. But what is left is the fact that the epochal change reproduces the same basic features of all epochs of capitalist production, the same set of social relations of production across the social body, the same rat race and corresponding social creation of scarcity, the same flows of winners and losers, the same horror statistics; only on a greater scale, with a different set of commodities, with different degrees of 'deepening' across the social body and different socio-cultural relational fabrics.

Indeed, in order to be subsumable, struggles must to some extent be dispersed across the social field, because their dispersion and relative isolation facilitates their integration into capitalist markets. If struggles circulate and coagulate, there emerges a political recomposition that is able to articulate all these values opposing capital's value, to sustain them, to give force to their constitutive action as a new mode of relations, an *absolute* limit to capital in that it is a limit to the production of its value.

The struggle for alternatives to this must find a way to go beyond *that* struggle, the struggle the subsumption of which gives rise to the mechanisms described in the last chapter, the constitution of norms of production throughout the social body behind the backs of the producers themselves. To overcome this is to go beyond the value-generating powers of the *system* and pose new social relations on the basis of new values and new ways of articulating values. The search for new value practices however, cannot be defined in abstract. The issue of alternatives to a mode of articulation is not an 'ethical' question that can be addressed with the correct application of abstract principles and norms. Abstract principles must be seen as the emergent properties of concrete subjects positing their concrete values in different contexts. Values of this kind, I would argue, can only emerge from communities in struggle constituting their own measures, their own commons.

14
Market freedom and the prison: Hayek and Bentham

As we have seen in Chapter 7, we can distinguish processes of disciplinary integration *within productive nodes* from those occurring *among productive nodes*. Those from *within* productive nodes are those that emerge in specific organisations, within which market exchange relations do not occur. Relations among productive nodes that are linked by relations of market exchange characterise the others. In the first, power relations, surveillance and information flow through all sorts of media (emails, cameras, reports, direct supervision, control of output and performance, management systems); in the second, the same flows occur through the feedback processes of the price system, as discussed in the previous chapter. From the point of view of the system of disciplinary integration as a whole, this is the *main* difference, which is a difference not in terms of the rationales and effects of discipline, but in the means of communication it employs.

To clarify this, I argue in this chapter that a socially pervasive market order such as the one we inhabit presents organisational and disciplinary characteristics that are similar to those of a prison, not just any prison, and not merely a prison, but an 'inspection house', as understood by Jeremy Bentham who, in the late eighteenth century, enthusiastically designed what he called 'the panopticon' in order to extract work from the inmates and deal with emerging problems of social control. The reader may find this comparison odd, if not paradoxical. After all, the market and the panopticon seem to inhabit two different universes. The former, following the narrative of its promoters, is the galaxy of freedom, the order of a *cosmos*, emerging as an unintended result of the interaction of choices freely made by individuals. The latter is the constellation of dungeons, the *taxis* designed by the freedom of the planner who holds in a vice the lives of the subjects of the plan and who has a project in mind and wants to put it to work. Hayek, the paladin of market freedom and spontaneous order, seems so distant from Jeremy Bentham and his likes, the rationalist constructionists with their designed orders.[1]

Yet, in this chapter I argue that there is a common theoretical plane between the market mechanism understood in Hayek's terms as a mechanism of coordination of individual plans, and Bentham's principle of panopticism, understood as a disciplinary device for the secure management of a multitude and the extraction of labour. Clearly, this common theoretical plane cannot be found in what Hayek and Bentham supposed were the sources of their respective mechanisms (the market for Hayek and the panopticon for Bentham). Here they obviously differ. While Bentham's panopticon is designed, Hayek believes that the market order is the result of spontaneous evolution, and he does not acknowledge a substantial role for power, struggles and states in the emergence of property rights, for example, through a variety of enclosures.[2] Hayek's understanding of the role of the market order and Bentham's understanding of the panopticon can be compared once we abstract from Hayek's metaphysical views on the spontaneous evolution of markets, and regard Hayek's market and Bentham's panopticism as two given mechanisms, considering their rationales rather than their believed genealogy.

But again, even abstracting from their perceived genealogical differences, a prison, even loosely defined as an 'inspection house', is different from a market. The fact that they may share something in common does not make them similar. A pine tree is certainly different from an oak tree, and this difference is not even overcome when one notices that they share the basic processes of photosynthesis, although the latter is the basis for their general classification as plants. So, in a sense, in this comparison I am interested to find out the common ground between these prima facie so diverse social organisations. It is this common ground that, as in the case of different trees, would allow us to recognise them as two different *forms* of the same thing. The implication of this is important. If the capitalist market and the 'inspection house' (the plan) are two forms of the same thing, and this thing, as I shall show, is ultimately a disciplinary mechanism in which the individuals' freedom is limited to a choice from a given menu and they are prevented from defining the *context* of their interaction, then emancipatory political theory and practice must find a way beyond this dichotomy, to discover *forms* of social interaction that cannot be reduced to the disciplinary and organisational features of the market or the prison.

As far as I know, the common ground between the market order and the panopticon has never been highlighted by a comparative analysis. There is of course a good reason for this. The two authors belong to two different strands of liberal thinking. Bentham was regarded by Hayek as a rationalist constructivist who, together with Descartes, Hobbes and Rousseau, held the 'erroneous conception' that societies can give themselves 'laws' in accordance with some high principle of justice (Hayek 1973: 95). For utilitarianism, optimisation of pleasure provides the only rule by which to judge the institutions governing human behaviour ('the greatest happiness for the greatest number'). For Hayek this rule would rely on the assumption of omniscience, an assumption the challenge of which is at the basis of all Hayek's major theoretical contribution.

With Bentham's panopticon, however, unlike in his general utilitarian philosophy, omniscience is *not* a pre-given assumption, nor a result of the social interaction organised by the panopticon. Instead, the need for the panopticon as a mechanism of inspection arises, so to speak, out of the acknowledgement of the ignorance of the 'central planners'. Like the market for Hayek, the panopticon for Bentham provides a mechanism for overcoming this ignorance. In the order of the panopticon there is never the presumption that power 'knows everything', only that the inspected, the unwilling participant in this order, would *conceive* power as omniscient. On the other hand, power in this order acknowledges the 'tacit' aspect of this 'knowledge of the inspected', and the panopticon order is designed precisely to capitalise on this. Prima facie, therefore, there are important similarities between Hayek's and Bentham's systems. The similarities that emerge in an initial superficial comparison are, I believe, confirmed when one analyses the two systems in detail.

In this chapter I review the broad features of both Hayek's idea of market order and Bentham's *panopticism*. I then discuss the overlap between the two systems, while in the next chapter I briefly discuss the implications of the common theoretical plane between these two apparently opposite systems. Here I suggest that the current global market order can be theorised in terms of a 'fractal panopticon', that is a series of overlapping and interrelated virtual 'inspection houses' in which competition *and* the configuration of property rights combine to constitute a global disciplinary mechanism in the form of market freedom.

MARKET ORDER

Hayek's spontaneous order vs. designed order

Hayek's general theory of spontaneous order points out that capitalism is the unintended outcome of the widespread observance of certain 'non-designed', unplanned norms. Hayek identifies an important dualism between designed and spontaneous order, 'a profound tension between the goals of designed institutions and the resulting spontaneity of an evolving order' (Sciabarra 1995: 31).[3] This tension between two extreme ordering principles of individual activities *within* a systemic whole constitutes the horizon of intervention of Hayek's academic and political work.

To put the problem of order at the centre and to point to its spontaneous emergence implies a conceptualisation of the individual as *social* individual. This is not only because 'Living as members of society [we are] ... dependent for the satisfaction of most of our needs on various forms of co-operation with others' (Hayek 1973: 36). Adam Smith had already recognised this social dimension of production. But unlike Smith and the methodological individualism of neoclassical economists, Hayek's whole is more than the sum of its parts, because it includes *relations* among the members. In this order, 'each element affects and is affected by the others, jointly constituting and being constituted by the whole' (Sciabarra 1995: 31). Because of these relations, the whole is not apprehensible through a synoptic understanding. The structure of social order can only be grasped from a specific vantage point (ibid.).

We should not be enchanted by Hayek's social individual. The latter is a social individual of a particular kind, defined *ex post*, after a given configuration of property rights poses individuals as *private* individuals.

The problem of order emerges from this definition of individuals as private (in Marx's sense (1975), as alienated). By virtue of being fragmented private individuals, they have expectations and plans that do not match. The 'matching of the intentions and expectations that determine the actions of different individuals is the form in which order manifests itself in social life' (Hayek 1973: 36).

This matching of expectations of *private* individuals can, according to Hayek, be the result of two ordering principles, one of which 'derives ... entirely from the belief that order can be created only by forces outside the system (or "exogenously")' (ibid.). This is the authoritarian ordering principle. In the other principle, an order is 'set up from within (or "endogenously") such as that which the general theory of the market endeavours to explain. A spontaneous order of this kind has in many respects properties different from those of a made order' (ibid.).

The superior character of spontaneous order in relation to designed order resides in the use that this order makes of knowledge in society (Gray 1998:28). Because 'knowledge ... exists ... solely as the dispersed bits of incomplete and frequently contradictory knowledge which all the separate individuals possess' (Hayek 1945: 77), the economic problem of society is thus not merely a problem of how to allocate 'given' resources – if 'given' is taken to mean given to a single mind, which deliberately solves the problem set by these 'data'. It is rather a problem of how to secure the best use of resources known to any of the members of society, for ends whose relative importance only these individuals know. Or, to put it briefly, it is a problem of the utilisation of knowledge which is not given to anyone in its totality (ibid.: 77–8).

The problem of social order is thus a problem of how social knowledge is created and distributed among private individuals, and what rules or patterns are created to connect and match their independent plans.[4] Knowledge thus not only takes up the form of individual plans, i.e., private purposes, but also that of *praxis*, of rules followed by private individuals in their interaction.[5]

Private individuals follows three kinds of rules, and these 'chiefly negative (or prohibitory) rules of conduct ... make possible the formation of social order'. First, there are those 'rules that are merely observed in fact but have never been stated in words'. Second, 'rules which we are able to apply, but do not know explicitly'. The second type of rules, 'though they have been stated in words, still merely express approximately what has long before been generally observed in action'. Finally, there are those 'rules that have been deliberately introduced and therefore necessarily exist as words set out in sentences'. The problem with all kinds of constructionist approaches is that they 'would like to reject the first and second groups of rules, and to accept as valid only the third group' (Hayek 1970: 8–9).

The first and second groups of rules constitute tacit knowledge. It is precisely because of tacit knowledge that, according to Hayek, a central authority cannot solve the coordination problem. The latter would not only face the impossible task of collecting all the information from individual agents, including the tacit components, but it would also have to feed back to agents, the information necessary to adjust individual plans to the central authority's master plan. The only way to solve this problem is through a *mechanism* that uses *individual knowledge*, but at the same time in which each individual is *ignorant* of the overall outcome. The solution lies in the duality between individuals' *absolute sapience* of (and engagement with) their private spheres and purposes (which include tacit components), and individuals' *absolute ignorance* of (and indifference to) the forms and outcomes of their interactions. The model is a characteristic model of utter systemic opportunism; 'I am only doing my job,' says Hayek's individual, never pondering about the social meaning of that 'job'. That is, about how that job is articulated within the whole.

The market

Let us now see the qualities of 'spontaneous order' understood as market order. The market system is, according to Hayek, the best example of this evolved set of institutions. It is an impersonal *mechanism* with a problem to solve, that of coordinating individual knowledge and plans. This problem is discernible only if we drop the unrealistic assumptions of neoclassical economics that can show the benefit of competition only in the presence of an unlimited number of suppliers of a homogeneous commodity.[6] Unlike neoclassical economics, which discusses competition using assumptions which '*if* they were true of the real world, would make it wholly uninteresting and useless', because if everybody knew everything, then competition would result in a wasteful method of coordination among individuals, Hayek proposes to consider competition as a 'discovery procedure' (Hayek 1978: 179).

Mainstream economic theory cannot understand the true function of competition, because its starting point is a *given* supply of scarce goods (ibid.: 181). However, the discoveries of what and how much to produce; of 'which goods are scarce goods, or which things are goods, and how scarce and valuable they are' (ibid.: 182); of the 'minimum cost of production', or of the desires and attitudes of unknown customers (Hayek 1946: 100–1; Hayek 1978:182); these are all precisely what the market is supposed to find out. Note that, this 'finding out' by the market is at the same time a material force. Scarcity is a result produced by market interaction, not a presupposition, since the process of competition in the market creates needs and wants. Unlike the classical political economy tradition, prices are not only the expression of past activity, but are the information signals that excite future activity, that allow individuals to focus their attention on what is worth producing and what is not. The price system is a communication system. Knowledge that is widely dispersed throughout society can thus become effectively utilised (Hayek 1978:181–2, 188), not simply as the *know-how* necessary for the production of individual commodities, but as a social force that makes it *necessary* to produce in certain ways and for certain purposes.

This compulsory aspect embedded within Hayek's liberal philosophy of freedom acquires a systemic character, and pervades the context within which he argues that private individuals can exercise their liberty. By letting themselves be guided by these common indicators (ibid.: 60) private individuals have learnt to substitute abstract rules for 'the need of known fellows' and for coercive, imposed ends (ibid.: 61). In this condition, the relation of the individual with the 'other' is not direct, but mediated by 'a system of abstract relations' in which 'individual man can be directed by the private knowledge of his own purposes, and not by the knowledge of other people's needs, which is outside the range of his perceptions' (ibid.: 268).

The order brought about by the market is one that never reaches the equilibrium position that neoclassical economists talk about, but only ever approximates it. This is because individual plans never finish mutually adjusting through a series of negative feedback signals, the same ones defined by Smith under the category of the 'invisible hand' that regulate prices in a market (ibid.: 184). Mutual adjustment of expectation is only one of the unintended outcomes of the market order. The other is efficiency. The market 'also secures that whatever is being produced will be produced by people who can do so more cheaply than (or at least as cheaply as) anybody who does not produce it ... and that each product is sold at a price lower than that at which anybody who in fact does not produce it could supply it' (ibid.: 185).

These aggregate demand and supply curves of economic analysis, therefore, are not, in reality, pre-given, 'but results of the process of competition going on all the time' (ibid.: 187). Thus the formation of prices resembles the incessant and continuous process of formation of socially necessary labour time that Marx (1976a) refers to (see Chapter 13 and De Angelis 2004b). Like any disciplinary process (Foucault 1977), this one too is constructed through the dynamic duality of rewards and punishments. Thus Hayek presents the social setting as a drawing that awaits the colouring of flesh-and-blood power relations. The forces of social change are portrayed in their strategic setting, but the power relations within which these forces are embedded are completely invisible. Power is left as a merely implicit issue. Changes may occur only if 'the few willing and able to experiment with new methods *can make it necessary for the many* to follow them, and at the same time to show them the way' (Hayek 1978: 187, my emphasis). The ways to 'make necessary' the 'required changes in habits and customs' are of course in principle endless, and all have to do with a form of power. But implicit in Hayek's point is that, ultimately, there are two camps: those who are for change and those who are not, because it is not in their interests. Competition creates a continuous compulsion and a resistance to this compulsion:

The required discovery process will be impeded or prevented, if the many are able to keep the few to the traditional ways. Of course, it is one of the chief reasons for the dislike of competition that it not only shows how things can be done more effectively, but also confronts those who depend for their incomes on the market with the alternative of imitating the more successful or losing some or all of their income. Competition produces in this way a kind of impersonal compulsion which makes it necessary for numerous individuals to adjust their way of life in a manner that no deliberate instructions or command could bring about. (Hayek 1978: 189)

But why is continuous 'change' necessary? In the presence of Hayek's rejection of a 'hierarchy of ends' to evaluate human societies, the criteria brought forward by Hayek that justify this continuous compulsion are the identification of an abstractly defined 'progress' as an end in itself: 'Progress is movement for movement's sake' (Hayek 1960: 41). This idealisation of movement for movement's sake, irrespective of the direction of the movement, its social outcome, what is produced and how needs are formed and met, and irrespective of the nature of social interaction, makes Hayek the quintessential capitalist apologist.[7]

There are two implications of this. First, that 'competition is valuable *only* because, and so far as, its results are unpredictable and on the whole different from those which anyone has, or could have, deliberately aimed at'. Second, 'that the generally beneficial effects of competition must include disappointing or defeating some particular expectations or intentions' (Hayek 1978: 180). The latter means that in the functioning of the market order (ibid.: 185) 'a high degree of coincidence of expectation is brought about by the systematic disappointment of some kind of expectations'. The market order rewards some, punishes others. The continuous process of compulsion and the series of rewards and punishments 'going on all the time', that is, the process of competition, have the property identified by Foucault (1977) as that of a 'disciplinary mechanism'. Bentham's panopticon is also one of these devices.[8]

PANOPTICISM

A 'new mode of obtaining power'

Bentham certainly does not claim the panopticon to be an emergent order. Prima facie, in his model of the 'inspection house' there is little rhetoric of the

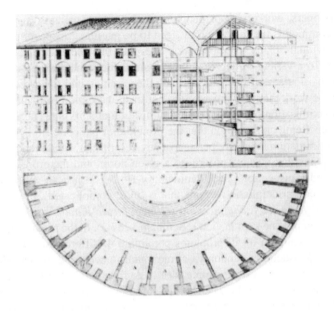

Figure 9   Plan of the panopticon.
Source: Bentham (1787)

evolution of freedom. The panopticon is unmistakably an institution of confinement, intended to facilitate the extraction of labour, and one designed precisely for this double purpose.

The panopticon is a circular building with at the centre a watchtower with large windows. The peripheral ring is subdivided into cells, each of which has a window facing the outside and one facing the tower. The light coming from the outside window, therefore, allows the occupants of each cell to be seen, as if in many little shadow theatres (Foucault 1977). Meanwhile the inspectors in the central tower, protected by blinds and by an opposite source of light, are at all times invisible to the eye of the occupant of each cell.

The cover of the 1787 project document boasts the general principle of the panopticon (here called, following Foucault (ibid.), *panopticism*). Its applicability, according to Bentham, is generalisable to any circumstance in which, to use Hayek's terms, individual plans do not match (of course, in the case of the panopticon, the plans that do not match are those of the individual inmates vis-à-vis those of the inspector). As described on the front cover, the panopticon contains

the Idea of a New Principle of Construction applicable to any Sort of Establishment, in which Persons of any Description are to be kept under Inspection. And in Particular to Penitentiary-Houses, Prisons, Houses of Industry, Work-Houses, Poor-Houses, Manufactories, Mad-Houses, Hospitals, and Schools.

What prisoners, workers, poor people, 'mad' persons, patients, and students have in common is the fact that they need to be put under inspection, because their individual 'plans' do not match the plan that Bentham has in mind for them. To a variety of degrees, they all share the same desire for *escaping* from the particular confinement in which they are put, and for *exercising less effort* in the work that they are asked to perform. Inspection fulfils this double role of maximisation of security and minimisation of shirking. The innovation arises from Bentham's opinion that the principle of panopticism is generalisable to any situation in which 'persons of any description' would tend to follow or make plans that do not conform to a given norm, and therefore require to be kept under inspection. The 'Penitentiary-House' is just an application of the panopticon principle, in fact one that is 'most complicated', in which 'the objects of *safe-custody, confinement, solitude, forced labour,* and *instruction,* were all of them to be kept in view' (Bentham 1787:3). In the preface, Bentham promises the solution of all problems pertaining to different spheres (health, education, production, economy, crime management and public finance) through the application of 'a simple idea of Architecture', that is, by a spatial configuration of *relations* between bodies, through the arrangement of bodies in space: 'Morals reformed – health preserved – industry invigorated – instruction diffused – public burthens lightened – Economy seated as it were upon a rock – the Gordian knot of the Poor-Laws not cut but untied – all by a simple idea of Architecture!' (ibid.: iii).

This is a principle for the management of power relations, and nothing else. In particular, it is a principle to increase the power of the 'inspectors' over the 'inspected', thus allowing the latter to be put into 'useful use'. The norm is usefulness of the inspected body. Without proper application of the principle of the panopticon, 'persons of any description' would tend not to conform to a given norm, and would therefore require to be kept under inspection. This 'new mode of obtaining power, of mind over mind, in a quantity hitherto without example,' offered by the panopticon, is based on a simple principle: 'the *centrality* of the inspectors' situation, combined with the well known and most effectual contrivances for *seeing without being seen*' (ibid.: 21).

This introduces immediately a quality in the relation of power. Power is exercised not just by the actual presence of the inspector over the inspected. The inspected does not need to *have full knowledge* of being inspected and the inspector *does not have* full knowledge of the plans and behaviour of the inspected. In fact, this 'ideal perfection' is not possible, because it 'would require that each person should actually be … constantly … under the eyes of the persons who should inspect them'. Thus, 'this being impossible, the next thing to be wished for is, that, at every instant, seeing reason to believe as much, and not being able to satisfy himself to the contrary, he should *conceive* himself to be so' (ibid.: 3).

This situation would enable 'the *apparent omnipresence* of the inspector ... combined with the extreme facility of his *real presence*' (ibid.: 25). The *conception*, rather than the reality, of constant surveillance is what gives the inspector a god-like character (omnipresence). To paraphrase Hayek, Bentham knows that the individual in authority – the inspector – cannot have full knowledge of the inspected, his actions and his plans. But Bentham uses an architectural design to reverse this potential ignorance and turn it into a potential knowledge to the advantage of the inspectors.

Modularisation and productivity of power

Another aspect of the generalisable character of the panopticon principle is in the modularisation of its constituent parts: the peripheral ring, the central tower and the relations among them. This means that the principle of the panopticon could cover 'an area of any extent.' For example:

If the number of rotundas were extended to *four*, a regular uncovered area might in that way be inclosed: and, being surrounded by covered galleries, would be commanded in this manner from all sides, instead of being commanded only from one.

The area thus inclosed might be either *circular* like the buildings, or *square*, or *oblong*, as one or other of those forms were best adapted to the prevailing ideas of beauty or local convenience. A chain of any length, composed of inspection-houses adapted to the same or different purposes, might in this way be carried round an area of any extent. (Ibid.: 18)

The panopticon therefore does not need a *singular centre*; it may well be constituted by a series of centres, as long as they are *integrated*.

Another aspect of the panopticon is that it leads to an emergent property, that of economy of scale in the production of inspection, the '*inspection force*':

On such a plan, either one inspector might serve for two or more rotundas, or, if there were one to each, *the inspective force*, if I may use the expression, would be greater in such a compound building than in any of the number, singly taken, of which it was composed: since each inspector might be relieved occasionally by every other. (Ibid.: 19)

It must be pointed out that this increased productivity of inspection depends on the increased pervasiveness of the panopticon principle, to *see without been seen*, once more 'rotundas' are integrated. In other words, the greater the number of integrated rotundas, the more efficiently power can be organised through a panopticon principle. This panoptical 'efficiency of scale' of inspections is therefore an important quality that allows the panopticon to be extended beyond the confinement of a single institution.

Unwaged work of inspection

As part of the increased efficiency of inspection, the panopticon also allows the co-optation of the inspector's family's unwaged labour. Provided

that room be allotted to the lodge ... for the principal inspector ... and his family, ... the more numerous ... the family, the better; since, by this means, there will in fact be as many inspectors as the family consists of persons, though only one be paid for it. (Ibid.: 23)

Bentham is very clear on why this should be the case, why the members of the family of the head inspector would want to perform the duties of the family head. It is an utterly *free* choice, but one which arises out of a *context* that has been entirely engineered, planned, designed.

Neither the orders of the inspector himself, nor any interest which they may feel, or not feel, in the regular performance of his duty, would be requisite to find them motives adequate to the purpose. Secluded oftentimes, by their situation, from every other object, they will naturally, and in a manner unavoidably give their eyes a direction conformable to that purpose, in every momentary interval of their ordinary occupations. It will supply in their instance the place of that great and constant fund of entertainment to the sedentary and vacant in towns, the looking out of the window. The scene, though a confined, would be a very various, and therefore perhaps not altogether an unamusing one. (Ibid.: 20)

Here, what from the perspective of the family members appears as leisure, entertainment, is turned into surveillance work from the perspective of the mechanism of the panopticon. This free-choice co-optation of the inspector's family's work is very similar in context to what we will see later as the free-choice co-optation of the prisoners' work.

The rest of the world

The principle of modularisation of the panopticon can also be seen in another aspect. The panopticon, a discrete building, can be interfaced with the outside world through an administrative device, bookkeeping and the publication of accounts. In Letter 9 Bentham envisages high rewards for those who will manage the panopticon. The chosen contractor will be the one who offers 'the best terms'. The contractor will be given 'all the *powers* that his interest could prompt him to wish for, in order to enable him to make the most of his bargain; with only some reservations ...' (ibid.: 39). 'On pain of forfeiture or other adequate punishment ... and that upon oath', the contractor would have to publicise the panopticon's accounts, 'the whole process and details of his management', as well as 'all history of the prison' (ibid.).

The advantage of this is that it provides a mechanism that signals profits and losses to the rest of the world, and therefore enables a form of competition to take place. Bad management is demonstrated by loss of profit, 'for it is one advantage of this plan, that whatever mischief happens must have more than eaten out all *his* profits before it reaches *me*' (ibid.: 41). The publication of the accounts is a way to increase the productivity of surveillance, its effectiveness, to maximise the panopticon principle. It is the means through which the disciplinary mechanism set in place can operate efficiently:

After such publication, who should I have then? I should have every body: every body who, by fortune, experience, judgement, disposition, should conceive himself able and find himself inclined, to engage in such a business: and each person, seeing what advantage had been made, and how, would be willing to make his offer in proportion. What situation more favourable for making the best terms? (Ibid.: 42)

Collateral advantages and 'synergies'

The panopticon also offers a series of important 'collateral' advantages. The first one is that the number of inspectors required is relatively lower than for a comparable establishment (ibid.: 25). Second, the principle of the panopticon also applies to all layers of the staff forming the inspection force:

the *under* keepers or inspectors, the servants and subordinates of every kind, will be under the same irresistible control with respect to the *head* keeper or inspector, as the prisoners or other persons to be governed are with respect to *them*. (Ibid.: 26)

This allows the panopticon be beneficial not only for the maximisation of the discipline of the inmates, but also of the discipline of the inspectors, because 'in no instance' (ibid.: 26) could they 'either perform or depart from their duty, but [the inspector] must know the time and degree and manner of their doing so' (ibid.: 26). The panopticon therefore provides a satisfactory answer 'to one of the most puzzling of political questions, *quis custodiet ipsos custodes?*' Inspectors and inspected are both locked into a mechanism of surveillance. The panopticon is 'no less beneficial to what is called *Liberty* than to necessary coercion; no less powerful as a control upon subordinate power, than as a curb to delinquency; as a field to innocence than as a scourge to guilt' (ibid.: 27). The panoption principle disciplines everyone, free and unfree.

The third advantage is a sanitised exercise of power, through the elimination of 'disgust' and risks of infection due to face-to-face interactions by making sure that the job of inspection is replaced by an impersonal mechanism. Through this device, those who exercise power can minimise their contact with their subordinates.[9]

Fourth and finally, the panopticon ought to be open to visitors so as to give rise to a *system* of inspection. Again, Bentham here is referring to the ability of the system to capitalise on the *unintended* results of the action of the visitors. The visitors, 'without intending perhaps, or even without thinking of, any other effects of their visits, than the gratification of their own particular curiosity' do contribute to the system of competition. A multi-layered system of inspection could emerge, in which 'these spontaneous visitors' play the unintended role of 'assistants, deputies' to the superintendant 'in so far as he is faithful' or 'witnesses and judges, should he ever be unfaithful, to his trust'. The motives of the visitors are for this purpose 'perfectly immaterial; whether the relieving of their anxieties by the affecting prospect of their respective friends and relatives thus detained [over time], or merely the satisfying that general curiosity, which an establishment, on various accounts so interesting to human feelings, may naturally be expected to excite' (ibid.: 29).

The motivations of individual agents is irrelevant. What counts is their role within a system of inspection. Whatever their intentions and motivations to visit the establishment, by so doing they become *integrated* within the purpose of a system of inspection.

MARKET AND PANOPTICISM: TWO OVERLAPPING ORDERS

There are striking similarities and complementarities between Hayek's and Bentham's systems. These are summarised in Box 1 and discussed below.

Origins

In the first place, and very briefly, there are, quite surprisingly, some similarities of origination between the two mechanisms. While for Bentham the construction of this mechanism resides squarely on the ingeniousness of the planner of the panopticon, for Hayek, the market would be an emergent order *if* it were not for those like Keynesians and socialists who put limits to the market evolution. But in Hayek, the policy implication is the same as in Bentham: the role of the state is not that of coordinating individual actions, but one of allowing the emergence of an order in which individual actions are coordinated spontaneously. Similarly, the belief that the market is a spontaneous order implies that the state ought to *promote* policies that create and facilitate the market as the *condition* in which private individuals operate.[10]

Impersonal mechanism of coordination

Both systems are impersonal mechanisms of coordination of individual subjectivities that give form to social labour. The impersonal aspect of the coordinating mechanism is enthusiastically recommended by Bentham and it is a quality that makes it suitable for application to a large variety of social subjects 'in need' of inspection. As we have seen, in Hayek's market the

---

Box 1   Market and Panopticism: Two Overlapping Orders

1. Origins. The 'planner' plays an important role in the design of the *parameters* of the order/mechanism.
2. Impersonality and efficiency. The impersonal mechanism of coordination of individual subjectivities (plans) is functional to the maximisation of extraction of labour (Bentham) or maximisation of efficiency (Hayek).
3. Extension and integration. The order/mechanism can be generalised through the social field by means of the modular properties of the panopticon (Bentham) or commodification of new areas of life.
4. Imperfect knowledge. There is the recognition that power (inspectors in Bentham's panopticon or the state in Hayek's market) has imperfect knowledge of individual plans.
5. Freedom of *private*, not social, individuals. The order/mechanism relies on freedom of private individuals (*given* a menu). The consequent strategic intent of power is the emphasis on co-optation of unintended consequences of individual freedom.
6. Role of 'enclosures'. Individual confinement is a *condition* of individual freedom. In Bentham, the confinement is created by the cell's walls, while in Hayek it is created through property rights, which turn individuals into private individuals.
7. Disciplinary order. The mechanism of coordination (watchtower or competition) distributes punishments or rewards and is 'invisible' to individuals. In Bentham, this is the power behind the watchtower, in Hayek it is the emergent and ongoing compulsion of the competitive process.
8. Fetishism and signalling. Both mechanisms function through 'shadowy projections' of real life activities. In the panopticon these are light signals, in the competitive market these are price signals.

---

emphasis is on abstract rules of conduct, which bind together private individuals so that there is no need for them to develop common aims.[11] As an impersonal mechanism, the market frees individuals from the 'need of known fellows' and yet allows them to socially cooperate in their labour. There are also some important parallels in the 'aims' of this impersonal mechanism. For Bentham we are clearly and explicitly talking about a mechanism aimed at extraction of labour and maximisation of profit (see Letter 13 on 'the means of extracting labour' and the discussion below on individual freedom). We can discern the same preoccupation in Hayek once we look at the mode of functioning, the *process* of the market order, rather than its end result.

For Hayek, the end result of the market order (say a particular distribution of income, or any other particular 'snapshot' of the socio-economic condition) cannot be judged 'by criteria which are appropriate only to a single organised community serving a given hierarchy of ends', because such a hierarchy of ends is not relevant to the 'complex structure composed of countless individual economic arrangements' (Hayek 1978: 183). The word 'economy' is in fact inadequate to describe a multitude of individual ends, because it refers to 'an organisation or arrangement in which someone deliberately allocates resources to a unitary order of ends'. Instead, the market order, or catallaxy, does not have any particular end. But if this is the case, 'what, then, do we mean when we claim that [it] produces in some sense a maximum or optimum?' If the market order cannot be said to have a purpose,

it may yet be highly conducive to the achievement of many different individual purposes unknown as a whole to any single person, or relatively small groups of persons. Indeed, rational action is possible only in a fairly orderly world. Therefore it clearly makes sense to try to produce conditions under which the chances for any individual taken at random to achieve his ends as effectively as possible will be very high – even if it cannot be predicted which particular aims will be favoured, and which not. (Ibid.: 183)

The catallactic order of the market is for Hayek the optimum condition within which individual freedom can be organised. It is not possible to predict the result of this discovery process because 'the only common aim which we can pursue by the choice of this technique of ordering social affairs is the general kind of pattern, or the abstract character, of the order that will form itself' (ibid.: 184).

If the market order cannot be judged by its ends, we can develop an understanding of its rationale by regarding it an incessant *process* in which social labour is caught up. As we have seen, this process never reaches the equilibrium position that neoclassical economists talk about, because there is no pre-established equilibrium to reach. While in orthodox welfare economics, the role of the market is that of a 'social computational device' (Kirzner 1973: 214) – which computes pre-established hidden prices given perfect information – in Hayek the role of the market, as a discovery mechanism that communicates information, is to *create* reality.

If the market cannot be said to have a 'unitary order of ends', it prioritises a unitary rationale for human social interaction: the endless promotion of efficiency, the endless unqualified 'progress', the never-ending rat race, the competitive compulsion that 'goes on all the time'. This is not an external 'end product' of Hayek's market order, but its *raison d'être*.

Extendibility of the system

Another similarity is in the potential spatial realm of the two mechanisms. It is true that prima facie Bentham's panopticon is a closed system, clearly limited in space, while Hayek's market order is an open one, which spans over the social field without inherent limit. Yet Bentham's micro-technology of power is generalisable thanks to the *modular* properties of the panopticon, which allow a series of watchtowers to be integrated so as to control larger areas (Bentham 1787: 18). Hayek's market, on the other hand, is the representation of a social organism, but one whose dynamics of interaction among individuals is particularisable to any area of the social field, so long as individuals are turned into private individuals with no 'need of known fellows'. The last three centuries of commodification of many spheres of social life are a clear extension of Hayek's market principle. Therefore, though their starting sphere of application is different, the two systems can be imagined as 'convergent'.

Authority's imperfect knowledge of individual plans

In both Bentham's and Hayek's orders, power's knowledge of individual actions and plans is not perfect, and the rationale of both orders is to tap into human knowledge held by private individuals. In both cases, this co-optation of knowledge and tacit plans is at the basis of the system's maximisation of efficiency. Within their respective orders, power's acknowledgement of its imperfect knowledge becomes an opportunity to channel individual actions into the efficiency of an order, and thereby, given the structure of power relations embedded in that order, to promote profit.

Freedom of private individuals

It follows from the previous point that both orders rely on the freedom of *private* individuals, understood as a free choice of options from a *given* menu. While this is obvious in Hayek's market order, it is not immediately so in Bentham.

We have discussed how Bentham intends to co-opt the free choice and intentionality of the inspector's family and visitors into the systemic work of inspection of the panopticon. This unwaged work by the family members and visitors is unintended, exercised by free individuals operating within a *context* that has been designed for the purpose of surveillance *and* labour extraction. A similiar principle applies to the inmates.

Letter 13 is titled 'on the means of extracting labour.' These means are based on putting the prisoners in a condition of exercising a *choice* and thereby reaping a reward.[12] Here, individual freedom of choice is disconnected, as in Hayek, from the collective freedom to choose the constraints of that choice. This choice amounts to a *means* of extracting labour![13] And what an efficient mechanism of labour extraction this is!

What hold can any other manufacturer have upon his workmen, equal to what my manufacturer would have upon his? What other master is there that can reduce his workmen, if idle, to a situation next to starving, without suffering them to go elsewhere? What other master is there, whose men can never get drunk unless he chooses they should do so? And who so far from being able to raise their wages by combination, are obliged to take whatever pittance he thinks it most for his interest to allow? (Bentham 1787: 76)

In Hayek, the question of freedom is at the core of his investigation, and it assumes not so much the connotation of a moral theory (Gamble 1996: 41), as one of politics. The notion of freedom informs the strategic horizon of his legacy. For example, he writes:

My aim will not be to provide a detailed program of policy but rather to state the criteria by which particular measures must be judged if they are to fit into a regime of freedom .... Such a program ... must grow out of the application of a common philosophy to the problem of the day. (Hayek 1960: 5)

Here Hayek's strategic horizon is clearly *deployed*. His philosophy of freedom is a weapon that serves as a yardstick to make judgements, to measure concrete instances and to evaluate them in order to see whether they conform to a 'regime of freedom' understood in liberal terms. In a word, it is a liberal *line in the sand*. In this sense, Hayek is one of those economists who provide a flexible and adaptable conceptual grid, and is aware of this role. This conceptual grid represents the glasses through which liberal and neoliberal economists in different contexts and times can filter out their reality, circumstances and historical contexts, and adapt their basic principles to these realities with policies.

This filter sees freedom as a relation between individuals as defined by private property. For Hayek, liberty has nothing to do with social individuals being able to define the conditions of their interaction. Freedom is defined negatively, as the state of 'independence of the arbitrary will of another' (Hayek 1960: 12). Freedom is taken away from an individual when 'in order to avoid greater evil, he is forced to act not according to a coherent plan of his own but to serve the ends of another' (ibid.: 12). In this sense, freedom is to be free to choose from a given menu, in which the emphasis is not so much on the range of choices listed on the menu, but on the 'given character' of the menu:

'freedom' refers solely to a relation of men to other men, and the only infringement on it is coercion by men. This means, in particular, that the range of physical possibilities from which a person can choose at a given moment has no relevance to freedom. (Ibid.: 12)

Coercion exists in Hayek when a specific individual bends another to his will; when it is done by impersonal market forces, it is not coercion, by definition. But the 'given character' of the menu is a form of coercion. The fact that some choices are not contemplated – such as the freedom to choose the kind of rules of social interaction, the freedom to choose not to be governed by abstract rules, but by mutual recognition, or solidarity for example – is a way to force people into choosing the remaining options. Let us briefly explore this.

There are five fundamental freedoms in Hayek, including ownership of property. These are 'legal status as a member of the community; immunity from arbitrary arrest; the right to work at any trade; the right to free government and the right to own property' (Steele 1993: 33). Gamble (1996) and others have noticed that the freedom represented by ownership of property, is positively, rather than negatively, defined.[14] This implies that as far as property is concerned, the negative, relational definition of freedom arises out of property monopoly. In other words, constriction arises from monopolising the means of existence, as revealed by his often-noted 'spring in the desert' monopoly case (Hayek 1960:136).[15] In this case coercion arises when ownership of the means of existence reaches such an extent that it deprives *others* from access to the means of existence.

In both Hayek and Bentham we have a clear emphasis on the emergence of unintended consequences out of given parameters, or rules. Whether these are embedded in a designed architecture (Bentham) or are the (naively believed) products of an evolutionary order (Hayek), the point that interests both is the resulting system-like mechanism of coordination. The system-like coordination can emerge only if the individuals are allowed a sphere of freedom within which to operate. For both Bentham and Hayek this mechanism is rooted in a system of individual free choice, but an individual free choice that always comes with a rigid *given* set of 'constraints.' In the microcosm of Bentham's panopticon, this constraint is the result of an ingenious project. In the organic system of Hayek's market, constraints are believed to be a natural evolutionary result. Yet, in both cases, individual freedom is the main condition for the system to operate at maximum efficiency and to turn 'individual plans' into social efficiency.

Individual confinement as a systemic condition of individual freedom

Another similarity is that in both cases we have confinement as a presupposed basis of the extent of individuals' freedom. In the case of the individuals of the panopticon, the walls of the cells are the physical barriers that allow the creation of confinement. The purpose of 'safe confinement' is to prevent escape and enforce labour. Safe confinement *isolates* the inspected from each other in order to dash their *hopes*, and dangerous *'concert among minds'* (Bentham 1787: 32), which might enable them to overpower the guards. In the case of Hayek, the barriers are social, and constructed in the forms of *property rights*. In both cases, however, the very existence of these barriers is *naturalised*.

Mechanism of coordination is 'invisible' to individuals

Another similarity is the notion that the coordinating power, which distributes punishments and rewards to individual singularities, is invisible. In both cases, there is an automatic mechanism that coordinates individual subjectivities, and in both cases the latter do not relate to each other *directly* but through the mediation of other things. In the case of the panopticon, it is the central power of the inspectors' apparatus that mediates between individuals and thus coordinates the division of labour of a multitude. In Hayek's case, it is money as an expression of relative prices that provides the mediation.

The role of 'shadowy projections'

Finally, both these mechanisms use projections of real-life activity as data to feed the mechanism of control and coordination. In Bentham's panopticon, these are the mechanical products of an ingenious architectural design. In Hayek, prices fulfil the same role. There is of course an important difference between the two mechanisms. The knowledge embedded by market pricing in Hayek is knowledge that all individuals can in principle use (Gray 1998: 38), while that yielded by the shadowy projections of the panopticon is not. But this difference is ultimately the difference in how the 'watchtower' is constituted in the two systems. We have to understand the watchtower as the centre of disciplinary power, as the dispenser of punishments and rewards. While in Bentham the watchtower is a material physical presence, that is presupposed and stands outside individuals subjectivities, in Hayek's market order the centre of disciplinary power is the emergent property of individual competitive interaction. The knowledge embedded in Bentham's shadowy projections gives the inspectors in the watchtower the same thing that market prices give to competing agents in the market: 'systemic or holistic knowledge, knowledge unknown and unknowable to any of the elements of the market system, but given to them all by the operation of the system itself' (ibid.).

15
The fractal panopticon and ubiquitous revolution

The overlap between Bentham's and Hayek's apparently opposite systems of coordination of social labour opens up an understanding of the current global market order under construction as being imbued with the property of *panopticism*. This is, according to Deleuze, an abstract formula arising from the panopticon, which implies the discrete character of disciplinary power: power is not visible and it operates through a mechanism within which the multitude is fragmented. Panopticism is 'no longer "to see without being seen" but *to impose a particular conduct on a particular multiplicity*' (Deleuze 1998). But, we may add, in such a way that the multiplicity is so immersed in this conduct that the latter becomes naturalised, and when there is naturalisation of conduct there is invisibility of the power behind it: a fish cannot see the sea (McMurtry 1998).

Panopticism and neoliberal globalisation

Panopticism is a principle that wants to establish the automatic functioning of capital's power by means of an arrangement of activities and bodies through space, in which individuals are not subjects who specify the norms of their interrelations – they are not subjects of communication – but the norms governing their relation to the whole are pre-given and embedded within a mechanism – individuals are objects of information.

The panopticon is an architectural apparatus, that is an arrangement of space for the control of a multitude through its classification. The parallels with neoliberal economic globalisation are striking. Capitalist economic globalisation too is an arrangement of space; its walls are old and new property rights, and flows of foreign direct investments, capital and commodities are signals of information telling how efficiently a node of the global factory in competition with others (an industry, a city, a region, a nation) has organised all the activities of its citizens *in relation to* those of corresponding nodes. Through competitiveness, relational features such as love, affects, social bonds, trust, nature, become objects of comparison and accumulation as social capital, human capital, physical capital, financial capital. As with the panopticon, the global factory too has a centre where this information is collected and analysed. This centre, as we have seen in Chapter 12, is actually of two types: a strategic centre and a parametric centre; and both are in turn constituted by a plurality of centres. In the first case, with Hardt and Negri (2000), this plurality of centres, through which sovereignty is articulated in *Empire*, is made up of various levels of national and supranational political powers (national governments, the IMF, the WB, the WTO), which enforce enclosures and introduce markets in new areas, and attempt to articulate conflicting value practices through the coupling of reproduction or production loops in urban regeneration or development projects. The biopolitical process of coupling is then pitted against similar couplings in different parts of the world, in what ends up as biopolitical competition *within* the global social body. As we have seen, this ongoing competition, whether actually occurring or threatened, constitutes the process of formation of socially necessary labour times. When these are translated by the market into monetary terms, they in turn constitute the parametric centres around which co-producing singularities construct the terms of reference for defining their actions within the global rat race.

The panopticon, says Foucault, is a wonderful machine, it's a generalisable model of functioning, a way of defining the relation of power in the daily life of people. 'By moving from the most diverse desires, it produces homogeneous effects of power' (Foucault 1977: 220). The global marketplace can meet this panoptical promise: through the commodification of everything it ensures that everything can go through the same discipline, the same system of rewards and punishment. In this way, modernity and postmodernity complement each other, as the master narrative of the former (the market norm) enriches itself by means of the 'diversity' promoted by the latter (an ever expanding universe of life practices turned into commodities).[1]

This generalisable model of functioning, this homogenising effect of power, entails the promotion of automatisms of behaviour obtained through the interiorisation of market normative principles. This interiorisation in turn opens the way to 'developing power' to the various peripheries of the big social machine – power understood here as the power to choose subject to given budgetary constraints. The greater the disciplinary character of the mechanisms of socialisation of labour, the more pervasive is the biopolitical competition among the couplings of production and reproduction. The more the web of social interactions constituting the social labour of production and reproduction is held together by market norms of behaviour, the less visible is power and the more freedom can be devolved to individual nodes within the global machine. Freeedom here refers to individual choices of instances, but not to the definition of the norms that regulate their interaction.

The pervasiveness of the market principle to all spheres of life brings with it the danger of social fragmentation, of dissolution of the social fabric. If individual interactions are increasingly of the kind compatible with market norms, if markets are everywhere because everything is commodified, value practices such as reciprocity, trust, honesty, loyalty and 'social responsibility', however culturally and contextually defined, are increasingly squeezed out. And so markets destroy the fabric that they most need to rely on in order to enhance social cooperation. At this juncture there arises the problematic of 'social capital' (Fukuyama 1995), which acts as a bonding force for cooperation between the various economic agents. Social capital is a euphemism for values that are at the basis of 'a genuine willingness to engage in cooperative endeavours to promote the collective good' (Dunning 2000: 477), but as a form of *capital* it is ambiguous. Because either we reconstruct social cohesion through value practices that are also able to challenge the value practices reproduced by capitalist markets, or the concept of social capital only sees social cohesion as instrumental to the mobilisation of intellectual capital and labour in general, with the aim of participating in the competitive battle. In the latter case, social capital only refers to a less confrontational and more cooperative social stance for the purpose of enhancing 'societal competitiveness',[2] that is, of threatening someone else's 'cooperative endeavour' and social cohesion. In this contradictory sense, the rhetoric of 'social capital' is no more than old-fashioned apologetics for capital.

As the global competitive struggle is partly played out in terms of how much capital a country is able to attract and keep within its borders, societal competitiveness – as opposed to industry, or sector competitiveness – increasingly acquires strategic importance. The annual Global Competitiveness Report of the World Economic Forum <www.weforum.org> suggests key areas of public policy for helping to attract FDI, such as improvement in the efficiency of institutions, investment in education and infrastructure, together, of course, with the traditional recipe of financial discipline and sober public spending.

The emphasis on 'education', and continuous training, in the context of a flexible labour market, is an attempt to engineer a workforce that is both able and willing to sustain the continuing process of restructuring captured by the flying geese model and embedded in trade as a disciplinary device. In this way, the political problem that Kalecki (1943) saw emerging with full employment is neutralised: the fluidity of modern working practices and 'flexible' labour markets, combined with inflation-targeting monetary policies, allows that even at near full employment a national economy (a node in the global factory) will not inflate.

The drive towards a continuous upgrading and expansion of the infrastructure throughout the globe, whether in the form of new motorways, dams, high speed railways or airports, is largely associated with patterns of new enclosures and the struggles opposing them, and must be read in the context of the management of social productivity and the intensification of capitalist relations of production. Ultimately, infrastructural projects of this kind depend on over-coming resistance and managing the conflict provoked by the environmental and social cost that these market-driven developments necessarily involve. Once again, this is a cost generally paid by unwaged reproduction work.

As competition develops among similar industries and services that have parallel global commodity chains, the nodes of these commodity chains are subsuming their surrounding territory (socially, economically and ecologically defined) as part of the factory. The work of production and reproduction is inte-grated within these nodes and across nodes, infrastructures are needed to speed up production and circulation time, the 'environment' is turned into a resource subordinated to the management of competition in these nodes. In this way, even 'sustainable development' – originally formulated as an alternative to capital's growth – becomes a paradigm of capital's own sustainability. Also, as these nodes within global commodity chains develop their competitive strength and the enclosures threaten the livelihood of millions, the same nodes attract migrant labourers, who require 'careful' management and regulation, for the sake of furthering international competitiveness (Mittelman 2000).

The fractal panopticon

If, following Bentham, we regard panopticism as a modality of power that rests on the principle of 'seeing without being seen', made possible by a flow of information that turns real subjects and activities into *data*, shadowy projections of real subjects, then, combining these principles of panopticism with its property of *modularisation* and Hayek's characterisation of the market as the coordinating mechanism of the action of private individuals, we can under-stand the rationale of the neoliberal project as one aiming at the construction of a system of interrelated virtual 'inspection houses', which we may call the 'fractal panopticon'.

Each panopticon, that is each set of interrelationships of control and resistance defined by a scale of social action, is in turn a singularity within a series of singularities, which stand in relation to each other in such a way that their action constitutes a 'watchtower' that is external to them, thus forming a greater panopticon – and so on, in a potentially infinite series. In Figure 10, each singularity (an individual or set of individuals, such as a 'firm', sector, city, nation, region, and so on, along an organisational hierarchy of social co-production) relates to a 'watchtower', which sees, classifies, acts, punishes and rewards according to the modality of the market, or of markets, simulations as in the case of many public services. These 'watchtowers' are invisible, but their effects are tangible and emerge through the process of competition described in previous chapters. At any given scale of social action, each singularity relates to others through a disciplinary mechanism, and in thus doing it consti-tutes itself as a node of a larger and more pervasive disciplinary mechanism. Sets of individuals compete among themselves in flexible labour markets. Sets

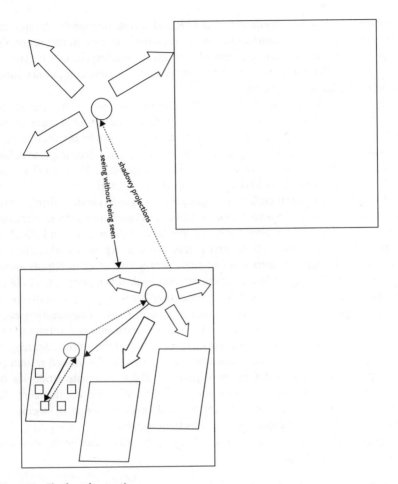

Figure 10   The fractal panopticon

of firms (made of those competing individuals) compete among themselves within a branch of industry. Sets of cities/states (made up of those firms, branches and individuals) compete among themselves within regions. Sets of regions compete among themselves throughout the globe.

The panopticon of the global market is 'fractal', in that each level of social aggregation, each node or singularity, is 'self-similar' to others. In the geometrical theory of fractals the property of self-similarity means that every feature of a fractal shape is reproduced by the same ratio at different scales, that is in a reduced or enlarged picture. In this way, the disciplinary process of competition becomes socially pervasive and touches areas not previously organised by the market.

The watchtower of this fractal panopticon of the neoliberal age is also invisible, because decentred, and is constituted by pervasive market-like interactions. However, its effects are tangible and operate through the disciplinary processes of competition described in the previous chapters. In this sense, the watchtower is an emergent property of competitive markets, in which Hayek's 'competition that goes on all the time' embeds the systemic compulsory functions of Bentham's central tower.

It must be pointed out that, as in Bentham's panopticon, the role of the planner in the fractal panopticon is to provide the design of a mechanism, which is then left to operate out of its internal logic of power between inspectors and inspected. Neoliberal policies can thus be regarded as attempts to define the *conditions* of interaction among private individuals, by extending and defending the realm of enclosure and competitive interaction.

Each 'scale' of social productive aggregation, (an individual, a 'firm', a city, a district, a country, a macro-region or a free-trade area) faces strong pressure to turn into a node set against the respective 'rest of the world'. An individual versus other individuals, a firm versus other firms, a city versus other cities, a country versus other countries, a free-trade area versus other free-trade areas. In the sense of engaging in a competitive race, each social node, each field of coupling between production and reproduction loops, appears as self-similar with respect to the others. At each of these scales, or levels of aggregation, each node has to cope with limited resources (budget constraint) and submit to the rules of a competitive drive vis-à-vis their own 'rest of the world'. Scarcity is endemic in the way the social organism is structured. These limited resources presuppose of course a definition of property rights and state strategies of enclosure analogous in their function to Bentham's safe confinement. In neoliberal policies, the aim is to restrict and preclude forms of social co-production that do not capitulate to competitive games.

Some of the main properties of the fractal panopticon can be discussed in terms of the following:

1. Operational mode of power: seeing without being seen
2. Real human activity represented through 'shadowy projections'
3. Contextual relation between 'inside' and 'outside'
4. Individual freedom and socially constructed cells
5. Pervasiveness of the 'watchtower'
6. Articulation between control and disciplinary mechanisms

1. Seeing without being seen

The relation between each singularity and a watchtower is constituted by the principle of 'seeing without being seen'. In Bentham, this enables 'the *apparent omnipresence* of the inspector ... combined with the extreme facility of his *real presence*' (Bentham 1787: 25). The apparent omnipresence of the inspector is obtained through an act of imagination in which the singularity 'conceives' the inspector to be omnipresent. *Fear* of omnipresence is the guiding force of the panopticon's mechanism of control. On the other hand, fear needs to be nurtured by exemplary action, thus power must show the extreme facility of its *real presence*. The process of competition, combined with the flexibilisation of labour markets and the reduction in entitlements, contributes to the formation of a conception of a pervasive threat and the actualisation of fear.

2. Real human activity represented through shadowy projections ('data')

Power has the ability to act when it has the ability to watch. Shadowy projections represent the flow of information at the disposal of the 'watchtower'. In Bentham's panopticon, from the position of the watchtower, the inspector does not have a correct and comprehensive knowledge of the reality of subjects, but one which is sufficient to exercise power over them. Shadowy projections are the edited information of life activity, and the kind of selection that goes to form that information is that which is sufficient for the mechanism of control.

Shadowy projection can take many forms. In Bentham's panopticon, as in Chinese shadow theatre, they took the form of human figures projected by an outside light source to the watchtower at the centre of the building. In contemporary capitalism, as in Hayek, they take the form of prices, and, when these are not possible, of performance indicators of a variety of kinds that institutions operating in fields such as health and education are increasingly required to adopt. Prices and other performance indicators embed that kind of edited information that allows an 'agent' located outside the singular panopticon to compare, control, and act, thus dispensing judgement *and* at the same time, acting as a virtual omnipresent inspector. Like shadows, their visibility depends entirely on the real subjects and their life experience being hidden; they offer only an edited information of real life activity. What is left out of prices is the lived, flesh-and-blood experience of work. Prices and performance indicators *are* pervasive and operational simulacra of real life, and represent the interface between one panopticon and another. As devices of 'visibility', of representation, of 'openness', they project the life activity within a singularity to the disciplinary force of the outside, a discipline the effect of which is to turn back on the activities of the doers, to shape their rhythms of work, to keep up the pressure of an endless rat race. Even Bentham (1787: 40), from his late-eighteenth-century perspective, could see the virtues of 'open government' for his panopticon, calling for the disclosure of accounts and, the possibility of its being taken over if a different manager was able to envisage more efficient ways of extracting work from the inmates.

3. Contextual relation between 'inside' and 'outside'

The mechanism of competition vis-à-vis an external 'watchtower' – among individuals on the labour market, schools, shopfloors, regions, etc. – coexists with a mechanism of discipline and control within each singularity. Thus, each singularity is part of a system vis-à-vis the set of interrelated 'watchtowers', and is at the same time a singularity incorporating a 'watchtower', an internal mechanism of discipline specific to that singularity. The extent to which external or internal 'watchtowers' predominate in specific cases is a contextual and empirical matter.

4. Individual freedom

Unlike freedom in Bentham's panopticon, the individual freedom in a fractal panopticon is in principle not restricted to choosing between work and non-work (corresponding to reward as opposed to 'bread and water'), but among a multiplicity of waged and unwaged occupations, which, however, all tend to turn into work because all are regulated within the overall mechanism of the fractal panopticon and are subject to ongoing capitalist measurement imposed from the outside. It is as if the individuals being inspected in Bentham's panopticon had also the choice of leaving their specific places of confinement, but as soon as they walk out of the front door, they enter another panopticon. It is in this context that we must study the rhetoric of flexibility and the corresponding restructuring of education that aims at teaching students to cope with the demands of the market. Of course, as we have seen, individual freedom here arises out of a context. In the fractal panopticon, barriers are social, given by property rights, entitlements and the continuous character of enclosures.

5. Pervasiveness of the 'watchtower'

The most insidious aspect of the fractal panopticon is that the material presence of the 'watchtower' is combined with its apparent immateriality. It is for this reason that we have put the word in scare quotes. This is the trick of the market. Once we forget the genealogy and preservation of property rights as a process of enclosures, a genealogy that continuously creates the *context* of competitive interaction within and between different nodes of social fields, all 'agents' participating in the framework of the fractal panopticon are at the same time 'inspected' as well as being constituent parts of what Bentham called the 'inspector force'. In Bentham's panopticon this is the case for the inspectors, who would in turn be inspected by visitors to the premises. However, it is only in the fractal panopticon that the lower ranks of the inspected, through actively engaging in the process of competition, also constitute an inspection force.

It is for this reason that a radical process of emancipation from capital's fractal panopticon as the mechanism for the imposition of work, cannot consist only in overcoming the 'watchtower', as this is not constituted independently of the actions of the inspected, as in Bentham's panopticon. *The inspected must recognise themselves as part of the inspection force and posit new commons and new forms of co-production if they want to move beyond the system of inspection and the endless production of scarcity it gives rise to.*

6. Articulation between control and disciplinary mechanisms

Foucault (1977) pointed out that the punishment–reward polarity embedded in disciplinary mechanisms is a factory of ethics. More recently, several authors have argued that as disciplinary institutions were thrown into crisis by the struggles in factories, homes, schools and rice paddies of the 1960s and 1970s, capital was forced to recapture this flight of desire by deterritorialising discipline and turning disciplinary societies into control societies (Deleuze 1990; Hardt and Negri 2000). While in disciplinary societies individual subjectivities faced a discrete sequence of institutions of confinement, in control societies the mechanism of co-optation is deployed on a continuous basis, with a blurred distinction among institutions.

The family, the school, the army, the factory are no longer distinct analogical spaces that converge towards an owner – state or private power – but coded figures – deformable and transformable ... Even art has left the space of enclosure in order to enter into the open circuit of the bank. The conquest of the market is made by grabbing control and no longer by disciplinary training, by fixing the exchange rate much more than by lowering costs, by the transformation of the product more than by specialisation of production ... Marketing has become the centre or the 'soul' of the corporation ... The operation of the market is now the instrument of social control and forms the impudent breed of our masters ... Man is no longer man enclosed, but man in debt. (Deleuze 1990: 181)

But debt of course is at the same time a form of enclosure, not in terms of physical confinement, but in the original sense of separation from social wealth, a separation that acts as a material force to turn activity into abstract labour and therefore accumulation. All the same, the instruments of monetary economic policies not only attempt to control monetary flows, but to reconfigure costs of production over the social field, thus operating as a disciplinary force. In the global fractal panopticon, the continuous reconfiguration of global production chains is not simply the attempt to direct flows of subjectivities, but also to discipline them along classic parameters of accumulation and work vis-à-vis their struggles.

In other words, as we have already discussed in Chapter 9, the distinction between discipline and control is not so neat. On the contrary, they are complementary, and always have been in the history of the capitalist mode of production. What changes within this history is the *form* of their articulation. As we have seen, in cybernetics, every control mechanism is based on *given* parameters, that is norms or, in the social sense, 'ethics', 'values', normalised modes of operation. There is, of course, a distinction between how these parameters are set, whether from the outside or, as in 'learning systems', from within control mechanisms (Skyttner 1996). The ideal within the fractal panopticon is that only the contextual parameters are set as discrete policies, i.e., liberalisation policies and new enclosures. Then the competitive market mechanism set in place by these parameters, with the help of the enforcement of 'law and order', is supposed to normalise, in disciplinary fashion, the cracks arising out of struggles.

BEYOND PANOPTICISM

Bentham however gives us a further insight. His panopticon is a place of safe custody, i.e., safe confinement, preventing escape, and of labour (Bentham 1787: 31). Safe confinement is due to the fact that inmates are isolated from each other and communication among them is prevented. As we have seen, there are two interrelated reasons for Bentham's strategic choice of power's control of communication, and these are the ability to frustrate the hope of the inmates to escape from their condition, and power's attempt to avoid dangerous 'concert among minds'.[3] In the condition of the neoliberal fractal panopticon, the reduction of hope brought about by the *pensée unique* of our age seems to have received the first blows from the new alter-globalisation movements that have begun to question competition as a mechanism of coordination and instead to explore new forms of communication and 'concert among minds'. By building bridges between political issues and subjectivities, women, precarious workers, labour, environmentalists, farmers, the indigenous and other movements are increasingly faced with the problem of exploring and thinking about new ways of social coordination of production and reproduction that moves beyond the one inspired by the combination of Hayek's market order and Bentham's panopticon. To do so, however, these movements will face the greatest challenge of all, and this is to redefine for themselves practices of freedom that break with those that simply see people as self-interested individuals with budget constraints making free choices from a given menu. The beginning of history is any time in which social individuals who recognise their sociality exercise freedom, and refuse the subordination of their lives to the value practices of capital by rearticulating social powers through alternative value practices. Within the fractal panopticon, revolution must be ubiquitous, which is another way of saying that it must take the features of *common* sense. 'Concert among minds' will have to come together with 'concert among bodies', which is another way of saying that the different struggling singularities will have to overcome their concrete divisions by becoming other than capital and co-producing commons. How? Well, that is a political-communicational question that only the people involved in struggle can address. In the next two chapters I can provide only some general reflections.

Part IV

'By Asking Questions We Walk': the Problematics of Decoupling

16
The 'outside'

This book may have provided food for thought in deconstructing the system of social relations we call capitalism, perhaps may have helped to clarify what the power of capital is predicated upon, and I hope it has been clear from both the contents of the discussion as well as the mode of presentation that I was pointing at the ruptures within this system. Yet, whenever we approach things in a system-like manner – even if, as we have seen, capitalism is only a subsystem of social co-production, and even if the system-like manner is full of cracks, ruptures and struggles, as we have described – we always run the risk of providing space for hopelessness and desperation: after all, who are we when the system is so powerful, so able to counter struggles, to integrate them into its own dialectic?

In this and the next chapter, I shall try to address and problematise this question. But it is important to keep in mind that we could of course have gone all the way and made use of the title of this book by portraying the 'beginning of history' as the inevitable destiny of our march towards 'progress' (as many traditional Marxists used to do), due to the internal contradictions of the systems, or as the already-given present reality emerging from the immateriality of our labour (as Negri's version of autonomist Marxism does). Instead, we have chosen a middle ground, one that recognises the simultaneous presence of war and peace, capitalism and communism, enclosures and commons, rat race and community, capital's measure and measures emerging from horizontal relational processes, value practices geared to accumulation of money and fragmentation of the social body and value practices geared to the living, nurturing and enjoyment of convivial life. Our understanding of the 'beginning of history' is located at this juncture and as such it is a clash, a conflict that is experienced in forms and degrees that are certainly influenced by positionality within the wage hierarchy and background; it is a general conflict nevertheless.

The awareness that we live in a system or, better, that our lives and livelihoods are articulated through systemic forces, does not need to lead us to despair. Knowledge of these forces does not make us weaker; on the contrary, it make us stronger, because the system reveals its Achilles heel by showing what it must do in order to survive: it *must* promote enclosures and it *must* pit producers, both waged and unwaged, against each other, thus creating the appearance of abundance, but instead reproducing scarcity. We have also argued that the struggles within the social body are everywhere and we have interpreted struggles within the circuits of capital as value struggles. We have discussed the homeostatic processes through which capital attempts to recuperate and displace these struggles, processes the result of which is the ongoing reproduction of a global hierarchy of reproduction fields. Finally, the working of capital's systemic articulation of different singularities also shows that what is called 'the global economy' is fractal-like, that in each scale of social action the value practices of capital tend to reproduce the two coordinates of enclosures and disciplinary integration in a self-similar way.

It is within these conditions, which are not outside our own daily practices, but that we reproduce through our actions and daily struggles to the extent that they are recuperated, that we must conceive the problematisation of the overcoming of capitalism. The fact that capital depends on recuperating struggles through homeostatic mechanisms does not mean that we must give up fighting. This is impossible, since social conflict understood as value struggles has been our ontological starting point: we are agents of social conflict either as individuals facing in isolation the struggles for our survival and sanity, or as part of networks of collective action. And the fact that we recognise our own implication in the reproduction of the system does not mean we should stop blaming *them* (states, transnational corporations and other elites of economic, political and ideological powers) for designing, promoting and enforcing conditions within which livelihoods are reproduced in alienating and exploitative forms. The acknowledgment of our being implicated means only and simply this: there is no changing the world without changing our own lives, and there is no changing our own lives without changing our modes of relations to others. The plurality of existing struggles needs to be reconfigured and recoded as a force of social transformation beyond capital's value practices rather than as the driving engine of its development. We need to decouple from the mechanism of capital's self-preservation, from the mechanism of homeostasis through which capital derives its oxygen, and ground the reproduction of our livelihoods on a different terrain. This process of decoupling and constitution coincides with the problematisation of the *outside*. In a word, we must ask again and again how do we (re)produce, sustain and extend an *outside* to capital's value practices?

THE 'OUTSIDE'

The 'outside' is not an academic category. It is a theoretical construct that is given life, texture and relevance by concrete life practices and struggles at the *front line* of the clash among *conati*. When we reflect on the myriad of community struggles taking place around the world for water, electricity, land, access to social wealth, life and dignity, one cannot but feel that the relational and productive practices giving life and shape to these struggles give rise to values and modes of doing and relating in social co-production (shortly, value practices). Not only that, but these value practices appear to be *outside* corresponding value practices and modes of doing and relating that belong to capital, what we have described in terms of enclosure and disciplinary integration. The 'outside' with respect to the capitalist mode of production is a problematic that we must confront with some urgency, if we want to push our debate on alternatives onto a plane that helps us to inform, decode, and intensify the web of connections of struggling practices.

The urgency can also be detected in the desire of many activists involved in the local ripples and translocal rivers of the global justice and solidarity movement to run away from the claustrophobic, devious and ecumenic embrace of the agents of neoliberal governance in their attempts to deflate and co-opt the value practices posited by our many movements. Listen, for example, to Paul Wolfowitz, one of the inspirers of the butchery of Baghdad, and now respected president of the World Bank. In his first speech at the annual IMF and WB meeting in September 2005, he said:

We meet today at an extraordinary moment in history. There has never been a more urgent need for results in the fight against poverty. There has never been a stronger call for action from the global community. The night before the G8 summit in Gleneagles, I joined [sic] 50,000 young people gathered on a soccer field in Edinburgh for the last of the Live 8 concerts. The weather was gloomy, but the rain did not dampen the enthusiasm of the crowd. All eyes were riveted on the man who appeared on the giant video screens – the father of South Africa's freedom. And the crowd roared with approval when Nelson Mandela summoned us to a new struggle – the calling of our time – to make poverty history. (Wolfowitz 2005)

In the words of the World Bank president, the 'fight' against poverty is a spectacular event – neoliberal supranational institutions and neoliberal national governments marching together with youths wearing sweatshop-produced wrist bands and rock stars with cool sunglasses, announcing to the CNN audiences that 'good governance' is indeed the practical solution to such a calamity.[1] As 'poverty' is no longer a concrete condition of life and struggle, it is turned into an abstract enemy, an outside that is supposed to be fought with corresponding abstract policies, that is, to recite a recent World Bank document assessing South Africa's investment climate, 'macroeconomics and regulatory policies; the security of property rights and the rules of law; and the quality of supporting institutions such as physical and financial infrastructure'

(World Bank 2005c: 5). With the definition of this abstract 'outside', concrete struggles of the poor, which turn poverty into the condition for the production of community, social cooperation and dignity, can be locally criminalised: after all, they threaten macro-economic stability, they threaten 'property rights and the rules of law', and they threaten the roles of infrastructures qua vehicles of capital accumulation, demanding instead that they are devoted to the repro-duction of the needs of communities. With the proclaiming of poverty as an outside to struggle against, Paul Wolfowitz and the discourse promoted by the institution he presides, can declare war on the poor, and kill *three* birds with one stone: first, by continuing to promote neoliberal policies that reproduce the poor as poor, through further enclosures and the promotion of disciplinary markets and their homeostatic mechanisms; second, by persevering in the cre-ation of a context in which the struggles of the poor are criminalised whenever they oppose neoliberal discourse and reclaim commons; and, third, by dividing the struggling body into good and bad, the good being the 'responsible' move-ments holding hands with Paul Wolfowitz and the like, while the bad are the 'irresponsible' rest of us. The basis of neoliberal governance depends on games and selecting principles like these.[2]

Listen instead to critical ethnographic accounts of struggles of the poor:

This was another defining moment for the struggle of the flat dwellers [in Chatsworth, Durban, South Africa]. Indian women had stood in the line of fire in order to protect an African family who had no mother. If they had lost, the Mhlongos would have been forced into the nearby bush. The council, too, had shown its hand. For them the broader issues of the sense of building non-racial communities from the bottom up meant nothing. The fact that Mhlongo was respected by the community and was working hard as a mechanic to give his family a chance in life was equally irrelevant. The council was a debt collector, fighting on moral terms. Their sense of morality was frighteningly clear. Mhlongo was an undesirable because he got in the way of their collection of (apartheid's) debts. (Desai 2002: 53)

Here too we can envisage an implicit problematisation of the 'outside', but here the outside presents itself in a more complex dimension. It is not posited by abstract principles, but it is constituted as a concrete and sensuous process, in which 'outsideness' and the corresponding reclaiming of 'otherness' emerge out of the refusal of an outside measure, an outside value practice, and they are reclaimed as qualities of a living relational practice. In the constitution of this 'outside' to capital's measure we find the poor's way of making poverty his-tory, by beginning, again and again and again, *their own history*. The outside here, let us call it, with provocation, *our outside*, emerges and becomes visible on the *front line*. This is the place of the clash against the 'out there' imposing its rules, as when opposition is deployed against the debt collector who comes to knock at the door with a rifle butt or, on a different scale, against the government and corporate managers conveying the messages that global market signals have decreed the destruction of an industry and of corresponding communities. The 'outside' created by struggles is an outside that emerges from within, a social space created by virtue of creating relational patterns that are other than and incompatible with the relational practices of capital. This is *our* outside, that is, the realm of value practices outside those of capital and, indeed, clashing with it. The value practices of Indian women defending an African's family (and thus contributing to the creation of a common and the reformulation of identities)[3] versus the value practices of a debt collector evicting another African family in the name of 'respect for property, rule of law and contract'.

Our outside is a process of *becoming other than capital*, and thus presents itself as a barrier that the boundless process of accumulation and, in the first instance, processes of enclosure, must seek to overcome. It goes without saying that this outside is contingent and contextual, since it emerges from concrete struggles and concrete relating subjectivities. And it is also obvious that the emergence of this outside is not a guarantee of its *duration and reproduction*. The point I am making is only this: 'our outside' is the realm of the production of commons. To this we shall shortly return, after a detour taking us back to revisit the issue of enclosure and dispossession.

ENCLOSURE, DISPOSSESSION AND THE OUTSIDE

The problematic of the outside has always been ambiguous in the Marxist literature that has addressed it, whether implicitly or explicitly. On the one hand, capital's own 'revolution' depends on the overcoming of conditions that, in given contexts and on given scales, are not suitable for accumulation, hence 'outside' its value practices. This overcoming of conditions may well be simply the coupling of circuits of 'pre-capitalist' production to those of capital (as discussed, for example, in Wolpe's (1972) work on the articulation of modes of production in the case of South Africa); or the destruction of these 'pre-capitalist' communities by the enclosures of land and other resources, as Marx points out in his discussion of the 'so called primitive accumulation'. On the other hand, radical thinking is supposedly entirely devoted to the problematisation of and search for an outside to the capitalist mode of production: what, in traditional terms, is the symbolic value of 'revolution' but this great event delivering us a field of social relations 'outside' those of capitalism?

More in general, within traditional Marxist discourse we face a key problem in the conceptualisation of the 'outside'. It seems to me that this presents itself either as historical pre-capitalist *ex ante*, or a mythological revolutionary post-capitalist *ex post*. In the middle, there is the claustrophobic embrace of the capitalist mode of production, *within which*, there seems to be *no outside*.

In these terms, it is clear how the historical process of moving from one to the other has tended to be conceived in terms of Lenin's deus ex machina of the party bringing consciousness to the masses ... from where? Precisely, from a fetishised 'outside'.

A brief review of some conceptions of the 'outside' within recent non-dogmatic Marxist literature reveals both the strength with which the many traditions have characterised capital's relation to the outside, but at the same time the weakness with which the processes of constitution of 'our outside' have been brought into the spotlight of the problematisation.

The work of Harold Wolpe (1972), in the fashion of Luxemburg, envisages the outside as the pre-capitalist mode of production that came to an end in South Africa with industrialisation and apartheid. Arguing that segregation and apartheid were two distinct phases of capitalist regimes in South Africa, Wolpe was able to clarify the role of the reserves in the pre-apartheid regime as a 'pre-capitalist' outside, which was instrumental in reducing the cost of the reproduction of labour time. Here the concept of the *articulation* of modes of production (one outside the other, yet coupled) was developed. This came to an end with the process of impoverishment of the reserves due to migration of the adult population and underinvestment associated with the expropriation of land. The apartheid regime therefore, with an escalating element of coercion, had to be decoded as a capitalist strategy of subordination of the increasingly rebellious urban black working class. With apartheid, in other words, we move from a dual to a single mode of production. Hence ultimately, in Wolpe's work, at the end of this historical process there seems to be no outside to the capitalist mode of production, at least in South Africa.

From a completely different perspective, and one which is less equipped to problematise and account for the hierarchies being reproduced within the 'global multitudes', Hardt and Negri (2000; 2004) reach the same conclusion and state it explicitly: the outside is part of the 'inside–outside' dialectic belonging to modernity, while in postmodernity and empire there is no outside. One could read this in terms of the fact that in the current phase of neoliberal globalisation there is no outside to capitalist relations of production, that is, 'inside–outside' relations of a particular nature. But this interpretation is also problematic once we see that in Hardt and Negri the paradigmatic process of capitalist relations of production – the process of measuring human activity from the outside of the direct producers and turning it into work, i.e., 'the law of value' – is supposedly coming to an end thanks to immaterial labour; or, at least, this is supposed to be the 'tendency'. As we have seen in Chapter 12, this is far from the case, and when the issue of capital's measure is brought back to the theoretical investigation (since it applies not only to communities facing enclosures, but also to both waged 'material' and 'immaterial labour'), then we can account for the reproduction and hierarchy as it emerges from the ongoing disciplinary processes of the market.

I will now digress a little further to discuss David Harvey's *The New Imperialism* (2003). In this book he builds on Luxemburg's position, and argues that the outside is the object of the 'accumulation by dispossession' that capital needs in order to overcome crises of overproduction, rather than of underconsumption. In his view, 'what accumulation by dispossession does is to release a set of assets (including labour power) at very low (and in some instances zero) cost. Overaccumulated capital can seize hold of such assets and immediately turn them to profitable use' (ibid.: 149). The outside thus is soon to be internalised by capital's loops which, benefiting from lower costs, will overcome the overaccumulation crisis until the next round of enclosures is required.

There is a theoretical weakness in Harvey's turning of the problematic of 'enclosures' into one of 'accumulation by dispossession'. This term, although evocative of the horrors of ripping apart communities and expropriating land and other means of life, is ultimately theoretically weak, since it posits 'dispossession' as a *means* of accumulation, rather than as what accumulation is all about. Indeed, in the context of accumulation of which *both* continuous (and spatialised) enclosures and market disciplinary processes are two constituent moments, separation of producers and the means of production means essentially that the 'objective conditions of living labour appear as *separated, independent* values opposite living labour capacity as subjective being, which therefore appears to them only as a value of *another kind*' (Marx 1974: 461). In an office or factory, in a neighbourhood of the global South threatened by mass eviction or in the Northern welfare claimant office playing with single mothers' livelihoods if they do not accept low-paid jobs, the many who are subject to capital's measure are at the receiving end of strategies that attempt to channel their life activities according to the priorities of this heteronymous measure that defines for them what, how, how much and when to exercise their powers (i.e., that turns their activities into 'labour' for capital). What is common to *all* moments of accumulation as social relation is a measure of things, which traditional Marxism has conceptualised in terms of the 'law of value', but which in so doing it has fetished as purely an 'objective' law and not as an objectivity that is continuously contested by subjects in struggles, who posit *other* measures of things *outside* those of capital.

To the extent to which capital's measure of things takes over the lives and practices of subjects, that is, *to the extent to which* their livelihoods are *dependent* on playing the games that the disciplinary mechanisms of the markets demand from them, dispossession occurs. The 'surplus labour' and corresponding 'surplus value' extracted from both waged and unwaged workers is only one side of the occurring dispossession. The other is the *detritus*[4] inscribed in the bodies and in their environments by the exercise of capital's measure on the doing of the social body, and their life activity. This *detritus* that is around subjects and inside subjects helps us to read dispossession not as an occurrence *out there*, but as a condition of life practices coupled to capital's circuits, to a variety of degrees and at different levels of the wage hierarchy. The *detritus* points at the problematic of social reproduction.

Indeed, as pointed out in different ways by George Caffentzis (2002), Sharad Chari (2005) and Gillian Hart (2002; 2005), there is no guarantee that, following dispossession, the 'released' labour power will find means of reproduction in the capital's circuits.[5] This means that enclosure always puts onto the agenda the problematic of social reproduction and the struggle around it. The outside thus turns from the object of expropriation into the *detritus*. By *detritus*, I understand the layers of waste inscribed in the body and in the environment and that emerge out of the articulation of life practices following their own *conatus* to capital's loops (and their *conatus*). In this sense, *detritus* is the common material condition (although diversified along different contexts and point at the wage hierarchy) in which the problematic of social reproduction is uniquely in the hands of waged and unwaged 'dispossessed' and their *organisational reach*. In other words, social reproduction outside capital dramatically depends on the effectiveness, organisational reach and communal constitution of struggles and the ability to reclaim and constitute commons in condition of *detritus*.[6]

In the diverse approaches I have briefly reviewed, I have difficulty in detecting any tendency towards overcoming the ambiguity about the treatment of the 'outside' to which I referred at the beginning of this section. Whether it is an outside that has come to an end due to increasing dependence on wages by the proletariat (Wolpe) or to the reaching of the phase of real subsumption and the hegemonising tendency of labour to become immaterial (Hardt and Negri), or whether the presence of the outside is still with us as a necessary component of accumulation (Harvey), in all these cases the definition of the outside in terms of its presence or absence is a function of something that is created *ex ante* and that, in this fashion, can come to an end through the development of capitalist processes (Wolpe, Hardt and Negri) or is in the *process* of coming to an end by ongoing dispossessions (Harvey).

What is implicitly left out here is that processes of struggles are continuously generating the outside. *Our* outside, or, maybe plural, our *outsides*, seem to have been left out of the picture, left unproblematised in at least three dimensions:

1. in their constituent *communitarian* features, that is the production of commons and of value practices, degrees of reproduction/challenges/overcoming of gender, racial or other hierarchies – in a word the shape and form of the production of commons in different contexts;
2. in processes of articulation of these commons – emerging in context-specific places[7] – to global disciplinary markets, that is degrees and forms of subsumption into capital's disciplinary processes;

3. in the nature and effectiveness of the challenge that these constituent processes pose to broader capital's loops and global markets' disciplinary processes, that is, the question of the crisis of social stability.

In a word, what is left out is very obvious to the eyes of many participating in struggles and to those providing ethnographical accounts: only people in struggle, deploying specific discourses empowering them in their specificity, are *co-producers of alternatives*.[8] And if this is the case, much work is needed to relate the multitude of existing or possible ethnographies of struggles to the 'great scheme of things', that is, the general problematic of combating a social force whose *conatus* of self-preservation depends on a boundless drive to dispossess, measure, classify and discipline the global social body and to pit singularities against each other by withdrawing their means of existence – unless one participates *successfully* in a race that threatens somebody else's livelihood (they call this the 'market').

VERY BRIEF DETOUR ON IMPERIALISM

I feel compelled now to make a detour to address the currently much debated question of 'imperialism'. Indeed, many of the radical approaches to the 'outside', such as those we have addressed, are linked to the question of imperialism in one way or in another. In Rosa Luxemburg, Wolpe and Harvey (the latter two both inspired by Luxemburg) and Hardt and Negri, the problematic of the outside is in different ways the problematic of colonisation of an 'out there', or, in Hardt and Negri's case, this is a problematic that comes to an end with Empire. In the classic treatment of Lenin, imperialism was the highest stage of capitalism, in which the conflicting interests of *national* bourgeoisies were leading to war. In contemporary debates within the movement of movements, the rhetoric of imperialism has accelerated following the occupation of Iraq by the United States and its allies. I cannot survey these debates in detail, but for our purposes it is important to point out that the various strands of contemporary discourse on imperialism are heavily cast in terms of 'interests' (national interests, US interests, etc.), and are not problematised in terms of the value practices of capital, enclosure and disciplinary integration, or the clash among value practices. I have the impression that in discourses emerging from within the movements, there is a tension between these two ways of problematising things, a tension that sometimes emerges in the literature, as for example on the occasion of the appointment of Paul Wolfowitz at the World Bank. In one commentary, for example, the appointment 'was a calculated move to ensure that the US is able to continually secure its economic and geopolitical interests' (Guttal 2006: 80–1); hence, in this respect, the move can be read within the traditional framework of 'imperialism', that is national interests. In another section of the same commentary, we learn that for 'the World Bank, post-war reconstruction is an opportunity to apply the most egregious form of structural adjustment to countries emerging from war or natural disasters, undergoing violent internal conflicts, under foreign occupation, and/or under-going "transition" from communism to capitalism' (ibid.: 86). Now this latter frames the issue in terms of the value practices of capital: Wolfowitz's appointment as president of the World Bank must be read in terms of how it might help capital (whatever its nationality) to make further inroads and expand its value practices on the social body upon which its preservation depends. This does not mean that 'national interests' or, in this case, US geopolitical and economic interests are not related to the promotion of capital's value practices. It is very difficult to avoid making this connection: the US has the largest military in the world; hence, even if we concede to the thesis of networked sovereignty in contemporary Empire, as argued by Hardt and Negri (2000), there is no way in which we can conceive the expansion of the social and political conditions necessary for the preservation of global capital without going back to the role of the United States.

However, from the perspective of the clash of value practices we are interested in, those upon which the beginning of history and the constitution of *our outside* depends, what we are opposed to is not so much the 'interests' of the United States or other nations. What the World Bank and its sister organisations do is not so much to defend US interests, but to promote a context in which those *types* of interests (the pursuit of money with no limit) are valued, while other types of 'interests' (dignity, food, freedom, commons, and so on) are not, or are subordinated to the former. In other words, *on the front line of social reproduction* the clash is about different value practices.

Thus, the danger we face by pursuing discourses on imperialism rather than on *capital* is to lose the sense, the meaning of the struggle *at the front line*! It is worth pointing out that 'interests' and 'value practices' are of course related; so, in opposing a certain value practice of capital (enclosure or disciplinary integration, for example), struggles also oppose someone's interests in pursuing that value. But we must bear in mind that the difference between the two is cast in terms of the dimension of time they refer to. 'Interests' are cast in linear time, since they are actualised in the aims of interested parties, in goals to be achieved. Value practices, however, are cast in cyclical time, since they refer to the formation of norms and modes of doing and relating, in the context of social interaction and co-production.

DETRITUS–CONATUS

In the first section of this chapter I have argued that the outside is the process of becoming other than capital. The problematic we have before us is thus how we can produce commons among so diverse and place-specific struggles, so as to constitute a social force that threatens the self-preservation of capital and *at the same time* posits its own self-preservation, predicated on a different type of *conatus* and different types of value practices. But this is too big a question, for which I do not have an answer. Only a suggestion for where to look: the *detritus* as a condition for the production of commons and the tension *detritus–conatus* as its driving energy.

This *detritus–conatus* process of becoming other then capital is more trivial than we might think. Although it often appears as a heroic outburst in which the new emerges through the 'phase time' dimension of struggles recounted by many ethnographies, its underlying character is rooted in the daily preoccupations that find expression in circular time and the routines necessary to reproduce life that give form to a singularity's *conatus* of self-preservation. And this is in a world that puts us all in the condition of articulating our *conatus* of self-preservation to that of capital. Let me give an example.

A woman clears up the rubbish in a tube train in 'postmodern' London. She might be from Eastern Europe or Western Africa, only the colour of her skin might tell. In one of the most expensive cities on earth, she is paid £5.05 an hour, regardless of whether it is night or day, a holiday or not; she even has to pay for transport by tube to the station in which she will clean carriages. Her daily return fare will cost her about one hour of her daily work. On Friday and Saturday nights she will have to clean the orange vomit produced by stressed out 'immaterial workers', drowning their frustrations for not having met targets set at the office, or celebrating a promotion (a step in the wage-ladder that differentiates social bodies in the eyes of capital), or simply attempting to recover a sense of the self by loosening up from the codes and measures that define their character in formal business contexts.

What is it that makes the woman take up a lousy job for a lousy wage but her *conatus of self-preservation* and that of her community – perhaps a child, a younger sister and a mother somewhere else in the world, may be waiting for her to send some cash under the threat of 'dispossession' of their land or house? Or perhaps her *conatus* of self-preservation led her to take up a lousy job far away from home because it allowed her to escape from violent conditions in the community in which she was born and bred – a violent man, a husband, a father, a brother? And what is her daily struggle to turn up for work and maintain sanity vis-à-vis the ongoing humiliating measuring processes of her doing, continuously attempting to 'minimise cost', to 'minimise waste', hence 'maximising' the *detritus* inscribed in the body of this woman and others like her? And when this woman and others like her come together to articulate their lives in the struggle for better working conditions, wages, or a free travel card, what is this struggle but the turning of *detritus* into the condition for reclaiming commonly produced wealth and asserting dignity? And what is the *production of this common wealth* if not part of the commons emerging from all struggles, presenting themselves in the twofold character of repossession of social wealth if the struggle succeeds *as well as* the constitution of new relational practices and new communities among the struggling subjects?

What I am trying to say here is this: *detritus* is a common *condition* of life practices and corresponding *conati* articulated to the *conatus* of self-preservation of capital, because the latter certainly demands its toll, hence produces *detritus* in our bodies and in our environments. In this respect, *detritus* is a common yet stratified ground or condition, with its own manure, out of which *desires flourish* and, to use the expression of Gilles Deleuze, produce reality. But they produce reality in different conditions. Some of these desires are siphoned back into the circuits of capital through commodity exchanges and connection with the disciplinary and enclosure processes of global loops. Some are siphoned back into these circuits by necessity; others by 'free consumer' or 'citizen' choice; others as a result of the successful strategies of marketing agencies; and others still by a mixture of these. In so far as this happens, and it happens increasingly often, the social force we call capital can preserve itself.

However, other desires emerging from the *detritus* do not reproduce the reality of the circuits of capital. As I have argued in Chapter 2, social reproduction is a larger set than 'capitalism' and its circuits, and it is predicated on webs of relational practices, which far exceed those constituted by capital's measure and the outside that capital successfully articulates to its *conatus* (for example, the reproduction of bodies qua labour power).

Some of these desires-creating-reality posit a direct relation to nature, whether this is in a productive relation with the land, to reproduce one's community's livelihoods as autonomously with respect to disciplinary markets as possible; or simply, at a different level of the wage hierarchy, a re*creative* relation to nature, in which reproduction is not uniquely of the commodity 'labour power', but of values and perspectives that are *other than* capital. Other desires still are constituted out of clashes and conflicts within the social body. In these cases, *detritus* is a condition of reproduction of racial, gender, and other hierarchies in which power, understood with Foucault as the effect on action, pushes the receiving ends in these hierarchies to challenge (through communication, negotiations and struggle) the meanings of the 'community' of which they are allegedly part. Alternatively, the *detritus* is a condition of escape, of exodus. Indeed, sometimes the *conatus* of self-preservation of identities gives rise to dangerous games, especially when the identities in question put their bearers at the receiving end of behaviour that might be called 'sexist', 'racist', 'homophobic', and so on.

Finally, still other desires emerging from the condition of *detritus* create convivial and horizontal commons, whether this happen in the context of the daily struggle for the reproduction of necessity and self-preservation, or in heroic and intense outbursts of collective activities that constitute struggle as the limiting of capital's *conatus* and the terrain of new commons. The outside, or better, *our outsides* are all here, in the diverse processes of the constitution of commons and in the problematic of their articulation, preservation, reproduction and *political recomposition* at greater scales of social action.[9] This means that the outside is constituted by living and relational practices, in their strategic problematisation, in the subjects' participation in the production of commons at the point of division.

17
Commons

THE PRODUCTION OF COMMONS

To talk about political recomposition is not only to raise the issue of the *overcoming* of divisions within the struggling body. It is to problematise these divisions as object of our overcoming, in full awareness that these cannot be overcome by abstract and ideological calls for unity *or* brushed aside by theoretical frameworks that dismiss their ongoing reproduction through the application of capital's measure and value practices. The problematic of overcoming division is one with the problematic of the production of commons.

It seems to me that the question/problematic of commons *emerges* and must be posited at a point/moment of *division* of a struggling body, at whatever scale of social action. It is at that juncture that the ability to problematise the commons and recompose struggles on that new terrain allows the struggle to move forward onto a new plane, to climb a step in the ladder of the fractal panopticon and contribute towards extending the articulation among struggles. This, of course, does not mean to call for unity, as the socialists do all the time – a unity *not* rooted in real concrete commons that struggling and diverse subjects can produce beyond a hierarchal and divided social body, but predicated on ideology *brought from a metaphysical outside* (the party). To say that at the point of division struggling subjects must seek to produce commons is not to be prescriptive: commons are often produced by struggles, whether an author calls for it or not. Rather it is to warn that the failure to produce commons, while the struggle loses momentum and external pressure to break it up increases, implies ripping apart the fabric holding together subjects in struggle, and the movement flows out in a thousand ripples. This, of course, might all be perfectly understandable, depending on the context: if, for one section of the movement, the price of finding a common is the annihilation of ones desires and needs, it is perhaps better to maintain full autonomy. The time is not ripe for the production of that type of commons. In these contexts, when *articulation* of conditions and desires across subjects in struggles is not possible or carries insurmountable limits, hence new value practices articulating different subjects cannot be established, the market might even offer the taste of liberation. For many women, the struggle against patriarchy involved getting a job, hence achieving financial autonomy vis-à-vis men. As we have seen in Chapters 5 and 6, capital has of course accommodated that, recoding patriarchy in a new international division of labour and making it necessary to recast the struggle against patriarchy on new terrain.

But we must keep in mind that the production of commons occurs at the point of division within the struggling body, precisely because it is a proactive creation to resist the division of the social body on the basis of immediate *material interests*. The production of commons can overcome these divisions not by ignoring them, but by rearticulating them around new value practices. Indeed, the production of commons to recompose a divided struggling body coincides with what might be called *articulation*, that is the production of meanings.[1] The answer to the context-specific question of how diverse and interconnected struggles can be articulated together is the question of how *common* meanings can emerge. Bearing in mind what we discussed in Chapter 2, that values are the socially produced meanings people *give to action*, the problematic of the circulation of struggle, the question of the effectiveness and organisational reach of struggle, is one with that of the production of *common* value practices in opposition to the value practices of capital.

It is through the production of commons that new value practices emerge and *divide-and-rule* strategies dividing the social body on the basis of material interests can be contrasted. That process of reflection/communication/negotiation aimed at identifying and crafting a specific contingent commons is a philosophy born in struggle, a necessary moment of the production of struggle itself, a philosophy that is grounded, but also that aspires, and hence *develops* a strategic look that helps to make clear what it is up against; hence it has the potential to be a material force 'that grips the masses', because the same struggling 'masses' (i.e., a 'whole' of relating subjects) are the producers and the product of this philosophy. Also, we must recognise that the ability to identify and generate a common means to go to a *deeper* level, the effect of which is to achieve a 'higher' organisational reach, to travel towards the root of things, is to 'kick asses' at the top!

The clash in perspective between a social force that produces enclosures and one that produces commons means this: capital *generates* itself *through* enclosures, while subjects in struggle generate themselves *through* commons. Hence 'revolution' is not struggling *for* commons, but *through* commons, not for dignity, but through dignity. 'Another world is possible', to use an under-problematised current slogan, to the extent that we *live* social relations of different types. Life *despite* capitalism, as a *constituent* process, not *after* capitalism, as a constituted future state of things.

FREEDOM, COMMUNITY ...

Indeed, the beginning of history must be lived, because only living subjects can participate in the constitution of the mode of their interrelation, and the *mode* of relation between individual singularities/fragments and the whole is the central kernel of the problematic of the beginning of history. Only living subjects can work out among themselves the meaning of going *outside* the value practices of capital and its disciplinary markets.

 The discussion of capitalist markets as disciplinary does not make them 'good' or 'evil' per se, but simply recasts the problematic of freedom and democracy onto a different plane than 'bourgeois' discourse. Our discussion has simply problematised the fact that markets imply specific forms of social relations and corresponding specific processes of doing, of positing heteronymous measures and of negotiating social norms behind the back of the actual doers, whether waged or unwaged. To individual singularities, capitalist markets are simply what they are, whether they are at the receiving end of a restructuring process that ruins them, or at the cutting edge of an innovative process that allows subjects to embark in a rapid and flourishing career. The fundamental point I have stressed about capitalist markets is that they are a system of social relations that take away from singularities with needs and desires the need to *articulate* things among themselves, since it is the market that does the *articulation* for them, that puts them into relation with each other in given forms and, therefore, through the repetition of feedback processes under the code of the 'law of value', that gives rise to norms of social production. Direct and free articulation, that is the active engagement with others in the production of meanings, values and, ultimately, the creations of *commons*, of parametric centres grounding co-production, is inversely proportional to the pervasiveness of market measures on the life practices of the producers. Hence freedom and democracy must be understood as the freedom and democracy of social individuals. The outside, *our outside*, is the space in which freedom and democracy, by taking on full meaning because they are lived and practised, become highly destabilising of the current social order.

 In another little-quoted passage, Marx addresses the question of freedom and democracy grounded in commons, in this subversive sense of the term, as the positing of the 'beginning of history': 'Let us finally imagine, for a change, an *association of free [individuals]*, working with the means of production held in *common*, and expending their many different forms of labour-powers in full *self-awareness* as one single social labour force' (Marx 1976a: 171; my emphasis). There are three elements of this sentence that I believe define 'human history' as Marx understands it as opposed to 'human prehistory'. First, the members of the association are *free* individuals. A freedom that is further qualified by, second, a *self-awareness* of being part of a whole producing and reproducing the conditions of their own life. In this sentence therefore, the 'working' referred to can be better conceptualised in the more general sense of social doing, whether this relates to raising children or building bridges. But the point is that, unlike Hayek's defence of the market order discussed in Chapter 14, this is not the freedom of bourgeois private individuals on the market whose choice is restricted to a selection of items on a *given* menu. Rather, individual freedom *and* self-awareness of being part of a whole implies that individuals are, *and* recognise themselves to be, *social individuals*, members of a community. Also it implies that their freedom not only applies to their individual spheres, but also to the definition of the *context* of their interaction. In a word, the menu is a result of their self-aware freedom, not a given product of their blind interaction as in the market mechanism or, alternatively, the authoritarian imposition of a self-proclaimed workers' state. Finally, third, this freedom of social individuals can be exercised only if the means used to produce their own conditions of life are considered precisely as such, as means, through which the aspirations and needs of human beings are met. This freedom cannot be exercised if these means of production, knowledge, and communication are enclosed. This freedom cannot be exercised if they are the means for private accumulation – accumulation, that is, not as a safeguard for rainy days as in agricultural societies or as precondition for *plotoch* as in 'stone-age' practices. Rather, to use King George Bush II's justification for terrorising Iraqi's population into submitting to market reforms, accumulation 'as a way of life', a way that splits the social body, separates production and consumption, and targets these alienated activities with the curse of *bound-lessness*. It is in the domain of the shared that limits can be set. For Marx, therefore, means of production, whether socially produced or part of the natural endowment of the context of human life (e.g. water, air, land, etc.), are held in *common*. But if this is the case, who decides what to use and for what purpose? Back to square one: decisions are taken by the association of *free* individuals who at the same time are self-aware as being part of the whole and as constituting a web of relations, decision processes and feedback loops through which the art of social living is constituted. This circularity is not a defect of Marx's argument; on the contrary. I read this as the positing of human freedom as a collective *process* of engagement, which balances roots and creativity, conditions and overcoming. It is the proclamation of human self-reliance and self-determination, understood neither as the abstract idea of a master narrative, nor as the particularist idea of the fragment.

'What a utopia!' one might say. Indeed, for some strange reason, in the English language a hyphen can do miracles. To be a living force, utopia must be able to articulate its twofold dimension: from no-where, we come back down to earth, now-here. And now-here, there are contingent problems of reproducing livelihoods, there are concrete struggles, concrete horizons, concrete conditions of *detritus*, contingent issues, needs, demands and aspirations. In the now-here, there is nothing that theoretical speculations about the no-where can tell us. But there is contingently defined *detritus*, there is desiring *conatus*, there is naked social cooperation, antagonistic to the extent that capital and patriarchy have pervaded the social body, in which productive communities make decisions and follow practices the effect of which is to threaten the livelihoods of other communities, to turn them into fragments. Now-here the problematic of the beginning of history is the daily praxis of reconstituting communities of social cooperation predicated on different value practices.

This problematic is open. In the sentence quoted above, Marx presupposes and does not explicitly discuss *how* what he calls 'free producers' decide for themselves, what is the mode of their interaction, *what is the organisational form of their mode of social cooperation*. Indeed, he leaves the question open, and in the next few pages following this passage he explicitly makes assumptions only regarding alternative modes of distributions of the products of labour according to labour time (Marx 1976a: 172). What however is clear is that what is hidden and presupposed in Marx's thinking here is the question of *community*, by which I mean the domain of relational modes, the problematic of how *free individuals* who are self-aware as being part of a social body in which they are related to each other, articulate their co-production. Neither Marx nor anybody else could answer this question. Only living social subjects in struggle and cooperation can pose the question of community as part of the problematic of the beginning of history, of *their* history.

What we can say, however, is that the plurality of subjects' struggles in the last few decades in many parts of the world has created a new context within which to reformulate the problematic of communities. The so-called 'single-issue' campaigns have questioned and undermined in society at large norms, values and institutions that meant exclusion, hierarchy, oppression and obscurantism for 'community'. Women struggling on the production, reproduction and interpersonal fronts problematised and rewrote meanings and roles, politicising self-awareness and inclusiveness. The widespread anti-authoritarianism of the 1960s and 1970s longed for respect and disrupted hierarchies. Gays and lesbians 'came out' and disturbed people's certainties about sexuality, opening up horizons and posing the question of relations with the 'other'. Anti-racist struggles faced society at large with the question of equal rights, respect and dignity within the social body. Indigenous struggles amplified the demands for dignity, autonomy and self-reliance, and forced the issue of respect for non-mainstream, non-Western forms of knowledge. The contemporary struggles of migrants inside the European metropolis is exposing the third world in the first as well as the hypocrisy of governments which make 'human rights' their reason for going to war but yet put migrants in detention camps to regulate their access to their labour markets. Decades of environmental struggle have made us aware of our natural context, of our being part of nature, and of the need for us to be responsible for each other, for other species and for the ecosystem, however we want to problematise that 'responsibility'. Farmers across the world reclaiming land, demanding respect, have helped us to make the link between what we eat and how we produce, and how this is the basis of what we are.

In retrospect, all these struggles, which not long ago many 'revolutionary socialists' at worst dismissed as secondary and at best tried to subordinate and co-opt to the priorities set by self-delusional leaders, have produced a cultural milieu that envelops *detritus* and make possible not simply the conception, but also new practices of local and translocal *communities* outside the value practices of capital. Responsibility for the whole, but also dignity of the parts understood as autonomously positing *their own* measures; trust for the 'other', but also critique of one's position within the whole; inclusiveness of needs and aspirations, but also respect for different voices; participatory horizontality of political processes, but also definition of priorities; urgency of action, but also time for communication: these, in my experience, are all dynamic principles that are emerging in the many relational fields of *community*, and in networks and webs springing out of the universe of the alter-globalisation movements.

... AND COMMONS

The opening up of *communities* to the value practices embedded in diverse struggles creates the precondition for helping us to posit the question of community of producers, of *how* we engage in social reproduction, how we relate to each other, at every scale of social action. But this relational field of community always presupposes and, through social practices, gives rise to *commons* around which the activities of the subjects are articulated. Every mode of doing needs commons. Indeed, to pose the question of commons is simply to recognise the social character of our doing, the fact that individuals are *social* and hence they *must share something* (language, land, sea, air, values, etc.); and, at the same time, what is shared is the result of a social co-production. Different modes of production differentiate on the basis of *how* commons are reproduced and of *what* are commons and what are not, which is to say, how communities of producers relate to each other. Thus, in capitalist production, each 'community' of producers (in private or state companies, or cooperatives), is pitted against others in an endless race to succeed and/or survive in the market. Through this antagonism, they reproduce the common conditions of their livelihoods. They are also locked in a structural drive for money; they all share rules and practices that reproduce their antagonism. Money, or the desire for money, is their common, a common still reproduced by the actions of communities, as *all* commons are, but in such a way that the product-thing of human action (money) command the doing of the co-producers. This upside-down world, the other side of which is generally analysed in terms of commodity fetishism, alienation and abstract labour, is at the same time

a world in which the relations between commons and communities are disjointed, because for capital what is common (the product of social production)
can only appear as private, as appropriable, as the means of accumulation, as
the condition for some community of producers to take advantage of *other*
communities of producers.

A different understanding of commons is re-emerging from the webs and
networks of the alter-globalisation movement. Indeed, many of today's
struggles deployed against global neoliberal capital contain several demands
for *commons*. On issues of land, water, knowledge, electricity, social entitlement, education, health, nature, habitat and others, a large variety of struggles
longs for recomposition and articulation with others, within the same locality
and around the world. There is an increasing awareness in these networked
movements that the general question of alternatives to neoliberal capital must
involve some form of end (as well as *reversal*) of enclosures, and consequent
establishment of commons. But it seems to me that the struggles of various
social movements in the last decades has also made clear that 'commons' and
'communities' are interlinked, that is that the dimension of *what* is shared and
of *how* is shared must go hand in hand. Hence, the great emphasis, in many
interesting sections of the movement, on questions of direct democracy, on the
exploration of new modes of horizontal decision making; and the fascination
with indigenous practices of consensus decision making and, in general, with
horizontal practices as an ongoing laboratory of co-productions.

In these movements there is also general awareness that commons do not
necessarily mean 'the state'. In other words, that the alternative to the antagonistic and alienated community of the market is not what Marx calls the
'illusionary community' of the state. The demands for new commons spring
from the search for a way forward, away from ideological constructs, and
requiring wide participation in decision making.

From this account, the beginning of history therefore seems to pose itself as
a problematic defined along two main coordinates: commons and communities. In this sense, the beginning of history is the beginning of the *constitution*
of the thinking and praxis that look upon the world's fragments as free and
dignified voices, and the whole of their interactions as 'objectal' – that is,
under the form of object – rather than objective – that is, independent from the
subjects.[2] While apologists for neoliberal globalisation pose the intersubjective
global interaction as *objective*, as a reality individual fragments *must bow to*
and that is independent from subjects – and this is false of course, precisely
because states, transnational corporations, global economic institutions, and so
on are the creators of this objectivity – to put the interaction among the fragments as *objectal* means not only that the fragments/singularities pose the
question of their self-awareness of the form of their interaction, but it is a problematising self-awareness, one that poses the question of the overcoming of
existing exploitative, oppressive and alienating forms of social interaction.

ANARCHISM, COMMUNISM AND SOCIALISM

Self-awareness. To begin the journey of self-awareness is not to recite a doctrine, a credo, a belief. Rather, it is to confront the meanings we deploy in the articulation of our practices to those of others, and to problematise them. Let me exemplify this journey of self-awareness, starting from the mythological home of the writer going to demos (and readers can of course exemplify for themselves, by starting from their own mythological homes, and dissolving the identities frozen therein by measuring them in terms of their process-like meanings). In the many marches and rallies, and debates in social centres and bookshops, in many parts of the world, we fly flags with different labels, symbols and colours. Three classic terms come to mind at this juncture, three concepts describing three ways of being implicated in the battle to overcome capital: anarchism, communism and socialism. Too often these terms have been regarded as brands requiring our loyalty and thus producing identity walls that divide the struggling body. Instead, I understand them as describing horizons of practices and processes of decoupling, and *not* as ideologies, models or brands.

Anarchism is about anti-authoritarianism; it is the belief that we can organise co-production on a voluntary basis, with no coercion, neither that of the market nor that of the state, and that we can take decisions together horizontally, democratically, non-violently. Anarchism is the principle that gives form to the mode of government we want to have over our lives, which is self-government, autonomy and freedom. Anarchism is the fun part of *our outsides*, and its subject is plural and diverse: a multitude of subjectivities.

Communism is about the practice of self-government, a process of co-production, so to speak, which involves the sharing of resources held in common among members of a community (or communities) who, for this reason, engage in relational processes to shape their norms and values. Communism is the relational part, to each other and to nature, constituting *our becoming outsides*. Its subjects are local and translocal communities.

Socialism is about ... Chavez, let us say ... governing capitalism through the state in such a way as to facilitate the increase in the degree of anarchism and communism among us all and then see what happens. Socialism is, for most of us, the theatrical part – it could be a farce, a drama, a tragedy or a comedy. The subject of socialism is always the illusionary community, bearing in mind that illusions bring results that are sometimes good and at other times devastating.

Anarchist practices without communist practices are individualistic or ghettoising. Communism without anarchism is hierarchical and repressive. Anarchism and communism without socialism, that is, without a struggle within/against/beyond the state, are fantasy (I do not say utopian, because utopias are not fantasies to me). Socialism without communism and anarchism is neoliberal.

I believe that within the many movements comprising the alter-globalisation movement there are many who seek to find ways to articulate anarchist, communist and socialist practices and overcome the ideological divisions that have characterised the history of anti-capitalism. Their practices of co-production of space–commons, such as the *encuentros*, or within social forums, are also a demonstration that these three horizons can come together to create common spaces, common meanings and values.

Yet, when I reflect on these horizons with respect to the measure of the enemy they are confronting (capital's value practices) I notice that it is 'communism' that seems to capture for me what goes on at the front line. The way I use this old and battered term is not as an ideology, but as a web of *value practices* that, thanks to the anarchist influences of self-government, cannot be defined, that escapes definition by individuals, parties and 'great leaders' and that is a '*real* movement which abolishes the present state of things' (Marx 1976c: 49); hence it abolishes capital's value practices, and hence, because the latter are constituted through organised political violence (the state), it must find ways to struggle within it (socialism), against it (anarchism), and beyond it (communism). But since by value practices we are talking about forms of livelihoods, co-production, I cannot conceive any abolition of the present forms of co-production without *at the same time* conceiving alternative forms of co-production. Therefore, I can only conceive communism in the same general way as I conceive capitalism, as ongoing process and articulation among singularities, predicated, of course, on *opposite* value practices. In this sense, communism is an ongoing practice of self-definition by individuals and communities who take matters into their own hands in the reproduction of their own livelihoods, and hence posit new norms and values of social co-production. Communism is the realm generated by the commoners striving to get outside of capital's value practices, into the realm of lived democracy and freedom.

Communists therefore are not those who 'fight for communism', as if communism were a fixed thing, a fixed set of rules, of norms we could fight for. There is nothing static in communism understood as social force; all of it is dynamic, flowing and relational, because the commoners create it. Communists are those who take part in the value struggles we are *all* involved in with awareness that alternatives linking our particular struggles to those of others can only be constructed beyond enclosures and beyond disciplinary integration. These, as we have seen, are really the bottom line for the preservation of the social force we call capital and the social system articulating clashing value practices that we call capitalism. Communists in this sense are not enchanted by the parables of reform or revolution, since neither of these is the point of the beginning of history. The point is to live a different type of life, linked to others and to nature through different value practices.

The only difference between communists and any other struggling subjects whatever their identity, is that communists confront capital while holding a mirror in their hands. The alternative to capital, at whatever scale of social action, is a social force that creates a world within the space defined by that reverse image: the image of commons and democratic communities instead of enclosures and market disciplinary integration. Communists are those who seek to create alternative ways to meet needs and follow desires at whatever scale of social action, wherever they are, knowing that the means can be shared, while the goals and the modes of doing that those means make possible can emerge from direct engagement with the other. Just as the social force we call capital seeks to preserve itself by extending and defending enclosures and the realm of the markets, so the social force we call communism can preserve itself only by extending and defending the realm of commons *and* grass-roots democratic processes and practices. The bottom-line ground within which to problematise alternatives, or the beginning of history is, in my opinion, all here.

But since enclosures and sites of disciplinary integration are almost everywhere, then their mirror image, which we have called the beginning of history, is also everywhere. Because, when you look at it systemically, as feedback mechanisms, there is no more split between individual and society, agents and structure. There is no split between 'in here' and 'out there'. Our split personalities, the contradictory roles we are called to lead, the schizophrenic oscillations in modes of doing between Dr Jekyll and Mr Hyde, in which the same *body* is called to act along conflicting value practices – as when we work under the imperative of meeting capital's measure when we know that this measure clashes with our own measure of things – reveal what Marx calls the class struggle to be as much a struggle within individuals as a struggle among groups in society. Communism in this sense is a social force of progressive decoupling from the monetary circuit of capital, and this can only be done through progressive extension of commons *and* corresponding communities. The beginning of history is everywhere and promises conviviality and abundance. The only thing that prevents us from being part of it is our needs and desire for it and the effectiveness of our powers, that is the organisational reach of our needs and desires. But the discussion of this cannot be part of this book; an author must be silent when the topic is a matter of concrete articulations to the other, concrete processes of constitution. These are rather a matter of strategy, networking, affects and community in specific contexts; they are a matter of free individuals seizing the conditions of production and reproduction of their own lives, and no theoretical generalisation is adequate to describe what ultimately is the flow of life as lived by beautiful free subjects. The beginning of history must be lived, otherwise it is the end of it.

Notes

1 THE BEGINNING OF HISTORY

1. Paradoxically, the ideological conviction was that the end of history had arrived with the 'end of ideologies'. Francis Fukuyama was the original proponent of the thesis according to which liberal democracy marked the 'end point of mankind's ideological evolution' and the 'final form of human government'. Liberal democracy 'remains the only coherent political aspiration that spans different regions and cultures around the globe'. That is, 'while earlier forms of government were characterized by grave defects and irrationalities that led to their eventual collapse, liberal democracy was arguably free from such fundamental internal contradictions'. This does not mean that these democracies 'were not without injustice or serious social problems', only that these problems 'were ones of incomplete implementation of the twin principles of liberty and equality on which modern democracy is founded, rather than on flaws in the principles themselves' (Fukuyama 1992: xi). It goes without saying that from the perspective of this book, these 'imperfections', when truly addressed, imply reverting the pervasiveness of capitalist markets that reduce 'liberty' to consumer choice and reproduce and widen inequalities across the planetary social body. In other words, the beginning of history here coincides with the end of discursive practices predicated on the horizons of the end of history.

2. Luce Irigaray, among other feminist scholars, emphasises the centrality of cyclical time in the production of male and female subjectivities, in her analysis of breathing, co-breathing and relational identity. She also recognises how, 'the time of life is always, at least in part, cyclical, like the time of seasons' or the time of plants and vegetation (1997: 47). Also, critical anthropology has acknowledged the importance of cyclical time in the production of subjectivity, as in the case of British anthropologist Chris Knight (1991), who links the emergence of human language to the production of solidarity among women made operationally possible by the synchronisation of their menstrual cycles to the moon cycle.

3. To clarify, by phase time I mean the time dimension peculiar to phase transitions. I borrow this from physics, which defines phase transitions in terms of sudden changes in one or more physical and organisational properties of matter. In my use, I intend to evoke the time of sudden changes in social and experiential 'phases' that are pervasive in human experience. A man or a woman falling in love, soldiers in the heat of battle, demonstrators reclaiming a square for a carnival under the watchful eye of powerless riot police, a car accident, a community of land squatters preparing to resist eviction, or, at larger scales of social action, the sudden change in the context of co-production of livelihood. In social theory, several concepts used to highlight transition and rupture have somehow to do with phase time. See, for example 'lines of flights' (Deleuze and Guattari 1988); 'exodus' (Hardt and Negri 2000; Virno 1996b); 'moments of excess' (Harvie and Milburn 2006). Sometimes these different concepts refer to an existential experience, at other times to a mass action. It goes without saying that social processes of radical transformation articulate both, and the distinction is purely analytical.

4. See, for example, Foucault (1991).

5. For a classic review of this tradition in relation to other forms of Marxism, see the introduction in Cleaver (1979).

6. According to the 'stage theory' version of Marxism, Marx divides world history into stages, each of which has its own economic and social structure. The transition from an 'inferior' to a 'superior' stage must follow a logical path, and it is not possible to skip stages of development. This interpretation, which was dominant until not long ago, constitutes the basic framework of classic historical materialism. It is linked to the historical interpretation of primitive accumulation, which we critically discuss in Chapter 10, in that a temporally clear-cut primitive accumulation would create the conditions for the transition to the capitalist stage of world history. Unfortunately, Marx wrote against turning the English experience into a model for the universal history of social and economic development. For example, in the French edition of *Capital*, the last edited by Marx himself, Marx clearly limits his analysis of primitive accumulation to *Western* Europe (Smith 1996: 54). In a clear statement against the universal stage theory, Marx's famous reply to Vera Zasulich is self-explicatory: 'The "historical inevitability" of a complete separation of ... the producer from the means of production ... is therefore *expressly* restricted to *the countries of Western Europe*' (Marx 1983: 124).

7. For a similar critique applied to the construction of women subjects, see Mohanty (2003).

8. The overcoming of this antagonism does not mean compromise between the poles of antagonism. There is nothing wrong with compromise per se in specific contingencies. Compromise however does not solve the contradiction; it just perpetrates it into the future. Overcoming implies a particular concept of temporality and history and of the nature of social change.

9. See Mario Tronti's classic text *Operai e capitale* (1966). For an English translation of sections of this book, see Tronti (1972).

10. For example, we exclude the question: How do the people on a dollar a day actually live, when they do live? What forms of exchange do they have with each other when so little among them is market exchange? For a critique of the paradigms of the third world as 'underdeveloped', and, correspondingly, of the mechanisms through which 'development' discourse was constructed as a strategy of control and power, see Escobar (1994), Esteva (1992), Esteva and Prakash (1998), Latouche (1993).

11. What might seem a naive observation is actually quite relevant even to someone who is no ascetic. In March 2006, the British government acknowledged that its own targets for cutting CO_2 emissions could not be met. Hence it embarked on a campaign of energy efficiency addressed to households: change the light bulbs, use double glazing, install roof insulation and all that. Not a word came from the government requiring shopkeepers in the high streets to contribute by switching off useless lights kept on all day and night to light useless commodities (often in the ratio of one light bulb for one commodity); or about switching off those huge commercial moving advertisements boards, such as the one in London's Piccadilly Circus, that for 24 hours a day proclaim to the world the virtues of MacDonalds and Coca Cola; or, more generally, to start to problematise the sacrality of money-measured economic growth and profitability and subordinate it to other values.

12. While 66 per cent of the money from the 2001 and 2003 tax cuts in the United States went to the wealthiest 1 per cent (Walker 2004), the poverty statistics of the 'only remaining superpower' are alarming. The U.S. Census Bureau reported in August 2003 that since 2000, an extra 4 million have been added to the number of poor Americans. The number of people below the official poverty line of $18,819 reached 35.9 million, a figure 1.3 million higher than the 34.6 million in poverty in 2002 (U.S. Census Bureau 2003). In any case, a quick estimate of the expenditures of an average household to provide only basic needs would leave the family on this income about $1,500 in debt (see CCHD 2004). On average, 16 per cent of children live in poverty in the United States, but, according to the US Census 2000, in some urban areas it reaches rates of 40 to 45 per cent (such as Brownsville, Tex., 45.3 per cent or New Orleans, La., 40.5 per cent). By 2002, 34.9 million, a little less than the population of Poland, were living in the land of freedom and democracy with not enough food for basic nourishment, a figure that had risen from 31 million in 1999. The official number of people experiencing hunger in the United States is almost 9.4 million (Nord et al. 2003), about the population of Sweden.

13. It is well known that US blacks in inner cities have a life expectancy which is lower than people living in the Indian region of Kerala, or Sri Lanka or China (Sen 1999). After all, campaigners of all persuasions have been extensively arguing that the (often broken) promise of an expensive college education and a job are among the key factors motivating poor people to join the US army (American Friends Service Committee 2004), thereby providing labour and brain power, as well as lives, to the empire's strategies of the day. According to federal statistics, the proportion of African Americans in the armed forces is 21 per cent, while they count for only 12 per cent of the entire population (Roy 2003). While army recruitment is concentrating on the growing poor Latino population in areas such as Puerto Rico, and private companies such as Halliburton are recruiting 'privatised' military personnel to send to Iraq in poverty ridden Central America (Democracy Now 2004), growing protests against army recruitment, linking it to poverty and vulnerability, are reported throughout the United States, as well as falling army recruitment. As reported by Mariscal (2005), 'One of the more dramatic protests targeting a recruitment station took place in late November of 2004 in Philadelphia. Increasingly frustrated by the lack of response from the Office of Housing and Urban Development to the needs of local homeless families, members of the Kensington Welfare Rights Union (KWRU) moved out of the Bushville Tent City they had established and staged a sit-in at the city's main Army recruiting station. Carrying signs that read, "Bring the Money Home" and "Billions for War, Still Nothing for the Poor," they briefly took over the office and issued a list of demands including affordable housing and domestic violence shelters. Several homeless families stated that they had relatives fighting in Iraq. The sit-in ended peacefully when fire and police officials arrived, and the homeless families returned to their encampment.'

14. As we shall briefly discuss in Chapter 7, competition across social nodes (organisations) must be rooted in some form of cooperation at the point of production, so when we talk about competition, we are really talking about *competition of cooperative nodes*. All the different models of capitalist organisation of production, whether they are more or less hierarchical, whether they are more similar to the modern 1920s' Ford or the postmodern twenty-first-century Google, need to find ways to structure cooperation by managing internal conflict vis-à-vis some 'other' out there. For a classic discussion of cooperation and division of labour from early capitalism to modern industry, see Chapters 13, 14 and 15 of Marx's *Capital* (Marx 1976a). Contemporary discussions on the importance of 'social capital' for the 'growth', 'economic success' and 'competitiveness' of nodes of social production at whatever scale (firms, cities, regions, countries) can be understood in terms of the need to counter the fragmenting forces of markets and reproduce some degree of cohesion necessary for capitalist production to occur. For a link between social capital and 'development', see Fukuyama (1995).

15. Classic statements of this relation are Marx's discussion of primitive accumulation in *Capital* (Marx 1976a), here discussed in Chapter 5, and Karl Polanyi's *The Great Transformation* (Polanyi 1944). Current literature is of course filled with references to the role of states in the promotion of global markets. For example, see Helleiner (1995) for a discussion of the role of the state in the shaping of global financial markets.

16. It is well known that historically pro-free trade countries such as Britain have begun to promote liberalisation only after they have protected their own industries and allowed them to grow strong. For a review, see Went (2002), or for a more detailed analysis, see Hudson (1992).

2   VALUE STRUGGLES

1. See, for example, the case of the Make Poverty History and Live 8 campaign on the occasion of the G8 meeting in 2005 at Gleneagles, Scotland. Hailed by rock star Bono as the occasion on which 'the world spoke and the politicians listened' and closed off by Bob Geldof's verdict of 'mission accomplished', the campaigners were keen to sing the praises of G8 leaders

and even called the 200,000 march against the G8 a 'walk ... to welcome the G8 leaders to Scotland'. See Hodkinson (2005) for a discussion of how the promised debt cancellation was peanuts in relation to total interest flowing from the global South to financial centres and how the promise of debt reduction is part of the neoliberal agenda to further structural adjustment and market reforms. It is then no surprise that on CNN, rock star Bono, liberal ex-president Bill Clinton, and 'good guy' development economist Jeffrey Sachs can share the same platform with neo-con engineer of the Iraq war and now World Bank president Paul Wolfowitz and all agree that market reforms, under the code name of anti-corruption, are central to debt and poverty reduction. See, for example, World Bank (2005a) for a video tester.

2. The article in the *Guardian* was reporting on the United Nation 2003 annual human development report (United Nations 2003), which mapped increased poverty in more than a quarter of the world's countries through a combination of HIV and Aids, famine, debt, and government policies.

3. 'Analysts at Goldman Sachs estimate that the global beauty industry – consisting of skin care worth $24 billion; make-up, $18 billion; $38 billion of hair-care products; and $15 billion of perfumes – is growing at up to 7 per cent a year, more than twice the rate of the developed world's GDP. The sector's market leader, L'Oreal, has had compound annual profits growth of 14 per cent for 13 years. Sales of Beiersdorf's Nivea have grown at 14 per cent a year over the same period' (*Economist* 2003). The same report argues that the 'beauty industry' is worth about $160 billion a year. On the other hand, there is a general consensus that to meet all the major 'development goals', among which only halving (not eliminating) poverty, hunger, malnutrition and reversing the impact of HIV/Aids and major diseases by 2015 would require about $100 billion a year, that is roughly doubling world aid of $56 billion (Johansson and Stewart 2002). Of course, these estimates are silent about the fact that the third world today pays back on debts to the North more than it receive in aid. In 1999 for every £1 in grant aid to developing countries, more than £13 came back in debt repayments (World Bank 2001). In aggregate, developing countries have become net capital exporters to the high-income world (World Bank 2005b). Also, these figures for the cost of basic 'development needs' are dwarfed when we assess them in relation to the cost of $3.8 million for each Cruise missile (750 of which were launched in just the first month of the latest Iraq war), or the cost of $42.9 million for a B-52 bomber (Brookings Institution 1998). Not to mention the $420 billion in US military spending, and the Bush administration's plan to spend over $2.2 trillion on the military over the next five years (Center for Arms Control and Non-Proliferation 2005).

4. Scarcity is a relation between needs and means. Contemporary mainstream economic discourse posits ends as 'unlimited' and means as limited (Robbins 1984). From this relation derives the naturalisation of scarcity, that is the belief that scarcity is a natural condition of humanity. In reality, scarcity in this sense is a discursive practice, predicated on the idea of individuals as fragmented and atomised and disconnected from a community, what economists call *homo economicus*. As individuals constructed as fragments, as singularities alienated from the powers of the social body, we do indeed live in a world of scarcity that we reproduce on a daily basis through disciplinary markets, that is forms of social relations in which we co-produce our livelihoods by pitting livelihoods against each other. The overcoming of scarcity is one with the overcoming of isolation and fragmentation, as demonstrated by those authors who describe how autonomous indigenous communities set ends and means through social processes involving direct relations among members rather than through abstract mechanisms of capitalist markets. For a critique of the notion of scarcity from this perspective see Esteva and Prakash (1998).

5. According to UN estimates, close to 1.2 billion, or a fifth of the human population on the planet, live in conditions of extreme poverty. About 800 million go chronically hungry. There is of course a debate over what counts as 'poverty', which we cannot survey here. In any case, an

interesting entry point of this debate are those studies that, faced with increasing evidence that there is not a direct relation between economic growth and poverty reduction (United Nations 2004) – something that no economist would like to hear – are suggesting that perhaps a revision of the measure of poverty should be considered (Deaton 2003). Others instead criticise the World Bank methodology of measuring poverty by the number of people earning below $1 or $2 a day, on the basis that this grossly underestimate it by relying on an abstract monetary measure that does not allow meaningful intertemporal and interspatial comparisons. The statement that world poverty is decreasing would not be justified on the basis of these criticisms. Some propose procedures that do not focus on 'whether the incomes of poor people are sufficient in relation to an abstract "money-metric" international poverty line but rather on whether they are sufficient to achieve a set of elementary capabilities' (Reddy and Pogge 2003: 32).

6. See, for example McMurtry (1998; 1999; 2002).
7. 'A value system connects together goods that are affirmed and bads that are repudiated as an integral way of thinking and acting in the world' (McMurtry 1998: 7).
8. 'A value system or ethic becomes a program when its assumed structure of worth rules out thought beyond it' (McMurtry 1998: 15). Thus, for example: 'When the Hindu does not think of a reality beyond cast dharma, and when the marketer cannot value beyond market price, we see examples of value programmes at work. A social value programme is a jealous God. Consciousness and decision, preference and rejection are imprisoned within it. Whatever is against it is repelled as alien, evil, abnormal. The modalities of role and individuation, personal gratification and avoidance, become elaborations and differentiations of the programme internalized as the self. Lived alternative to the role-master is taboo. In the adolescence of the species, all members of the group see as the group sees. All experience as the group does. All affirm and repudiate as the group does. There is no reality beyond it save the Other' (McMurtry 1999: 21).
9. 'Most of the highly fertile soil of the sea coasts and Mekong Delta area allocated for the high-price prawn crops in eight densely populated countries was rapidly degraded and sapped of nutrients, oxygen, water-holding capability, and tree roots by repeated cycles of salt-water flooding. Ground water was polluted and rendered unsafe for drinking. Large-scale prawn plantations moved in with the support of tax-incentives for investment. They secured peasants' plots by rent or purchase, flooded the land, pressured peasants to sell their livestock so it did not consume prawn stocks, and moved on to other profitable sites as soon as the land was exhausted. Whether small-plot farmers had rented, sold, or used their own small plots for prawn farming in dynamically increased market activities and transactions, they were all left with desertified land to live on. It had been sown with salt as surely and destructively as if an invading army had done it deliberately as a punitive raid. Yet everything that transpired consistently expressed the market system's principles of preference and worth' (McMurtry 1998: 8–9).
10. Quoted in McMurtry (1998: 15).
11. According to McMurtry it is possible to criticise this value system as in itself 'bad'. But in order to do so we have to expose it, by going around its 'armour of protective rationalisations'. Each value system has one such armour, to the extent that its predicaments are presented for the 'good' of humanity as a whole. So, for example, a racist paradigm claims to hold to certain values (such as freedom, Western civilisation and other buzzwords used by white supremacists) but instead holds other values. The problem is to expose this gap between the values a value system claims to hold and the values that in reality it holds. This is, in other words, to hold the value system to account. I am not convinced this is a sufficient 'method' to dispose of a value system that reproduces oppression, especially one that does this through coordinating people's livelihoods like capital. It is too rationalist, and it is not clear to whom one should hold the 'armour of protective rationalisations' to account. It is a few decades now since sophisticated critics like Noam Chomsky began exposing the lies behind the 'armour of protective rationalisations' of US foreign policy, but that has not contributed an iota towards changing the values

around which it is centred. Also, market mechanisms ultimately allow reproducing livelihoods and coordinating social production, although in a way that continuously produces losers and winners. To the extent that critics point at the problems of the former, the supporters point at the success stories of the latter.

12. See Dobuzinskis (1987: 119).

13. We must clarify here that the value practices I am referring to are principles of selection used by subjects within a system of values, not the set of ethical principles and mores that a particular agent is said to believe in. The latter may deviate from those values a particular singularity is called on to be guided by, value practices that emerge from the system as a whole and impose themselves upon individual singularities. For example, an 'ethical capitalist' might indeed subordinate profit considerations to labour rights or environmental concerns. But the 'ethic of capital' as played out by the systemic forces that articulate together ethical and non-ethical capitalists will never accept subordinating profit to anything. Capital's ethic is an emergent property of a multitude of ethics (hence of subjectivities, affects, perspectives, positionalities, and so on) interacting with each others in particular modes. It is a property that continuously recreates the capitalist order of things. It is a property that acquires the force of an 'objective' reality for any particular individual producer, whether waged or unwaged, that sets constraints on the actions of every single individual.

14. There is indeed something very problematic in this view that empire exhausts the real and indeed, if in reality it does not exhaust it yet, the political implication would be to favour its development. A case in point is for example Negri's controversial position in favour of a yes-vote for the French referendum on the neoliberal European constitution held in May 2004, which ended with the victory of the no-vote. Negri's argument for a yes-vote was that 'the constitution is a means to fight Empire, that new globalised capitalist society' (De Filippis and Losson 2005: 829). In our view of contemporary capital, the neoliberal European constitution promoting marketisation in social services and global markets in always new areas cannot be separated from the project of constituting a unified European foreign policy. It is not a European state that can offset US unilateralism, when the project of this state is a global order in which livelihoods are pitted against each other in the same way as in the global project of the US. In both cases, security is understood primarily in terms of security of global business operations, which, given the boundless character of capital's accumulation, includes the need for ongoing global capitalist growth (hence further enclosures, blood and tears). The threat to US unilateralism and, indeed, even to possible future multilateral wars for empire, is US and European grass roots ability to sabotage war, refuse it in practice, practise other values and value other practices. It is here that we find the node that must be problematised when reflecting on the failure of the unprecedented anti-war mass movements to prevent the Iraq carnage. To channel our hopes of peace and social transformation into a neoliberal constitution for Europe because there are no alternative projects on the table, because 'there is no one project of social reorganisation put forward by trade union or civil society that has accomplished real advances after a generation' (ibid.) seems to me to be precisely a radical normalisation of the 'end of history'.

15. Take for example this episode, reported in Ashwin Desai's (2002) book on South African community struggles after apartheid, in which by putting up resistance to threatened eviction by the local council, flat-dwellers in Chatsworth also develop new value practices among themselves, which overcome their identities and establish new commons. I briefly discuss this in Chapter 16. Here we do not have just a clash among moralities, of systems of values, but of value practices, informed by clashing measures of things, but that actively construct the 'social' and in different and indeed, clashing ways: the ways of the neoliberal debt collector and the ways of the community in struggle.

3   CAPITAL AS A SOCIAL FORCE

1. I am of course not the only one to be suspicious of the word 'capitalism'. The great critic of capital, Karl Marx, did not use the word once in his oeuvre, preferring instead the much more evocative terminology: capitalist mode of production (Smith 1996). More recently, the French historian Braudel, discussing the sixteenth-century origin of what is generally called capitalism, wrote: 'How could one possibly take it to mean a "system" extending over the whole of society? It was nevertheless a world apart, different from and indeed foreign to the social and economic context surrounding it. And it is in relation to this context that it is defined as "capitalism," not merely in relation to new capitalist forms which were to emerge later in time. In fact capitalism was what it was in relation to a non-capitalism of immense proportion. And to refuse to admit this dichotomy within the economy of the past, on the pretext that "true" capitalism dates only from the nineteenth century, means abandoning the effort to understand the significance – crucial to the analysis of that economy – of what might be termed the former topology of capitalism. If there were certain areas where it elected residence – by no means inadvertently – that is because these were the only areas which favoured the reproduction of capital' (Braudel 1982: 239).
2. Non-market relations are described using new terms by a stream of theoreticians and political activists: the sector of 'unwaged labour' (Dalla Costa and James 1972), the 'social factory' (Tronti 1973), the 'shadow economy' (Illich 1981), the 'general economy' (Bataille 1988), the 'moral economy' (Thompson 1991), the 'informal economy' (Latouche 1993). As pointed out by Caffentzis, with these new concepts, 'a new set of social-economic polarities has emerged: formal/informal, production/reproduction, market/moral, rational/customary, modern/post-modern, and a deconstruction of social forms has begun. For no sooner were apparent dichotomies identified, than their presumed positive and negative poles were displaced, or inverted, to reveal new fields of relations. Once, for instance, reproductive work, including subsistence farming, was made visible, it could no longer be ignored that the quantity of unwaged labor dwarfs the mass of wage labor, which was previously given pride of place in economic analysis, Marxist and non-Marxist alike' (2002: 3).
3. There is of course a long tradition discussing the relation between the non-capitalist and the capitalist spheres, spanning from Rosa Luxemburg (1963) (according to whom non-capitalism is what capital must colonise in order to expand) to Meillassoux (1981) (according to whom capital relies on the world's non-capitalist domestic economies for the cheap reproduction of labour power).
4. See, for example, Ivan Illich's notion of vernacular, which he uses as a 'simple, straightforward word to designate the activities of people when they are not motivated by thoughts of exchange, a word that denotes autonomous, non-market related actions through which people satisfy everyday needs – the actions that by their own true nature escape bureaucratic control, satisfying needs to which, in the very process, they give specific shape' (Illich 1981: 5–58). Or alternatively, Karl Polanyi's analysis of gift exchanges that do not reconcile with the rationalities and processes of market exchanges (Polanyi 1944, 1968).
5. As seems to be the case with the 'moral economy' in E.P. Thompson (1991).
6. For example, in his studies of the 'psychodynamics of work' the French author Christophe Dejours (1998) has extensively documented the fact that forms of organisations from below always imply more than just doing what you are told. As De Marcellus (2003: 2) points out, 'only doing what you are told to do is the definition of a classic form of sabotage on the job: the slowdown'. Dejours shows that cooperation and social creativity resolve the problems of production and organisation, independently from managers and bosses, day in and day out. Contrary to the conventional perception that workers couldn't do without the bosses to organise them, the opposite seems to be the case, and in order for patients to be cared for, students to be 'educated', or public services to run, the essential aspects of work must remain hidden from

management and its measures. It is precisely this dimension outside capital's measure that in the last two decades has become the target of New Public Management practices, through which markets, or their simulations, are introduced. The front-line clash of value practices is destined to intensify in public services in the next few years, and its problematisation in terms of values is politically essential. Other authors working with the MAUSS school sought to extend to contemporary societies the work of French ethnologist Marcel Mauss on the central role played by gift exchange in traditional indigenous societies. For example, Godbout (2000) and other researchers of the MAUSS discovered that contemporary societies conserve traditional forms of gift exchange with family and friends (that is, networks that are comparable in size to small traditional societies), but have also developed new practices of 'gifts to strangers'. Together with the development of the state and the market, this form of social relations seems to have developed as societies got larger, more fragmented and anonymous. In this category the authors include all kinds of associations and social activities belonging neither to the state nor to the market, such as volunteer work, charities, giving blood, self-help groups, the gift of body organs. In Canada, this form of unpaid work offered within family relations or as *gifts to strangers* was calculated to be 34 per cent of GNP in 1998, and has been rising since the 1980s. It is especially in periods of economic crisis that the practices of the gift to strangers become much more important. It would be interesting and important to engage in a systematic study of the range of strategies used to co-opt gift and commons to capitalist development.

7. However, coming back to the social system that is capitalism, we must make here a distinction between hierarchy between systems and hierarchy among people within a system, as bearers of social roles. The difference is in the direction of the information flows that constitute organisational patterns. Thus, hierarchies within social systems are characterised by top-down control, in which the higher layers set the parameters within which the lower layers are supposed to organise their interaction. A company's organisational chart or state's bureaucracies are examples of this type of hierarchy within systems. On the other hand, the hierarchies among systems we are talking about are not constituted from the top, but from the bottom. It is the interplay and thus the organisational form of the components of a system (themselves systems at lower levels) that give rise to the properties of a system that comprises them. Thus, for example, a system of social cooperation among a given number of producers gives rise to a higher productivity than the same production carried out by the same number of producers working in isolation from each other (Marx 1976a, ch. 12). This is an 'emergent' property of a system of social organisation, which is not present in the individual components, themselves being a system. An organism presents features that are not discernible in the cells that comprise it, although cells are also systems. The organising force for the reproduction of the system comes from below, and the organisational thrust to constitute different systems can only be bottom up.

8. This definition of capital as a thing is also the patrimony of classical political economy and modern economics. See, for example Perelman (2000).

9. For the definition of human capital, see the classic treatment of Gary Becker (1993). For social capital, see, for example Fukuyama's (1995) discussion of trust. For a critical review of the current use of social capital by modern international and development institutions, see Fine (2001).

10. The 'fallacy of composition' is the logical fallacy governing all types of methodological individualism, including contemporary economic discourse, and which informs much of public policies discourses. The fallacy of composition simply states that rules and properties applying to the activities of individuals do not necessarily apply to the whole resulting from the interaction of those individuals. It means that societies are not the sum of their parts (individuals) governing social life. Examples of the fallacy of composition embedded in modern policies are numerous. Just to cite a few, take the international financial institutions' effort to promote growth and development by 'structurally adjusting' individual countries and force them to promote cash crops so as to earn the cash revenue necessary to repay their international

debts. The diligent following of this advice by all the countries leads them to try to out-compete each other and to the perpetration of debt and poverty, since the resulting outcome of their interaction is an overproduction of cash crops and a consequent fall in prices (FAO 2005). Another example is the UK Labour government promising that 'education' will be the way to better and wealthier lives, justifying the dismantling of entitlements and the introduction of tuition fees on the basis that average graduate income is higher than non-graduate, hence individualising responsibility for university payment. What a trick! The resulting expansion of higher education in a context of flexible labour markets increasingly linked to globalisation processes and exposed to competition will have moved the goalpost for all. While a few years ago a university degree was an enviable entry point to a good salary and job security, for many today this is no longer the case, and tomorrow even less so. As more and more graduates compete against each other in 'flexible' labour markets, they will increasingly be put in the position of using their skills, knowledge and powers as the means for undercutting each other in the market and so will (re)produce scarcity.

11. See Spinoza's Ethics (1989), part 3, propositions 6,7 and 8.
12. The discourse of sustainability and its adaptation to capital's agenda can well illustrate a discursive strategy linked to the self-preservation of capital. See Chapter 7 on governance.
13. As clearly stated by the then managing director of the IMF, 'Countries cannot compete for the blessings of global markets and refuse their disciplines' (Camdessus 1997: 293).
14. For a theoretical foundation of this political reading of capital, see Cleaver (1979).
15. For an account of the disciplinary role of finance in the post-Bretton Woods scenario, as well as the fact that this strategy has itself entered into crisis (as seems to have been so in the case of Argentina), see Herold (2002).
16. We shall return to this problematic in the last two chapters. Here suffice to say that very insightfully Negri (1984: 188) puts the negation of capital's dialectic in terms of working-class 'self-valorisation' as distinct from capital's valorisation process: 'The relation of capital is a relation of force which tends toward the separate and independent existence of its enemy: the process of workers' self-valorization, the dynamic of communism. Antagonism is no longer a form of the dialectic, it is its negation.' Cleaver locates the genealogy of the concept of self-valorisation in the tradition of Autonomist Marxism, and it thus 'grew out of the early work by Panzieri, Tronti and others to grasp simultaneously the full extent of capitalist power (such as its attempts to convert all of society into a "social factory" and the full potential and expression of the working class power of "refusal," of its power to subvert capitalist domination' (Cleaver 1992: 128–9). Cleaver interprets Negri's concept of 'self-valorisation' in such a way as to define a strategic field. The concept in other word is important for 'showing how the power of refusal could and must be complemented by the power of constitution' (ibid.: 129). In our last two chapters we shall discuss the problematic of the overcoming of this dialectic.

4   WITH NO LIMITS

1. For Marx's discussion of what he calls 'Money circuit of capital', see Chapter 4 of Volume 1 of *Capital* (Marx 1976a). In Volume 2 (Marx 1978) he offers a systematic exposition. Examples of contemporary uses of the circuit as analytical framework include Bell and Cleaver (2002), in their discussion of crises; Caffentzis (2002), who discusses the circuit in relation to the problematic of social reproduction; and Dyer-Witheford (1999) who uses the notion of circuit to discuss high-technology capitalism.
2. To understand this intuitively, try the mental experiment: imagine you are part of a large company whose business is precisely to make money, and you are in a position of great responsibility: you are a corporate executive, a banker, a financial tycoon whose main concern qua agent of the business is to make money. Ask yourself: How much money is enough? Is 2 million pounds enough? Is 5 million enough? Is 10? Is a trillion sufficient? In reality of

course at any given time a limit is set by circumstances, but the point is this: from the perspective of profit making the 'pig principle' rules, and the more the better, especially because someone else will take the opportunity you have foregone; you must endeavour to survive the iron law of the market in which the big fish eats the small.

3. I have assumed here for convenience that the portion of this money deducted for the aim of life reproduction of the investors themselves is nil. Nothing changes with the main thrust of the argument if this assumption is dropped.

4. 'The circulation of money as capital is an end in itself, for the valorization of value takes place only within this constantly renewed movement. The movement of capital is therefore limitless' (Marx 1976a: 253).

5. It is for this reason, as Negri correctly observes, that for capital, 'limits exist and are considered as obstacles only in order to find again limits and proportions' (Negri 1984: 189).

6. The study of the conditions of production and reproduction of the ancient Greek social body has been the subject of debate for a long time. In the late nineteenth century the debate was cast in terms of whether, given the existence of trade and the use of money, the ancient Greek economy from the fifth century B.C. was 'primitive' or 'modern', that is, whether it resembled or not a 'modern' capitalist economy with interconnected markets, commodities and prices. In the mid twentieth century Karl Polanyi brought new terms to the debate. He argued that there are other forms of human exchange than market exchange and that even in the presence of markets, economies do not need to be organised around the self-regulating institutions of a market system. Drawing from anthropological and social studies, he distinguished between two forms of economic analysis, which he called 'formalist' and 'substantivist'. The former only applies to modern 'self-regulating' markets centred on impersonal interconnected market mechanisms and the forces of demand and supply that set prices. In the latter, goods may be produced and exchanged as well as valued by non-market and non-economic institutions (that is cultural, social and political) and therefore the value of these goods is derived from practices other than market practices, such as gift exchange and the state's redistribution and administrative price setting. To understand these practices, he argued, other tools of analysis were necessary, which he bundled together into what he called 'substantivist' economics. Polanyi argued that until the Hellenistic period the set of activities devoted to the reproduction of livelihood, what we would call today 'the economy', could not be identified as a separate and independent institution. Rather, these activities were 'embedded' in other social, political and cultural institutions.

In a seminal work, Moses Finley (1973) followed this line and argued that the ancient Greek economy was fundamentally different from contemporary market economies, both in scale and organisational characteristics. Although the Greeks engaged in market exchange, including long-distance trade, had a monetary system and coinage, and were involved in the production and consumption of goods, these activities were not seen as constituting a separate sphere, an 'economy'. Contemporary normalised economic activities, such as wage labour and investing money to make more money, were despised, since they were not tied to the management of the family farm and subsistence production. These latter activities were predicated on householding and self-sufficiency and were rooted in farm production that left enough free time for male, non-slave citizens to actively participate in the activities of the *polis*. On the other hand, wage labour and money making were rooted in principles of dependence rather than autonomy and subsistence. Market exchange and production were tied to personal and family needs, or were for the benefit of friends and the broader community, that is as means to ends, not to make profit, or to achieve 'economic growth', that is as ends in themselves.

Also, Finley argued that among the ancient Greeks there was neither a 'market mentality' nor impersonal mechanisms of markets price setting. Each individual city state had its *agora*, that is the open market and meeting place. However, these *agorae* were not interconnected, meaning that prices were set in accordance with local customs, local conditions and personal relationships rather than through the impersonal forces of supply and demand. This was not only because of the autarchic principles of self-sufficiency emphasised in Greek city states, but also because different city states in the eastern Mediterranean tended to produce similar goods. Therefore, trade was a type of 'vent-for-surplus' trade, that is limited to 'goods not available on the spot', to paraphrase Polanyi (1977). This is quite unlike today's 'disciplinary trade' (Chapter 9), whose main purpose is not to make available goods not available/producible on the spot, but is to discipline the social body through pervasive competition. For a general review of the debate, including contemporary debates on Finley's classic model, see Engen (2004).

7. For Marx, 'it is ... clear that in any economic formation of society where the use-value rather than the exchange-value of the product predominates, surplus labour will be restricted by a more or less confined set of needs, and that no boundless thirst for surplus labour will arise from the character of production itself' (Marx 1976a: 345). Marx goes on to explain that exceptions to this rule within non-capitalist modes of production can be found in cases in which the product of production is directly money. Thus for example, in antiquity 'over-work becomes frightful only when the aim is to obtain exchange-value in its independent monetary shape, i.e. in the production of gold and silver. The recognised form of over-work here is forced labour until death' (ibid.).

8. Against this, feminist authors such as Luce Irigaray (1997), among others, pose the question of definition of the 'I's' and the 'we' starting from a consciousness of limit, that is 'from an individual and collective responsibility that does not erase the singularity of each' (97, my translation).

9. In his seminal work *The Great Transformation*, Karl Polanyi exposed the myth of self-regulating markets and the neoclassical conception of the 'economy' as a realm of human action that is independent and separated from society (Polanyi 1944). Studying the working of classic antiquity as well as other self-sufficient social organisations, he argued that the economy, rather than being a distinct realm, is embedded in society, and therefore the distinction within spheres is problematic.

10. The Mercantilists, typified by Thomas Mun (1571–1641) and William Petty (1623–87) for example, believed in the complementary positive 'economic' effect of luxury consumption for the rich and poverty for everyone else. While the former would create jobs for the poor, the latter would help to keep down wages and force people to work in order to survive by limiting their capacity to resist work discipline: 'Penury and want doe make a people wise and industrious' (Mun 1664). William Petty demanded that wages should be kept low and poverty used to force people to work. This was because if wages were too high people just wouldn't work: 'when Corn is extremely plentiful, that the Labour of the poor is proportionably dear: And scarce to be had at all (so licentious are they who labour only to eat, or rather to drink)' (Petty 1690).

11. For example, Linebaugh and Rediker (2000) discuss the waves of struggles and resistance at different moments of the slave trade circuit. Yann Moulier Boutang (2002: 392) argues that the abolitionist movement in New England gained momentum thanks to the massive waves of escapes from slavery, which some accounts put at one hundred thousand fugitives, that is about one fifth of the overall slave population.

12. This narrow geographical confinement often implicit in the traditional Marxist historical approach has of course been subject to some criticism. For example, in his famous study on African underdevelopment, Walter Rodney (1972: 101) writes: 'The ideological gulf is responsible for the fact that most bourgeois scholars write about phenomena such as the industrial revolution in England without once mentioning the European slave trade as a factor of primary accumulation of capital ... But even Marxists (as prominent as Maurice Dobb and E.J. Hobsbawm) for many years concentrated on examining the evolution of capitalism out of feudalism inside Europe, with only marginal reference to the massive exploitation of Africans, Asians and American Indians.'

5   PRODUCTION AND REPRODUCTION

1. See Rowling (1987).
2. In the framework I use, the classical debate that picked up in the 1970s among radical political economists to establish whether the capitalist 'cause' of crisis was overproduction, underconsumption, falling rate of profit, or profit squeeze, is not relevant. If for the purposes of this book, they are all manifestations of the conflict among value practices, constituting the regulatory process of homeostasis of capitalist systems.
3. A fall in the work of reproduction in P* in the upper circuit means for example a reduced labour power for production, thus a negative effect on P. All the same, capital may try to find ways to increase reproduction work P* by shifting onto unwaged labour the cost of, say, cuts in public expenditure so as to reduce the social wage it pays. This simple relation can also be seen in terms of what Harvey (1999) calls 'spatial fix', that is the solution of a given capital's problems of profitability through outward capital expansion and various forms of territorial domination. But when understood in terms of the relation of production and reproduction, the 'spatial fix' does not call for a separation of the dimensions of accumulation and imperialism, as Harvey, and indeed most of Marxist literature, does, since M-C-M', accumulation, can only operate within time–space. This means that the 'outer expansion' (to reduce the value of labour power, to create more markets, to access raw materials, etc.) is nothing else but enclosure and the coupling of the enclosed spaced to disciplinary markets. See Chapter 16 for a brief comment on the relation between accumulation and imperialism.
4. In Chapter 14 I discuss how Jeremy Bentham saw in the co-optation of the unwaged labour of the 'inspector's family' one of the tools for making the panopticon prison cost-effective.
5. This outsourcing of education to unwaged work at home, according to Furedi, is at the root of the dramatic trend in plagiarism experienced in UK higher education and generally attributed to easy access to the internet. In reality, he argues, 'the internet turns plagiarism into child's play, but it does not possess the moral power to incite otherwise honest students to pass off other people's work as their own. Blaming the internet simply distracts attention from the responsibility that the system of education bears for cultivating a climate where cheating is not seen as a big deal' (Furedi 2006: 28). The big deal, in this increasingly competitive educational system, is the wage to which a degree is seen to give access.
6. For example, as expressed by Dalla Costa and James, women are of service to capitalism for two reasons: 'not only because they carry out domestic labour without a wage and without going on strike, but also because they always receive back into the home all those who are periodically expelled from their jobs by economic crisis. The family, this material cradle always ready to help and protect in time of need, has been in fact the best guarantee that the unemployed do not immediately become a horde of disruptive outsiders' (1972: 34).
7. One of the least reported and discussed phenomena in today's global factory is the role of witch-hunting. Silvia Federici (2004: 237) argues that 'as a consequence of the life-and-death competition for vanishing resources, scores of women – generally old and poor – have been hunted down in the 1990s in Northern Transvaal, where seventy were burned just in the first four months of 1994. Witch-hunts have also been reported in Kenya, Nigeria, Cameroon, in the 1980s and 1990s, concomitant with the imposition by the International Monetary Fund and the World Bank of the policy of structural adjustment which has led to a new round of enclosures, and caused un unprecedented impoverishment among the population.'
8. Women in the patriarchal families are exploited by men and as housewives by capital. If they also enter the sphere of waged work, they are also exploited as wage-workers (Dalla Costa and James 1972; Mies 1998). However, it must be noted that a man's exploitation of women in the house is done to meet his own needs and desires, not to extract a surplus value, a profit. On the other hand, men's exploitation of women 'is only the form through which capitalist exploitation is carried on' (Fortunati 1981: 146).

9. As Dalla Costa and James put it, 'if we fail to grasp completely' that unwaged work of reproduction of labour power is the 'very pillar of the capitalist organization of work, if we make the mistake of regarding it only as a superstructure, dependent for change only on the stages of the struggle in the factories, then we will be moving in a limping revolution that will always perpetuate and aggravate a basic contradiction in the class struggle, and a contradiction which is functional to capitalist development'. In other words, we would be perpetuating the error of considering the unwaged workers of reproduction as 'producers of use values only' and not of capitalist value. 'As long as housewives are considered external to the class, the class struggle at every moment and any point is impeded, frustrated, and unable to find full scope for its action' (1972: 34).
10. See, for example Anderson (2000) and Parreñas (2001).
11. The horror stories regarding the food industry are numerous and widely reported by the press and popular books. This is not the place to survey the topic. One example that particularly strikes me is the case of chicken nuggets, the consumption of which had reached £79 million worth and 21,000 tons in 2000, just for those consumed at home. Adults away from home consumed a corresponding amount. In the United Kingdom, children are also stuffing themselves with this delicacy, since it is served in school canteens and used as an instant pacifier in homes around the country. The sick also eat them in their beds in UK hospitals. When deconstructed, this little golden treat for an increasing number of Western children presents itself as a concentration of horrors, epitomising our commodified and alienated relations with nature, our bodies and each other. 'It depends on the industrialisation of livestock, on an endless supply of uniform factory birds to fit standardised factory machines. It depends, too, on the mass migration of workers, both legal and illegal, since adding the value to it requires an equally endless supply of low-value labour' (Lawrence 2002: 2). A typical product of modern capitalist transnational production, the chicken nugget hides a reality of horrors behind the succulent and crunchy skin. 'Like much of our diet today, the nugget is processed so highly that its taste and texture depend as much on engineering and additives as on any raw ingredients, making it an easy way to disguise cheap or adulterated food. And just as the nugget's form is far removed from its contents, so we have become completely divorced from the source of those contents, from the animals that provide them and from the people who transform them. The nugget is, in fact, the product of a transnational chain so fragmented and complex that even those in the business do not fully understand how some parts of it work' (ibid.). In these transnational chains, as in any other, it is possible to externalise costs to others (waged and unwaged workers producing it, consumers and nature). Thus, 'DNA tests specially developed by Sandford with the public analyst laboratory in Manchester enabled the English food standards agency to identify lots of water (in one case 43%) and traces of pork proteins in samples of Dutch chicken breasts labelled "halal". Six months later, Irish authorities made an even more unsettling discovery in chicken: undeclared bovine proteins. Seventeen samples from Dutch processors contained them. Some manufacturers were using a new technique – injecting so-called hydrolysed proteins. These are proteins extracted at high temperatures or by chemical hydrolysis from old animals or parts of animals which are no use for food, such as skin, feathers, hide, bone and ligaments, and rather like cosmetic collagen implants, they make the flesh swell up and retain liquid.' These discoveries raised the spectrum of the possibility of BSE in chicken meat. On the other hand, frozen chicken is shipped for export to fast-food and supermarket chains in Europe and England from huge factories outside Bangkok in Thailand, and 'produced' by miserly paid migrant workers, many of them women, from a variety of nationalities. In these factories, 150,000 birds are killed a day, each worker killing up to 190 birds an hour, and then cleaning, cutting, chopping, deboning, rearranging parts and packaging for 165 baht (£2.50 or $3) a day, six days a week, for a nine-hour day, which includes a one-hour break. Overtime of two or three hours a day allow workers to send more money home. Most of them in fact 'are the first of their families to go into the factories; their parents were rice farmers' (Lawrence 2002).

In recent years, the growth of a variety of struggles linking the questions of food, land, bio-diversity and 'good life' has not only helped to spread public awareness and resistance to the methods and ingredients of profit-driven food industry, but also to posit an agriculture based on value practices other than those of capital (Dalla Costa and De Bortoli 2005). But it is clear that we cannot approach the question of food without at the same time facing the problematic of the value practices through which we construct the modes of our interrelations with each other, waged and unwaged, within a system of reproduction of our livelihoods that is competitive and alienating. The picture of the chicken nugget stares at me, and embedded in its golden image is contained every thing that is wrong with capitalist production and that needs to be overcome!

12. As Maria Mies puts it, 'this view that the productivity of the female body is identical with animal fertility – a view which is presently propagated and popularized the world over by demographers and population planners – has to be understood as a result of the patriarchal and capitalist division of labour and not as its precondition' (Mies 1998: 54).

6 PRODUCTION, REPRODUCTION AND GLOBAL LOOPS

1. C-M-C, selling (C-M) in order to buy (M-C) applies to all transformations, which have use values as ends, including both the selling of waged labour and petty commodity production. Formula 3 in the previous chapter is the expanded formula of C-M-C, which accounts for housework in the case of the reproduction of wage workers.
2. 'The environment is by definition a set of things outside us, with no essential structure, while an ecology is a whole defined by internal relations. Environments can be listed and numerically evaluated. Ecologies offer no such packaging and *the boundaries between them are sites of active transformation*, without a fixed line between inside and outside. In particular, the boundary between humanity and nature becomes highly dynamic, and a matter to be understood historically and transformed politically. It is in this spirit that we would approach the question of an ecological crisis' (Kovel 2002: 17; my emphasis).
3. See Capra (1997: 92–4).
4. In Volume 2 of *Capital*, Marx describes the movement from the micro to the macro with the tools of the mechanical theory of heat. According to Caffentzis, this was 'developed by mid-19th century physics, [and] explains macroscopic phenomena as the products of millions of microscopic events and entities (2). In conformity with this method, Marx described the macroscopic aspects of capitalism as the product of millions of micro-events, and accounted for the reproduction of social capital on the basis of the circuits of individual capitals, with their microphysical orbits, different velocities and periods' (Caffentzis 2002: 5). Thus Marx writes: '… the circuits of individual capitals are interlinked, they presuppose one another and condition one another, and it is precisely by being interlinked in this way that they constitute the movement of the total social capital. Just as, in the case of simple commodity circulation, the overall metamorphosis of a single commodity appeared as but one term in the series of metamorphoses of the commodity world as a whole, now the metamorphosis of the individual capital appears as one term in the series of metamorphoses of the social capital' (Marx 1978: 429–30).
5. See for example the detailed annual 'competitiveness reports' published by the world economic forum (http://www.weforum.org).
6. On the features of the new slavery and its interconnection to the global economy, see for example Bales (2004).
7. 'Our societies are constructed around flows: flows of capital, flows of information, flows of technology, flows of organizational interactions, flows of images, sounds and symbols. Flows are not just one element of social organization: they are the expression of the processes dominating our economic, political, and symbolic life. … Thus, I propose the idea that there is a new spatial form characteristic of social practices that dominate and shape the network

society: the space of flows. The space of flows is the material organization of time-sharing social practices that work through flows. By flows I understand purposeful, repetitive, programmable sequences of exchange and interaction between physically disjointed positions held by social actors' (Castells 2000: 412).

7 ENCLOSURES AND DISCIPLINARY INTEGRATION

1. The term *homeostasis* 'stands for the sum of all control functions creating the state of dynamic equilibrium in a healthy organism. It is the ability of the body to maintain a narrow range of internal conditions in spite of environmental changes' (Skyttner 1996: 57). See also Capra (1997: 58). We should be aware that term of *homeodynamics* might be preferable because 'it suggests the process of seeking an adjustment rather than a fixed point of balance' (Damasio 2003: 302). See also Steven Rose (1998). In any case, I shall keep with the term homeostasis to keep with standard conventions.
2. Positive and negative feedback do not refer to quantitative changes in value but in the direction of change of the linked elements. So for example, plus signs indicate movements in the same direction and minus signs movements in the opposite direction. See Capra (1997: 60).
3. The American physiologist Walter Cannon (1932) developed the concept of homeostasis.
4. '*Stasis* clearly is one of those Greek word names that have almost the inner contradictory complexity Freud taught us to associate with products of the subconscious. It means an act which correspond with the root *estēn* ("to hold straight, to be standing up"), signifying at once "the fact of standing up", hence site, position, stability, firmness (*stasimos* is said of all that which is calm and well planted, just like *stasimon* in a tragedy denotes the text fragment which the choir sings without moving about), and "the fact of getting up", hence uprising, rebellion (*stasiōdēs* means "seditious"). In political terminology the word *stasis* came to signify, at the public level, the "state" (Polybus, 16, 34, 11) – and at the individual level, the "position" of a person in society (Polybus, 10, 33, 6). *Stasis* refers therefore to state, estate, government, establishment, standing; sometimes the "party," sometimes the "faction" (Herodotus, 1, 59), and, more generally, the "civil war" itself (Thucydides, History, 3, 68–86). *As if the state found itself necessarily linked to insurrection, as to its shadow or its condition of possibility*' (Cassin 2002: 2–3; my emphasis).
5. It goes without saying that in both cases the problem of scale must be kept in mind in order to analyse the relevant context (Harvey 2000).
6. This invisibility of the basic social processes producing and reproducing command over daily activities may account for what seems to be the greatest fallacy upon which an otherwise productive and inspiring tradition of political and philosophical thought has constructed its thinking about the contemporary condition. Authors from Gilles Deleuze to Antonio Negri, among others, argue that we live in a post-disciplinary society when in fact in the last quarter of a century we have witnessed and endured, through the hammers of structural adjustment and war, the largest expansion of the most pervasive disciplinary mechanism known to humanity, what Hayek called the market order. See Chapter 9 for a discussion.
7. See Marx's (1975) analysis of alienation in his 'Economic and Philosophical Manuscripts'.
8. This is, to me, a way to ground the 'study of the body ... in an understanding of real spatio-temporal relations between material practices, representations, imaginaries, institutions, social relations, and the prevailing structures of political-economic power' (Harvey 2000: 130) without abandoning the problematic of the front-line clashes of value practices.
9. The key issue is that these 'things' with which governments are concerned are in fact people in their relations, 'their links, their imbrication with those things that are wealth, resources, means of subsistence, the territory with its specific qualities, climate, irrigations, fertility and so on'. Also, their relation to 'those other things that are customs, habits, ways of acting and thinking, and so on' as well as 'their relation to those still other things that might be accidents and misfortunes such as famine, epidemics, death, and so on' (Foucault 2002: 208–9).

10. One key feature of this disposition of government, which Foucault traces in its origin in the sixteenth century in anti-Machiavellian authors such as La Parrière and political economists such as Quesnay, is the introduction of 'economy' into political practice, that is, as Rousseau poses the problem, 'to set up an economy at the level of the entire state, which means exercising toward its inhabitants, and the wealth and behavior of each and all, a form of surveillance and control as attentive as that of the head of a family over his household and his goods' (ibid.: 207). The problematic of government is therefore different from that of sovereignty and the prince as in Machiavelli. 'Whereas the doctrine of the prince and the juridical theory of sovereignty are constantly attempting to draw the line between the power of the prince and any other form of power – because its task is to explain and justify this essential discontinuity between them – in the art of government the task is to establish a continuity, in both an upward and downward direction.' Upward continuity implies that 'a person who wishes to govern the state well must first learn how to govern himself, his goods, and his patrimony, after which he will be successful in governing the state' (ibid.: 206). On the other hand, 'we also have a downward continuity in the sense that, when a state is well run, the head of the family will know how to look after his family, his goods, and his patrimony, which means that individuals will, in turn, behave as they should. This downward line, which transmits to individual behavior and the running of the family the same principles as the good government of the state, is just at this time beginning to be called "police". The prince's pedagogical formation endures the upward continuity of the forms of government, and police the downward one. The central term of this continuity is the government of the family, termed "economy"' (Foucault 2002: 207). The role of the family here should be taken loosely. What matters is the exemplification unit. In neoliberalism, this unit was the firm.

11. Networks are understood currently as sets of interconnected nodes of people and resources, as well as their links, their relations. See Castells (2000).

12. Among an extensive literature, see Cleaver (1979), De Angelis (2000a), Midnight Notes Collective (1992), Negri (1968).

13. These include *fiscal discipline* (strict criteria for limiting budgets); *public expenditure priorities* (away from subsidies and administration towards 'neglected fields with high economic returns …'); *tax reform*: broadening the tax base and cutting marginal tax rates; *financial liberalisation*: interest rates should ideally be market-determined; *exchange rates*: they should be managed to induce rapid growth in non-traditional exports; *trade liberalisation*: tariffs not quotas, and declining tariffs; *foreign direct investment*: no barriers and 'equality' with domestic firms; *privatisation* of state enterprises; *deregulation*: abolition of regulations that restrict competition by limiting market entry to new firms; *property rights*: secure rights without excessive costs and available to the informal sector (Williamson 1990).

14. For example, in May 2002 the British NGO Oxfam launched a report in support of exports promotion for tackling poverty in third world countries (Oxfam 2002). The position was seen as too dangerously close to World Trade Organisation rhetoric and thus generated a lively debate from within the world of NGOs and CSOs. Contributors included Colin Hines, Vandana Shiva and Walter Bello, among others. See the debate reported in Oxfam (2002) as well as at http://www.theecologist.org.

15. See for example the American Enterprise Institute, the most powerful think tank in Washington, and having close connections with the Bush administration and large corporations such as Motorola, American Express and ExxonMobil on its board. On 11 June 2003, the institute – itself an NGO – launched 'NGO Watch' with the aim of monitoring NGOs activities, in the same way that NGOs generally monitor corporate activities. 'In fact, it is a McCarthyite blacklist, telling tales on any NGO that dares speak against Bush administration policies or in support of international treaties opposed by the White House' (Naomi Klein 2003a).

16. This however must be qualified. There are major differences between NGOs emerging form grass-roots communities working to catalyse communities' participation in local projects and

international NGOs implanting their modes of doing things and their priorities into local areas. As reported to me by several NGO workers, international NGOs often arrive in local impoverished areas in the Global South and, because they are well funded, out-compete local ones. This exposes local communities to the risk of seeing the provision and delivery of foods, medical, educational and engineering services vanish when they are most needed, that is as soon as a 'security crisis' affect the locality and international NGOs pack up and go home.

17. See, for example Martin (2000).

18. It is perhaps worth mentioning the anti-Nafta campaigns in the early 1990s, the first recent experiment in the Northern hemisphere of cross border and cross issue organising and of meshing of identities. A few years later, in 1996, during the Zapatistas promoted *Encuentro*, a diverse composition of participants experienced the first glimpses of a different type of politics, in which anarchist, feminists, communists, farmers, workers, indigenous and academics from a variety of languages and political backgrounds started learning to build on difference rather than ghettoising through difference. The more recent experience of the World Social Forum, begun in Porto Alegre in 2000, is the direct result of that experience spread throughout the political circuits of the world.

19. As we have seen in Chapters 4 and 5, Silvia Federici (2004) shows how the brutal strategies of the 'enclosure of the body' were part and parcel of the emergence of biopolitical strategies in Europe during the 'transition' to capitalism.

20. To clarify, another useful way to understand the meaning of governance is to contrast it, using a variety of criteria, with the more intuitive concept of policy. In both cases we have some kind of government action. This is true even in the case of 'corporate governance', as proposed by the UN Global Compact (United Nations 2000a; United Nations 2000b) discussed at the end of this chapter, where the government acts by *abstaining* from regulating important areas such as human rights, issues linked to labour and environment, and so on. However, in terms of its purpose and rationale, in the case of policy we have a type of government action that has clearly defined objectives and clearly defined means. In the case of fiscal and monetary policies, for example, we have policy instruments (the 'means' of interest rate, tax rate, government expenditure or monetary aggregates) that are used to reach certain objectives such as employment growth or a particular level of inflation targets. On the other hand, the purpose and rationale of governance is not so clear-cut and 'linear'. The main problematic of governance is the accommodation and articulation of conflicting interests, not the achievement of goals, which are external to the process itself. Thus, the emphasis with policies is on causal relations and the corresponding transmission mechanisms. Behind policies there are questions such as 'What goals are important?'; 'How do we reach these objectives?'. Different theoretical and policy approaches and paradigms help shed light on these different questions by identifying different causal relations. On the contrary, in the case of governance, the emphasis is on the organisational principles through which those articulations of conflicting interests arise.

Another important difference is the role of government institutions. In the case of policy the role is to formulate and implement, while with governance it is to promote and to a certain extent enforce compliance, but mostly to set the framework and contribute to the definition of the process of selection of the actors involved in governance action. Another important difference between these two types of government action is the role of non-governmental actors. In the case of policy, this role is to obey norms, which are given from the top. In governance, it is to participate in the definition of rules, again with certain limitations, depending whether these are games about rules or games under rules (Stoker 1998). The occurrence in time is the other important difference. Policies are discrete events, while governance is a continuous process.

21. 'Civil society might through its various positive influences enhance social cohesion. Contributions to public education, stakeholder voice, policy debate, transparent and accountable governance, and material welfare can all help to counter arbitrary social hierarchies and

exclusions that global finance might otherwise encourage. As a result, global finance would contribute less to social conflict and more to social integration, vigilance and monitoring' (Scholte and Schnabel 2002: 25).

22. 'Banks have recognized this general principle with their recent attention to issues of policy "ownership". Civil society can offer a means for citizens to affirm that certain rules and institutions of global finance should guide – and where necessary constrain – their behaviour. Likewise, civil society can also provide a space for the expression of discontent and the pursuit of change when existing governance arrangements are regarded as illegitimate' (Scholte and Schnabel 2002: 25).

23. For example, more than 11 million young children die every year, the risk of dying in childbirth is one in 48 in the developing world and HIV/Aids, malaria and other diseases are rampant. Yet, 'from 1975 to 1996, 1,223 new genres of medicines were developed, but only 13 genres were intended to cure deprived people from major tropical diseases. In 1998, from the total budget of US$70 billion allocated for research of the giant medicine corporations, only $300 million (0.43 per cent) was allocated for Aids vaccine research and $100 million (0.14 per cent) for malaria medicine research.' Instead, the great bulk of research funding 'was allocated to the research of cosmetics, obesity and other "vanity" drugs' (Nugroho 2002). Surely, a 'partnership' based on the priority of profit and market values will not change this trend.

24. Richter (2002) for example proposes the following: 'Instead of "dialogue," for instance, words such as meeting, talks, discussion, debate or negotiation would be more exact. Using other terms would limit the impression that communications between industry and other actors aim at a free and open exchange of views between equal partners. Instead of "partnership", the following terms could be used:

- corporate sponsorship or funding (for donations in cash and kind);
- tenders (for instance, for negotiations to achieve lower prices for industrially-manufactured products such as medicines);
- outsourcing or contracting out (of public services such as water supply and health care to for-profit entities);
- collaboration (such as on research into new pharmaceuticals and vaccines, which is often publicly subsidised);
- consultation (for example, on scientific standards which affect industry products or practices);
- co-regulation (for mutually-agreed arrangements governing corporate conduct);
- personnel secondment (for corporations placing and paying for their employees to work in international agencies such as those of the UN and the World Bank).'

25. See, for example the case of Shell in Durban (Friends of the Earth 2002: 7).
26. See Friends of the Earth (2002: 9).
27. See, for example Friends of the Earth (2002: 14).
28. As reported to me by an informant who has worked with an NGO engaged in a brief partnership with the World Bank.
29. See note 15 above.
30. With their insistence on reducing the 'other' into an integrated element of global markets, the institutions of global capitalism seems to perpetuate the Western habit of not being able to 'recognize the "you" as irreducible to "us", not knowable, nor perceivable in its totality by us' (Irigaray 1997: 118, my translation).

8   GLOBAL LOOPS

1. However, it must be pointed out that there is much more to be said with respect to the privatisation of basic resources like water than the increase in the price charged for it and the consequent increase in profit for the water companies. Due to people's basic need for water, its privatisation is also an opportunity for micro-strategies that aim at creating individualised

'rational' consumers, trained to the modalities of economic calculus and 'resource management'. Prepaid water meters, which water companies are introducing in townships and slums around the world, are a tool for this micro-management. See, for example, Naidoo (2005) for a discussion of water privatisation and struggle in Soweto, South Africa.

2. See Gray (2004) for a survey of the literature on flexible labour markets, as well as a discussion of them in terms of 'flexploitation', a regime of welfare benefits forcing the unemployed into low-paid, temporary or part-time jobs, known in the USA as 'workfare' and increasingly adopted in Europe.

3. For an up-to-date critical analysis of the current states of negotiations, the division lines among the countries involved, the issues at stake, the arm-twisting tactics used, and the translation of the technical vocabulary of trade into common language, check the material on websites such as Focus on Global South (www.focusweb.org) or Global Trade Watch at Public Citizen (www.citizen.org/trade/).

4. See World Trade Organisation (2003).

5. See also Glyn and Sutcliffe (1992: 91).

6. The following section is derived from a paper David Harvie and I wrote to problematise the sceptics' thesis and open up the 'economic' point of view to contamination with issues of power and qualitative change. We did this by recasting the quantitative measures of foreign direct investment proposed by the sceptics in terms of a unit of measurement that can be better seen to capture relations of power in capitalist economies. Following classical political economy, the unit of measurement we thus adopted was that of labour commanded. See De Angelis and Harvie (2004).

7. It is known that Marx, like Ricardo, rejects Smith's theory of labour commanded, as a theory of value. Instead he founds his value theory on the labour socially necessary to produce it. However, if labour commanded is not for Marx the immanent measure of value, it gives us another important indication, in that 'the increase of wealth, the increase of the value contained in the commodity, and the extent of this increase, depends upon the greater or less quantity of living labour which the materialised labour sets in motion'. He also adds that 'put in this way', Smith's view 'is correct'. (Marx 1969: 77).

This acknowledgement of 'something deeper' (ibid.: 71) in Smith's argument has generally been overlooked by the extensive exegetic literature on Marx's theory of value. If the value of labour power is not an indication of the value of commodities, it is certainly an important factor in determining the amount of living labour that can be put to work by a given quantity of capital; therefore it can provide us with an idea of the increase in wealth (in value terms) that a certain quantity of capital (still in value terms) can set in motion.

This meaning, in which Marx refers to labour commanded as that quantity of living labour which is set in motion by a given amount of capital, is also evident in other contexts in his writing (see, for example, Marx 1981: 323). There is however another sense in which we can gain insight by the term labour commanded. This is the potential living labour that can be put into motion by a certain money value of capital. This understanding, in fact, relates back to Hobbes' insight that wealth is power, and to Smith, who also links labour commanded with power. This power consists precisely of 'command over all the labour' (Smith 1970: 134). Marx, in turn, argues that 'The power which each individual exercises over the activity of others or over social wealth exists in him as the owner of exchange value, of money. The individual carries his social power … in his pocket' (Marx 1974: 177).

This conception of labour commanded stresses the power of money to control others' time, to put people to work, to command labour, whether or not this power is actually exercised. Indeed, the command over labour and the exercise of this command refer to two different concepts within Marx's theory of value and surplus value, which is based on the distinction between labour and labour power. The former is not a commodity, but a life activity creating value. The latter is a commodity to be exchanged on the market and has a price like any other commodity.

Labour commanded therefore is not yet a measure of labour expended, although it gives us an indication of the amount of labour that can be expended, that can potentially be set in motion.

Changes in quantities of labour commanded, therefore, as reflected in changes in monetary FDI patterns translated into labour commanded, for example, do not give us an indication of labour expended or embodied; rather, they point to changes in the quantity of waged labour that can be set in motion within the accumulation process. However, this quantity is also dependent upon the level of wages, which in turn depends upon general conditions of labour-power reproduction, or unwaged work. Thus, in this context, the notion of labour commanded opens up the problematisation of a variety of factors, including relations between classes and between waged and unwaged sections of working classes, that the simple monetary measures of FDI disguise.

8. The Sardar Sarovar Project, the largest single dam in the Narmada Valley Development Project, was only able to start through a World Bank loan of $450 million. Following international pressure and an independent review, however, the Bank was forced to withdraw its support of the project. See Caufield (1998: chapter 1).
9. See for example Hildyar (1998).

9   THE GLOBAL WORK MACHINE

1. For an earlier discussion of global capitalist production using the money circuit of capital, see the classic paper by Palloix (1975).
2. These were originally defined by Terence Hopkins and Immanuel Wallerstein (1986: 159) as 'network[s] of labor and production processes, whose end result is a finished commodity'. Clancy (1998) reviews the literature on global commodity chains and discusses the implications for the service industry. In his definition, 'commodity chains trace the social and economic organization surrounding the global "life" of a product, ranging from the first stage of raw material extraction through consumption of a finished good. The key questions to be answered along the way are why particular processes or stages of production take place in specific locales, how the industry in question is organised and governed, and, ultimately, where the economic surplus goes' (Clancy 1998: 123). He identifies the explanatory aspect of commodity chains along three 'primary dimensions. First, an input–output structure that is both sequential and temporal identifies the various steps of the production process, ranging from raw material to final assembly, marketing and sometimes even consumption. Second, a spatial dimension examines where different stages of production actually take place. This also involves an explanatory element in that it asks why nations or regions play a particular role in the division of labour (or for that matter do not). Finally, an organisational or governing dimension examines structural characteristics of the industry itself by identifying ownership patterns as well as transactions between agents along the commodity chains' (ibid.: 124–5).
3. We must take into consideration that 'the boundary between internalisation and externalisation is continually shifting as firms make decisions about which functions to perform "in-house" and which to "out-source" to other firms'. The reality is thus 'a spectrum of different forms of co-ordination which consist of networks of interrelationships within and between firms structured by different degrees of power and influence. Such networks increasingly consist of a mix of intra-firm and inter-firm structures. These networks are dynamic and in a continuous state of flux' (Dicken 2003: 8–9).
4. According to Subcomandante Marcos (the main spokesperson of the Zapatistas), globalisation is a world war, it is a war waged against humanity, and its aim is the distribution of the world: 'A new world war is waged, but now against the entire humanity. As in all world wars, what is being sought is a new distribution of the world' (DOR 1996).
5. See various years of the annual Trade and Development reports published by the United Nations Conference on Trade and Development (UNCTAD).

6. Also much pre-capitalist trade – especially that predicated on patriarchal social relations – has its origins in plunder. 'The examples from pre-colonial Africa make clear that the predatory mode of production of men, based on the monopoly of arms, could become "productive" only when some other, mostly female, production economies existed, which could be raided. It can be characterized as non-productive production. They also show the close link between pillage, loot and robbery on the one hand, and trade on the other. What was traded and exchanged against money (kauri shells) was not the surplus produced over and above the requirements of the community; but what was stolen and appropriated by means of arms was, in fact, defined as "surplus"' (Mies 1998: 65).

7. 'Operationally defined', argues Polanyi (1977: 81), 'trade is a method of acquiring goods not available on the spot.' At this extremely high level of generalisation, trade seems to be a natural product of human social metabolism, as it allows human communities to satisfy needs which otherwise would be unmet, but also to engage in social relations with 'the other', the foreigner, the outside of the immediate community. Trade 'is something external to the group, similar to activities we tend to associate with quite different spheres of life: namely, hunts, expeditions, and piratic raids. In every case, the point is acquiring and carrying goods from a distance. What distinguishes trade from other activities is a two-sidedness, which also ensures its peaceful nature, absent from quests for booty and plunder' (ibid.).

8. This has been theorised in terms of time–space compression as those 'processes that so revolutionize the objective qualities of space and time that we are forced to alter, sometimes in quite radical ways, how we represent the world to ourselves' (Harvey 1989: 240). So for example, the transportation and communication technologies introduced by corporations shrank space through increases in the speed of sending material goods, information, and people.

9. For a review, see Hoogvelt (1997).

10. One important implication that we cannot treat here is that the stronger the relevance of intra-firm trade, the greater is the corporate power to transfer value along its chain. This administrative value transfer – which was noted by Palloix's (1975) classic study of global capitalist production – may as well contribute to the appearance of the severed link between work and value. As we shall discuss in Chapter 12, this appearance has been taken as reality by several critical observers.

11. These two broad characteristics of deep integration, have led some authors to point out the distinction between internationalisation and globalisation processes. The former 'involve the simple extension of economic activities across national boundaries'. These processes therefore involve the simple spatial extension of patterns of economic activity and can be measured in quantitative terms. Globalisation processes instead 'are qualitative processes. They involve not merely the geographical extension of economic activity across national boundaries but also (and more importantly) the functional integration of such internationally dispersed activities' (Dicken 2003: 5). See also Hoogvelt (1997: 116).

12. As an example of the link between processes of economic globalisation, work of reproduction and war, see Federici (2002). As we have seen, competition not only reduces the cost of reproduction and the value of labour power in relatively high-wage countries, but also puts pressure on workers to work more efficiently and intensively, and on the unemployed to intensify job searching, with the effect of exerting downward pressure on wages, and so on.

13. See, for example Skyttner (1996).

14. See also Hoogvelt (2001).

15. 'The phantasmagoria of abstract possibilities in which the opportunist acts is colored by fear and secretes cynicism. It contains infinite negative and private chances, infinite threatening "opportunities." Fears of particular dangers, if only virtual ones, haunt the workday like a mood that cannot be escaped. This fear, however, is transformed into an operational requirement, a special tool of the trade. Insecurity about one's place during periodic innovation, fear of losing recently gained privileges, and anxiety over being "left behind" translate into

flexibility, adapability, and a readiness to reconfigure oneself. Danger arises within a perfectly well known environment. It grazes us, it spares us. It strikes someone else ... In contrast to the Hegelian relation between master and slave, fear is no longer what drives us into submission before work, but the active component of that stable instability that marks the internal articulations of the productive process itself' (Virno 1996a: 16).

16. This in turn is at the root of the legitimisation of a continuous rat race underpinning the human condition within the capitalist mode of production. 'In order for someone to conceive the possibility of escaping from a particular condition, it is necessary first to feel that one has fallen into that condition. For those who make up two thirds of the world's population today, to think of development – of any kind of development – requires first the perception of themselves as underdeveloped, with the whole burden of connotations that this carries' (Esteva 1992: 7).

17. The global cyclical patterns linking struggles and capital relocation have recently been documented and extensively empirically studied by Beverly Silver (2003). Using the World Labour Group's extensive database of labour unrest in the period 1870–1996, she found, in the automobile and textile industries, the emergence of three 'fixes' to working-class struggle: 'Capitalists respond to a squeeze on profits in a given industry, with geographical relocation (a spatial fix) or process innovations (a technological/organizational fix), but they also attempt to shift capital into new innovative and more profitable product lines and industries', that is, a 'product shift'. 'Successive new labor movements have risen (and established labor movements declined) with these shifts' (Silver 2003: 76). It is unfortunate that the database does not also allow the tracing of what we might call a 'reproduction fix', so as to take into account the struggle of the unwaged workers' reproducing labour power, as discussed in our framework.

10   MARX AND THE ENCLOSURES WE FACE

1. For a critique of Hardin's approach, see for example Anderson and Simmons (1993). Ronald Coase offers a parallel argument to that of Hardin. The theorem that goes under his name, the Coase Theorem, proposes that pollution and other 'externalities' can be efficiently controlled through voluntary negotiations among the affected parties (that is both the polluters and those harmed by pollution). A key to the Coase Theorem is that many pollution problems emerge with common-property goods that have no clear-cut ownership or property rights. With clear-cut property rights, 'owners' would have the incentive to achieve an efficient level of pollution. Thus, pollution can be reduced through voluntary negotiation by assigning private property rights to common-property resources and the consequent development of a market in property rights. Now the problem with this is that every human action is a social action and therefore bound to produce externalities. In Coase's framework, therefore, everything becomes enclosable. See Coase (1988).

2. For a discussion of the relation between commons and communities, see De Angelis (2003) and De Marcellus (2003). For an application of this analysis in the area of higher education, see Harvie (2004).

3. The literature here is truly, and fortunately so, very extensive. For some examples, see Shiva on intellectual property rights and enclosure of knowledge (2002b) and on water enclosures (2002a). On the subject of an important wave of struggles against water privatisation in Cochabamba, Bolivia, see Web 5. On the impact of dams on local populations and their struggles see, for example, the case of the Narmada Valley in Web 1 and Web 2. On the massive integrated system of enclosures across Central America under Plan Puebla-Panama, see Hansen and Wallach (2002). The campaign against GATS (General Agreement on Trade and Services) has highlighted the corporate agenda of 'locking in' past privatisation and 'enclosures' as well as promoting new ones. See Web 3 and Web 4, as well as Wasselius (2002). On the denunciation of the effects of debt and struggles against it see Web 6. For a

broad survey of the struggles against the enclosures imposed through structural adjustment policies, see Walton and Seddon (1994).

4. Exceptions coming from three different perspectives are provided, for example, by the work of John McMurtry who tries to pull it all together by identifying the market as an ethical system and counterpoising commons to marketisation; see McMurtry (1998; 1999; 2002). Another exception is the work of John Holloway (2002), and his important and refreshing analysis of the problematic of revolution today. Finally, Hardt and Negri (2000) open the way for what they call 'commonwealth'. Whatever their strengths and weaknesses, these bodies of work leave in the background the strategic question raised by the problematic of capital as enclosing social force, and fail to tackle it directly. In this sense, this chapter is intended to complement these other works.

5. See Bonefeld (2001), De Angelis (2001a; 2004a), Federici (1992), Midnight Notes Collective (1992), Perelman (2000) among others. The web journal *The Commoner* (www. thecommoner.org) is largely dedicated to pursuing this line of research. For a critique of this approach, see Zarembka (2002) and, for a counter-critique, see Bonefeld (2002a).

6. In De Angelis (2001a) I discuss the main horizons of interpretation of primitive accumulation within the Marxist tradition. I identify a 'historical primitive accumulation' deriving from Lenin and an 'inherent-continuous primitive accumulation' from Luxemburg. More recent interpretations seem to share the basic characteristics of these two approaches. For example, in his classic studies on the development of capitalism, Maurice Dobb (1963: 178) uses the category of primitive accumulation to indicate a well-defined age of accumulation of property rights better known as the mercantile age. According to Dobb, therefore, primitive accumulation is accumulation 'in an historical sense'. It is worth noticing that Paul Sweezy, Dobb's main opponent in the famous debate on the transition from feudalism to capitalism published in *Science and Society* 1950–53, acknowledges Dobb's 'excellent treatment of the essential problems of the period of original accumulation' (Sweezy 1950: 157). The now historic debate on 'transition' (collected in Hilton 1978) and its later developments and transfigurations, such as the Brenner debate on the pages of the journal *Past and Present* of the 1970s (collected in Astor and Philperin 1985) and later exchanges in *Science and Society* (Gottlieb 1984; Leibman 1984; McLennon 1986; Sweezy 1986), is characterised by a common acceptance of this historical definition of primitive accumulation. It is fair to point out however, that the approach taken by Samir Amin (1974: 3) is different from Dobb's approach of setting primitive accumulation in a historically prior period and is closer to the notion of inherent and continuous primitive accumulation that occurs through what Amin defines as transfer of value within the world economy. Another interpretation within this general framework is Wallerstein's notion of a world system (see Wallerstein 1979). In contrast with the approach taken here, the continuous character of primitive accumulation in these accounts seems to stress only 'objective' mechanisms of accumulation and circulation of capital.

7. The capitalism that Marx never refers to, referring instead to the capitalist mode of production, see Smith (1996). This opens the way to conceptualising its coexistence with other modes of production, other modes of doing things and relating to each other, hence to regarding the social field as a strategic field of relations among forces.

8. See Hardt and Negri (2000).

9. For a discussion of this model of power – understood as 'power-over' or *potestas*, vis-à-vis another emancipatory model of power, 'power-to', or *potentia*, see Holloway (2002). In De Angelis (2005b) I argue against the idea that power-over is opposed to power-to. Rather it is a modality of powers-to, it is an emergent result of the exercise of different powers-to and a corresponding organisational reach running in the opposite direction.

10. In this book I use the terms 'primitive accumulation' and 'enclosure' as interchangeable theoretical terms.

11. See Perelman (2000).

12. Marx (1976a: 874).
13. Marx (1976a: 874).
14. Marx (1976a: 874–5). We can also find indications of Marx's emphasis on class relations in the structure of this section of *Capital*. Marx dedicates two chapters of this section to the formation of the working class (Chapters 27 and 28) and three chapters on the formation of the bourgeoisie (Chapters 29, 30 and 31).
15. In Volume 3 of *Capital* Marx stresses that accumulation proper is nothing else than primitive accumulation – which he defined in Volume 1 in terms of separation – 'raised to a higher power' (Marx 1981: 354). In the *Theories of Surplus Value* he is even more precise, writing that accumulation 'reproduces the separation and the independent existence of material wealth as against labour on an ever increasing scale' (Marx 1971: 315, my emphasis) and therefore 'merely presents as a continuous process what in primitive accumulation appears as a distinct historical process' (Marx 1971: 271, 311–12). Again, in the *Grundrisse* he states: 'Once this separation is given, the production process can only produce it anew, reproduce it, and reproduce it on an expanded scale' (Marx 1974: 462).
16. Marx (1974: 461).
17. See Holloway (2002).
18. 'The objective conditions of living labour capacity are presupposed as having an existence independent of it, as the objectivity of a subject distinct from living labour capacity and standing independently over against it; the reproduction and realization, i.e. the expansion of these objective conditions, is therefore at the same time their own reproduction and new production as the wealth of an alien subject indifferently and independently standing over against labour capacity. What is reproduced and produced anew is not only the presence of these objective conditions of living labour, but also their presence as independent values, i.e. values belonging to an alien subject, confronting this living labour capacity' (Marx 1974: 462).
19. Marx (1974: 462).
20. Marx (1974: 462).
21. See Marx (1975).
22. Marx (1976b: 989). For a more detailed analysis of the connection between reification and commodity fetishism in Marx's analysis, see De Angelis (1996).
23. Marx (1976a: 342).
24. Marx (1976a: 724).
25. Marx (1976a: 775).
26. 'It is in fact this divorce between the conditions of labour on the one hand and the producers on the other that forms the concept of capital, as this arises with primitive accumulation ... subsequently appearing as a constant process in the accumulation and concentration of capital, before it is finally expressed here as the centralization of capitals already existing in few hands, and the decapitalization of many' (Marx 1981: 354–5).
27. Marx (1974: 460–1).
28. Marx (1974: 459).
29. Marx (1976a: 899–900).
30. Marx (1976a: 900).
31. Marx (1976a: 879).
32. In the case of environmental commons, for example, the discourse of carbon credit and the creation and consequent development of markets in 'pollution rights' stands in opposition to the discourse of environment as global common.
33. Another way to put it would be through Karl Polanyi's concept of 'double movement' (Polanyi 1944). On one side there is the historical movement of the market, a movement that has no inherent limits and that therefore threatens society's very existence. On the other there is society's propensity to defend itself, and therefore to create institutions for its protection. In Polanyi's terms, the continuous element of Marx's primitive accumulation could be identified

in those social processes or sets of strategies aimed at dismantling those institutions that protect society from the market. The crucial element of continuity in the reformulation of Marx's theory of primitive accumulation arises therefore once we acknowledge the other movement of society. Of course, unlike Polanyi, we believe the actors of this 'double movement' are the grass-roots, not simply 'states'.

34. Marx (1971: 271; my emphasis).

35. Accumulation relies on 'the silent compulsion of economic relations [which] sets the seal on the domination of the capitalist over the worker'. In this case, '[d]irect extra-economic force is still of course used, but only in exceptional cases. In the ordinary run of things, the worker can be left to the "natural laws of production", i.e. it is possible to rely on his dependence on capital, which springs from the conditions of production themselves, and is guaranteed in perpetuity by them' (Marx 1976a: 899–900).

In contrast, 'during the historical genesis of capitalist production. The rising bourgeoisie needs the power of the state, and uses it to "regulate" wages, i.e. to force them into the limits suitable for making a profit, to lengthen the working day, and to keep the worker himself at his historical level of dependence. This is an essential aspect of so-called primitive accumulation' (ibid.).

36. Marx (1976a: 899–900).

37. 'As soon as the workers learn the secret of why it happens that the more they work, the more alien wealth they produce ... as soon as, by setting up trade unions, etc., they try to organize planned co-operation between the employed and the unemployed in order to obviate or to weaken the ruinous effects of this natural law of capitalist production on their class, so soon does capital and its sycophant, political economy, cry out at the infringement of the "eternal" and so to speak "sacred" law of supply and demand' (Marx 1976a: 793).

38. Marx (1976a: 794).

39. Marx (1976a: 775).

11 ENCLOSURES WITH NO LIMITS

1. See Hardt and Negri (2000).

2. See, for example Federici (1992), and the other contributions in the 1992 issue of Midnight Notes on the new enclosures. See also Caffentzis (1995).

3. On Sunday 1 April 1649 a small group of poor men collected on St George's Hill just outside London and at the edge of the Windsor Great Forest, hunting ground of the king and royalty. They started digging the land as a 'symbolic assumption of ownership of the common lands' (Hill 1972: 110). Within ten days, their number grew to four or five thousand. One year later, 'the colony had been forcibly dispersed, huts and furniture burnt, the Diggers chased away from the area' (ibid.: 113). This episode of English history could be consistently included in Marx's Chapter 28, entitled 'Bloody Legislation against the Expropriated'. Yet, while most of that chapter deals with Tudor legislation aimed at criminalising and repressing popular behaviour induced by the expropriation of land (vagrancy, begging, theft), this episode goes a step further, by making clear that primitive accumulation acquires meaning vis-à-vis patterns of resistance and struggle. This episode entails the active and organised activity of a mass of urban and landless poor aimed at the direct reappropriation of land for its transformation into common land. Paraphrasing Marx, it was an activity aimed at 'associating the producer with the means of production'. It is clear therefore that the force used by the authorities to disperse the Diggers can be understood, consistently with Marx's theory, as an act of 'primitive accumulation', because it reintroduces the separation between producers and means of production. Although Marx did not include this episode in his treatment of primitive accumulation in Chapter 28 he does refer to a handful of cases in which struggles are counterpoised to state

legislation, which represent either 'retreats' of capital vis-à-vis these struggles or attempts to contain them.

4. See Branford and Rocha (2002).
5. See McMurtry (2002).
6. See IFG (2002).
7. See Klein (2001; 2003b).
8. See Kovel (2002).
9. See Perelman (2000).
10. For example, petroleum extraction by Shell in Nigeria has been blamed for land pollution and the consequent endangering of the livelihoods of villagers and farmers, as spillages have affected crops and sources of drinking water, reduced soil fertility, polluted ponds and thereby threatened animal livelihood, biodiversity, and so on. For a general background discussion of this case, see Web 7. For a general discussion of the link between oil production and environmental damage (and the consequent threat of enclosure for those who depend on the ruined resources, and their consequent struggles), see Web 8.
11. See, for example Holloway (1998). For an analysis of the impact of the Zapatistas methodology of struggle outside Chiapas, see De Angelis (2000b) and Midnight Notes Collective (2001).
12. See Branford and Rocha (2002).
13. Federici (2002) and Caffentzis (1983/2004).
14. See Davis (1990: 235).
15. See Piven and Cloward (1972).
16. See Costello and Levidow (2001) for casualisation strategies; also Gray (2004). See Bonefeld (2002b) for a class analysis of EMU (European Monetary Union). See also the anthology edited by Abramsky (2001) on struggles in Europe, many of which can easily be identified as anti-enclosure struggles.
17. See, for example Levidow (2002), Rikowski (2002) and Tabb (2001).

12   THE 'LAW OF VALUE', IMMATERIAL LABOUR, AND THE 'CENTRE' OF POWER

1. See Chapter 14, in which I develop this, building on Foucault's analysis (1977) of Bentham's model prison, the panopticon.
2. George Caffentzis points out that in Marx's *Capital* 'There are many explicitly stated laws (e.g., the law of the tendency of the falling rate of profit, the general law of capitalist accumulation) and many explicitly identified values (e.g., use-value, exchange-value, surplus value) in Marx's texts, but there is little evidence of a "Law of Value." Although Engels seems to have used it often, Marx rarely employs the phrase in Capital I, II, III or in the letters and unpublished manuscripts, and, when he does, he uses the phrase loosely and in passing. For example, in the 860 pages of Capital III attributed to Marx there are only seven uses of the phrase according to the index and it is difficult to "abstract" a law-like statement of the Law of Value from simply putting all these different uses in Marx's texts side-by-side' (Caffentzis 2005: 88–9).
3. In their effort to go beyond Marx, Hardt and Negri (2004: 130) have argued that there is no longer a reserve army because there is not an 'industrial army' and there is not an unproductive 'reserve'. In the first case, 'industrial workers no longer form a compact, coherent unity but rather function as one form of labour among many in the networks defined by the immaterial paradigm'. This of course defies the truism according to which the unwaged, in a condition of lacking alternative means of livelihood, help to push down wage levels, whether for 'material' or 'immaterial' production. How else can we explain the fact that, for example, immaterial workers in Bangalore, meeting up in 'cool' cafes and restaurants to perform their 'directly social' production processes, earn a fraction of what is earned by immaterial workers

located in Silicon Valley and meeting in correspondingly 'cool' cafes and restaurants? Wouldn't this have to do with the fact that the conditions of reproduction of the same labour power in India are much cheaper than in Silicon Valley, due to the massive reserve of unwaged workers, bonded labourers and small farmers who, in conditions of abject poverty, help to reproduce their livelihoods through cheaper food and cheaper services? And wouldn't this also imply that a 'reserve' does exists, since if it is true that 'no labour power is outside the process of social production' (Hardt and Negri 2004: 131), it is also true that there is plenty of labour power outside *waged* social production but coupled to it through the compulsion of earning a living?

4. See also Cleaver (1979).

5. For an overview of the terms of the debate, see the articles collected in Freeman and Carchedi (1996), as well as Freeman, Kliman and Wells (2004).

6. These, according to Kliman (2004), are things that the TSSI replicates that the equilibrium/simultaneist interpretations do not. There are also some more technical issues, such as: the determination of the general profit rate includes also productive conditions in the luxury sector (which is negated by Ricardo and Ricardian interpretations of Marx); aggregate profit cannot be negative if aggregate surplus value is positive, and vice versa (which is possible in the equilibrium interpretation of Marx); commodities with positive values cannot have negative prices, and vice versa (again possible within equilibrium interpretations of Marx). On surplus labour being the sole source of profit, see Kliman (2001).

7. Thus Caffentzis argues that 'the struggle over the transformation problem has been largely a game of "gotcha" with the bourgeois academics (whenever they are politically threatened) pointing out the logical and mathematical infelicities of *Capital* III and Marxists rushing to provide ever more weighty mathematical retorts. The animus on all sides of the debate is a struggle of worth (of the preservation of tradition and honour) instead of use' (Caffentzis 2005: 109). Indeed, this is a type of 'value struggle' that would be utterly self-referential in its academic dimension if it were not articulated to the current problematic of the 'beginning of history' and of why the 'law of value' is important to the anti-capitalist movement.

8. For a more detailed and grounded analysis of how capital measure is a terrain of struggle in UK higher education, see De Angelis and Harvie (2006).

9. As observed in the case of the recent cycle of anti-globalisation struggles, for example, 'Theorists of "new social movements" and "identity politics" will have no trouble in identifying familiar subjects – green, feminist, anti-racist – in the throng. But such analysts, who have often been energetic to deny the importance of "old" class struggles – might be given pause by the fact that these agents now appear in coalitions that often exceed single issues and specific identities precisely by the assertion of common "anti- corporate", and sometimes overtly "anti-capitalist", perspectives. Similarly, while "post-Marxists" such as Ernesto Laclau and Chantal Mouffe [1985] might be keen to discuss the "discursive articulation" of such coalitions, they should be abashed that these processes of connection occur around the very issues of globalized commodification, internationalized production and financial capital from which they have so assiduously distanced themselves' (Dyer-Witheford 2002: 3).

10. It is here worth pointing out that despite their marked differences from traditional orthodox Marxism, Hardt and Negri share with it a conception of history in 'stages'. The important difference is in the meaning given to the current 'stage' of capitalism. See Chapter 1 (p. XX and note 6).

11. The socially necessary labour time is, using Marx's terms, from the first chapter of Volume 1 of *Capital*, the average labour time that is required to produce a commodity under the 'normal' conditions of production and with the average degree of skill and intensity of labour prevalent in a given space–time (see Marx 1976a: 129). In Chapter 13 I interpret this socially necessary labour time within an ongoing process. See also note 4, p. 276.

12. For a brief review see Wright (2005). For a series of critical engagements with Hardt and Negri's *Empire*, see the essays collected in Balakrishnan (2003).
13. In *Multitude* (2004), Hardt and Negri distinguish between two forms of immaterial labour, intellectual or linguistic and affective labour. The first involves 'problem solving, symbolic and analytical tasks, and linguistic expressions. This kind of immaterial labor produces ideas, symbols, codes, texts, linguistic figures, images, and other such products.' On the other hand, 'unlike emotions, which are mental phenomena, affects refer equally to body and mind. In fact, affects, such as joy and sadness, reveal the present state of life in the entire organism, expressing a certain state of the body along with a certain mode of thinking. Affective labor, then, is labor that produces or manipulates affects such as a feeling of ease, well-being, satisfaction, excitement, or passion. One can recognize affective labor, for example, in the work of legal assistants, flight attendants, and fast food workers (service with a smile). One indication of the rising importance of affective labor, at least in the dominant countries, is the tendency for employers to highlight education, attitude, character, and "prosocial" behavior as the primary skills employees need. A worker with a good attitude and social skills is another way of saying a worker adept at affective labor' (Hardt and Negri 2004: 108).
14. On the occasion of the 2005 French referendum over the European constitution, which many critics condemned for wanting to inscribe neoliberal principles into constitutional law, Negri argued in favour of a 'yes' vote, on the basis that 'the constitution is a means to fight empire, that new globalised capitalist society.' See note 4, p. 253.
15. For a sympathetic critique of Holloway's (2002) book, see De Angelis (2005b).

13   THE VALUING AND MEASURING OF CAPITAL

1. 'We are back, then, to a "politics of value"; but one very different from Appadurai's Neoliberal Version. The ultimate stakes of politics, according to Turner, is not even the struggle to appropriate value; it is the struggle to establish what value is ... Similarly, the ultimate freedom is not the freedom to create or accumulate value, but the freedom to decide (collectively or individually) what it is that makes life worth living. In the end, then, politics is about the meaning of life. Any such project of constructing meanings necessarily involves imagining totalities (since this is the stuff of meaning), even if no such project can ever be completely translated into reality – reality being, by definition, that which is always more complicated than any construction we can put on it' (Graeber 2001: 88).
2. 'The magnitude of the value of a commodity ... expresses a necessary relation to social labour-time which is inherent in the process by which its value is created. With the transformation of the magnitude of value into the price this necessary relation appears as the exchange-ratio between a single commodity and the money commodity which exists outside it. This relation, however, may express both the magnitude of value of the commodity and the greater or lesser quantity of money for which it can be sold under the given circumstances. *The possibility, therefore, of a quantitative incongruity between price and magnitude of value, i.e. the possibility that the price may diverge from the magnitude of value, is inherent in the price-form itself. This is not a defect, but, on the contrary, it makes this form the adequate one for a mode of production whose laws can only assert themselves as blindly operating averages between constant irregularities'* (Marx 1976a: 196, my emphasis). In terms of the argument I will develop in this chapter, this discrepancy between 'magnitude of value', hence the socially necessary labour time constituting this magnitude, and its monetary expression, is 'adequate' to the price form because of the nature of the social feedback mechanism (process) involved. For Marx's discussion of the process of formation of prices of production, see *Capital*, Volume 3, Part 2 (Marx 1981).
3. There are in principle three ways of defining value norms of production for society as a whole. First, through administrative decree, a 'state body' or a management body that

decrees what must be standard. Second, through community's consensus, that is the community of the co-producers defining ways of setting standards. Third, through ongoing homeostatic mechanisms, such as market forces, that force individual producers to catch up with or surpass the norm. In reality, all these three are present in capitalist-dominated societies and the question is how they are articulated. While the second type, however, presupposes individual producers' definitions of their own standards, in the first and the third types discipline come from outside the individual producers. In the first case, the outside is represented by a 'foreman', a 'line manager', a person holding the whip. In the second case, disciplinary forces of norm creation come from a mechanism, a *dispositif*, that hides, rather than highlights, particular types of relations among people. There is nobody in particular holding the whip – or at least so it appears for most of us – but still the whip is cracked: restructuring, flexibility, cuts in social spending, debt repayment, structural adjustment, ongoing scarcity, competition, the rat race; and the carrots are distributed: promotions, new cars, credit lines, debt forgiveness.

It is this impersonal disciplinary mechanism (re)producing the norms of our social cooperation that must be tackled. There are, however, actual designers of the mechanism, as we have seen in Chapters 10 and 11 on enclosures, and as we shall see in Chapter 14 on Hayek.

4. Marx defines socially necessary labour time as the 'labour-time required to produce any use-value under the conditions of production normal for a given society and with the average degree of skill and intensity prevalent in that society' (Marx 1976a: 129). One could interpret this as a given average and turn it into a coefficient in an input–output table in which prices of input and of output are the same. Alternatively, we can wander how this average can be *both* the result of past labour *and* the premise against which new labour is measured. Thus, Marx continues: 'The introduction of power-looms into England ... probably reduced by one-half the labour required to convert a given quantity of yarn into woven fabric. In order to do this, the English hand-loom weaver in fact needed the same amount of labour-time as before; but the product of his individual hour of labour now only represented half an hour of social labour, and consequently fell to one-half its former value' (ibid.). Thus, socially necessary labour time does not strictly refer to 'embodied' labour, yet it does lead to an understanding of the mental and bodily labour of hand-loom workers attempting to catch up with the new standard. To keep their market, hand-loom products will now have to sell for half price (external measure), with direct and indirect consequences on the lives and livelihoods of the producers (immanent measure).

5. To give voice to this 'limit' is perhaps the deepest rationale of John Holloway's theoretical starting point, the 'scream', the 'no': 'When we write or when we read, it is easy to forget that the beginning is not the word, but the scream. Faced with the mutilation of human lives by capitalism, a scream of sadness, a scream of horror, a scream of anger, a scream of refusal: NO' (Holloway 2002: 1; see De Angelis (2005) for a discussion of Holloway's book). The main weakness of Holloway's approach, also revealed in his reply to my intervention (Holloway 2005), is the one-sided privileging of negativity, the no, the limit to capital, while judging the constituent processes, the 'yeses', with what can be described as a deflating 'also important for revolution ... but'. What I have tried to emphasise in this book is that we should be able to grasp the problematic of the NO to capital's value *and* the articulation of the 'yeses', of other values, as *both* being complementary aspects of the constitution of a new world.

6. See Cleaver (1992).

14 MARKET FREEDOM AND THE PRISON: HAYEK AND BENTHAM

1. Hayek (1988: 52) writes: 'Long before Auguste Compte introduced the term "positivism" for the view that represented a "demonstrated ethics" (demonstrated by reason, that is) as the only possible alternative to a supernaturally "revealed ethics" ... Jeremy Bentham had developed the most consistent foundations of what we now call legal and moral positivism: that is, the

constructivistic interpretation of systems of law and morals according to which their validity and meaning are supposed to depend wholly on the will and intention of their designers. Bentham is himself a late figure in this development. This constructionism includes not only the Benthamite tradition, represented and continued by John Stuart Mill and the later English Liberal Party, but also practically all contemporary Americans who call themselves "liberals".'

2. On this point see Gray (1998: 151) and on the role of the state in shaping markets see the classic statement by Polanyi (1944). See Chapters 26 to 33 of Marx's *Capital* (Marx 1976a) for a historical and theoretical discussion of the emergence of capitalist markets with an emphasis on power and expropriation in complete opposition to Hayek's belief in spontaneous order.

3. Order, on the other hand, is defined as 'a state of affairs in which a multiplicity of elements of various kinds are so related to each other that we may learn from our acquaintance with some spatial or temporal part of the whole to form correct expectations concerning the rest, or at least expectations which have a good chance of proving correct. It is clear that every society must in this sense possess an order and that such an order will often exist without having been deliberately created' (Hayek 1973: 36).

4. Note that precisely because the starting point is private individuals, the problem of coordination of individual plans is often the problem of coordinating conflicting plans. Let us take a classic example, the coordination problem of capitalists and workers. The workers have a plan, to get a wage. They have knowledge of how poor life is without it. The employers have knowledge of the conditions of the market. The mechanisms that coordinate their conflicting knowledge, rooted in conflicting standpoints within society, is one that enables them to coordinate their actions without challenging the premises that are at the basis of their actions.

5. Incidentally, therefore, the problem of social order in Hayek overlaps with the question of forces of production in a society.

6. Thus 'it need hardly be said, no products of two producers are ever exactly alike, even if it were only because, as they leave his plant, they must be at different places. These differences are part of the facts which create our economic problem, and it is little help to answer it on the assumption that they are absent' (Hayek 1946: 98).

7. This philosophical stand is in fact close to what Marx identifies as the nature of the capitalist movement, i.e., 'production for production's sake' or 'accumulation for accumulation's sake'. The continuous process of accumulation implies the continuous need for individual private agents to blindly adapt to its movement.

8. It has been correctly argued that Hayek's emphasis on progress for progress sake internalises also an important contradiction between 'a conservative attachment to inherited social forms and a liberal commitment to unending progress' (Gray 1998: 156). This contradiction is mostly revealed when the 'unending progress' actually destroys the authoritarian basis which helped to establish the premises of its movement, by, for example, destroying social cohesion through the undermining of patriarchal relations.

9. 'Another advantage ... is the great load of trouble and disgust, which it takes off the shoulders of those occasional inspectors of a higher order, such as judges, and other magistrates, who called down to this irksome task from the superior ranks of life, cannot but feel a proportionable repugnance to the discharge of it' (Bentham 1787: 27). The technology of power given by the panopticon makes it possible to avoid entering the cells one by one to inspect them. Thus, 'by this new plan, the disgust is entirely removed; and the trouble of going into such a room as the lodge, is no more than the trouble of going into any other' (ibid.: 27–8).

10. For example, since 'rational action is possible only in a fairly orderly world', then 'it clearly makes sense to try to produce conditions under which the chances for any individual taken at random to achieve his ends as effectively as possible will be very high – even if it cannot be predicted which particular aims will be favoured, and which not' (Hayek 1978: 183). The production of these conditions, in the world of Hayek, is the state creation of markets. The story of markets as constituting a spontaneous order turns therefore into a self-fulfilling

prophecy. Because markets are believed to be emerging spontaneously, the state must promote the conditions for their emergence, which, even if the thesis of spontaneous order is proved wrong, would result, in any case, in the creation of markets.

11. On Hayek's abstraction, see Gamble (1996: 44–6).

12. 'If a man won't work, nothing has he to do, from morning to night, but to eat his bad bread and drink his water, without a soul to speak to. If he will work, his time is occupied, and he has his meat and his beer, or whatever else his earnings may afford him, and not a stroke does he strike but he gets something, which he would not have got otherwise' (Bentham 1787: 67).

13. The British Library copy of the 1787 edition has a stamp of the 'Patent Office' right above the title of this letter 'on the means to extract labour'. It would be interesting to uncover the history of this 'intellectual property right'.

14. Gamble (1996: 42) rhetorically asks: 'In a society in which the opportunities to own and acquire property were limited not by the arbitrary decision of rulers but by laws which allowed only members of one minority group to hold property, would it be justifiable to advocate the redistribution of property to increase the total sum of liberty?'

15. See Gamble (1996: 42). See also the discussion in Kuhathas (1989).

15   THE FRACTAL PANOPTICON AND UBIQUITOUS REVOLUTION

1. This polarity between modernity and postmodernity is, of course, embedded in the commodity form and, specifically, in the general form of value (Marx 1976a).

2. In one formulation, a competitive society is 'a society which has found a dynamic equilibrium between wealth creation on one side and social cohesion on the other ... A competitive society is one which identifies and actively manages all the facets of its competitiveness – from infrastructure to education' (Prokopenko 1998: 3). The cost (threatened punishment) for not meeting the requirement of this society is wage erosion and the condition of 'survival' is identified with the management of society as a whole; government policies are instrumental in this. Investment in 'social capital' is paramount for this strategy.

3. 'Overpowering the guard requires an union of hands, and a concert among minds. But what union, or what concert, can there be among persons, no one of whom will have set eyes on any other from the first moment of his entrance? Undermining walls, forcing iron bars, requires commonly a concert, always a length of time exempt from interruption. But who would think of beginning a work of hours and days, without any tolerable prospect of making so much as the first motion towards it unobserved?' (Bentham 1787: 32). In Letter 8, Bentham addresses the issue of how this confinement can be applicable 'to the joint purposes of punishment, reformation, and pecuniary economy', because it may be disputable that solitude may serve a purpose to reformation. But 'In the condition of our prisoners ... you may see the student's paradox, nunquam minus solus quam cum solus [never less alone than when alone] realized in a new way; to the keeper, a multitude, though not a crowd; to themselves, they are solitary and sequestered individuals' (Bentham 1787: 35).

16   THE 'OUTSIDE'

1. Following the G8 July meeting in Gleneagles and before the World Bank meeting on 24 September 2005, CNN produced a programme called *CNN Connects: a Global Summit*. This was about focusing on what CNN and the World Bank described as 'key challenges of our time – poverty, corruption, climate change, and religious conflict'. In this programme, 'The World Bank President Paul Wolfowitz was one of six panelists who discussed these issues and practical ways of addressing them. Mr Wolfowitz was joined by former US President Bill Clinton; rock star and activist Bono; Her Majesty Queen Rania Al-Abdullah of Jordan; Jeffrey

Sachs, Special Adviser to Kofi Annan on the MDGs; and Nobel Peace Prize winner Wangari Maathai.' Bono and Wolfowitz 'expressed concern about the impact of corruption on development progress'. Check World Bank (2005a) and the material on the 'office of the president' link at www.worldbank.org.

2. For a critical analysis of neoliberal governance and the role of selection principles, see the discussion on neoliberal governance in Chapter 7.

3. Creation of commons at the point of division reconfigures identities. Take, for example, this other episode from Desai's book, in which the communities were successful in preventing the local council from selling houses and dividing the communities along hierarchical lines: 'As the Council officials retreated, a defining moment in the struggle for Chatsworth occurred. One of the designer-bedecked (African) councilors began castigating the crowd. She had once lived in a shack, she screamed. Why were Indians resisting evictions and demanding upgrades? Indians were just too privileged. One elderly aunty, Girlie Amod, screamed back: "We are not Indians, we are the poors." The refrain caught on as councilors hurried to their cars. As they were leaving they would have heard the slogan mutate as Bongiwe Manqele introduced her own good humored variant, "We are not African, we are the poors." Identities were being rethought in the context of struggle and the bearers of these identities were no respecters of authority' (Desai 2002: 44).

4. I borrow this term from Chari (2005).

5. This has been pointed out in different ways by George Caffentzis (2002), Sharad Chari (2005) and Gillian Hart (2002; 2005).

6. The problematisation of this *detritus*, the struggles emerging therein and their *positing* alternatives, is hardly present in Harvey's framework, apart from some scant references to the fact that 'accumulation by dispossession' provokes community struggles. The same applies with respect to the *relational and feedback patterns* between the *conatus* of self-preservation of these communities in struggle and the *conatus* of self-preservation of capital. So, for example, Gillian Hart (2002; 2005) points out that we should not see 'dispossession from the land' as a necessary condition for rapid industrial accumulation, or at least not within the same locality. As her analysis of Taiwanese investments in South Africa argues, industrialisation in Taiwan was an unintended consequence of redistributive land reforms in the late 1940s and early 1950s brought about by revolt in the countryside. This operated as a social wage and later became the precondition for Taiwan capital's investment in South Africa. By the 1980s, when wage pressures had arisen in Taiwan, Taiwanese capitalists found a welcome in South Africa. Not only was the apartheid regime providing massive subsidies for national and international investors to move into racialised, decentralised industrial areas such as Ladysmith-Ezakheni, but the millions of black South Africans whose land had been expropriated in previous years, and who were packed into townships in the rural areas, provided an opportunity for investment for labour-intensive production techniques and labour practices that would later become socially explosive.

7. I am using here a naively non-geographic intuitive understanding of place, although, more rigorously, I would subscribe to the definition proposed by Gillian Hart (2005: 21) for whom 'place is most usefully understood as nodal points of connection in wider networks of socially-produced space'.

8. At the end of its ethnography of communities in *We are the Poors* Ashwin Desai's remarks find an echo in my experience of struggle: 'It is striking that the actual demands of people are almost always within what is possible, what can be achieved. The problem is – it won't be given or it is busy being taken away. This is the power these community movements have. They can "realistically" achieve their immediate goals but only through struggle. It is, I think, in light of these two factors – the expectation of a certain level of social good and the sense that it is being deliberatelly witheld or taken away – that people are willing to resist the UniCity's demand for payment. And in so doing there is an actual and cumulative disruption of the logic of capital and not a mere dispute with it no matter how comprehensively footnoted'

(2002: 143). For a discussion of how discourses far removed from and often opposed by 'left wing' ideologies can become meaningful to radicals, see Sharad Chari's (2005) discussion of pentacostalism as a vehicle for meanings and practices of struggles. These ethnographic approaches, grounded on people's processes of struggle, contrast sharply with rationalist approaches such as that provided by David Harvey for whom 'not all struggles against dispossession are equally progressive' (2003: 177). And who is to judge of the degree of 'progressiveness' of their struggle, but the struggling subjectivities themselves? And how is this 'judgement' being obtained, but through the involvement of subjectivities in contextually grounded political processes of communication, negotiation *and* struggle among value practices?

9. The radical analysis of survival and the creation of commons (the outside to the capitalist mode of production) can only be the work of ethnographers – people who live with and struggle with the community in struggle. From my experience as a non-professional ethnographer – that is simply as someone who participated in struggles, who has average ability for (self)-reflection, and who tries to link these reflections to critical political economy's preoccupations – I came to the following hypothesis: to really understand struggle – that is to draw insights from the experience in the contextual that can be enriching for a plurality of contexts of struggles – the ethnographer must seek to *couple* her own experience of struggle (in terms of the tension between *conatus* and *detritus*) to those of those communities, so as to problematise what is common and what is not among them.

17 COMMONS

1. See, for example Stuart Hall (1980).
2. The term 'objectal' is a neologism, and was introduced by Serge Latouche (1984).

References

Abramsky, Kolya (ed.) (2001) *Restructuring and Resistance, Diverse Voices of Struggle in Western Europe*, resresrev@yahoo.com.

American Friends Service Committee (2004) *Military Recruitment*, http://www.afsc.org/youthmil/Military-Recruitment/default.htm (last accessed 5 May 2005).

Amin, Samir (1974) *Accumulation on a World Scale: a Critique of the Theory of Underdevelopment*, London and New York: Monthly Review Press.

Anderson, Bridget (2000) *Doing the Dirty Work? the Global Politics of Domestic Labour*, New York: Zed Books.

Anderson, Terry L. and Randy T. Simmons (eds) (1993) *The Political Economy of Customs and Culture: Informal Solutions to the Commons Problem*, Lanham, Md.: Rowman & Littlefield.

Anheier, Helmut and Nuno Themudo (2002) 'Organisational Forms of Global Civil Society: Implications of Going Global', in Marlies Glasius, Mary Kaldor and Helmut Anheier (eds) *Global Civil Society 2002*, Oxford: Oxford University Press, pp. 191–216.

Aristotle (1948) *The Politics*, Oxford: Oxford University Press.

Aristotle (1985) *Nicomachean Ethics*, Indianapolis, Cambridge: Heckett Publishing.

Balakrishnan, Gopal (ed.) (2003) *Debating Empire*, London: Verso.

Bales, Kevin (2004) *Disposable People: New Slavery in the Global Economy*, Berkeley: University of California Press.

Barratt Brown, Michael (1974) *The Economics of Imperialism*, Harmondsworth: Penguin Books.

Bataille, Georges (1988) *The Accursed Share*, New York: Zone Books.

Becker, Gary S. (1993) *Human Capital: a Theoretical and Empirical Analysis, with Special Reference to Education*, London: University of Chicago Press.

Bell and Cleaver (2002) 'Marx's Crisis Theory as a Theory of Class Struggle', reproduced in *The Commoner*, 5, Autumn, http://www.commoner.org.uk/cleaver05.pdf and http://www.commoner.org.uk/cleaver05_pr.htm. Originally published in *Research in Political Economy*, 5, 1982, pp.189–261.

Bentham, Jeremy (1787) *Panopticon: or the Inspection-House*, Dublin: Thomas Byrne.

Bologna, Sergio (1991) 'The Theory and History of the Mass Worker in Italy', *Common Sense* 11, pp. 16–29; 12, pp. 52–78.

Bonefeld, Werner (2001) 'The Permanence of Primitive Accumulation: Commodity Fetishism and Social Constitution', *The Commoner*, 2, September, http://www.commoner.org.uk/02bonefeld.pdf.

Bonefeld, Werner (2002a) 'History and Social Constitution: Primitive Accumulation is not Primitive', *The Commoner*, Debate on Primitive Accumulation, http://www.commoner.org.uk/debbonefeld.pdf.

Bonefeld, Werner (2002b) 'Class and EMU' *The Commoner*, 5, Autumn, http://www.thecommoner.org.uk/bonefeld05.pdf.

Boutang, Yann Moulier (2002) *Dalla schiavitu' al lavoro salariato*, Rome: Manifestolibri.

Branford, Sue and Jan Rocha (2002) *Cutting the Wire: The Story of the Landless Movement in Brazil*, London: Latin American Bureau.

Braudel, Fernand (1982) *The Wheels of Commerce: Civilization and capitalism 15th–18th Century*, vol 2, London: Collins.

Braudel, Fernand (1984) *The Perspective of the World: Civilization and capitalism 15th–18th Century*, vol 3, London: Collins.

Brookings Institution, The (1998) *What Nuclear Weapons Delivery Systems Really Cost*, http://www.brook.edu/fp/projects/nucwcost/delivery.htm (last accessed 6 May 2005).

Burnham, Peter (1996) 'Capital, Crisis and the International State System', in Werner Bonefeld and John Holloway (eds) *Global Capital, National State and the Politics of Money*, Basingstoke: Macmillan.

Caffentzis, George (1983/2004) 'Freezing the Movement: Posthumous Notes on Nuclear War', *The Commoner*, 8, Autumn/Winter, http://www.commoner.org.uk/08caffentzis.pdf.

Caffentzis, George (1995) 'The Fundamental Implications of the Debt Crisis for Social Reproduction in Africa', in Mariarosa Dalla Costa and Giovanna F. Dalla Costa (eds) *Paying the Price: Women and the Politics of International Economic Strategy*, London: Zed Books.

Caffentzis, George (1999) 'The End of Work or the Renaissance of Slavery? A Critique of Rifkin and Negri', *Common Sense*, 24, pp. 20–38. Also available at www.autonomedia.org.

Caffentzis, George (2002) 'On the Notion of a Crisis of Social Reproduction: a Theoretical Review', *The Commoner*, 5, Autumn, http://www.commoner.org.uk/caffentzis05.pdf

Caffentzis, George (2005) 'Immeasurable Value? An Essay on Marx's Legacy', *The Commoner*, 10, http://www.commoner.org.uk/10caffentzis.pdf.

Camdessus, Michel (1997) 'Managing Director's Opening Address: Camdessus Calls for Responsibility and Solidarity in Dealing with the Challenges of Globalization', *IMF Survey*, 26, 18, 6 October.

Cannon, Walter B. (1932) *The Wisdom of the Body*, New York: Norton.

Capra, Fritjof (1997) *The Web of Life: A New Synthesis of Mind and Matter*, London: Flamingo.

Cassin, Barbara (2002) 'The Politics of Memory: How to Treat Hate', *Quest: An African Journal of Philosophy / Revue Africaine de Philosopy*, 16, 1–2. Available at http://www.quest-journal.net/vol_XVI/QUEST%20XVI%20FINALFINALFINAL4TXT.txt (last accessed 10 March 2006).

Castells, Manuel (2000) *The Rise of the Network Society*, vol 1. Cambridge, Mass.: Blackwell Publishers.

Caufield, C (1998) *Masters of Illusion: The World Bank and the Poverty of Nations*, London: Pan.

CCHD, Catholic Campaign for Human Development (2004) Poverty Tour, http://www.nccbuscc.org/cchd/povertyusa/tour2.htm (last accessed 5 May 2005).

Center for Arms Control and Non-Proliferation (2005) 'Highlights of the FY05 Budget Request', http://64.177.207.201/static/budget/annual/fy05/ (last accessed 5 May 2005).

Chandhoke, Neera (2002) 'The Limits of Global Civil Society', in Marlies Glasius, Mary Kaldor and Helmut Anheier (eds) *Global Civil Society 2002*, Oxford: Oxford University Press, pp. 35–53.

Chari, Sharad (2005) 'Political Work: the Holy Spirit and the Labours of Activism in the Shadow of Durban's Refineries', in *From Local Processes to Global Forces*, Centre for Civil Society Research Reports, vol. 1, Durban: University of Kwazulu-Natal, pp. 87–122.

Clancy, Michael (1998) 'Commodity Chains, Services and Development: Theory and Preliminary Evidence from the Tourist Industry', in *Review of International Political Economy*, 5, 1, Spring, pp. 122–48.

Cleaver, Harry (1979) *Reading Capital Politically*, Austin: University of Texas Press.

Cleaver, Harry (1984) 'Introduction', in Antonio Negri (1984) *Marx beyond Marx: Lessons on the Grundrisse*, South Hadley, Mass.: Bergin & Garvey.

Cleaver, Harry (1992) 'The Inversion of Class Perspective in Marxian Theory: from Valorisation to Self-Valorisation', in W. Bonefeld, R. Gunn and K. Psychopedis (eds) *Open Marxism*, Pluto Press.

Cleaver, Harry (2005) 'Work, Value and Domination: on the Continuing Relevance of the Marxian Labor Theory of Value in the Crisis of the Keynesian Planner State', *The Commoner*, 5, http://www.commoner.org.uk/10cleaver.pdf.

Coase, Ronald H. (1988) 'The Problem of Social Cost', in Ronald H. Coase, *The Firm, the Market and the Law*, Chicago and London: University of Chicago Press.

Cohen, G. A. (1988) *History, Labour and Freedom*, Oxford: Clarendon Press.

Costello, Anne and Les Levidow (2001) 'Flexploitation Strategies: UK Lessons for Europe', *The Commoner*, 1, May, http://www.commoner.org.uk/Flex3.pdf.

Crozier, M., Samuel P. Huntington and Jdju Watanuki (1975) *The Crisis of Democracy: Report on the Governability of Democracies to the Trilateral Commission*, New York: New York University Press.

Dalla Costa, Mariarosa and G. F. Dalla Costa (eds) (1999) *Women, Development and the Labor of Reproduction: Struggles and Movements*, Trenton, N.J. and Asmara, Eritrea: Africa World Press.

Dalla Costa, Mariarosa and Dario De Bortoli (2005) 'For Another Agriculture and Another Food Policy in Italy', *The Commoner*, 10, Spring/Summer, http://www.thecommoner.org/10dallacostadebortoli.pdf.

Dalla Costa, Mariarosa and Selma James (1972) 'The Power of Women and the Subversion of the Community', in E. Malos (ed.) *The Politics of Housework*, Bristol: Falling Wall Press.

Damasio, Antonio (2003) *Looking for Spinoza: Joy, Sorrow and the Feeling Brain*, London: William Heinemann.

Davis, Mike (1990) *City of Quartz: Excavating the Future in Los Angeles*, London: Verso.

De Angelis, Massimo (1996) 'Social Relations, Commodity-Fetishism and Marx's Critique of Political Economy', *Review of Radical Political Economics*, 28, 4, pp. 1–29.

De Angelis, Massimo (2000a) *Keynesianism, Social Conflict and Political Economy*, London: Macmillan.

De Angelis, Massimo (2000b) 'Globalization, New Internationalism and the Zapatistas', *Capital and Class*, Spring, 70, pp. 9–35.

De Angelis, Massimo (2001a) 'Marx and Primitive Accumulation: the Continuous Character of Capital's "Enclosures"', *The Commoner*, 2, September, http://www.commoner.org.uk/02deangelis.pdf.

De Angelis, Massimo (2001b) 'Hayek, Bentham and the Global Work Machine: the Emergence of the Fractal-Panopticon', in Ana Dinestern and Michael Neary (eds) *The Labour Debate: An Investigation into the Theory and Reality of Capitalist Work*, Ashgate: Aldershot.

De Angelis, Massimo (2002) 'The Market as a Disciplinary Order: a Comparative Analysis of Hayek and Bentham', *Research in Political Economy*, 20.

De Angelis, Massimo (2003) 'Reflections on Alternatives, Commons and Communities', *The Commoner*, 6, Winter, http://www.commoner.org.uk/deangelis06.pdf.

De Angelis, Massimo (2004a) 'Separating the Doing and the Deed: Capital and the Continuous Character of Enclosures', *Historical Materialism*, 12, 2.

De Angelis, Massimo (2004b) 'Defining the Concreteness of Abstract Labour and its Measure', in Alan Freeman and Andrew Kliman (eds) *Current Issues in Marxian Economics*, Cheltenham: Edward Elgar.

De Angelis, Massimo (2004c) '"Opposing Fetishism by Reclaiming our Powers": the Social Forum Movement, Capitalist Markets and the Politics of Alternatives', *International Social Science Journal*, 182, December.

De Angelis, Massimo (2005a) 'The Political Economy of Global Neoliberal Governance', *Review*, 28, 3, pp. 229–57.

De Angelis, Massimo (2005b) 'How?!?! An Essay on John Holloway's *Change the World without Taking Power*', *Historical Materialism* 13, 4, pp. 233–49.

De Angelis, Massimo and Dagmar Diesner (2005) 'The "Brat Block" and the Making of Another Dimension', in David Harvie et al. (eds) *Shut Them Down! The G8, Gleneagles 2005 and the Movement of Movements*, Leeds: Dissent! and Brooklyn, N.Y.: Autonomedia, 207–12. Also available at http://www.shutthemdown.org (last accessed 18 April 2006).

De Angelis, Massimo and David Harvie (2004) 'Gobalisation? No Question: Foreign Direct Investment and Labour Commanded', paper presented at the Heterodox Economics Conference, July, City University, London.

De Angelis, Massimo and David Harvie (2006) 'Cognitive Capitalism and the Rat Race: How Capital Measures Ideas and Affects in UK Higher Education', paper presented at the conference Immaterial Labour, Multitudes and New Social Subjects: Class Composition in Cognitive Capitalism, April, King's College, Cambridge.

Deaton, Angus (2003) 'Counting the World's Poor: Problems and Possible Solutions', *The World Bank Research Observer*, 16, 2, Fall.

De Filippis, Vittorio and Christian Losson (2005) 'Référendum 29 mai. Toni Negri, figure alter-mondialiste, appelle à approuver la Constitution: "Oui, pour faire disparaître cette merde d'Etat-nation"', *Liberation*, 13 May 2005, http://www.liberation.fr/page.php?Article=296227#.

Dejours, Christophe (1998) *Souffrances en France: la banalisation de l'injustice sociale*, Paris: Seuil.

Deleuze, Gilles (1990) 'Postscript to the societies of control', *L'autre journal*, 1, May. Available at http://www.watsoninstitute.org/infopeace/vy2k/deleuze-societies.cfm (last accessed 5 February 2005).

Deleuze, Gilles (1998) *Foucault*, Minneapolis and London, University of Minnesota Press.

Deleuze, Gilles and Felix Guattari (1988) *A Thousand Plateaus: Capitalism and Schizophrenia*, London and New York: Continuum.

De Marcellus, Olivier (2003) 'Commons, Communities and Movements: Inside, Outside and Against Capital', *The Commoner*, 6, Winter, http://www.commoner.org.uk/demarcellus06.pdf.

Democracy Now (2004) 'A New Poverty Draft: Military Contractors Target Latin America for New Recruits', 23, December, http://www.democracynow.org/article.pl?sid=04/12/23/1541224#transcript (last accessed 10 March 2006).

Desai, Ashwin (2002) *We are the Poors: Community Struggles in Post-Apartheid South Africa*, New York, Monthly Review Press.

Dicken, Peter (2003) *Global Shift: Transforming the World Economy*, London: Sage.

Dobb, Maurice (1963) *Studies in the Development of Capitalism*, London: Routledge.

Dobuzinskis, Laurent (1987) *The Self-Organizing Polity: An Epistemological Analysis of Political Life*, Boulder: Westview Press.

DOR (1996) 'First Declaration of la Realidad', EZLN, http://www.actlab.utexas.edu/~zapatistas/declaration.html.

Duffield, Mark (2001) *Global Governance and the New Wars: The Merging of Development and Security*, London: Zed Books.

Dunning, John H. (2000) 'The Future of the WTO: a Socio-Relational Challenge?', *Review of International Political Economy*, 7, 3, pp. 475–83.

Dyer-Witheford, Nick (1999) *Cyber-Marx: Cycles and Circuits of Struggle in High-Technology Capitalism*, Urbana: University of Illinois Press.

Dyer-Witheford, Nick (2002) 'Global Body, Global Brain/ Global Factory, Global War: Revolt of the Value-Subjects', *The Commoner*, 3, January. http://www.commoner.org.uk/03dyer-witheford.pdf

Economist, The (2003) 'Special Report: Pots of Promise: the Beauty Business', *Economist*, 22 May.

Ehrenreich, Barbara and Arlie Russell Hochschild (2002) *Global Woman: Nannies, Maids and Sex Workers in the New Economy*, New York: Metropolitan Books.

Elster, Jon (1985) *Making Sense of Marx*, Cambridge: Cambridge University Press.

Elliott, Larry (2003) 'Lost Decade', *Guardian*, 9 July.

Engen, Darel (2004) 'The Economy of Ancient Greece', EH.Net *Encyclopedia*, edited by Robert Whaples, August, http://eh.net/encyclopedia/article/engen.greece.

Escobar, A. (1994) *Encountering development: the making and unmaking of the third world*, Princeton, N.J.: Chichester, Princeton University Press.

Esteva, Gustavo (1992) 'Development', *The Development Dictionary*, London: Zed Books.

Esteva, Gustavo and Madhu Suri Prakash (1998) *Grassroots Post-Modernism: Remaking the Soil of Cultures*, London: Zed Books.

FAO (2005) 'Food Trade Deficits Threaten Poorest Countries', Food and Agriculture Organization of the United Nations, http://www.fao.org/newsroom/en/focus/2005/89746/index.html (last accessed December 2005).

Federici, Silvia (1992) 'The Debt Crisis, Africa and the New Enclosures', in *Midnight Notes*, reproduced in *The Commoner*, 2, September 2001, http://www.commoner.org.uk/02federici.pdf.

Federici, Silvia (2002) 'War, Globalisation and Reproduction', in Veronika Bennholdt-Thomsen, Nicholas Faraclas and Claudia von Werlhof (eds) *There is an Alternative: Subsistence and Worldwide Resistance to Corporate Globalization*, London: Zed Books.

Federici, Silvia (2004) *Caliban and the Witch: Women, the Body and Primitive Accumulation*, New York: Autonomedia.

Fine, Ben (2001) *Social Capital versus Social Theory: Political Economy and Social Science at the Turn of the Millennium*, London: Routledge.

Finley, Moses I. (1973) *The Ancient Economy*, London: Chatto & Windus.

Fortunati, Leopoldina (1981) *L'arcano della riproduzione. Casalinghe, prostitute, operai e capitale*, Venice: Marsilio.

Foucault, Michel (1977) *Discipline and Punish: The Birth of the Prison*, translated by A. Sheridan, London: Penguin Books.

Foucault, Michel (1981) *The History of Sexuality, vol. 1*, London: Penguin.

Foucault, Michel (1991) *Remarks on Marx: Conversations with Duccio Trombadori*, New York, Semiotext(e).

Foucault, Michel (2002) 'Governmentality', in James D.Faubion (ed.) *Power: Essential works of Foucault 1954–1984*, London: Penguin.

Freeman Alan and Guglielmo Carchedi (1996) *Marx and Non-Equilibrium Economics*, Cheltenham and Brookfield: Edward Elgar.

Freeman, Alan, Andrew Kliman and Julian Wells (eds) (2004) *Current Issues in Marxian Economics*, Cheltenham: Edward Elgar.

Friends of the Earth (2002) *The Other Shell Report*, http://www.foe.org (last accessed 4 June 2005).

Fukuyama, Francis (1992) *The End of History and the Last Man*, London: Hamish Hamilton.

Fukuyama, Francis (1995) *Trust: The Social Virtues and the Creation of Prosperity*, London: Hamish Hamilton.

Furedi, Frank (2006) 'What's wrong with cheats: The cooption of parents as unpaid teachers is at the root of Britain's plagiarism epidemic', *Guardian*, 28 March, p. 28. Available at http://education.guardian.co.uk/higher/comment/story/0,,1741131,00.html (last accessed 10 April 2006).

Gamble, Andrew (1996) *Hayek: The Iron Cage of Liberty*, Cambridge: Polity.

George, Susan (1988) *A Fate Worse than Debt: A Radical New Analysis of the Third World Crisis*, London: Penguin.

Gereffi, Gary and Miguel Korzeniewicz (eds) (1994) *Commodity Chains and Global Capitalism*, Westport, Conn.: Greenwood Press.

Giddens, Anthony (1990) *The Consequences of Modernity*, Cambridge: Polity Press.

Glyn, Andrew and Bob Sutcliffe (1992) 'Global but Leaderless? The New Capitalist Order', in Ralph Miliband and Leo Panitch (eds) *New World Order: The Socialist Register*, London: Merlin Press.

Godbout, Jacques (2000) *Le Don, la Dette et l'Identité: Homo Donator vs Homo Oeconomicus*, Paris: La Découverte / MAUSS.

Gordon, David (1998) 'The Global Economy: New Edifice or Crumbling Foundation?', *New Left Review*, 168, pp. 24–65.

Gottlieb, Roger S. (1984) 'Feudalism and Historical Materialism: a Critique and a Synthesis', *Science and Society*, 48, 1, pp. 1–37.

Graeber, David (2001) *Toward an Anthropological Theory of Value: The False Coin of our Dreams*, New York: Palgrave.

Graeber, David (2005) 'Value as the Importance of Action', *The Commoner*, 10, Spring/Summer, http://www.commoner.org.uk/10graeber.pdf (last accessed 10 March 2006).

Gray, Anne (2004) *Unsocial Europe: Social Protection or Flexploitation?* London: Pluto Press.

Gray, John (1998) *Hayek on Liberty*, London: Routledge.

Guttal, Shalmali (2006) 'Reconstruction's Triple Whammy: Wolfowitz, the White House and the World Bank', in *Destroy and Profit: Wars, Disasters and Corporations*, Bangkok: Focus on the Global South. Available at http://www.focusweb.org/pdf/Reconstruction-Dossier.pdf (last accessed 10 April 2006).

Haffner, Friedrich (1973) 'Value, Law of Value', in C. D. Kernig (ed.) *Marxism, Communism and Western Society: A Comparative Encyclopedia*, New York: Harder & Herder.

Hall, Stuart (1980) 'Race, Articulation and Societies structured in Dominance', in *Sociological Theories: Race and Colonialism*, Paris: UNESCO.

Hansen, Tom and Jason Wallach (2002) 'Plan Puebla-Panama: The Next Step in Corporate Globalization', *Labor Notes*, April, http://www.labornotes.org/archives/2002/04/a.html (last accessed December 2003).

Hardin, Garrett (1968) 'The Tragedy of the Commons', *Science*, 162, pp.1243–8. Reproduced in Garrett Hardin and John Baden, *Managing the Commons*, San Francisco: W.H. Freeman, 1977.

Hardt, Michael and Antonio Negri (1994) *Labor of Dionysus: A Critique of the State-Form*, Minneapolis: University of Minnesota Press.

Hardt, Michael and Antonio Negri (2000) *Empire*, Cambridge, Mass.: Harvard University Press.

Hardt, Michael and Antonio Negri (2004) *Multitude: War and Democracy in the Age of Empire*, New York: Penguin Press.

Hart, Gillian (2002) *Disabling Globalization: Places of Power in Post-Apartheid South Africa*, Pietermartzburg: University of Natal Press.

Hart, Gillian (2005) 'Denaturalising Dispossession: Critical Ethnography in the Age of Resurgent Imperialism', in *From Local Processes to Global Forces*, Centre for Civil Society Research Reports, 1, Durban: University of Kwazulu-Natal, pp. 1–25.

Harvey, David (1989) *The Condition of Postmodernity: an Enquiry into the Origins of Cultural Change*, Oxford: Basil Blackwell.

Harvey, David (1999) *The Limits to Capital*, London: Verso.

Harvey, David (2000) *Spaces of Hope*, Edinburgh: Edinburgh University Press.

Harvey, David (2003) *The New Imperialism*, Oxford: Oxford University Press.

Harvie, David (2004) 'Commons and Communities in the University: Some Notes and Some Examples', *The Commoner*, 8, Autumn/Winter, http://www.commoner.org.uk/08harvie.pdf.

Harvie, David (2005) 'All labour produces value for capital and we all struggle against value', *The Commoner*, 10, Spring/Summer, http://www.commoner.org.uk/10harvie.pdf.

Harvie, David and Keir Milburn (2006) 'Moments of Excess', edited version of a paper presented at Life Despite Capitalism, November 2004, London; available at http://www.le.ac.uk/ulmc/doc/dharvie_excess.pdf (last accessed 10 June 2006).

Hayek, Friedrich (1945) 'The Use of Knowledge in Society', *American Economic Review*, 4, pp. 519–30, reprinted in Friedrich Hayek, *Individualism and Economic Order*, Chicago: Chicago University Press, 1948.

Hayek, Friedrich (1946) 'The Meaning of Competition', in Friedrich Hayek, *Individualism and Economic Order*, Chicago: Chicago University Press, 1948.

Hayek, Friedrich (1960) *The Constitution of Liberty*, London: Routledge.

Hayek, Friedrich (1970) 'The Errors of Constructivism', in Friedrich Hayek, *New Studies in Philosophy, Politics, Economics and the History of Ideas*. Chicago: Chicago University Press, 1978/1985, pp. 8–9.

Hayek, Friedrich (1973) *Law, Legislation and Liberty, vol. 1: Rules and Order*, Chicago: University of Chicago Press.

Hayek, Friedrich (1978) *New Studies in Philosophy, Politics, Economics and the History of Ideas*, Chicago: Chicago University Press.

Hayek, Friedrich (1988) 'The Fatal Conceit: the Errors of Socialism', in W.W.Bartley III (ed.) *The Collected Works of F.A. Hayek*, vol. 1, Chicago: University of Chicago Press.

Held, David et al. (1999) *Global Transformations: Politics, Economics and Culture*, Cambridge: Polity.

Helleiner, Eric (1995) 'Explaining the Globalization of Financial Markets: Bringing States Back In', *Review of International Political Economy*. 2, 2, pp. 315–41.

Henderson, Jeffrey et al. (2002), 'Global Production Networks and the Analysis of Economic Development', *Review of International Political Economy*, 9, 3, pp. 436–64.

Herold, Conrad M. (2002) 'On Financial Crisis as a Disciplinary Device of Empire: Emergence and Crisis of the Crisis', *The Commoner*, 5, Autumn, http://www.commoner.org.uk/herold5.pdf.

Hildyar, Nicholas (1998) 'The Myth of the Minimalist State: Free Market Ambiguities', *The Corner House*, Briefings 5, http://www.thecornerhouse.org.uk/item.shtml?x=51960 (last accessed 10 March 2006).

Hill, Christopher (1972) *The World Turned Upside-Down: Radical Ideas during the English Revolution*, London: Penguin.

Hilton, Rodney (ed.) (1978) *The Transition from Feudalism to Capitalism*, London: Verso.

Hirst, Paul and Graham Thompson (1999) *Globalization in Question: The International Economy and the Possibilities of Governance*, 2nd edn., Cambridge: Polity.

Hodkinson, Stuart (2005) 'Is this History?' *Independent*, 26 October.

Holloway, John (1996) 'Global Capital and the National State', in Werner Bonefeld and John Holloway (eds) *Global Capital, National State and the Politics of Money*, Basingstoke: Macmillan.

Holloway, John (1998) 'Dignity's Revolt', in J. Holloway and E. Pelaez (eds) *Dignity's Revolt: Reflections on the Zapatista Uprising*, London: Pluto Press.

Holloway, John (2002) *Change the World Without Taking Power*, London: Pluto Press.

Holloway, John (2005) 'No', *Historical Materialism* 13, 4, pp. 265–85.

Holloway, John and Eloína Peláez (1998) *Zapatistas: Reinventing Revolution in Mexico*, London: Pluto Press.

Hoogvelt, Ankie (1997) *Globalization and the Postcolonial World: The New Political Economy of Development*, London: Macmillan.

Hoogvelt, Ankie (2001) *Globalization and the Postcolonial World: The New Political Economy of Development*, Baltimore, Md.: Johns Hopkins University Press.

Hopkins, Terence and Immanuel Wallerstein (1986) 'Commodity Chains in the World Economy Prior to 1800', *Review*, 10, 1, Summer, pp.157–70.

Hudson, Michael (1992) *Trade, Development and Foreign Debt: A History of Theories of Polarisation and Convergence in the International Economy*, London: Pluto Press.

IFG (2002) 'A Better World is Possible: Alternatives to Economic Globalization. Summary', *International Forum on Globalization*, http://www.ifg.org/alt_eng.pdf (last accessed December 2003).

Illich, Ivan (1981) *Shadow Work*, London: Marion Boyers.

Irigaray, Luce (1997) *Tra oriente e occidente. Dalla singolarita' alla comunita'*, Rome: Il manifesto libri.

Jameson, Fredric (1991) *Postmodernism, or The Cultural Logic of Late Capitalism*, London: Verso.

Johansson, Claes and David Stewart (2002) 'The Millennium Development Goals: Commitments and Prospects', New York: Human Development Report Office. Working paper, 1, 7 October.

Kalecki, Michael (1943) 'Political Aspects of Full Employment', in Osiatynski (ed.) *Collected Works of Michael Kalecki, vol. 1*, Oxford: Clarendon Press.

Kirzner, Israel M. (1973) *Competition and Entrepreneurship*, Chicago and London: University of Chicago Press.

Klein, Naomi (2001) 'Reclaiming the Commons', *New Left Review*, 9, May/June, pp.81–99.

Klein, Naomi (2003a) *Bush to NGOs: Watch Your Mouths*, appearing in the *Global and Mail*, 20 June 2003, http://www.globeandmail.com.

Klein, Naomi (2003b) 'Fences of Enclosures, Windows of Possibilities', http://www.nologo.org/ (last accessed December 2003).

Kliman, Andrew (2001) 'Simultaneous Valuation vs. the Exploitation Theory of Profit', *Capital and Class*, 73.

Kliman Andrew (2004) 'Marx vs. the "20th-Century Marxists": a reply to Laibman', in Alan Freeman, Andrew Kliman and Julian Wells, *The New Value Controversy*, Cheltenham: Edward Elgar.

Kleinknecht, Alfred and Jan ter Wengel (1998) 'The Myth of Economic Globalisation', *Cambridge Journal of Economics*, 22, 5, pp.637–47.

Knight, Chris (1991) *Blood Relations: Menstruation and the Origins of Culture*, New Haven and London: Yale University Press.

Koestler, Arthur (1967) *The Ghost in the Machine*, London: Hutchinson.

Kovel, Joel (2002) *The Enemy of Nature: The End of Capitalism or the End of the World?* London and New York: Zed Books.

Kuhathas, Chandran (1989) *Hayek and Modern Liberalism*, Oxford: Clarendon Press.

Laclau, Ernesto and Chantal Mouffe (1985) *Hegemony and Socialist Strategy: Towards a Radical Democratic Politics*, London: Verso.

Laing, Ronnie D. (1960) *The Divided Self: A Study of Sanity and Madness*, London: Tavistock.

Latouche, Serge (1984) *Le procès de la science sociale. Introduction à une théorie critique de la connaissance*, Paris: Anthropos.

Latouche, Serge (1993) *In the Wake of the Affluent Society: An Exploration of Post-Development*, Atlantic Highlands, N.J.: Zed Books.

Latouche, Serge (2001) *L'invenzione dell'economia*, Bologna: Arianna editrice.

Lawrence, Felicity (2002) 'Fowl Play', *Guardian*, G2, July 8, p.2.

Leibman, David (1984) 'Modes of Production and Theories of Transition', *Science and Society*, 48, 3, pp.257–94.

Levidow, Les (2002) 'Marketizing Higher Education: Neoliberal Strategies and Counter-Strategies', *The Commoner*, 3, January, http://www.thecommoner.org.uk/03levidow.pdf.

Levidow, Les (2003) 'Trans-Atlantic Governance of GM Crops', seminar paper presented at the University of East London, 7 June.

Linebaugh, Peter (1991) *The London Hanged: Crime and Civil Society in the Eighteenth Century*, London: Allen Lane Penguin Press.

Linebaugh, Peter (forthcoming) *Magna Carta and the Commons: the Lost Charters and the Struggle to Reclaim Liberty and Subsistence for All*, Berkeley: University of California Press.

Linebaugh, Peter and Marcus Buford Rediker (2000) *The Many-Headed Hydra: Sailors, Slaves, Commoners, and the Hidden History of the Revolutionary Atlantic*, Boston: Beacon Press.

Luxemburg, Rosa (1963) *The Accumulation of Capital*, London: Routledge & Kegan Paul.

Lyotard, Jean-François (1984) *The Postmodern Condition: A Report on Knowledge*, Manchester: Manchester University Press.

Mariscal, Jorge (2005) 'Fighting the Poverty Draft: Protests Move to Recruiting Offices', *CounterPunch*, 28 January, http://www.counterpunch.org/mariscal01282005.html (last accessed 5 May 2005).

Martin, Brendan (2000) *New Leaf or Fig Leaf? The Challenge of the New Washington Consensus*, London: Bretton Woods Project and Public Services International.

Marx, Karl (1969) [1905–10] *Theories of Surplus Value*, Part 1, London: Lawrence & Wishart.

Marx, Karl (1971) *Theories of Surplus Value*, vol. 3, Moscow: Progress Publishers.

Marx, Karl (1974) [1858] *Grundrisse*, New York: Penguin.

Marx, Karl (1975) [1844] 'Economic and Philosophical Manuscripts', in *Early Writings*, New York: Vintage Books.

Marx, Karl (1976a) [1867] *Capital*, vol. 1, New York: Penguin Books.

Marx, Karl (1976b) [1863–6] 'Results of the Immediate Process of Production', in *Capital*, vol. 1, New York: Penguin Books.

Marx, Karl (1976c) [1847] 'German Ideology', in Karl Marx and Frederick Engels, *Collected Works*, vol. 5, London: Lawrence & Wishart.

Marx, Karl (1978) [1885] *Capital*, vol. 2, New York: Penguin Books.

Marx, Karl (1981) [1894] *Capital*, vol. 3, New York: Penguin Books.

Marx, Karl (1983) [1881] 'Reply to Vera Zasulich', in Teodor Shanin (ed.) *Late Marx and the Russian Road*, New York: Monthly Review Press.

Marx, Karl (1987) [1859] 'Preface', *A contribution to the Critique of Political Economy*, in Karl Marx and Frederick Engels, *Collected Works*, vol. 29, London: Lawrence & Wishart.

McLennon, Gregor (1986) 'Marxist Theory and Historical Research: Between the Hard and Soft Options', *Science and Society*, 50, 1, pp.157–65.

McMurtry, John (1998) *Unequal Freedoms: The Global Market as an Ethical System*, Toronto and Westport, Conn.: Garamond & Kumarian Press.

McMurtry, John (1999) *The Cancer Stage of Capitalism*, London: Pluto Press.

McMurtry, John (2002) *Value Wars: The Global Market versus the Life Economy*, London: Pluto Press.

Meillassoux, Claude (1981) *Maidens, Meal and Money: Capitalism and the Domestic Community*, Cambridge: Cambridge University Press.

Midnight Notes Collective (1992) 'New Enclosures', in *Midnight Notes*, reproduced in *The Commoner*, 2, September 2001, http://www.commoner.org.uk/02midnight.pdf.

Midnight Notes Collective (2001) *Auroras of the Zapatistas: Local and Global Struggles of the Fourth World War*, Jamaica Plaine, Mass.: Autonomedia.

Mies, Maria (1998) *Patriarchy and Accumulation on a World Scale: Women in the International Division of Labour*, London: Zed Books.

Mittelman, James (2000) *The Globalization Syndrome: Transformation and Resistance*, Princeton: Princeton University Press.

Mohanty, Chandra Talpade (2003) *Feminism Without Borders: Decolonizing Theory, Practicing Solidarity*, Durham, N.C. and London, Duke University Press.

Mun, Thomas (1664) *Englands Treasure by Forraign Trade*, http://socserv2.socsci. mcmaster.ca/~econ/ugcm/3ll3/mun/treasure.txt (last accessed 10 March 2006).

Naidoo, Prishani (2005) 'The Struggle for Water, the Struggle for Life: the Installation of Prepaid Water Meters in Phiri Soweto', Centre for Civil Society *RASSP Research Report*, 1, pp. 1–23.

Negri, Antonio (1968) 'Keynes and the Capitalist Theory of the State Post-1929', in *Revolution Retrieved: Selected Writings on Marx, Keynes, Capitalist Crisis and New Social Subjects 1967–83* (1988), London: Red Notes, pp. 5–42.

Negri, Antonio (1984) *Marx beyond Marx: Lessons on the Grundrisse*, South Hadley, Mass.: Bergin & Garvey.

Negri, Antonio (1994) 'Oltre la legge di valore', *DeriveApprodi* 5-6, Winter.

Nord, Mark, Margaret Andrews and Steven Carlson (2003) 'Household Food Security in the United States', Food Assistance and Nutrition Research Report No. 35, October, Economic Research Service, United States Department of Agriculture, http://www.ers.usda.gov/publications/fanrr35/ (last accessed 10 March 2006).

Nugroho, Yanuar (2002) 'Essential Services in 2003', *Jakarta Post*, Business and Investment, 30 December.

Offe, Claus (1985) 'Work: The Key Sociological Category?' in C. Offe (ed.) *Disorganized Capitalism*, Cambridge, Mass.: MIT Press. pp. 129–50.

Oxfam (2002) *Rigged Rules and Double Standards: Trade, Globalisation and the Fight against Poverty*, http://www.marketradefair.com (last accessed 10 May 2004).

Palloix, Christian (1975) 'The Internationalization of Capital and the Circuit of Social Capital', in Hugo Radice (ed.) *International Firms and Modern Imperialism*, Harmondsworth: Penguin.

Parreñas, Rhacel Salazar (2001) *Servants of Globalization: Women, Migration and Domestic Work*, Stanford, Calif.: Stanford University Press.

Peng, D. (2000) 'The Changing Nature of East Asia as an Economic Region', *Pacific Affairs*, 73, 2, pp.171–92.

Perelman, Michael (2000) *The Invention of Capitalism: Classical Political Economy and the Secret History of Primitive Accumulation*, Durham, N.C. and London: Duke University Press.

Petty, William (1690) *Political Arithmetick*, http://socserv2.socsci.mcmaster.ca/~econ/ugcm/3ll3/petty/poliarith.html (last accessed 10 December 2005).

Piven, Frances Fox and Richard Cloward (1972) *Regulating the Poor: The Functions of Public Welfare*, New York: Vintage.

Polanyi, Karl (1944) *The Great Transformation: The Political and Economic Origins of our Time*, Boston: Beacon Press.

Polanyi, Karl (1968) 'Primitive, Archaic, and Modern Economies', in G. Dalton (ed.) *Essays of Karl Polanyi*, New York: Anchor Books.

Polanyi, Karl (1977) *The Livelihood of Man*, New York: Academic Press.

Potts, Lydia and Terry Bond (1990) *The World Labour Market: a History of Migration*, London: Zed Books.

Prokopenko, Joseph (1998) 'Globalization, Alliances and Networking: a Strategy for Competitiveness and Productivity', Enterprise and Management Development Working Paper, EMD/21/E.http://www.ilo.org/dyn/empent/docs/F111PUB105_01/PUB105_01.htm (last accessed 15 March 2006).

Reddy, Sanjay G. and Thomas W. Pogge (2003) 'How *not* to Count the Poor', Institute of Social Analysis, http://www.socialanalysis.org (last accessed 5 May 2005).

Richter, Judith (2002) 'Codes in Context: TNC Regulation in an Era of Dialogues and Partnerships', the *Corner House*, Briefing 26, http://www.thecornerhouse.org.uk/ (last accessed 15 September 2005).

Rifkin, Jeremy (1995) *The End of Work: The Decline of the Global Labor Force and the Dawn of the Post-Market Era*, New York: G.P. Putnam's Sons.

Rikowski, Ruth (2002) 'The Capitalisation of Libraries', *The Commoner*, 4, May, http://www.thecommoner.org.uk/04rikowski.pdf.

Robbins, Lionel Charles (1984) *An Essay on the Nature and Significance of Economic Science*, 3rd edn., New York: New York University Press.

Rodney, Walter (1972) How Europe Underdeveloped Africa, London: Bogle–L'Ouverture Publications.

Rose, Steven (1998) *Life-Lines: Biology beyond Determinism*, New York: Oxford University Press.

Rowling, Nick (1987). *Commodities: How the World Was Taken to Market*, London: Free Association Books.

Roy, Arundhati (2003) 'Instant-Mix Imperial Democracy (Buy One, Get One Free)', *Terra Incognita*, http://www.terraincognita.50megs.com/roy.html (last accessed 5 May 2005).

Schmid, Estella, Rochelle Harris and Sarah Sexton (2003) *Listen to the Refugee's Story: How UK Foreign Investment Creates Refugees and Asylum Seekers*, co-published by Ilisu Dam Campaign Refugees Project, the Corner House and Peace in Kurdistan, http://www.thecornerhouse.org.uk/document/refinves.html (last accessed 15 March 2006).

Scholte, Aart and Albrecht Schnabel (2002). 'Introduction', in Aart Scholte (ed.) with Albrecht Schnabel, *Civil Society and Global Finance*, London: Routledge.

Sciabarra, Chris Matthew (1995) *Marx, Hayek and Utopia*, New York: State University of New York Press.

Sen, Amartya Kumar (1999) *Development as Freedom*, New York: Knopf.

Shiva, Vandana (2002a) *Water Wars: Privatization, Pollution, and Profit*, Cambridge, Mass.: Southend Press.

Shiva, Vandana (2002b) *Protect or Plunder? Understanding Intellectual Property Rights*, London: Zed Books.

Sidebottom, Harry (2004) *Ancient Warfare: a Very Short Introduction*, Oxford: Oxford University Press.

Silver, Beverly J. (2003) *Forces of Labor: Workers' Movements and Globalization since 1870*, Cambridge: Cambridge University Press.

Simondon, Gilbert (2002) *L'individuazione psichica e collettiva*, Rome: Derive e Approdi.

Sklair, Leslie (2002) *Globalization: Capitalism and its Alternatives*, Oxford: Oxford University Press.

Skyttner, Lars (1996) *General Systems Theory*, London: Macmillan.

Smith, Adam (1970) *The Wealth of Nations*, Books 1–3, Harmondsworth: Penguin.

Smith, Cyril (1996) *Marx at the Millennium*, London: Pluto Press.

Spinoza, Benedictus De (1989) *Ethics*, London: Dent.

Steedman, Ian (1977) *Marx after Sraffa*, London: NLB.

Steele, G.R. (1993) *The Economics of Friedrich Hayek*, London: Macmillan.

Stoker, G. (1998) 'Governance as Theory: Five Propositions', *International Social Science Journal*, 50, 155, March, pp. 17–28.

Strange, S. (1996) *The Retreat of the State: The Diffusion of Power in the World Economy*, Cambridge: Cambridge University Press.

Sweezy, Paul (1950) 'The Transition from Feudalism to Capitalism', *Science and Society*, 14, 2, pp.134–57.

Sweezy, Paul (1986) 'Feudalism to Capitalism Revisited', *Science and Society*, 50, 1, pp. 81–95.

Tabb, William (2001) 'Globalization and Education as a Commodity', Professional Staff Congress, http://www.psc-cuny.org/jcglobalization.htm (last accessed 15 March 2006).

Thompson, Edward P. (1991) *Customs in Common*, New York: The New Press.

Tronti, Mario (1966). *Operai e capitale*, Turin, Einaudi.

Tronti, Mario (1972) 'Workers and Capital', *Telos*, 14, Winter, pp. 25–62; originally 'Poscritto di problemi,' in Mario Tronti, *Operai e Capitale*, Turin: Einaudi, 1966/1971, pp. 267–311.

Tronti, Mario (1973) 'Social Capital', *Telos*, 5, 17, pp. 98–121.

Tymieniecka, Anna-Teresa (1976) 'Man the Creator and his Triple *Telos*', in Anna-Teresa Tymieniecka (ed.) *The Teleologies in Husserlian Phenomenology*, vol. 3, London: D. Reidel Publishing, pp. 3–29.

U.S. Census Bureau (2003) *Income, Poverty and Health Insurance Coverage in the United States: 2003*, Current Population Reports, August, www.census.gov/prod/2004pubs/p60-226.pdf (last accessed 5 May 2004).

United Nations (2000a) *Global Compact Handbook*, http://www.unglobalcompact.org/Portal/ (last accessed 5 May 2005).

United Nations (2000b) *Global Compact Primer*, http://www.unglobalcompact.org/Portal/ (last accessed 5 May 2005).

United Nations (2003) *Human Development Report 2003. Millennium Development Goals: A Compact among Nations to End Human Poverty*, New York: United Nations; available at http://hdr.undp.org/reports/global/2003/ (last accessed 5 May 2005).

United Nations (2004) *Human Development Report 2004. Cultural Liberty in Today's Diverse World*, New York: United Nations; available at http://hdr.undp.org/reports/global/2004/ (last accessed 5 May 2005).

UNCTAD (1993) *World Investment Report 1993: Transnational Corporations and Integrated International Production*, New York: United Nations.

UNCTAD (1996) *Trade and Development Report 1996*, New York: United Nations.

Virno, Paolo (1996a) 'The Ambivalence of Disenchantment: Radical Thought and Italy. A Potential Politics', in Paolo Virno and Michael Hardt (eds) *Radical Thought in Italy: a Potential Politics*, Minneapolis and London: University of Minnesota Press.

Virno, Paolo (1996b) 'Virtuosity and Revolution: The Political Theory of Exodus', in Paolo Virno and Michael Hardt (eds) *Radical Thought in Italy: a Potential Politics*, Minneapolis: University of Minnesota Press.

Virno, Paolo (2004) *A Grammar of the Multitude: for an Analysis of Contemporary Forms of Life*, Los Angeles and New York: Semiotext(e).

Walker, Christopher (2004) 'Bush builds his Versailles as the poor go to ruin', *Independent on Sunday*, Business Section, 26 September, p.10.

Wallerstein, Immanuel M. (1979) *The Capitalist World-Economy: Essays*, Cambridge: Cambridge University Press/Maison des Sciences de l'Homme.

Walton, John and David Seddon (1994) *Free Markets and Food Riots: The Politics of Global Adjustment*, Cambridge, Mass.: Blackwell.

Wasselius, Erik (2002) 'Behind GATS 2000: Corporate Power at Work', *TNI Briefing Series*, 6, http://www.tni.org/reports/wto/wto4.pdf (last accessed December 2003).

Weiss, Linda (1997) 'Globalization and the Myth of the Powerless State', *New Left Review*, 225, pp. 3–27.

Weiss, Linda (1998) *The Myth of the Powerless State*, New York: Cornell University Press.

Went, Robert (2002) *The Enigma of Globalisation: A Journey to a New Stage of Capitalism*, London: Routledge.

Wiener, J. (2001) 'Globalisation and Disciplinary Neoliberal Governance', *Constellations*, 8, 4, December, pp. 461–79.

Williams, Eric (1964) *Capitalism and Slavery*, London: Deutsch.

Williamson, John (1990) 'What Washington Means by Policy Reform', in John Williamson (ed.) *Latin American Adjustment: How Much Has Happened*? Washington, D.C.: Institute for International Economics.

Williamson, John (2000) What Should the World Bank Think about the Washington Consensus? *The World Bank Research Observer*, 15, 2, August pp. 251–64.

Wolfowitz, Paul (2005) 'Charting a way Ahead: The Results Agenda', 2005 Annual Meeting Address, World Bank, Washington, D.C., September 24. Available at http://www.worldbank.org/ (last accessed 25 February 2006).

Wolpe, Harold (1972) 'Capitalism and Cheap Labour-Power in South Africa: from Segregation to Apartheid', *Economy and Society*, 1, pp. 425–56.

World Bank (2001) *Global Development Finance*, Washington, D.C.: World Bank; available in electronic format at http://www.worldbank.org/data/onlinedbs/onlinedbases.htm (last accessed 15 March 2006).

World Bank (2005a) 'CNN connects a global summit'; transcript and video available at http://web.worldbank.org/WBSITE/EXTERNAL/NEWS/0,,contentMDK:20649995~pagePK: 64257043~piPK:437376~theSitePK:4607,00.html (last accessed 16 November 2005).

World Bank (2005b) *Global Development Finance*, Washington, D.C.: World Bank; available in electronic format at http://www.worldbank.org/data/onlinedbs/onlinedbases.htm (last accessed 15 March 2006).

World Bank (2005c) *South Africa: an Assessment of the Investment Climate*, New York; available at http://www1.worldbank.org/rped/documents/ICA008.pdf (last accessed 15 March 2006).

World Trade Organisation (2003) '10 Benefits of the WTO trade system'; available in electronic format at http://www.wto.org/english/res_e/doload_e/10b_e.pdf (last accessed 25 March 2006).

Wright, Steve (2005) 'Reality Check: Are we Living in an Immaterial World?', in J. Slater (ed.) *Underneath the Knowledge Commons*, London: Mute.

Zarembka, Paul (2002) 'Primitive Accumulation in Marxism, Historical or Trans-historical Separation from Means of Production?' *The Commoner*, debate on primitive accumulation, http://www.commoner.org.uk/debzarembka.pdf.

Other Web Resources

Web 1, India's Greatest Planned Environmental Disaster: The Narmada Valley Dam Projects, http://www.umich.edu/~snre492/Jones/narmada.html (last accessed December 2003).

Web 2, One World Campaign: Narmada Valley, http://www.oneworld.org/campaigns/narmada/front.html (last accessed December 2003).

Web 3, GATS Campaign, Stop the GATSastrophe! WDM's campaign on the General Agreement on Trade in Services, http://www.wdm.org.uk/campaign/GATS.htm (last accessed December 2003).

Web 4, GATSwatch.org: Critical Info on GATS, http://www.gatswatch.org (last accessed December 2003).

Web 5, 'Globalization and War for Water in Bolivia', published by Jim Shultz and Tom Kruse, Cochabamba, Bolivia, http://www.americas.org/News/Features/200004_Bolivia_Water/Shultz_and_Kruse.htm (last accessed December 2003).

Web 6, 'Jubilee plus' material at http://www.jubileeplus.org/. Jubilee South, a radical network from the South, at http://www.jubileesouth.org/ (last accessed December 2003).

Web 7, Human Rights and the Environment, international campaigns, Nigeria ERA Monitor Report, 8: 'Six-Year-Old Spillage in Botem-Tai', http://www.sierraclub.org/human-rights/nigeria/background/spill.asp (last accessed December 2003).

Web 8, Trade Environment Database (TED) Projects, *Oil Production and Environmental Damage*, http://www.american.edu/ted/projects/tedcross/xoilpr15.htm. On international grass-roots campaigns, see *Oilwatch, A Southern-based activist network takes on petroleum dependency*, http://www.newint.org/issue335/action.htm (last accessed December 2003).

Index

Compiled by Sue Carlton